Responsibility for Negligence in Ethics and Law

OXFORD PRIVATE LAW THEORY

Oxford Private Law Theory publishes leading work in private law theory. It commissions and solicits monographs and edited collections in general private law theory as well as specific fields, including the theoretical analysis of tort law, property law, contract law, fiduciary law, trust law, remedies and restitution, and the law of equity. The series is open to diverse theoretical approaches, including those informed by philosophy, economics, history, and political theory. Oxford Private Law Theory sets the standard for rigorous and original work in private law theory.

ALSO PUBLISHED IN THIS SERIES

Relational Justice
A Theory of Private Law
Hanoch Dagan and Avihay Dorfman

Methodology in Private Law Theory
Between New Private Law and Rechtsdogmatik
Edited by Thilo Kuntz and Paul B. Miller

Responsibility for Negligence in Ethics and Law

Aspiration, Perspective, and Civic Maturity

VERÓNICA RODRÍGUEZ-BLANCO
Professor of Moral and Political Philosophy (Jurisprudence),
University of Surrey, UK

OXFORD
UNIVERSITY PRESS

OXFORD
UNIVERSITY PRESS

Great Clarendon Street, Oxford, OX2 6DP,
United Kingdom

Oxford University Press is a department of the University of Oxford.
It furthers the University's objective of excellence in research, scholarship,
and education by publishing worldwide. Oxford is a registered trade mark of
Oxford University Press in the UK and in certain other countries

Published in the United States of America by Oxford University Press
198 Madison Avenue, New York, NY 10016, United States of America

British Library Cataloguing in Publication Data
Data available

Library of Congress Control Number: 2024951454

ISBN 9780198948186

DOI: 10.1093/9780198948193.001.0001

Printed and bound by
CPI Group (UK) Ltd., Croydon, CR0 4YY

MIX
Paper | Supporting
responsible forestry
FSC® C013604
FSC
www.fsc.org

The manufacturer's authorised representative in the EU for product safety is
Oxford University Press España S.A. of El Parque Empresarial San Fernando de Henares,
Avenida de Castilla, 2 – 28830 Madrid (www.oup.es/en or
product.safety@oup.com). OUP España S.A. also acts as importer into Spain
of products made by the manufacturer.

To my daughter Eleonora, my husband Thomas and my parents Alejandro and Sonia, whose enormous love shaped my moral vision.

Acknowledgements

I would like to thank people who supported and inspired me in developing the ideas in this book with their intelligence and appreciation of this ambitious task. The seeds of this idea were planted during a workshop on 'Negligence and Responsibility' organized by the late John Gardner, George Pavlakos, and me at the University of Birmingham in 2015. The discussions helped me to start my ideas on responsibility for negligence, and I am grateful to my co-organizers and participants, including Ben Zipursky, Irit Samet, Constantin Sandis, Erasmus Mayr, and Ori Herstein. As a result, George Pavlakos and I published an edited collection on the philosophy of negligence. I am especially grateful to George Pavlakos for his enthusiasm and engagement with my own ideas. The members of the University of Surrey Centre for Law and Philosophy and the Surrey School of Law created a unique synergy of intellectual ideas and friendship that I have never encountered before. I am grateful for their wonderful collegial spirit, integrity, and love for knowledge and truth. I feel lucky to experience the perfect mix of true friendship and intellectual life within an institutional setting. Thank you to you all! The reading group on philosophy of action as a spin-off of the Surrey Centre for Law and Philosophy's seminars provided the perfect environment for exploring key thoughts of the book. I cannot thank enough Steve Bero, Ken Ehrenberg, Ambrose Lee, Emmanuel Lihnares, Daniel Peixoto-Murata, Armando Romero, and Chris Taggart, whose careful examination of readings in ancient and contemporary philosophy of action helped in the development of my own view.

A parallel reading group in philosophy of action run by Spanish speakers was an inspiring place to discuss key ideas on action, intention, and negligence. It has been a privilege to be part of this group, and I am grateful to Sebastian Agüero, Sebastian Figueroa Rubio, Julieta Rábanos, Gabriela Scataglini, and Pilar Zambrano for their perceptive discussions. During the spring of 2022, I was a Visiting Research Professor within the European Research Council-funded project 'The Normative and Moral Foundations of Group Agency' at the University of Vienna. It was a one-of-a-kind experience that gave me the space to develop my ideas and connect them to questions of group agency responsibility. It combined all the desired characteristics of scholarship and intellectual generosity. I am grateful to Herlinde Pauer-Studer, Nathan Biebel, Niels De Hahn, Olof Leffler, Veli Mitova, Lars Moen, Grace Paterson, and Anne Schwenkenbecker for their insightful comments on sections of this book and for enriching informal conversations. In autumn 2022, I was an Alexander Von Humboldt Fellow at the University of Munich, where I worked with Monika Betzler and her group. I am grateful for the perceptive feedback

I received from her colleagues and students. Finally, in spring 2023, I was a Max Planck Fellow at the Max Planck Institute for Legal History and Legal Theory in Frankfurt. The fellowship offered an ideal setting for refining my ideas, while Marietta Auer's colloquium on private law theory broadened my perspectives on related topics.

In these ten years, I have accumulated many debts of gratitude to outstanding scholars who have engaged with my work. I have been very fortunate to receive feedback on sections of the book from friends, colleagues, and audiences in different forums, including the Max Planck Institute at Freiburg, the Glasgow Legal Theory Group, the Belgrade Legal Theory Group, the Amsterdam Centre on the Legal Professions and Access to Justice, the Durham Centre for Law and Philosophy, and the Oxford Jurisprudence Discussion Group. Thank you to the University of Edinburgh legal theory group, which held a symposium on the book. I am grateful to the audience, and especially to the commentators, Martin Kelly and Arantxa Gutiérrez-Raymondova, for their thought-provoking views. I would like to thank the University of Girona Legal Philosophy Group, and especially Diego Papayannis for his comments on a chapter of the book. Thank you to Amalia Amaya-Navarro, Hrafn Asgeirsson, Eric Boot, Andres Botero, René Brouwer, Thomas Bustamante, Damiano Canale, Conor Casey, Emilios Christodoulidis, Mark D'Souza, Charlotte Elves, Timothy Endicott, Juan Bautista Etcheverry, Javier Gallegos, Marco Goldoni, Alexander Greenberg, Noam Gur, Antony Hatzistavrou, Ulrike Heuer, Heidi Hurd, Miodrag Jovanovic, Carlos Kohn, Hafsteinn Dan Kristjánson, Luciano Laise, Gerald Lang, William Lucy, Ronaldo Porto Macedo, Ewan McDonald, Maria Margarita Rosa Martínez, Claudio Michelon, Michael Moore, Antonio Chacón Moreno, Jorge Nuñez, Dennis Patterson, Joshua Pike, Jeffrey Pojanowski, Lorena Ramírez-Ludeña, Cristina Redondo, Henry Mauricio Reyes, Angelo Ryu, Alex Sarch, Trenton Sewell, Bojan Spaic, Sandy Steel, Christopher Tollefsen, Iris Van Domselaar, Fabiola Vethencourt, Neil Walker, and Kara Woodbury-Smith for their comments on sections of, or ideas related to, the book. I am extremely grateful to Brian Bix, who provided detailed feedback on the entire book. Thank you to Stephen Perry for his insightful comments and key suggestions that enabled me to improve the book. I would like to thank the referees for OUP. Their comments made this work better. Thank you to Anthea Connolly and Louise Chapman, whose meticulous editing significantly improved the text. Last but not least, my enormous gratitude to the editors of the series Private Law Theory at OUP, Paul Miller and John Oberdiek, for their trust and support of this work. Thank you to Brian Stone, Charlotte Kershaw, and their team at OUP for their excellent support and work producing this book.

Chapter 1 draws from material published in 'Backward-Looking Puzzle of Responsibility in Negligence: Some Preliminary Thoughts to Understanding Inadvertent Action' in Verónica Rodríguez-Blanco and George Pavlakos (eds), *Agency, Negligence and Responsibility* (CUP 2021); Chapters 4 and 5 rely on the article 'Ways of Inhabiting the Deliberative-Aspirational Point of View: Practical Reason and Objective Goods' (2022) 67 American Journal of Jurisprudence 293; and Chapter 9 draws from material published in 'Revising the Puzzle of Negligence: Transforming the Citizen Towards Civic Maturity' (2023) 68 American Journal of Jurisprudence 105.

Contents

Figures

Table of Cases

UNITED KINGDOM

NATIONAL CASES

United States

Table of Legislation

Introduction

It is a philosophical platitude that we are beings in the world, and that our actions and activities, as well as the institutions that come from them, are fundamentally and qualitatively different from those of non-human creatures. Thus, constitutions, states, laws, families, universities, corporations, and all the doings and activities within these institutions are distinct from hives of bees, beavers' dams, and the 'doings' of packs of wolves, herds of sheep, schools of fish, and so on. The differences between the 'doings' of non-human animals and human beings are multiple, but the starkest difference lies in the fact that we are the kind of creatures that need to 'make sense' of our doings, activities, and institutions. Through describing and re-describing what we are doing, our own actions, activities, and institutions become intelligible to us. At the same time, we use the activity of 'making sense' of our doings to move forward, so to speak, and to transform both ourselves and our institutions.

Many philosophers and social theorists would agree with this discussion so far. The disagreement emerges when we address the following questions: how should we understand the process of 'making sense' and its impact on our actions and institutions? How minimal or maximal should it be? Given the critical role that reasons and knowledge play in 'making sense' of actions, do we need a top-down approach? Or should we instead start from the self-understanding provided by our social practices, including our language, given the role of our social practices in determining the values in terms of which we 'make sense' of our doings?

If we add to these basic reflections the fact that we make *judgements of responsibility* about our 'doings', we begin to approach a complex and difficult landscape. Understanding why we should be responsible for our negligent actions in both legal and ethical contexts presents us with particularly challenging problems and questions. We can formulate the problem of responsibility for negligence as follows: the person who commits the negligent act cannot have beliefs or knowledge about what they are doing; otherwise, the act would not be inadvertent, and inadvertence is at the core of negligent action. This view inevitably places pressure on our conception of 'doing', in which belief has a central role. 'Doing', we might say, involves beliefs about what one is doing, and, therefore, the focus of control is intentional action. However, in our everyday normative experience, particularly in law and ethics, we are subject to judgements of responsibility for negligence. We perform numerous actions in a way that is forgetful, lazy, distracted, or ignorant, and the results of these actions are not what we intended. Moreover, we sometimes cause harm, and, on other occasions, hurt, ignore, or damage things that matter to others by acting carelessly towards them and their property.

Conceiving negligent action in terms of belief presents a number of challenges, one of which is attempting to pinpoint the moment and process of the agent's belief formation, in order to pinpoint the point at which the action's performer gains control. This view comes under pressure by sceptics who argue that the connection between the initial belief and the resulting action is weak and could lead either to an infinite regress or to clear-eyed *akrasia* (ie to a situation in which the agent has deliberated and knows what to do but decides to ignore her own deliberations on the matter). One complication here, however, is that it has proved difficult to understand what *akrasia* entails.

Responsibility for negligence in law and ethics is under threat not only from a number of sceptical positions concerning knowledge and control as the key factors of responsibility, but also from those philosophers who adhere to the view that moral luck is inevitable. These philosophers argue that because the idea that we can deliberate and control our actions is illusory, moral luck permeates our actions—a fact that complicates judgements of responsibility. These sceptical thoughts have spilt over into a legal philosophical reflection on responsibility in relation to the law of negligence. Indeed, scepticism and the moral luck problem have led philosophers to consider the merits of abolishing negligence law.

In this book, I aim to advance a theory of responsibility for negligence in both law and ethics. Starting from the philosophical platitude that we are inevitably in the world and that we need to 'make sense' of our doings, deliberation seems inescapable. But deliberating soundly and 'making sense' of our doings correctly are achievements. Beliefs and desires are not 'given', and in the process of deliberation, we need to think about and describe values to 'see' our actions in the correct light—or so I shall argue. However, the notion that deliberation is a top-down activity is unrealistic. We require an account of deliberation and our 'doings' that is sufficiently close to our animality but that at the same time explains how the emergence of our rational nature arises from this animality. In other words, we must elucidate what a 'doing' is and the process of 'making sense' in the context of our actions, including negligent ones. This explanation needs to respect our animal nature: the fact that we are human beings with feelings, emotions, passions, and desires. I contend that by comprehending the concept of deliberation and the processes involved in 'doings' and 'making sense', we can gain insight into the functioning of defective 'doings' and 'making sense' processes. The core argument posits that *akrasia, specifically, non-clear-eyed akrasia*, underpins the phenomenon of negligent action, not a 'glitch', or false, implicit, or unconscious beliefs. My explanation of the phenomenon of *akrasia* follows from the conception of deliberation and 'doing' that I put forward. I explain *akrasia* as the uneven development and integration of our thinking, our descriptions and re-descriptions of values, and our desires and passions. I also argue that law, as one of our most important social institutions, and, more specifically, the law of negligence, propounds descriptions and re-descriptions of values as *proleptic* thoughts that allow citizens to inhabit an aspirational perspective.

Court decisions can alienate their addressees and citizens. But we use our normative 'doings' to move forward and transform ourselves, and the law is inescapably part of this normative 'doing'; hence, it is possible for the law to contribute to the activity of 'making sense'. We can abolish the law of negligence, but doing so would deprive us of a means to make sense of an important category of actions, namely careless actions.[1] We can ground the law of negligence on alternative theories, for example, the law and economics theory, according to which the law of negligence should ensure the maximization of wealth. However, this approach reduces the process of 'making sense' of our actions to a focus on 'effective and technocratic actions', leading to a diminished understanding of practical reason.

Of course, judges can engage poorly with descriptions and re-descriptions of values as *proleptic* thoughts. The law of negligence may alienate us, leaving us unable to comprehend its meaning. On the other hand, if the law of negligence is engaged with citizens' deliberation and practical reasoning, in the form of serious engagement with descriptions and re-descriptions of values as *proleptic* thoughts, then it will not alienate citizens because it will emerge from both our empirical and rational agency. Furthermore, the law of negligence is in continuity with citizens' practical reasoning understood in a psychologically realistic manner. In general, law is an abstract matter, but to justify its doctrines, we must delve deeper into the connections between abstract doctrinal concepts and the human condition, the potential of self-transformation, and our moral psychology's ability to articulate these concepts. This book shows that we can justify our doctrinal and abstract concepts of negligence by thoroughly understanding the underlying structure of our own moral psychology, ie our excellent or defective engagement with practical reason.

In Chapter 1, I discuss the key features of negligent action and the puzzle that arises from the backward-looking and forward-looking perspectives of deliberation and action, as well as from the first-person and third- or second-person perspectives on deliberation and action. I argue that there is a tendency to think about negligent action as a matter of attributing a mental state to the agent, thereby reducing the agent's first-person perspective to the third- or second-person perspective on a negligent action. Parallel to this, there is a tendency to think about the negligent action solely from a backward-looking perspective, once the victim's harm

[1] In 1972, New Zealand introduced a non-fault universal insurance scheme and abolished the negligence law. See New Zealand Royal Commission of Inquiry, *The New Zealand Plan, Compensation for Personal Injury in New Zealand* (New Zealand, 1967) (Chair: Mr Justice Owen Woodhouse). The original plan was subject to a series of reforms from 1982, including The Accident Rehabilitation and Compensation Act 1992, the Accident Insurance Act 1998, and the Injury Prevention, Rehabilitation and Compensation Act 2001.

and the agent's action have come together. Once the agent performs the negligent action, the theorist considers the harm and establishes the grounds for responsibility for negligence, while ignoring the agent's complex process of forward-looking deliberation. This means that the forward-looking perspective collapses into the backward-looking perspective. I use the Wittgensteinian concept of 'seeing an aspect' to illuminate the agent's different perspectives, proving that 'seeing' our actions lacks an empirical component and demonstrating that the 'seeing' in deliberation and practical reasoning involves an *act of thinking*. The analysis concludes that there is no conceptual impossibility in grasping the forward-looking perspective on negligent actions from the backward-looking perspective. I argue, however, that we need to change our methodology based on action theory and practical reason.

Chapter 2 explores two sceptical positions regarding responsibility for negligent action in both law and ethics. The first is the sceptical view that we cannot be responsible for negligent actions because we lack knowledge of them while performing them. The position's core argument begins by tracing the moment when the agent formed beliefs about her action, examining the process of forming these beliefs, and evaluating whether the agent discharged her epistemic duties. This leads either to an infinite regress or to clear-eyed *akrasia*, in which the agent knew what to do but, despite this knowledge, performed the negligent act. However, the explanation of the negligent act transforms it into either an intentional or a reckless action. The second sceptical view argues that if the grounding of responsibility is based on character, and past actions are the cause of one's current character traits (eg laziness, sloppiness, forgetfulness, clumsiness), then there is no strong connection between multiple past actions and one's current character. Because of this, the agent could not have known that her past actions would shape her current character.

To scrutinize these sceptical challenges, I examine the role of knowledge and character in action, dispelling some misconceptions about the nature of deliberation, practical knowledge, and character. To achieve this, I examine in Chapter 3 an underlying premise in contemporary conceptions of rational agency and deliberation. Contemporary theories of deliberation presuppose that there is a bifurcation between desires and beliefs within our deliberative stance, a bifurcation that makes it mysterious how beliefs and desires could interact. We place our beliefs on one side and our desires on the other, simplifying, ignoring, or viewing their potential to merge or interact as problematic and implausible. Some contemporary theories of deliberation focus on beliefs, others on desires. Different ways of understanding beliefs and desires manifest this bifurcation, such as distinguishing between deliberations based on motives and deliberations based on reasons, between internal and external reasons for action, and between intellectualist and voluntarist conceptions of agency and deliberation. The result is a specific picture of deliberation that I call the 'balancing view'. All these theories share the common premise that our only task is to balance desires against beliefs, beliefs against beliefs, or desires against desires. As a result, desires and beliefs (and, consequently, desire-based and belief-based reasons) are 'given'. I show that this bifurcation results in an emaciated understanding of the complexity of deliberation and the exercise of practical reason.

Chapter 3 paves the way for a new understanding of deliberation based on Aristotle's ethics, which is the focus of Chapters 4 and 5. My aim in these chapters is not to present Aristotle's own conception of deliberation; rather, I draw inspiration from his texts and from Aristotelian commentators to advance a different understanding of deliberation and practical reason, one that rejects the contemporary bifurcation premise and the 'balancing' view of deliberation to which it leads. The Aristotelian model posits that both practical argument and deliberation constitute practical reason. If there is a hypothetical attribution of deliberation, we are closer to practical argumentation, in which the practical syllogism plays a key role.[2] We should contrast this with the deliberative stance (ie the stance we take when we are acting, and our action is forward-looking). From this stance, we are neither looking at a past action and reconstructing it, nor considering what to do from a purely theoretical perspective. A practical syllogism is generally a scheme for interpreting future or past actions, not something we engage with when we are actually acting.[3] In Chapter 4, my focus is on deliberation—specifically, the first-person perspective or deliberative stance.

Aristotle presents us with a unique model that differs from the Socratic idea of deliberation as the science of measurement—according to which deliberation can be reduced to a skill or craft—and the modern 'balancing' model.[4] Aristotle aims to show that deliberation and its outcome, a rational decision (*prohairesis*),[5] are

[2] 'Deliberation, as Aristotle represents it, does not take a form that remotely resembles an Aristotelian syllogism, and Aristotle never says or implies that it does.' John Cooper, *Reason and the Human Good in Aristotle* (Hackett Publishing 1986) 14. See also Heda Segvic, *From Protagoras to Aristotle* (Princeton UP 2008) 9–10, 148–50. On the idea that the core of practical argumentation is practical syllogism, see ibid 150–51. This is not true to life, and, arguably, the practical syllogism works only as an imputation or scheme of interpretation. See Elizabeth Anscombe, *Intention* (Harvard UP 1957, reprinted 2000) 78–79 and Sarah Broadie, *Ethics with Aristotle* (OUP 1991). See Broadie (this note) 157, for a criticism of the schematism of practical syllogism. Other commentators have highlighted that Aristotle's explanation of the incontinent person's reasoning in the form of practical syllogism is too sketchy. Bonnie Kent, 'Transitory Vice: Thomas Aquinas on Incontinence' (1989) 27 Journal of the History of Philosophy 199, 200. See Chapter 5 for a detailed discussion of the practical syllogism.

[3] See Agnes Callard, 'Aristotle on Deliberation' in Ruth Chang and Kurt Sullivan (eds), *Routledge Handbook of Practical Reason* (Routledge 2021).

[4] For the difference between the contemporary model and the Aristotelian, see ibid. Callard argues that balancing is only one aspect of the model derived from Aristotle. Karen Nielsen argues that Hardie also makes the comparison necessary, but this is difficult to square with the Aristotelian model; see Karen Nielsen, 'Deliberation as Inquiry: Aristotle's Alternative to the Presumption of Open Alternatives' (2011) 120 The Philosophical Review 383, 386. She also adds some intriguing notes on the comparative model of Aristotle's deliberation. ibid 387.

[5] There are a variety of translations of the Aristotelian term *prohairesis*. We can simply interpret it as the end or the conclusion of deliberation. Hardie offers an analysis of the word as 'efficient cause'. WFR Hardie, *Aristotle's Ethical Theory* (originally printed in 1968, Clarendon Press 2004) 160–64. According to Hardie, it is not an intellectual opinion; rather, after choosing and acting, we show our character (ibid

not skills or crafts, although deliberation has important elements that overlap with what we understand as a craft or skill. At the same time, Aristotle shows that there is an important overlap between theoretical reasoning and deliberation.[6] Because deliberation has a proper way of functioning, Aristotle's explanation successfully avoids the Scylla of conceiving of deliberation as a craft or skill and the Charybdis of assimilating deliberation to theoretical reasoning.[7] Aristotle's endeavour, if successful, reveals the possibility of practical reason.

In addition, I criticize the 'grand end' view of practical deliberation and defend what I refer to as the 'upward journey towards the specification of the *what*'. I argue that there is no need to recognize or validate the procedure's correctness. Does this imply a lack of reflection on the *what* and the *how*, as well as a lack of recognition in the deliberative process? I address this issue in Chapter 5, showing how recognition is possible within the 'upward journey towards the specification of the *what*' view. According to this perspective, recognition operates not externally but internally.

The 'upward journey towards the specification of the *what*' view acknowledges that, as we exercise our deliberative capacities, we are also perceiving, learning to perceive, and acquiring insights. The quality of this learning depends on the quality of deliberation and rational decision (*prohairesis*).[8] The particulars of the action are its essence rather than its products.[9] The particulars can be seen only from the deliberative perspective, and what is 'seen' can be improved through reflection—an idea I explain further in Chapter 5. Chapter 5 shows that desires are the work of intelligence, which implies a process of thinking and transformation. When making judgements about responsibility, we tend to focus on reasons for action and/or our rational capacities, as well as the agent's desires and beliefs. Desires and beliefs occur at specific times within the 'balancing' model of reasons for action. Action is a snapshot of what the deliberator happens to apprehend at any given moment. The standard 'balancing' model of deliberation focuses on desires as states that are 'given', and beliefs that make the necessary connection either with

165). In Chapter 5, using the Aristotelian model of deliberation, I explain the key element of becoming or transformation. Segvic asserts that Plato uses '*prohairesis*' only once in the *Parmenides*, see Segvic (n 2) 162, fn 25. Vigo distinguishes two senses of '*prohairesis*'. Alejandro Vigo, 'Deliberación y Decisión Segun Aristóteles' (2012) 43 Tópicos: Revista de Filosofía 51. He highlights that *prohairesis* is not a commitment, but rather the end of the investigation into the basic action with which the agent began. See Aristotle, *Nichomachean Ethics* (trs Sarah Broadie and Christopher Rowe, OUP 2002) 1139a30. To refer to Aristotle's works, I use the Bekker numbers. *Prohairesis* is a result of deliberation that combines cognitive and emotional elements. See Aristotle (this note) 1113a10ff.

[6] See Hardie (n 5) 225–28.

[7] The tendency to collapse the distinction between theoretical and practical reasoning leads to a mistaken view of the role of practical syllogism (see Chapter 6).

[8] Reeve highlights perception in deliberation. Christopher Reeve, *Action, Contemplation and Happiness* (Harvard UP 2012) 181–83. See also Cooper (n 2) 65.

[9] See Broadie (n 2) 205, 209, who uses the appropriate expression 'happiness is an activity'. This implies that achieving an understanding of living well necessitates deliberation and action.

normative reasons or with desires within the so-called 'motivational set'. By contrast, on the Aristotelian model of deliberation, thinking transforms our desires.

In Chapter 5, I demonstrate the importance of the deliberative-aspirational perspective. We learn of the possibility of a deliberative-aspirational perspective through others and through engaging in immersed deliberation—for instance, when our inadvertent action causes harm to others. In Chapter 1, I present the case of Alessandra, who leaves her dog in her vehicle on a hot day and, upon returning with her children, finds that her dog has died from heatstroke. Alessandra does not learn about the tragedy through a process of inference. Alessandra does not conclude that her dog died from the fact that it is a hot day, there is no fresh air in the car, and the dog is not breathing. There is no inference from the factual premises. She does not interpret what she sees and attributes responsibility to herself for what has happened. On the contrary, prior to acting, Alessandra deliberated and determined the *what* through the *how*; for instance, she registered her children in hockey lessons and encouraged their participation in hockey to foster in them a sense of team spirit and a healthy lifestyle. She did not know *what* the particular and core features of this good would be (namely, team spirit and a healthy lifestyle), but rather discovered that hockey is a good through deliberating on *how* to achieve this end. She also bought a pet for her children, hoping that they would learn to care for animals. Alessandra must combine being a mother who aims to cultivate camaraderie in her children with being a good pet owner. Prior to collecting the children from their hockey game, she deliberated over whether to bring the dog; she wanted the dog to have fresh air, to be able to greet the children, and perhaps to chase a stick after the game. Some of these deliberations took place prior to the fatal moment of the accident. When Alessandra returns to her car and sees her dog dead, she immediately understands what has happened. Similar to the Wittgensteinian duck-rabbit example discussed in Chapter 1, the tragedy 'dawns on her', causing her to 'see' aspects of both her own *actions* and her *thinking*. Aspects of our actions can be hidden by other aspects, and experiences can transform us by revealing different aspects of the particularities of our actions. Because Alessandra pursued her thinking in this case through narrow deliberation, she does *not* need any process of inference or interpretation. She knows what she has deliberated and thought about, and, as I shall argue, she avoids inhabiting the aspirational-deliberative perspective.

Suppose that Alessandra has heard in the news about recent high temperatures, and that, on a number of occasions, friends have warned her against attempting to juggle too many tasks and refusing to accept her limitations. Alessandra could inhabit the aspirational perspective and transform her desires and character, for instance, by buying a pet for the children only when they are more independent and sufficiently responsible to take care of it themselves.

Avoidance can lead to fantasy and a lack of attention. Recognition is the way in which we inhabit the deliberative-aspirational perspective. Once we recognize a particular feature in its specificity and context, we can think about it and change our views; at the same time, when this recognition and thinking become part of our deliberations, we transform our emotions and desires. Because this transformation includes our emotions and desires, it affects our character's development. However, transformation is not solely a result of training our desires, emotions, and character; it also occurs as a consequence of taking a perspective, which involves thinking about a subject matter and recognizing it, or avoiding it and failing to examine it.

But how does inhabiting this deliberative-aspirational perspective enable us to engage with medium- and long-term goals without losing the immersed or narrow deliberative perspective? We have learned that changing our perspectives through both thought and experience does not involve contemplating our inner experiences and thoughts as if they were mere events or objects. I reject the view that we can be impartial or detached from our experiences without losing something important. I also reject the perceptual model of self-reflection and the objectification of the self, advocating instead a model of transparent self-reflection on which the agent tries to settle the question '*what shall I do?*', paying careful attention to the subject matter, relationships, and what is right. The agent looks outward at the world and either recognizes or fails to recognize the deficiencies in her interactions with others. We can use this recognition or avoidance as a basis for further narrow deliberations. Relationships and experiences confront us with others, inviting us to either avoid or recognize them. By carefully paying attention to the features of the world and our relationships, we are able to aspire to medium- and long-term goals within the narrow or immersed deliberative perspective. The depth and richness of the latter process enable us to better understand whether (and if so, how) our current position is lacking. Grasping these medium- and long-term goals is possible because there is a trajectory from the immersed perspective to the deliberative-aspirational perspective. The latter is an expansive view that is continuous with the immersed perspective. Medium- and long-term goals, while uncertain, can form part of future immersed or narrow deliberations.

Chapter 6 argues that *akrasia* underpins and explains ethical blameworthiness and judgements of responsibility for negligent acts. This chapter advances the view that we act inadvertently because we act *akratically*. This, in turn, is explained as a specific defective engagement of the agent's practical reasoning, a failure of integration between character and thinking that should be understood as a *failure to inhabit the deliberative-aspirational perspective*.

At first glance, the concept of *akrasia* may not appear helpful due to its multiple interpretations and ambivalences. Moreover, in addition to the complexity of interpreting Socratic and Aristotelian technical notions, contemporary and ancient understandings of *akrasia* differ. This is because ancient and contemporary conceptions of practical reason and deliberation (see Chapter 3) differ. Consequently, *akrasia* appears to be an elusive and inscrutable phenomenon.

In §6.1, I distinguish the modern conception of *akrasia* from the view advocated by Socrates and Aristotle and explain how some contemporary models of *akratic* action are either deflationary or change the subject. I also argue that the Aristotelian practical syllogism is problematic as an explanation of how we act *akratically*. When we focus on how deliberation operates, we think about the diachronic structure of practical agency; in contrast, practical syllogisms are used as practical arguments once an action has been performed and cannot explain how deliberation actually works.[10] Practical syllogisms provide the structure of the agent's practical argument when we engage in justification or reconstruction of the action. Practical syllogisms, however, do not explain what happens to the agent when she acts *akratically*. In other words, the appeal to practical syllogisms falls short because it ignores the dynamic and complex aspects of deliberation. It has a dubiously artificial and schematic quality.[11] Arguably, in order to fully grasp the deliberative process and how the agent exercises practical reasoning, we must understand the diachronic structure of the first-person perspective.[12] This is at the core of a sound explanation of acting *akratically*.

In §6.2, I show how we can fail to integrate thinking and desire and how we can fail to inhabit the deliberative-aspirational perspective. This shows how the concept of *akrasia*, properly understood, underlies the concept of negligent action. Chapter 6 establishes the foundations for the discussion of responsibility for negligent action, deliberation, and diachronic agency that takes place in the following three chapters of the book.

Chapters 7 and 8 focus on the solutions offered by legal theorists and moral philosophers to the puzzle of negligence in law and ethics, respectively. Chapter 7 shows that contemporary general theories of tort law fail to address four key challenges that arise from the phenomenology of negligent action. First, *the abstract challenge* shows that all theories that focus on the *right/duty* pair in the law of negligence use an excessively abstract conception of action, obscuring the question of responsibility or blameworthiness for negligent action at the level of agency and deliberation. Secondly, *the deterrence challenge* shows that we should not conceptualize deterrence as an empirical engagement with action or as an intelligible connection to risk. For instance, Ripstein tells us that negligence always involves the realization that the defendant created a specific risk to the plaintiff.[13] Ripstein emphasizes the complete sequence of events that begins with the risk and ends with the defendant's injury; however, his attributive approach, which adopts a third-person

[10] See Segvic (n 2).

[11] See Broadie (n 2); Anthony Kenny, 'The Practical Syllogisma and Incontinence' (1966) 11 Phronesis 163–84; Anscombe (n 2).

[12] Walsh, for example, emphasizes the importance of an explanation of *akrasia* that considers the wider context of Aristotelian concepts (ie the concepts of practical reason and deliberation). James Walsh, *Aristotle's Conception of Moral Weakness* (Columbia UP 1963) 118.

[13] See Arthur Ripstein, *Private Wrongs* (Harvard UP 2016) 87.

perspective, fails to explain the law's role concerning deterrence when a citizen engages in or is deliberating about an action from a forward-looking perspective. Thirdly, *the particularity challenge* asserts that law's addressees cannot engage with negligence law based on general rules, directives, or principles. Nor can negligence law employ ways of thinking and concepts that are alien to our deliberative stance (eg risk and probability). Fourthly, *the guidance challenge* establishes that an adequate theory of negligence must explain how the law engages with the practical reasoning of the citizens it addresses. In this chapter, I explain why different existing theories of the grounds of the law of negligence cannot adequately respond to these challenges.

Chapter 8 analyses how the 'balancing view' has cast a spell over contemporary explanations of negligence in the context of ethics. The 'balancing' model of deliberation presents reasons as fully grasped by the agent, leaving no room for learning or the cultivation and transformation of our thinking, emotions, and desires. There is no diachronicity, and the moment of choice is interpreted as an evaluation of the different reasons—either desire-based or belief-based, either internal or external, but in any case 'given'—that provide the best answer to the question, 'What shall I do?' Defective executions, such as negligence or inadvertence, become problematic and puzzling. On the other hand, there exist a variety of non-sceptical strategies that aim to demonstrate that the agent had a moment of choice, also known as the 'tracing strategy', or the capacity to choose, that the executed action fell within the agent's rational competence, that there is a reasonable expectation that the agent will act in accordance with the right standard, that the agent should have exercised more thought and fulfilled her epistemic duties, that the agent exposed others to an unreasonable risk and should have foreseen it, or a combination of the above. I discuss all of these solutions to the sceptical problem of negligence in ethics, solutions that indirectly affect our understanding of the law of negligence. I show that all these strategies are based on the 'balancing model' of deliberation, which assumes that the appropriate task is either to find a *locus* of responsibility or to abolish the diachronicity of agency. I argue that the consequent explanations of responsibility for negligence and of the wrongness of negligence are unsatisfactory.

Chapter 9 concentrates on developing an account of negligence in the context of law based on the Aristotelian concepts of deliberation, *akrasia*, and the avoidance of the aspirational perspective. My account explains negligent wrongful conduct and provides a fruitful elucidation of negligence law. It also explains the role of the law of negligence in 'making sense' of both negligent and non-negligent actions.

I advance the idea that legal directives, principles, and rules that impose a duty of care on citizens play the role of *proleptic* thoughts (ie anticipated thoughts that are part of the deliberations of citizens when they engage in different activities; for example, a surgeon operating on a patient). Legal rules and directives impose duties of care and tell citizens to consider these duties in their deliberations. However, legal directives, principles, and rules are the result of descriptions and re-descriptions of values advanced by judges who engage with the particularities of legal cases *as if* they were in the position of the forward-looking perspective—or so I shall argue. Furthermore, citizens' practical reasoning cannot include duties and rights as general formulations of 'what one ought to do' unless they integrate them into both narrow (or substandard) and aspirational deliberations. This means that citizens are invited to think carefully about how the *specification* of the *how* can determine the *what*, while also paying attention to their own thoughts about the specific subject matter, in order to inhabit the deliberative-aspirational perspective.

If we apply the denial of the fantasy of a private language to our discussions of what is good, what is right, what is valuable, what is worth engaging with, and what 'makes sense', we see that there cannot be a private vision of the good. Legal decisions cannot have a private space in which the referent of the good, right, valuable, or worthwhile is intelligible only to judges or legal practitioners and inscrutable to others. At the same time, judges, in their legal decisions, are attempting to determine the deliberative-aspirational perspective and invite citizens to inhabit it. Judges justify the attribution of responsibility for negligence if citizens fail to adopt this perspective. The agent's failure to adopt the required deliberative-aspirational perspective, which resulted in injury to the defendant, explains why negligence is wrong. *In legal terms, we could say that the deliberative-aspirational perspective defines the contours of the reasonable standard of care.*

I shall also show that while the backward-looking insights of corrective justice theorists are important, the primary duty of citizens is to engage with the *proleptic* thoughts or reasonings of legal decisions that specify the way in which the *how* determines the *what* in settling the question, 'What shall I do?' However, legal decisions also demand that we inhabit a deliberative-aspirational perspective to further specify an answer to the question, 'What shall I do?' This final chapter shows the continuity of law and ethics in the domain of negligence law and discusses one important potential objection to the ideas defended in the book.

PART I
THE PUZZLE OF NEGLIGENCE

When (a) we have knowledge of our action and (b) we are not under coercion, it seems reasonable to assert that we are responsible for our intentional actions. Nevertheless, it is uncertain if we bear responsibility for actions when we exhibit flaws of character, such as laziness, distraction, social awkwardness, and so on.

Our actions are inadvertent and may eventually be considered negligent because they breach a standard or norm that a reasonable person would not have violated. Put simply, from an ethical and legal standpoint, we can conclude that the person acted negligently because the agent acted in an unreasonable manner.

However, it is paradoxical that I should be held responsible for acting unreasonably when my inherent character flaws or the circumstances of my action prevented me from being aware of or noticing them. It seems unfair to hold me responsible for things that are beyond my control, such as my distractions, laziness, and lack of attention, which stem from my passions and desires and ultimately are constitutive of my character. While I could exercise some control over my beliefs and knowledge of my actions, I do not control spontaneous passions and desires that can overtake my reasoning, as they are constitutive of who I am.

Apart from this significant challenge regarding the connection between character and the knowledge of my action, how should we characterize negligent or inadvertent action in theory-relevant ways? Theorists propose explanations that share a premise. The negligent or inadvertent act occurred due to 'absent' beliefs. We interpret them as mental states that were 'absent' when they should not have been.

However, I contend that this is an inaccurate explanation of negligent or inadvertent action. To understand inadvertent action, we must analyse how we act from a first-person or deliberative perspective. We think about our desires, perceiving their content as something worthy or valuable to pursue. As a result, we invariably engage in *how* we should obtain what we deem valuable or worthy. My contention is that our shared concepts play a key role in grasping value and learning to desire. Concepts are the background against which we engage with the world, come to 'see' matters in a specific way, and value or disvalue them. Therefore, I challenge the idea that our intentional actions stem from our beliefs and desires construed as mental states. I offer a more precise depiction of the agent's practical reasoning when she commits an inadvertent or negligent act. When she looks back at her action, her defective practical reasoning 'dawns' on her. She does not learn what she has done through inference or theory. She does not acquire knowledge by inferring that she should have been in a certain mental state when she committed the inadvertent or negligent act. On the contrary, she 'sees' an aspect of her own reasoning when she initiated her action and 'sees' the eventual harm that she has caused due to her defective exercise of practical reasoning.

This first part of the book discusses the key features of a negligent or inadvertent action, as well as the scepticism surrounding responsibility for negligent or inadvertent action.

1

The Puzzle of Negligence in Law and Ethics

§1.1 Basic Phenomenological Features of Negligence

A negligent act is the focus of the law of negligence, as are practices of blaming and holding responsible in ethics and morality. However, it is puzzling how we should characterize an action that is negligent—and therefore non-intentional—in such a way as to render it our own doing and hence susceptible to judgements of responsibility.

What kind of creatures are we that we can be responsible for negligent actions? We do things and make things happen in the world, even when we are forgetful or ignorant. This can seem counter-intuitive and even contradictory, given that the paradigm of action is intentional or deliberative action. Some theories of responsibility focus on the key feature of intentional action, commonly referred to as 'choice'. Other views on responsibility focus on the evaluative judgements that we attribute to the responsible agent. However, in our current legal and moral practices, we impose responsibility for careless or inadvertent acts, and in such cases, it is unclear whether evaluatively defective judgements or defective choices play a role. Arguably, we bear responsibility when our actions stem from inadvertence or forgetfulness, even if we feel some degree of alienation from them. It is clear that we can be responsible when we deliberate, as this allows us to exercise our capacity for practical reason and control our behaviour. It is less clear that we can be responsible when we are forgetful, distracted, inattentive, unfocused, or imagining things that are not our intended goal or end.

The question of what kind of creatures we are that we can be held accountable for negligent acts requires an answer to a more fundamental question: how can we say that we 'do X' when we perform X, which may involve acting in error, forgetfulness, or inadvertence in relation to our initial deliberation? In other words, we must address the question of how deliberation breaks down and whether this breakdown entails agency as partly alienated, or rather entails a continuity of our agency and therefore our action and responsibility.

To provide a satisfactory explanation of negligent actions, one must adequately account for the basic features of the phenomenology of inadvertent actions, as outlined below:

Inattention/Inadvertence:

(1) Cases of pure negligence are grounded in inattention or inadvertence.

Responsibility for Negligence in Ethics and Law. Verónica Rodríguez-Blanco, Oxford University Press.
 DOI: 10.1093/9780198948193.003.0001

Non-intentional:

(2) The agent is engaged in performing the action, and her deliberative stance is crucial, but, paradoxically, she brings about a state of affairs that is unintended.

Trivial:

(3) The agent perceives the portion of the action that involves the inadvertence or error as trivial or inconsequential at the time of performance.

Blameworthiness is grounded on failing to act in accordance with a standard:

(4) Blameworthiness is grounded on the idea that there are objective standards for right action and that negligent action falls below the standard and hence amounts to wrong action.

Failure to grasp the objective standard or the right action:

(5) At the moment of the performance of the action, the agent fails to grasp the objective standard for the right action.

Learning about the action after its performance:

(6) The agent learns about her action after seeing the harm or other effects of it.

Disappearance of triviality:

(7) The harm or other effects of the action make it apparent to the agent that the inadvertent part of the action is not trivial or inconsequential.

Before advancing a theoretical framework to shed light on the basic features of the phenomenology of negligent actions, we must make explicit the puzzle that arises as a result of the two different perspectives on responsibility for negligent actions. Responsibility for inadvertent or careless acts raises a puzzle about how the deliberative or first-person aspect of action can be grasped as past, given that the deliberative perspective is forward-looking while responsibility is backward-looking. To shed light on how agents engage in the performance of negligent actions and develop an adequate account of responsibility for negligence, I discuss the backward-looking puzzle.

§1.2 The Backward-Looking Puzzle of Responsibility for Negligence

We can think about inadvertent actions in relation to the paradigm case of action, which is intentional action. This entails delving into action from the first-person or deliberative perspective.[1] This method of explaining action is primarily

[1] This is different from the 'subjective' point of view that focuses on motivational or internal reasons. The idea of the first-person or deliberative stance concentrates on action and practical reason. See my book Verónica Rodríguez-Blanco, *Law and Authority Under the Guise of the Good* (Hart/Bloomsbury 2014) for further reflection on this.

forward-looking, meaning that it focuses on what we bring about with our bodily movements from the agent's point of view. This perspective focuses on the ideas of movement, change, and transformation. By contrast, in our practices of responsibility, attributing responsibility for an action involves focusing on the past; our assessment is backward-looking, and, arguably, the action is conceived, at least partially, as an *event*. There is no movement or transformation. Something happened, and the change and transformation in the world have already been effected at the point of the attribution of responsibility. I will initially formulate the puzzle of negligence intuitively as follows:

> When we individuate an inadvertent action using the deliberative or first-person perspective and its forward-looking description, which encompasses changes, movement, and their underlying logos or reasons, it becomes challenging to understand the action as a past event. Events are not progressive and do not involve future changes or movements. Philosophically speaking, we need something that seems conceptually impossible: we need a sound backward-looking perspective for the purposes of legal and moral responsibility for negligence, which at the same time grasps the forward-looking perspective. This seems conceptually impossible because it entails a concept that grasps both the changes and movements of inadvertent and intentional actions as seen from the deliberative stance and inadvertent and intentional actions as events occurring in the past.

The literature on negligence attempts to identify the key features that characterize negligence, but analyses tend to be too quick when it comes to establishing a sound conception of action as a basis for an account of negligence. Nearly all authors have assumed that there is a symmetry between the observer, or third-person perspective, and the deliberator, or first-person perspective. The tendency, therefore, is to collapse (a) the first-person or deliberative perspective into the third-person or observer perspective, and (b) the forward-looking perspective into the backward-looking perspective. Theorists propose this solution for intentional actions and speculate that it could also apply to inadvertent actions. In other words, as performers of an intentional action that happened and brought about a result, object, or state of affairs in the world, we give a report of what happened from the third-person or observer perspective.

With regard to negligent actions, legal theorists and philosophers aim to identify the action from the third-person perspective and determine what happened to the agent when she acted inadvertently. For instance, legal theorists and philosophers have engaged in attempting to determine the 'absent key element or condition' that will enable us to say that an agent acted negligently. Some examples of the questions posed are: did the agent fail to *form the belief* that her action posed a risk?[2]

[2] For a full discussion of the 'belief' account of responsibility for negligence, see Chapter 8.

Did she fail to *know* that there was a risk? Was there a process, resulting from the interplay of pre-conscious and conscious states, that would explain the control required for assuming responsibility for negligence?[3] Can we identify *the point at which the agent chose* a defective character that led her to the negligent action?[4] Other authors have concentrated on conscience,[5] unexercised capacities,[6] and character as factors in negligent actions,[7] but these accounts neither sufficiently explain nor satisfactorily theorize the kinds of action that are presupposed.

The following example might illustrate the symmetrical thesis. Let us suppose that I make a cup of tea while an observer watches my bodily movements. For example, I boil the water, place a teabag in the cup, and then, after a few minutes, place the tea on my kitchen table. The observer will attribute to me the mental state of believing that if I boil the water and pour it into a cup with a teabag in it, I can make a cup of tea, as well as the desire to make a cup of tea.

According to this view, if I ask myself whether I acted intentionally, I also explain the action in similar terms: I shall say that I was in the mental state of believing that I would produce a cup of tea and that I desired to make a cup of tea. This view assumes that there is a symmetry between the deliberative stance and the observer stance, namely a third-person perspective. Most importantly, within this position, there will be another symmetrical conflation between the backward-looking and the forward-looking perspectives. This means that when I was acting, I was acting because I was in the mental state of believing that I would produce a cup of tea and the mental state of desiring to make a cup of tea. When I look back at the result of my action, I will also explain it in terms of my mental states, namely, desires and beliefs.

When we think about our practices of responsibility, theorists tend to engage in a similar conflation. For instance, suppose that you make a cup of tea at work, approach a colleague whom you hate for spreading rumours about you, spill the tea on her, and pretend that it was an accident. An observer could attribute responsibility to you, stating that you had the intention to burn your colleague, both because you believed you could burn her with your actions and because you had the

[3] Kim Ferzan,'Opaque Recklessness' (2001) 91 The Journal of Criminal Law and Criminology 597.

[4] This is the so-called 'tracing view'; see Chapter 8.

[5] Gideon Yaffe, 'How Could You? The Moral Import of Obliviousness' in Verónica Rodríguez-Blanco and George Pavlakos (eds), *Agency, Negligence and Responsibility* (CUP 2021) 57.

[6] See HLA Hart, *Punishment and Responsibility* (OUP 1968) 149; Joseph Raz, 'Responsibility and the Negligence Standard' (2010) 30 Oxford Journal of Legal Studies 1; Joseph Raz, 'Being in the World' (2010) 23 Ratio 422; Andrew Simester, 'Responsibility for Inadvertent Acts' (2005) 2 Ohio State Journal of Criminal Law 601. For a discussion of the positions of Hart and Raz, see Ori Herstein, 'Responsibility in Negligence: Discussion of From Normativity To Responsibility' (2013) 8 Jerusalem Review of Legal Studies 167; cf Heidi Hurd and Michael Moore, 'Punishing the Awkward, the Stupid, the Weak and the Selfish: The Culpability of Negligence' (2011) 5 Criminal Law and Philosophy 147, 164–65. For a discussion of the 'capacity' view, see Chapter 8.

[7] See Yaffe (n 5); Antony Duff, 'Choice, Character and Criminal Liability' (1993) 12 Law and Philosophy 345; Antony Duff, *Intention, Agency and Criminal Liability* (Blackwell 1990); George Sher, 'Out of Control' (2006) 116 Ethics 285; George Sher, *Who Knew* (OUP 2009).

desire. The result of the action is that her skin is now burned. We can now attribute a causal link between the mental states (ie a belief that your actions will burn your colleague and the desire to burn a colleague, who is considered an enemy), and the result of the action (ie an injury). However, from a deliberative perspective, you focus solely on how she has disseminated malicious rumours about you, how your reputation has suffered, and how your actions represent a genuine act of revenge. You make a scalding cup of tea and contemplate how to casually walk by, pretending that the spillage was a mere accident. Your focus is on what actions are required to pretend that the hot cup of tea slipped from your hands, resulting in injury. Here, the structure of the agent's practical reasoning is present, giving a different kind of intelligibility to the act. The focus is on the action's becoming or unfolding (eg the process of exacting revenge and pretending to be the key to the appearance of an accident). In the previous description, we assume that there is a causal link between the individual's mental states and the state of affairs in the world, which we must disentangle to determine whether the individual is responsible. In the latter description, we focus on the process of practical reasoning and the becoming of the action. At first glance, there seems to be no substantive difference in explaining the action, so we can conflate the observer and the first-person perspectives.[8] However, problems arise when we consider inadvertent actions.

Let us imagine the following example:

DRIVING ABOVE THE SPEED LIMIT

You are driving slightly over the speed limit in a school zone; the speed limit is 20 miles per hour, and you are driving at 25 miles per hour, while listening to loud music. When a child crosses the street, you fail to notice him, and consequently run him over, causing him to be injured.

The observer will explain that your mental state of distraction caused you to drive at a high speed, which in turn caused the injury to the child. The 'but for' or counterfactual test of causation will explain that your mental state of distraction caused the injury to the child. The observer could also say that you missed a foreseeable risk that you ought to have grasped but did not.[9] How would we explain this in terms of mental states and the observer's perspective? We could argue that you were responsible because you *were not in* the mental state of believing in

[8] For a criticism of this conflation of intentional actions, see my monograph, Rodríguez-Blanco (n 1).

[9] I omit the complex doctrinal views of legal negligence because, in my judgement, a piecemeal approach to understanding negligence in the ordinary and philosophical senses will help us to illuminate and evaluate the doctrinal perspective in both criminal and tort law. For instance, in English Tort Law, we establish a defendant's negligence when we demonstrate that the defendant owed the plaintiff a duty of care, violated this duty, and demonstrated that her actions caused the harm. Both the conditions of proximity and foreseeability determine the duty of care (*Donoghue v Stevenson* [1932] AC 562; *Caparo v Dickman* [1990] 2 AC 605; *Bourhill v Young* [1943] AC 92), yet the interpretation of these terms remains ambiguous.

the foreseeable risk, even though you *should have been*. You *ought to have known or been aware* that the area was a school zone, which entails a lower speed limit and the likelihood of children being present. However, from the first-person perspective, you were enjoying your favourite radio station, which coincidentally was playing your most beloved piece of music. The music's beauty carried you away, causing you to press the pedal without realizing what was happening. We could add that the reasons for your action (ie pressing the pedal) were your emotions and thoughts about pleasure and beauty, flights of imagination aroused by the beauty of the music, etc.

In the case of inadvertent actions, the observer or third-person perspective does not explain the action but rather establishes the mental state that I should have to avoid responsibility.[10] Given this, how does the absence of this mental state, ie the failure to be in the mental state of foreseeing, forming the belief, or having the true and justified belief, provide an intrinsic and intelligible connection to the outcome of the action? In cases of inadvertent actions, the symmetry between the third-person and first-person perspectives seems to break down. In other words, how the agent sees her own action while acting and how she looks back and sees the action as an outcome or result are different. The symmetrical view fails to capture this difference. Observe the contrast with our everyday language, which typically grasps and clearly conveys this difference. In the context of our previous example, the speeding driver will say, 'At the moment of the accident, I did not mean to hurt the child; I was just listening to my favourite music.' By contrast, in an imaginary world in which our ordinary language reflects the symmetrical view, the speeding driver would instead say: 'At the moment of the accident, I was listening to my favourite music, and at the same time, unfortunately, the appropriate mental state that would have enabled me to prevent the accident was absent.' How should we understand this in relation to our current linguistic practices? Did the driver know, at the point of acting, that she lacked the requisite mental state? The latter statement makes sense only *after* the accident, but it is not part of the agent's practical reasoning structure when she is performing the action. It seems unintelligible that, while she is performing the action, the agent *knows* that the appropriate mental state is absent. How can she be aware of the absence of certain mental states? And how does this absence explain her action? Unsurprisingly, we must now turn to theoretical mechanisms such as pre-conscious states, which are unable to clarify how the agent, rather than an internal mechanism, initiated the action. If we accept the symmetrical view as the correct explanation for action and use it to explain

[10] The 'tracing' strategy does not rescue the symmetrical view. The problem of identifying the correct mental state applies to past actions in terms of the mental state the agent had, which determines culpability for the negligent act. For criticism of the tracing strategy, see Manuel Vargas, 'On the Importance of History for Responsible Agency' (2006) 127 Philosophical Studies 351; Matthew King, 'The Problem of Negligence' (2009) 35 Social Theory and Practice 577; cf John Martin Fisher and Neil Tognazzini, 'The Truth About Tracing' (2009) 43 Nous 531. For a criticism of the 'tracing account', see Chapter 8.

responsibility for negligence, it appears that sceptical positions will have the upper hand in the discussion.[11]

I will argue that we can think about backward-looking inadvertent actions and our practices of responsibility if we change the methodological focus of our inquiry. When we scrutinize inadvertent backward-looking actions, we do not look at facts—facts about mental states or facts about the world—as the consequences of our actions, because this way of thinking obscures the phenomenology of agency and responsibility. In contrast, I will draw an important analogy between 'seeing an aspect' and 'seeing an inadvertent act', arguing that both rely on our trained and reflexive capacities and dispositions. In §1.3, I explain the phenomenon of 'seeing an aspect' as advanced by Ludwig Wittgenstein in *Philosophical Investigations.* In §1.4, I show the analogies between 'seeing an aspect' and 'seeing an inadvertent action' and explain how 'seeing an inadvertent act' is immersed in our daily activities and practices of attributing responsibility, as well as how we can create a backward-looking perspective that grasps the first-person perspective or deliberative stance. Finally, in §1.5, I shall explore the implications of this new methodology for thinking about legal and moral responsibility for negligence.

§1.3 'Seeing an Aspect'

Wittgenstein introduces the idea of 'seeing an aspect' in the second part of *Philosophical Investigations* (Fragment XI)[12] with the puzzle of how we see two different figures in the same drawing while the physical properties of the picture—the lines, colours, shape, and organization remain intact. I have included a drawing below in Figure 1.1.

[11] Hurd and Moore (n 6) and Rosen represent the two main sceptical positions, although their positions differ. Gideon Rosen, 'Scepticism About Moral Responsibility' (2004) 18 Philosophical Perspectives 295. The former reject the notion that there can be a unified theory of negligence in the context of criminal law because '*negligence is not a single continent with a unified nature. It is more like an archipelago of islands, each with its own distinct nature*.' Hurd and Moore (n 6) 192. Like Hurd and Moore, Fitzpatrick also defends the view that negligence is not a unitary notion but argues that it should be based on 'reasonable expectations'. William Fitzpatrick, 'Varieties of Negligence and Complications for Moral Blameworthiness' in Verónica Rodríguez-Blanco and George Pavlakos (eds), *Agency, Negligence and Responsibility* (CUP 2021) 75. Rosen posits that we could explain negligence by tracing the agent's fault back to the moment when the agent had knowledge or awareness of the action, which they then disregarded. This is a case of *akrasia* but unfortunately, Rosen tells us, we do not sufficiently understand what this entails, or whether *akrasia* is even possible. Alexander, Ferzan, and Morse also offer an important sceptical position when they argue that responsibility for negligence is flawed. It cannot guide behaviour as it reaches the agent too late, and if there are cases of choice that later become cases of inadvertence, then these are not cases of negligence but rather collapse into recklessness (ie the agent consciously disregards the risks of her actions; see Larry Alexander, Kim Ferzan, and Stephen Morse, *Crime and Culpability* (CUP 2009) Chapter 3. For a discussion of sceptical views, see Chapter 2 of this book.

[12] See Ludwig Wittgenstein, *Philosophical Investigations* (originally published in 1953, Blackwell 2009).

Figure 1.1 Wittgenstein's 'Duck-Rabbit'

When we first look at the drawing, we see a duck, and we think about ducks in a pond and the feathers and colours of ducks. When we look again, more closely, we see a rabbit, and thoughts of rabbits and rabbit activities might come to mind (eg rabbits jumping in a meadow or rabbits eating carrots). We seem to relate to the two pictures, not in terms of their physical reality, as the lines of the drawing remain unchanged. We do not relate to the pictures in terms of their organization, because neither has changed.

What changes and enables us to see a rabbit at one time, and then, all of a sudden, a duck is *our perspective*—in other words, how we relate to the lines in the drawing. This is what Wittgenstein calls 'aspect dawning'. You do not choose the perspective; it imposes itself upon you. The picture imposes one aspect on us, compelling us to perceive a rabbit; suddenly, a shift takes place, revealing a duck. The description is reached spontaneously, swiftly eliminating alternative possibilities such as a donkey or a smiley face. We also think about the figure, as we have learned to respond to what it represents and how it relates to other objects, such as rabbits and meadows. We have learned that rabbits jump in meadows and that ducks swim in lakes, and we are reason-responsive through our reason-concepts to these objects in the world. In other words, we identify the figure based on what it represents. The visual experience is more than just physical; thoughts seem to be part of it. Therefore, my perception is not limited to my eyes alone, as I also perceive through my thinking. However, we should not regard thoughts as mere mental states or mysterious entities. We acquire them through our interactions with the world and in learning to respond to it with reason and emotions. The experience of seeing is learned through expressions of our language, and there is no other way of learning the experience. The expressions are learned in language-games, and this requires that we are reason-responsive. In other words, our concepts, reason-concepts, and language-games carve up both the world and our experiences.

Wittgenstein appears to be urging us to embrace the notion that perception and thought coexist when we see. There is no theoretical or inferential process that involves first seeing the physical features of an image, then creating a hypothesis, conjecture, or interpretation[13] of what the image might be, and subsequently inferring what the image represents. We at once see the rabbit and think about it. Then a change of perspective occurs, and we see the duck and think about that.

Why is the exercise of seeing this gestalt figure so puzzling? We are engaging at the same time with two thoughts and two sights, but with one single physical sign and organization. We are interacting with an animal that we are certain is called a 'rabbit', leaping across meadows; concurrently, we are interacting with another animal that we are certain is called a 'duck', swimming in lakes. In our thoughts and experiences of the world, these are two different animals, and we know that there is no single animal called a 'duck-rabbit'. But the drawing tells us something different.

Arguably, this perspective on pictures applies to actions. When we see others acting, we do not observe their movements as merely physical; in the majority of cases, we immediately grasp what they are doing. This means that, in opposition to what is advocated by the symmetrical view, we do not rationalize or interpret an action from the third-person perspective by attributing beliefs and desires to the agent to make their action intelligible. What actually happens is that the intelligibility of the action strikes us as a kind of 'seeing as', and therefore no attribution of beliefs and desires is necessary. For example, in the classroom, students are taking notes and learning; at the bus stop, people are waiting for the bus; and at the store, people are picking up fruit which they will buy. We perceive the actions of our bodies as meaningful. Like the 'duck-rabbit', we do not see *only* the physical properties and organization of other agents' bodies (eg the taking of notes, the buying of fruit, and so on). The *aspect* of the action dawns upon us.

§1.4 Implications for Legal and Moral Responsibility for Inadvertent Acts

We have said that we learn words such as 'rabbit' and 'duck' through what they do and in the contexts in which we refer to them (eg when, as children, we visit parks and meadows, and our parents explain to us what rabbits and ducks do). We also learned to be reason-responsive to these animals (eg we feed ducks with seeds

[13] For the position that 'seeing aspects' does not involve interpretation, see Stephen Mulhall, *Inheritance and Originality* (OUP 2001) 153–57.

and hop about in meadows in the hope of catching rabbits). If we have a domestic rabbit, we look after it and feed it with carrot tops.

All of this seems simple and obvious when we are referring to ducks and rabbits. But how might all of this apply to inadvertent actions? Let us recall that our puzzle is about cases of inadvertent acts in the past in which the results or outcomes of our actions strike us as events. They constitute the subject matter of our assessments of responsibility for negligence and are correctly grasped when action is really produced from the forward-looking perspective. People typically assert that we are responsible for our inadvertent actions, either because we ought to have done something, or because we ought to have known something and failed to do so. However, the way we engage with action is forward-looking; we occupy this perspective when we act according to reasons, as I shall argue later in this book. In these cases, reasons track values or good-making characteristics. In this way, reasons are inevitably involved in strong evaluations. When dealing with inadvertent actions, it seems that it is impossible to integrate the forward-looking perspective of action with the backward-looking view of past events. When someone acted inadvertently because she overlooked something or ought to have known something that she did not know, we do not consider the reasons that are *in her acting*, and we disregard her first-person perspective. On the contrary, when we evaluate her actions, we consider them to be *what she should have done*. It seems conceptually impossible to integrate both perspectives.

Let us think again about the duck-rabbit picture and how we engage with it. We see rabbits and ducks and we think of the picture in terms of what it represents. We can see rabbits and ducks, because we've learned what they do and how they relate to other animals and objects in the world. We can see the duck and think about ducks, their activities, and characteristics. In the absence of aspect blindness, another aspect can dawn on us: we can see the rabbit and have thoughts about rabbits.

However, actions are different and much more complex. What would we need to say to a child if we wanted to teach them about inadvertent actions? We do not intend inadvertent actions, and if we understand what it means to act neither intentionally nor involuntarily, we can understand them. We can reframe the question to ask: 'What would we teach a child about intentional action?' Consider some paradigmatic examples of intentional action that involve deliberation and practical knowledge. When teaching a child how to bake a cake, we teach them that we first need to mix the sugar and butter, then add milk, eggs, vanilla, and finally flour. We put the mixture into a cake tin and place it in a heated oven. If we accidentally forget to add the eggs, we can explain to the child that this is an example of an inadvertent action (ie you knew you should do X, but you forgot to do it or ignored it because you were preoccupied with something else). You intended to produce a state of affairs, namely a cake, but by mistake you have produced something else (ie an undigestible mix of sugar, butter, milk, vanilla, and flour).

The child has now learned a primitive concept of inadvertent action. As competent adults, we develop a mastery of understanding what inadvertent actions are. We engage with the world from the deliberative or first-person perspective. We act intentionally to pursue ends with good-making characteristics and values, but we also learn that occasionally we fail because we inadvertently produce the wrong state of affairs and fail to know what we ought to know.

Let us now try to understand how Wittgenstein's idea of 'seeing aspects' might shed light on the puzzle of the backward-looking perspective on responsibility for inadvertent actions. We shall focus only on the interpersonal understanding of our past actions and attributions of responsibility, but this also has ramifications for attributions of responsibility at the intrapersonal level. We will discuss this aspect in Chapter 9.

Let us closely examine a variation of an example from Sher's book *Who Knew?*[14] The example is called *Hot Dog*. In *Hot Dog*, Alessandra is collecting her children from a hockey game. It is a hot day, and she has her dog in the car. She quickly goes to collect the children and leaves the dog in the vehicle. When Alessandra arrives at the pitch, a dispute between the children arises, and she attempts to calm them down. Owing to the heated dispute, she forgets about her dog, and when the family returns to the vehicle, they discover the dead body of their beloved dog.

The question that arises is how Alessandra is able to attribute responsibility to herself when, from the first-person perspective, she engaged only in the action of collecting her children and was trying to resolve the dispute that had arisen between them. She knew why she was doing what she was doing at the moment. She knew why she parked her vehicle, left the dog in the car, started to walk to the hockey pitch, and tried to resolve the dispute among the children. She knew why she had returned to the car. She produced what she aimed to produce. However, she did not aim to cause the death of her beloved dog. In 'seeing' her past actions, she observes the state of affairs that they resulted in (ie a dead dog) and the fact that she did not have the precaution or practical knowledge that she ought to have had. But how can she infer what she ought to have thought, ought to have done, or ought to have known, to produce the state of affairs (ie the dead dog)? I shall argue that Alessandra is able to 'see' both the forward-looking perspective of her action (ie the deliberative and intentional action) and the backward-looking perspective of her action (ie the lack of precaution and practical knowledge that produced the death of her dog) *in the same way that we can see both animals in the image*. Similar to 'seeing' the duck-rabbit aspect, Alessandra can 'see' the *aspects* of her own past action (ie her lack of precaution and practical knowledge) and what she produced (ie the dead dog). Simultaneously, she can 'see' her forward-looking action as another aspect of her action. The aspect of the backward-looking action

[14] Sher, *Who Knew* (n 7).

dawns on her and is imposed on her. She neither sees her past action as a piece of materiality, nor as a fact or something physical. Nor does she infer from the facts (ie a dead dog) a conjecture or a hypothesis (ie this is my dog that I left in the car, and consequently, my failure of precaution and practical knowledge caused the death of my beloved dog). The primary understanding of her action, justifying the use of the adverb 'inadvertently', suggests that she overlooked something in her practical knowledge and execution of the action. As in the example of the mother baking a cake with her child, where an ingredient was missing, the steps that led to Alessandra's action were faulty and produced the wrong state of affairs—the death of her beloved dog. In normal circumstances and owing to the normal capacities of human beings, Alessandra recognizes herself and her actions from both perspectives and can grasp both the backward-looking and the forward-looking perspectives of the action as *aspects* of her own performance. She does not identify with her mental states or bodily movements; *she transcends the materiality and theoretical stance of her own mind and grasps all the aspects of her actions directly. Her actions dawn on her, and this is their primary meaning.*

All further interpretations of whether she is responsible or not, and re-enactments of her actions (eg in a courtroom), will need to rely on this primary meaning of her actions.

§1.5 A Method for a Sound Explanation of Negligent Acts

I have attempted to demonstrate that a desideratum for an adequate explanation of negligent acts and the corresponding grounding of responsibility for negligence must mirror our linguistic practices and the phenomenology of our actions *while* we are acting. This means that we need to explain inadvertent action *from* the deliberative perspective. This chapter began by reflecting on inadvertent acts from the deliberative view or first-person perspective, which is forward-looking, as opposed to seeing the result or outcome of our actions, which is essentially backward-looking. However, a puzzle emerges when we attempt to understand an action from both the past and the deliberative perspective simultaneously. *Philosophically speaking, we need something that seems conceptually impossible: we need a sound backward-looking perspective for the purposes of legal and moral responsibility for negligence, which at the same time grasps the forward-looking perspective.* Most authors have overlooked[15] the puzzle because they assume a symmetrical thesis

[15] For an exception, see Sher, *Who Knew* (n 7). He points out that 'the perspective of the agent and that of the person who encounters his actions *from the outside* are incompatible in the sense that no one simultaneously occupies them both'. Sher, *Who Knew* (n 7) 10, my emphasis. He thinks that the focus on 'knowledge' in action, which he calls the 'searchlight view', conflates the agent's perspective and our own (ie the third-person perspective of observers of the action). However, he is too hasty in dismissing the puzzle and offers an unsatisfactory solution. For further discussion of Sher's solution, see Chapter 8.

concerning intentional and inadvertent actions. Legal theorists and philosophers conflate both (a) the first- and third-person perspectives and (b) the forward- and backward-looking perspectives of action. I have argued that (a) the symmetrical thesis causes tension and, furthermore, can even commit violence to the way we think about and express our mistakes and the disastrous outcomes that result from inadvertent actions; (b) consequently, we need to rethink the methodology of grasping inadvertent action while we are acting (ie the deliberative or first-person perspective of engaging in action); and, finally, (c) I suggest that the methodology offered by Wittgenstein in *Philosophical Investigations* concerning 'seeing an aspect' of an image illuminates the way in which the two perspectives on inadvertent action could be made intelligible.

This method of inquiry demonstrates that there is no conceptual impossibility in grasping an action from the deliberative/first-person and forward-looking perspective and from the back-forward perspective as a past event. In my view, this is fertile ground for rethinking our notions of learned and reflective capacity, values, practical reason, and character in the context of inadvertent action. That is the enterprise with which this book engages.

The previous reflections invite us to consider three key issues:

1) Whether intentional action runs parallel to practical reason and whether we can establish that an action is intentional when an answer to the question 'why?' has application. The exercise of practical reason can break down due to forgetfulness or inadvertence. The structure of the agent's actions at the moment of the action is presented as bringing about a state of affairs in the world that is unintended. The agent did not intend what she produced.
2) does not hinder the agent's ability to identify an action as their own.
3) The agent learns about the action by observing the result. However, arguably, the entire form of the action and the way in which she actually engaged her practical reasoning (ie thoughts and desires) dawn on her when she sees the result of her action.

The concept of 'seeing as' helps us to comprehend the agent's change of perspectives. It also shows that responsibility for inadvertent acts depends partly, as a starting point, on the agent being able to recognize her own actions, even when they involve flawed practical reasoning and deliberation. This enables us to understand how the conflicting engagement happens from the first-person perspective or deliberative stance.

However, this view on negligence highlights an additional challenge. When the agent starts the action, her action is intentional, and therefore her practical reasoning is fully engaged. When the question 'why?' is asked hypothetically as she is performing the action, she is able to answer, 'because . . .' Let me use our previous example to illustrate this: when we ask Alessandra why she is leaving her house with her dog in the vehicle, she will answer that she is going to collect her children at the hockey match; when we ask her why she is parking her car, she will answer that she is parking so that she can go to the hockey pitch and come back with her children; when we ask her why she is leaving her dog in the car, she will reply that dogs are not allowed on the hockey pitch. This series of actions acquires intelligibility because she sees the actions as having good-making characteristics or manifesting values that she endorses (ie promoting sporting activities for her children, keeping safe, and following the rules of the hockey team). However, if we hypothetically ask 'Why?' after the action has caused harm, her response doesn't stem from values or goodness, but rather from her mental state at the time of the action. If we hypothetically ask, 'Why did you leave the dog in the car?', her action will be negligent if her response is along the lines of: 'I didn't realize that it would be dangerous and that there was a possibility of heat stroke'. Thus, forgetfulness, inadvertence, and inattention are not answers to the question 'why?'. The analysis then tends to immediately focus on the 'absent' mental state or the unexercised capacity that impedes the presence of the mental state. The inquiry can also ask whether what happened was foreseeable or whether there were substantive risks that she ought to have grasped. Positive responses suggest that it is reasonable to say that she could have done something different. It immediately locates the agent from a point of view closer to that of a theoretical deliberator. However, we fail to scrutinize the transition from human beings with specific constitutions, engaged in practical reasoning, to the position of omniscient or theoretical deliberators—or even what it means to be in this position. We fail to consider the agent's limited conditions and circumstances, completely ignoring her moral psychology. However, if we engage in practical reasoning that leads to defective performance, we must question why the agent's practical reasoning failed to incorporate the right reasons and truthful values involved in the action. The focus on mental states seems too narrow and cannot give us an accurate picture of the entire agent. We believe that the agent, or the self as a whole, acted and made a mistake. It was not only part of her (ie her mental states), as the question that arises is how we can change our mental states and be in the *right* mental state instead. Are our mental states something that just happens to us? Can *we* control and change our mental states (eg beliefs)? The challenge lies in the fact that when we detach our practical reasoning from the performance of a negligent action, we fail to identify it as our own. We end up with compulsive actions or other forms of alienation that cause the agent to suffer. On the other hand, if we combine practical reasoning with action, we have robust deliberative and intentional action, but not negligent action.

In our investigation, we shall focus on the question of how right action and truthful values can appear in our practical reasoning. The key methodological claim is that explaining how right action and truthful values appear in practical reasoning will enable us to understand *when* and *how* right action and truthful values fail to appear in our practical reasoning. This explanation illuminates how we can do better, perform correctly, and become truthful and right. Consequently, it sheds light on whether it is reasonable to think that agents could have done better.

Negligent action is not an omission (ie an intentional action that suffers a lapse owing to the absence of a mental state). Negligent action is in continuity with practical reason, although it involves the defective exercise of practical reason. This view will shed light on the phenomenology of negligent acts and the sound conception of legal and moral responsibility for negligence. But, before scrutinizing the theoretical framework that will unveil the interconnections between right action, truthful values, practical reasoning, and responsibility for inadvertent or negligent acts, I shall discuss, in the next chapter, the sceptical perspectives towards responsibility for negligence.

2
Scepticism about Negligence

§2.1 The Sceptical Challenge

The initial chapter presented a conceptual framework on the deliberative point of view or perspective of an individual who engages in an inadvertent or negligent act. In comprehending responsibility for negligent actions, I emphasized the significance of perspectives, which are the various ways in which we perceive our acts. In the subsequent four chapters, I look at how we deliberate to shed light on perspectives and situations in which our engagement with the world is flawed, ie when we act negligently. However, before proceeding, it is imperative to understand the challenges that arise while attempting to provide a comprehensive elucidation of responsibility for negligence.

The notion that knowledge is fundamental to responsibility is widely supported, as it implies that our actions are primarily driven by our views about them. The expression implies that we possess 'knowledge of our action' and that this information grants us control over our actions and the manner in which we execute them. The term used in the literature to describe this concept is 'the epistemic condition'.[1] For instance, when I am preparing chamomile tea, I am aware that the kettle is filled with boiling water. I believe that pouring this water into the cup with the teabag will result in the production of tea, and I am motivated to do this because I have a strong desire to make tea. But I can also stop in the middle of performing the action. I can exert control over the action, for instance, by deciding to make Earl Grey tea instead of chamomile tea. I can control my actions because I have knowledge[2] of my actions. However, the concept of responsibility for negligence underscores the notion that possessing knowledge is essential for exercising control over one's actions. We will now elucidate two forms of scepticism, namely 'Lack of Knowledge Scepticism' and 'Character Scepticism'.

[1] Phillip Robichaud and Jan Willem Wieland, *Responsibility: The Epistemic Condition* (OUP 2017).

[2] For our purposes in this chapter the terms 'ignorance' and 'lack of knowledge' are interchangeable. cf Rik Peels and Martijn Blaauw, *The Epistemic Dimensions of Ignorance* (CUP 2017). As will become clearer later in the chapter, we aim to avoid framing the debate as merely epistemic and in terms of ignorance, ie believing something that is not true, suspending one's beliefs, or having no beliefs about the matter.

Responsibility for Negligence in Ethics and Law. Verónica Rodríguez-Blanco, Oxford University Press.
 DOI: 10.1093/9780198948193.003.0002

§2.2 Scepticism Due to Lack of Knowledge

Arguably, in order to have responsibility for negligent or inadvertent acts, we need to show that either (a) there is blameworthiness or responsibility[3] for the lack of knowledge of the inadvertent original action, or (b) there is blameworthiness or responsibility for the lack of knowledge of past actions that are strongly connected to the original inadvertent action.

But how can I be responsible for the lack of knowledge about either the original inadvertent action or the strongly connected past action(s)? Let us go back to a modified version of our initial example. I mistakenly believe I'm preparing a chamomile tea, but in reality, I'm preparing a herbal tea for sleep, unaware that the teabag contains sleep-inducing herbs. Am I responsible for the accident that occurs as a result of my dangerous driving, which itself is a result of the effect of the herbs? The question should refer to the strongly connected past action, ie drinking the sleeping aid herbal tea. Let us give more context and suppose that the labels on the boxes of chamomile tea and sleeping aid herbal tea are clear and large. Should I bear the responsibility or blame for my ignorance, it implies that my inattention during the selection of the sleeping aid herbal tea sachet, my distraction from my favourite music, or my ignorance of my daughter's swapping of the two tea boxes' locations in the cupboard could have been the cause.

The 'lack of knowledge' sceptic asks, if I do not know the nature and character of the action, then how can I be responsible for what I am doing? The idea is that in order to be responsible, I need to be in control, but the sceptic tells us that, without knowledge, there is no possible control.

Rosen establishes a 'slippery slope' type of argument between circumstantial ignorance, ie knowledge of the particular circumstances of the act, and inadvertent ignorance. In a case of circumstantial ignorance, eg Oedipus kills a stranger on the road to Thebes without knowing that the stranger is actually King Laius, his father, Oedipus is responsible for killing a stranger but not for parricide, and his ignorance excuses him from parricide but not from homicide. As a result, there is a clear parallel between circumstantial ignorance and ignorance of inadvertent acts. In the tea example, I am unaware that the tea I'm drinking aids in my sleep. Therefore, similar to Oedipus, I bear responsibility for the action of 'drinking tea', but not for the action of 'drinking tea that aids in my sleep and causes me to drive dangerously and have a car accident'. As a result, we need to trace the action to the instance in which the agent has knowledge and control over her action. In other words, the point at which the agent knows the *character and nature of her action.*

[3] I refer to blameworthiness as ethical blameworthiness and use blameworthiness and responsibility as interchangeable. See Heidi Hurd and Michael Moore, 'Punishing the Awkward, the Stupid, the Weak and the Selfish: The Culpability of Negligence' (2011) 5 Criminal Law and Philosophy 147.

In the case of Oedipus, there is no moment in the past at which he could have discovered and known that the stranger was his father. In the tea example, we can scrutinize a previous action where I asked my daughter to reorganize the boxes and observed the new location of both the chamomile and the sleeping aid tea boxes. Am I responsible for the action that is performed in accordance with this knowledge? Why should this knowledge hold me accountable for the action that is generated by this knowledge?[4] A non-sceptical theorist might argue that I am responsible for my action because this is the point in which I choose to act; I have control through my beliefs, and therefore I am derivatively responsible for all the actions that are strongly connected to this action and its knowledge.

The non-sceptic could continue that the tea example is different from the case of Oedipus, in which there is an impossibility of knowing the nature and character of the action, because in the tea example I had the opportunity to know—without much effort—that the boxes had been put in different places. The sceptic might reply as follows. This is not a case in which I am responsible for my inadvertent action, ie 'drinking the sleeping aid tea', because the original inadvertent action is connected to an action of which I have knowledge and therefore control. Rather, using the example, my responsibility lies in 'knowing that the boxes have been put in a different location than usual' at t1 and then forgetting about it at t2. But why would I be blameworthy for forgetting, replies the sceptic? This appears to be a phenomenon that simply occurs to me, rather than something I actively control. This is a passive condition, a state of my mind. When I am forgetful, I do not have knowledge of my state of mind, and therefore I lack control.

A non-sceptic might counter-argue that the concept of epistemic obligation or duty plays a key role here. When we perform certain actions, we discharge our epistemic duties. However, argues the sceptic, this will not do. According to Rosen, these obligations are about things we must perform. This solution, continues Rosen, ignores the fact that, on some occasions, we discharge our epistemic duties but fail because things just happen to us. Furthermore, Rosen advances the distinction between passive and active as follows:

> Belief revision is a passive matter. I can take various active steps to influence the content of my opinion: I can consult my guru; I can read a book; I can sit and think about a question. But once I have taken these active measures, the change in view itself is something that simply happens in me or to me. It is not something I do.[5]

[4] Hurd and Moore raise the point that the action needs to be morally blameworthy in order to generate responsibility, as responsibility is desert-based (n 3). See Chapter 8 for a further discussion of this point.

[5] Gideon Rosen, 'Scepticism About Moral Responsibility' (2004) 18 Philosophical Perspectives 295, 302.

This is a familiar Cartesian epistemic scepticism. There is no guaranteed epistemic route between my beliefs and how things really are. True beliefs or knowledge derived from my investigation, but there is no certainty or trust-inspiring method between my state of mind and the actual state of things. Cartesianism restores certainty through a pure thought or idea of the true nature of the object. However, this process does not involve my will or desires; it simply happens to me. We view beliefs as separated from desires.[6]

Rosen points out that responsibility for negligence is responsibility for passive matters, and this is certainly paradoxical. In the tea example, I can take all reasonable steps to remember that the boxes are in a different location, such as placing a note on the fridge, but unfortunately, I can still forget to look at this note or glance at it without seeing it.

The idea that we are responsible because we failed to discharge our procedural epistemic duties can lead to an infinite regress. In the example above, we would need to enquire whether I am responsible for not noticing the note on the fridge. One could argue that I didn't take reasonable steps to prompt me to remember leaving a note on the fridge; for example, I also forgot to put a note in my diary to remind me that there was a note on the fridge. However, imagine that I also forgot to read my diary and that the precaution was therefore useless. Is it my fault that I neglected to read my diary before making my tea, which in turn holds me accountable for consuming a sleep-inducing beverage and, consequently, for driving dangerously? Aside from the fact that we are now losing the strong connection with the original inadvertent action, similar questions might arise concerning my failure to read my diary. *We believe that there is no logical point at which we can stop the infinite regress.*

A non-sceptic might say that the locus of responsibility is in the character, ie I am a forgetful person, and my failure is in my character. According to Rosen, passivity extends not only to our beliefs but also to character.[7] Scepticism about character will be discussed in the next section.

As an alternative to trying to find the *locus* of responsibility for inadvertent action and halting the infinite regress, one could argue that the inadvertent action should be a *'clear-eyed' akratic* action, where I knew I should perform action A, such as taking the sachet from the chamomile tea box, but I disregarded this knowledge in favour of performing the alternative action B, such as taking a sachet from the box of tea that aids in sleeping. Our locus of responsibility for negligence is a knowing sin. I knew the relevant fact, ie that this is not a chamomile tea but an sleeping aid tea. This is an odd approach, since it fails to explain certain fundamental aspects of the phenomenology of responsibility for negligence. The approach fails to clarify the inadvertent nature of the action from the deliberative

[6] For further analysis of this bifurcation between desires and beliefs, see Chapter 3.
[7] Rosen (n 5).

or first-person perspective, the non-intentional nature of some parts of the action, or the perceived triviality of the action from the deliberator's perspective.[8] Furthermore, Rosen argues that this alternative solution will not work as we do not fully understand what 'clear-eyed' *akrasia* is or how it operates, and it is unclear whether we can attribute this phenomenon to others.[9] Therefore, judgements of responsibility for inadvertent action cannot be certain, and *akrasia* is in continuity with weakness of the will, ie when we are irresolute about what we ought to do. Consequently, Rosen argues, on the basis of our own reflection on our actions, it is not possible to definitely ascertain whether we are identifying a distinct instance of *akrasia* or a manifestation of weakness of the will.[10]

§2.3 Character Scepticism

Let's assume, however, that my forgetfulness stems from laziness and that I am the kind of person who finds it difficult to recall the locations of different tea boxes. Why would I be responsible or blameworthy for my character, which is not really under my control? One could argue that my past actions, which shaped my current character, should bear responsibility. However, if we assume that I deliberately choose to act in order to justify the execution of these previous activities as my own, then the inadvertent action that arises from my flawed character is a consequence of past actions that do not appear to have a significant correlation with my present actions.

In the given example, my laziness and resultant forgetfulness are the result of my not listening, neglecting, and/or lack of engagement with actions that would have enabled me to improve my mental laziness, consider engaging in activities such as brain training, spiritual exercises, and practising mindfulness.

The current issue revolves around the correlation between my previous activities, my previous character, and my present actions and character, rather than solely focusing on the passivity of character, as Rosen argues. Am I also accountable

[8] See Chapter 1 for further discussion on this.

[9] Rosen (n 5) 308–09. Most of the authors that work on responsibility for negligence refer to *akrasia* as clear-eyed *akrasia* only. See eg Neil Levy, 'Culpable Ignorance and Moral Responsibility: A Reply to Fitzpatrick' (2009) 119 Ethics 729. They do not analyse and consider cases of simple *akrasia*. For a detailed analysis of the distinction, see Chapter 6.

[10] Rosen's reflection on this is reminiscent of Cartesianism. He asserts: 'The culpable bad actions have a distinctive sort of causal history—an inculpating history—in which the act either is, or derives from, an episode of genuine *akrasia*. There may be no obstacle in principle to identifying such episodes. God could manage it; a super-psychologist might manage it. But given the real limitations on our access to our causal histories of human actions and to the states of knowledge and opinions that underlie them, I claim that, as a matter of fact, we *are never entitled to any significant confidence* that the bad act under consideration satisfies the necessary condition we have identified. And this is just the thesis of scepticism about moral responsibility.' The emphasis is mine. Rosen (n 5) 309. See also discussion in §9.6.4.

for my failure to listen, disregard, and/or lack of involvement in actions that could have helped me enhance my mental laziness? Imagine a scenario where I previously enrolled in mindfulness training provided by my nearby community centre. I put a note on my fridge the day of the first lesson, but due to my hectic lunch schedule, I failed to read the reminder. It is far-fetched and counter-intuitive to say, 'I am responsible for driving dangerously because (a) I failed to have lunch on the first day of my mindfulness course, and consequently, (b) I forgot to read the reminder on my fridge about my mindfulness course, and consequently, (c) I forgot to attend my mindfulness course, and consequently, (d) I could not improve my mental laziness, and therefore, (e) I became a forgetful person. Consequently, (f) I failed to remember that my daughter had reorganized the tea boxes, (g) I mistakenly took the wrong tea box and drank tea to aid in sleeping, and (h) I drove my vehicle under the influence of tea that induces sleepiness.' The problem arises from the lack of a clear connection between (a) 'I neglected to have lunch on the first day of my mindfulness course' and (h) 'I drove my vehicle under the influence of tea that induces sleepiness'. The connection between the past actions, the past character, and the current character is unclear or mysterious.

In the context of this argument, let us consider a hypothetical scenario wherein a preceding action is intricately connected to the character exhibited in the unintentional action. In order to establish a meaningful connection, it is imperative to conduct a thorough examination of the process of character development and the active engagement of the individual. Nevertheless, the sceptic may contend that to establish this association, it is important to demonstrate that the individual has deliberately made a decision to engage in a specific action and that they were aware that this action would lead to a particular outcome. For instance, I was aware that refraining from taking any action would lead to laziness and consequently neglect the significant aspects of my life, yet I still opted to do nothing. In the tea example, I deliberately opted not to exert any effort in recalling my mindfulness training, thus demonstrating a deliberate decision to not enhance my cognitive indolence. I will, therefore, be primarily responsible for the intentional or reckless actions that are caused by my character and only derivatively responsible for the inadvertent actions. But there is no primary responsibility for the inadvertent action. Responsibility for an inadvertent action is defined by the intentional or reckless state of mind of the agent prior to the inadvertent action.

I am responsible for my mental laziness, which is the result of my intentional or reckless state of mind, but not for my inadvertent actions. Moreover, the persistence of scepticism poses a challenge in the realm of legal responsibility. How can the law hold us accountable for our flawed character?[11]

[11] Hurd and Moore (n 3).

In summary, we must demonstrate that (a) the inadvertent action bears a strong connection to previous actions, and (b) we bear responsibility for these past actions because we have failed to discharge our epistemic procedural duties. In the case of circumstantial knowledge of an action, ignorance excuses us because we cannot demonstrate that we have failed to discharge our epistemic duties. For instance, it was impossible for Oedipus to discharge his duties and discover that the stranger was his biological father. Similarly, when we engage in inadvertent action, we can trace it back to past actions where we failed to discharge our epistemic duties. However, this raises the question of whether we are also blameworthy for not discharging our epistemic duties. For example, if I experienced a sudden and unexpected episode of dizziness that prevented me from reading the labels on the tea boxes, it would have become impossible to acquire the necessary knowledge at that time. In this scenario, the inquiry can lead to an infinite regression, raising the question of whether I was responsible or blameworthy for this sudden and unexpected dizziness. We face the risk of severing the robust correlation between previous actions and the initial inadvertent action. We can halt the regress by attributing it to individual character traits, such as laziness, as exemplified by my failure to recall that my daughter had rearranged the boxes. However, the question emerges as to why I bear the responsibility for shaping my character. It is necessary to ascertain the character's origins by examining its historical activities, which give birth to two distinct challenges. Initially, it is important to note that there is no ethically blameworthy action that has contributed to the development of my present character. Consequently, the profound association with past actions becomes diminished. For instance, it would be absurd to attribute responsibility to me for consuming the herbal tea that facilitates sleep, given that I have deliberately refrained from enhancing my disposition through means such as brain training or mindfulness practices. Ultimately, we can halt the regression by asserting that at some juncture in the past, the performer knew what she ought to do and ignored it.

In order to answer the sceptical challenges, we need to scrutinize a number of premises concerning the nature and role of knowledge and character in action. The next four chapters of the book dispel some of the misconceptions about the nature of practical knowledge and character and advance an explanation of the phenomenon of negligence or inadvertent action as an underlying *akratic* action. The argument posits that understanding responsibility for negligence in law and ethics is possible *only if we understand the underlying or underpinning structure of practical reasoning and deliberation when we act inadvertently*. It is argued that the underpinning structure of deliberation when we act inadvertently is *akratic* action (not necessarily clear-eyed *akrasia*), conceived as an uneven or defective integration of our character and intelligent thinking in acting.

PART II

THE DELIBERATIVE-ASPIRATIONAL MODEL OF AGENCY

This section of the book advances an Aristotelian-inspired model of deliberation. The purpose is to provide insight into the occurrence of negligence or inadvertent action. Contemporary philosophical discussions on deliberation and reasoning commonly use a shared paradigm when theorizing about action and deliberation. The term I used to describe this paradigm is the bifurcation model and its corollary, the 'balancing' view of deliberation. Theorists assume that desires and beliefs do not interact or merge. They primarily assume that desires and beliefs are 'given'. According to these views, all we need to do is clearly define or 'pin down' our desires and beliefs, which are either mental states or pertain to the content within our mental states, specifically facts. Furthermore, we can pinpoint a specific time or instance when we formed our beliefs and desires. As a result, the sole purpose of deliberation is to weigh or 'balance' among various alternatives and, subsequently, 'choose' one of them. Deliberation is construed as a process of balancing beliefs against beliefs, or desires against beliefs, or desires against desires. The terminology varies according to the theory. Some theorists adhere to the distinction between normative and motivational reasons for actions. Some individuals opt to use the terminology of reason-based and desire-based, or internal and external reasons for actions. Some theorists distinguish between justificatory and explanatory reasons for actions. Nevertheless, the prevailing thought among all contemporary theorists is that we 'know' or are able to 'pin down' our desires and beliefs. For many contemporary theorists, the main conundrum seems to be how desires and beliefs operate, and which set of reasons should have priority.

I challenge the premise of a bifurcation between desires and beliefs and argue that the classical conception of action and deliberation, specifically Aristotle's conception of deliberation, supports a fundamentally different notion. I establish that the Aristotelian-inspired model is a sound, fruitful, and powerful explanation of action. Moreover, I contend that it is psychologically realistic and illuminates the entire spectrum of our agency, including negligent action. According to this approach, deliberation involves actively 'seeking' from the deliberative or first-person stance. This 'seeking' involves the agent determining the content and character of her ends, which I refer to as the '*what*' of deliberation, and elucidating the means, which I refer to as the '*how*' of deliberation. This Aristotelian-inspired model posits that the *what* illuminates the *how, and vice versa. This process happens while we act and within the agency's extended temporal dimension.* In this way, our beliefs or thoughts shape the content of our desires and what we value. Our desires and beliefs are not 'given' or easily ascertainable. On the contrary, *deliberation is the process of determining their content.* In addition, I contend that the goodness of our ends is indeterminate, rendering our desires and beliefs about our desires indeterminate as well. We are able to grasp our immediate ends by focusing on particulars, and the engagement of what is valuable operates at the level of specific circumstances.

A critic may contend that this model of deliberation seems effective only when we are immersed in the world and aim for immediate, indeterminate ends. The objector may argue that this model fails to explain our engagement with medium- and long-term ends. Nevertheless, I also demonstrate the feasibility of adopting a broader perspective, encompassing medium- and long-term ends. I defend the idea that when we engage with others and others confront us in a myriad of ways, we are inevitably forced to either avoid or inhabit an aspirational perspective that encompasses a wider view of ends. Simultaneously, we also bring with us the knowledge of values that we have acquired through our immersive deliberation.

Finally, the Aristotelian-inspired model of deliberation allows us to elucidate the occurrence of *akrasia.* I demonstrate that *akrasia* is the underpinning phenomenon that elucidates inadvertent or negligent action. When we act *akratically*, we act against what we have deliberated. The situation is perplexing because it appears that there is a breakdown in our deliberation, leading to a loss of agency and control over our actions. Acting *akratically*, however, is different from acting compulsively. Some theorists propose that *akrasia* occurs when the agent lacks the resolve to act in line with her deliberation. The *akratic* action really reflects a change of mind. Other theorists suggest that the *akratic* makes an insincere statement while deliberating. Nevertheless, these explanations fail to account for the struggles and regret stemming from our *akratic* actions. In contrast to these theorists, I provide an explanation of *akrasia* that revolves around the idea that *akrasia* occurs due to an uneven development of character and thoughts about what is right, dutiful, and good. When we act *akratically*, we fail to move ourselves forward and transform into an aspirational-deliberative perspective.

3
The Balancing Model of Deliberation

§3.1 The Bifurcation Thesis and the 'Balancing Model' of Deliberation as its Corollary

In the previous chapter, I examined the sceptical challenges pertaining to the notion that we are responsible for negligent actions. However, these sceptical positions assume a specific model of deliberation that remains ambiguous.

I aim to defend the view that acting *akratically* is indicative of flawed practical reasoning and deliberation and shows a failure of integration between our desires and beliefs. Acting *akratically* explains how we can be blameworthy for our negligent acts. However, to understand the nature of acting *akratically*, it is necessary to clarify how and what constitutes excellence in practical deliberation. Simply put, it is critical to understand sound deliberation and its relationship to ethical deliberation.

This chapter aims to provide a concise overview of the current status of motivation theories and the origins of limited or sceptical interpretations of practical reason and deliberation. The objective of this rudimentary and comprehensive analysis is not to establish the validity or invalidity of Hume's interpretations by his interpreters and adherents. Instead, my intention is twofold: (a) to illustrate the implications of the Humean bifurcation thesis, which posits a stark dichotomy between desires and beliefs, for our comprehension of deliberation and the nature and strength of practical reason; and (b) to demonstrate the pervasiveness of the bifurcation thesis in our understanding of responsibility and blameworthy action.

The next chapter will delve into the concept of sound deliberation within the Aristotelian-inspired model of deliberation, building upon the previous study on the limitations of the Humean model and its division between desires and beliefs. I propose the Aristotelian-inspired model of deliberation as a compelling alternative to the bifurcation idea of deliberation and its consequent 'balancing' method.

In this section, I delineate the picture of practical deliberation that has been predominant in contemporary analytical philosophy and give it the name 'balancing model'. An explanation of this model of deliberation will help us better grasp the Aristotelian-inspired model of ethical deliberation and practical reason.

The balancing model has its roots in an emaciated and, at times, sceptical conception of practical reason. It is the corollary of the idea that there is a bifurcation between beliefs and desires. The bifurcation thesis has several interpretations,

Responsibility for Negligence in Ethics and Law. Verónica Rodríguez-Blanco, Oxford University Press.
 DOI: 10.1093/9780198948193.003.0003

ranging from a weak form[1] to a stronger version that leads to the nihilism of robust practical reason. As per the balancing model, when we deliberate, we only engage with those beliefs that correspond to *how* we can achieve and succeed in doing what *we believe* we desire or must do. These beliefs correspond to what the world looks like and can be formulated as propositions that are either (susceptible to being) true or false. If we evaluate our desire-based ends, it's only because of our beliefs that our desires, when interpreted as ends, will be more effectively served. For example, I have a desire for either vanilla or chocolate ice cream, but the ice cream in front of me is actually pistachio ice cream. Therefore, if I desire this ice cream, I am in error. Similarly, at a more complex level, I desire to drive to Paris or Rome with a friend. My desire is to have a unique cultural experience. I read travel books and learn about the museums and other cultural activities in both cities to determine which one will give me the best cultural experience. According to the balancing model, we do not engage in shaping, determining, and discriminating between what is right, unjust, dutiful, good, or evil. We simply try to understand our desires and our current mental states prior to performing an action, and then find the best way to fulfil these desire-based ends. To fulfil these desires, I engage in beliefs about the means to achieve these ends, or beliefs about the level of satisfaction I will experience with these ends, depending on the option I choose. If I deliberate, I need to balance two or more options, eg going to Paris or Rome, and I need to calculate my level of satisfaction for each option, which can be characterized as pleasure, pain, or utility. This calculation can be expressed in terms of probability, but it's not mandatory. A consideration of the means might also play a role in deliberations. I need to consider, for example, whether I have sufficient money to cover the cost of a hotel room and museums in each city.

§3.2 The Bifurcation Model and the Internalist and Externalist Account of Reasons for Actions

The balancing model of deliberation is sometimes presented as the model of reasons for action.[2] Theorists present two conceptions of the deliberator's reasons

[1] Williams' theory of action and motivation is a good example of the weak version of the bifurcation thesis. See Bernard Williams, 'Internal and External Reasons for Actions' in *Moral Luck* (CUP 1981) 101 and Bernard Williams, 'Voluntary Acts and Responsible Agents' in *Making Sense of Humanity* (CUP 1995) 22.

[2] Elizabeth Anscombe, a notable exception, employs the concept of 'reasons for actions' to demonstrate how the term intention aligns with practical reason. She argues that an intentional action is characterized by reasons that are connected to other reasons, as perceived or imagined by the performer from a first-person perspective. In her work, *Intention* (Basil Blackwell 1957, reprinted by Harvard UP 2000), she does not address the role of desires when we engage in intentional actions or deviate from them. However, in 'Modern Moral Philosophy', she asserts that serious moral philosophy necessitates engagement with moral psychology, thereby hinting at the importance of considering questions of character and desire. However, I believe she would be frightened by the notion that reflections on

for actions. First, internalist conceptions establish a connection between the agent's subjective motivational set and the reasons for actions, acknowledging variations in its content. For example, in Williams' sub-Humean model[3] the content includes desires,[4] dispositions of evaluations, and patterns of emotional reaction.[5] Secondly, according to externalist conceptions, reasons for action do not need to refer to our motives, ie desires and passions, as the content of reasons for actions can be purely cognitive, pertaining to the domain of theoretical reason. Williams' example illuminates this distinction. Owen Wingrave, Henry James' character in his short story of the same name, does not have and cannot see any consideration in favour of the reasons for action provided by his family to join the army. Traditions, customs, history, and country are not reasons that can be connected to Owen's subjective motivational set. According to Williams, the externalist's mistake lies in believing that there is a process of deliberation and reasoning that will cause a *new* desire or motivation that has no connection with the subjective motivational set of the agent. According to Williams, the way deliberation operates is through a sound, deliberate route. Whatever character this deliberative route takes, it ought to have as its starting point the *locus* of our desires and passions, what he calls our subjective motivational set. However, he seems at points to amplify this motivational set in a non-Humean fashion to incorporate, for example, commitments and personal projects.[6] But they are all, according to Williams, our internal reasons construed from the basic elements of the subjective motivational set. We are deliberating between our divergent beliefs, as we strive to meet our subjective motivational set. For instance, we need to decide what would be the most convenient, pleasant, or cost-effective course of action.[7] Our deliberations could also include how to satisfy combined elements of our subjective motivational set or how to balance or prioritize elements of the motivational set that are in conflict.[8] However, Williams argues, the crucial question is *how we come to believe*, ie how an external reason can be transformed or converted into an internal reason. Williams'

virtue have evolved into an independent theory known as 'Virtue Ethics'. See Elizabeth Anscombe, 'Modern Moral Philosophy' (1958) 33 Philosophy 1. For an excellent critique of this move, see Martha Nussbaum, 'Virtue Ethics: A Misleading Category?' (1999) 3 The Journal of Ethics 163.

[3] Williams thinks that the Humean model oversimplifies and, in contrast to Hume, acknowledges the existence that there is practical reason, yet maintains its indeterminate and vague nature. 'It (the account of deliberation) is unclear, and I regard it as a basically desirable feature of a theory of practical reasoning that it should preserve and account for that unclarity. There is an essential indeterminacy in what can be counted as a rational deliberative process. Practical reasoning is a heuristic process, and an imaginative one, and there are no fixed boundaries on the continuum from rational thought to inspiration and conversion.' Williams, 'Internal and External Reasons for Actions' (n 1) 110.

[4] ibid 101.

[5] ibid 105.

[6] ibid 105. See also Monika Betzler, 'Personal Projects and Reasons for Partliality' (2014) 40 Social Theory and Practice 683.

[7] Williams 'Internal and External Reasons for Actions' (n 1) 104.

[8] ibid.

response is that the transformation cannot occur *qua* external reason but because the internal reason does all the work through imagination[9] and other vague and indeterminate deliberative routes. The neo-Humean or sub-Humean answer is that *belief cannot change anything.*

The primary premise in this analysis is undeniably the bifurcation thesis. Desires are inherently passive, despite our awareness of them,[10] but they can be altered through imagination and indeterminate deliberate ways. Reason and beliefs do not interact with the subjective motivational set, and, therefore, reason and beliefs cannot transform desires. If the transformation or conversion takes place, it is often due to the presence of an initial desire, or something very closely related to it.[11]

Contrast this model with Parfit, who argues that external reasons, as opposed to internal reasons, are non-reductive normative reasons.[12] This means that reasons for actions are external, as they are not reducible to a specific subjective motivational set. We have a reason to act because this reason is a normative fact that the agent has a strong reason to carry out, for example to protect her life, foster her well-being, and so on.[13] This normative reason is independent of the agent's desires and whether the agent actually wants to engage with them.

[9] Williams asserts: 'More subtly, he may think he has reason to promote some development because he has not exercised his imagination enough about what it would be like if it came about. In his unaided deliberative reason, or encouraged by the persuasion of others, he may come to have some concrete sense of what would be involved, and lose his desire for it, just as, positively, the imagination can create new possibilities and new desires.' ibid 105. It is unclear what 'imagination' means here. Iris Murdoch's conception of imagination, for example, involves reasoning and reflection. For a further analysis of this, see Chapter 5.

[10] Williams rejects unconscious desires and terms them 'symbolic'. ibid 103. We can be partially ignorant of some elements of our subjective motivational set, but for an element to play a role in our deliberations, it ought to be rationally related to other elements of the subjective motivational set.

[11] See Hallvard Lillehammer, 'The Doctrine of Internal Reason' (2000) 34 The Journal of Value Inquiry 507 for a criticism of this position. Lillehammer argues that if a transformation is possible, it is because of external reasons. I concur with him, but we should frame the dispute not on the existence or absence of external reasons, but rather on the potential for our desires to undergo transformation and the active and intricate role they play in shaping certain worldly states. The framing of the discussion over the existence of external reasons relies on bifurcationist dogma, which is a hindrance to reformulating the debate and asking further questions about the nature and character of our motivational set. Also note that the notion of desire, introduced by Altham as a potential way out of bifurcationist dogma, does not completely reflect the complexity and active role of desires. Jimmy Altham, 'The Legacy of Emotivism' in *Fact, Science and Morality: Essays on A.J. Ayer's Language, Truth and Logic* (Blackwell 1986) 275. It presupposes that desires and beliefs are *states* and that they can be combined to explain how we act and deliberate. It obliterates the question about how exactly beliefs and desire interact.

[12] Derek Parfit, 'Reasons and Motivations' (1997) 71 Proceeedings of the Aristotelian Society 94; Lillehammer (n 11) 108–09. For a more subtle and contemporary version of externalism, see Jonathan Dancy, *Practical Reality* (OUP 2000); Errol Lord, *The Importance of Being Rational* (OUP 2018); and Ruth Chang, 'Grounding Practical Normativity: Going Hybrid' (2013) 164 Philosophical Studies 163. For other subtle distinctions and ways to approach externalism, see Mark Schroeder, 'The Importance of Being in a Position to Know' (2020) 100 Philosophy and Phenomenological Research 457.

[13] Parfit (n 12) 102.

Reasons for actions are about the truth and not about what is useful for us.[14] Externalists, Parfit tells us, do not accept that the question of deliberation and motivation define what reasons for action we have in the normative sense. The normative question cannot be answered in terms of psychological facts.[15] We see here a distinction between our beliefs about factual truths that give us normative reasons for actions, for example there is a fire in the building, and this fact gives me a reason to leave the building, and desires and other motives that are separate and independent of our engagement with beliefs and theoretical reason. In the given example, despite the presence of a fire in the building, I may not feel compelled to save my own life. Even when we do not have the appropriate desire for an external reason, we can sensibly assert that there is a reason to do X, for example you have a reason to escape from a building on fire in spite of not having the desire to save your life.

The bifurcation thesis is palpable in the externalist model because normative truths and our beliefs about them are independent of our desires and subjective motivational set. We conceptualize moral psychological questions as purely empirical; Parfit instructs us to distinguish them from normative truths and normative questions. The balancing model requires considering the weight of certain normative facts, ie weighing some normative truths against others and deciding which would result in the best course of action. The balancing model, whether internal or external, entails weighing, considering, and balancing various reasons for actions.

The philosophy of action also employs the term 'reasons for actions' to elucidate the action. Desires and beliefs become a pair, construed as separate mental states that rationalize an action. Davidson,[16] for example, argues that they are the primary reasons for the action of an agent. Thus, if I want to eat vanilla ice-cream and I believe that the creamy stuff before me is ice cream, then I have a primary reason to eat the ice cream, and this primary reason rationalizes my action, ie my eating the ice cream. Davidson does not use the language of reasons for actions to explain practical reasoning, but rather to explain action itself. Nevertheless, this explanation has an impact on our contemporary ways of thinking about practical reasoning and, more specifically, on our contemporary understandings of *akrasia*. Davidson's explanation of action theory, *akrasia*, and practical reasoning presupposes the bifurcation thesis and its corollary, the balancing model. I will expand on this in §6.2.

[14] ibid 111.

[15] ibid 126.

[16] Donald Davidson, 'Actions, Reasons and Causes' (1963) 60 The Journal of Philosophy 685. For a criticism of Davidson's position, see my monograph, Verónica Rodríguez-Blanco, *Law and Authority Unde the Guise of the Good* (Hart/Bloomsbury 2014).

§ 3.3 The Bifurcation Model and the Diachronicity of Agency

In the 'balancing model' deliberation *does not* involve a 'seeking' where the transformation towards right desires is crucial, and it is impossible to re-direct or change our desires because *beliefs alone cannot change our desires.* Since our desires and passions simply occur to us, they cannot alter other desires; we remain passive towards them. Furthermore, deliberation as practical reasoning does not have a diachronic character, and if it does, the diachronic dimension just reveals the deficiency, limits, and futile optimism about the efficacy of prior deliberations. Deliberation involves a 'balancing' of multiple and conflicting alternatives of action, taking into account the person that I am at the point of the deliberation. Any deliberation within diachronicity and transformation poses insurmountable difficulties.[17]

According to Williams, the agent's perspective of choice is the actual deliberative moment, which he refers to as '*from here*', rather than the perspective of evaluation with better knowledge that the agent could have or should have had, which he refers to as '*from there*'. This is illustrated by Williams' example of Gauguin's actions. The painter abandons his wife and children to pursue a painting career. His success as a painter, ie giving a unique artistic legacy to the world and defining how human existence is meaningful, cannot be separated from any justification of his actions. However, neither Gauguin nor anyone else could have predicted his success at *the moment of his actions*. If Gauguin fails, he has made a mistake; if he succeeds, his actions may justify themselves.[18] Of course, this justification is not moral, but it is within a life that adheres to certain values, ie a life that is meaningful through aesthetic experience. Williams acknowledges that this justification is not towards others, ie the children will still have grounds for reproach, but the justification will operate retrospectively. Williams' point is that *at the moment of the action*, Gauguin cannot act in light of all the relevant rational considerations that apply to him[19] because much of the justification of his actions will depend on his talents, deliberative capacity,[20] and character, and how *he* successfully develops these talents. Gauguin's success adds additional evaluations and considerations to his initial deliberation, but it only shows the limits of our first-person deliberative stance.[21] This analysis is the result of the asymmetry between our first-person and third-person deliberative stances, which is presupposed in Williams' moral psychology.[22]

17 There are attempts to bring diachronicity into the balancing model. See eg Michael Bratman, *Faces of Intention* (CUP 1999). For a criticism of this attempt, see chapter 3 of my monograph Rodríguez-Blanco (n 16).

18 Bernard Williams, 'Moral Luck' in *Moral Luck* (CUP 1981) 20, 23.

19 ibid 24.

20 ibid 25.

21 For further discussion of this example and its impact on moral luck in ethics and law, see Chapter 7.

22 See Chapter 1.

Furthermore, we conceptualize deliberation as the process of making decisions to achieve medium- or short-term goals, which we perceive as preferences. Deliberation is conceived as akin to a moral dilemma, yet what is at stake is short- or medium-term desire-based ends.[23] In this view, beliefs and desires are two different entities that interact in a very particular way. If the interaction occurs before the action, it is considered causal; however, if it occurs after the action, it only serves as a reflection of the unpredictable and complex nature of our actions and deliberations. The interaction does not help us learn about ourselves, cultivate and transform ourselves, or develop self-knowledge for future actions. We do not project hard-learned lessons from past actions into future actions. Furthermore, when exercising reason in a reflective mode and following an action, the interplay between reason and desires, as demonstrated by Williams in Gauguin's case, merely highlights the shortcomings of our actions and the boundaries of our first-person deliberative perspective. Reasons justify, explain, and illuminate the new factors and elements in this conception, for example descriptions of the action's success and/or failure.

§3.4 The Bifurcation Model and the Humean Empirical Conception of Human Agency

David Lewis's view of the bifurcation model, as well as its corollary, the balancing model, is another paradigmatic example.[24] He argues in favour of the Humean position in the following terms. Decision theory is the best possible account of the role of our beliefs and desires.[25] Therefore, we should reject anti-Humean views that aim to show how beliefs can transform desires, as they contradict Decision Theory. However, we could take the argument in the opposite direction: Decision Theory, a paradigmatic example of the balancing model and a corollary of the bifurcation thesis, makes it trivial and obvious that any anti-Humean theory of the interaction of desires and beliefs would clash with any proposal that deviates from the bifurcation thesis. Lewis's argument commits the *petitio principi* fallacy.

The Humean empirical conception of action and motivation directly or indirectly inspires the bifurcation thesis. This bifurcation is pervasive and it is the key

[23] Karen Nielsen, 'Deliberation as Inquiry: Aristotle's Alternative to the Presumption of Open Alternatives' (2011) 120 The Philosophical Review 383.

[24] David Lewis, 'Desire as Belief' (1988) 97 Mind 323.

[25] Richard Jeffrey, *The Logic of Decision* (Chicago UP 1965). The Bayesian principle, which is the core element of Decision Theory, establishes that an agent chooses an action of maximum expected desirability. The agent's notion of the probabilities of the specific circumstances and the desirability of the outcomes of the potential actions are represented by numbers that reflect the agent's actual beliefs and preferences. The bifurcation thesis is one of the core premises of the model. It says that we need to establish the most coherent set of beliefs about the means to obtain maximum satisfaction from our desire-based ends.

premise of the balancing model. It has three key features. First, there is the prevalent belief that our desires and passions are *given*, unchangeable, and uncultivable due to the lack of discernible connection between our emotions and volitions in general.[26] In a similar fashion, because all the relationships between passions and desires are causal, it is not possible to reason one's way out of a desire. In other words, reasoning does not affect desires, though beliefs can causally affect them. For example, I want to satisfy my thirst, and my belief that there is a glass of water in front of me can lead to a derived desire to take and drink the water. Therefore, no reasoning can alter a desire, and beliefs only influence desires by creating a causal link between the agent's desire and the means to fulfil it.[27] Just as natural phenomena such as molecules, the sun, rain, the descent of my pen, or the appearance of grey hairs in my hair emerge spontaneously, so too do desires and passions. We conceptualize desires and passions as integral components of the 'furniture of the universe', integrating them into various states of affairs or events, yet maintaining a distinct *locus* within our own being. However, the concept of 'us' does not refer to a separate or distinct entity from the bodily movements that occur within the natural environment. The Humean conception of action does not disrupt the continuity of our actions, including ethical actions, with the natural world and reassures us that our actions are also part of the empirical world.

Secondly, Hume defends the view that reason operates only theoretically, and therefore he casts doubts on the possibility of robust practical reason,[28] the reasoning that guides us in bringing about, producing actions, shaping, and defining ends. We can obtain theoretical knowledge either through proofs, such as the relationships between causes and effects, or through probability.[29] Consequently, propositions about the world can only be either true, false, or probable. However, when we act, we move our bodies, and only our desires can motivate us to act. Desires are not susceptible to being true or false, and evidence of this, Hume argues, is our profound and irresolvable disagreements.[30] It also appears that if, for example, I desire to go to the cinema, I am actually able to succeed in doing so. At some point, beliefs ought to interact with desires. Hume's solution to this difficulty is that desires can be of two kinds. The first kind are primary desires or instincts that arise from bodily states, for example thirst or hunger.[31] Other things

[26] David Hume, *Treatise of Human Nature* (first published 1739, Penguin Classics 1985) 462, 415.

[27] Enç derives a logical conclusion from Hume's analysis, ie 'reason can never oppose passions in the direction of the will because it is in the nature of original desires to be capable of resisting pressures from reasoning—that is, no *reasoning process* can by itself force an agent to abandon an original desire.' See Berent Enç, 'Hume's Unreasonable Desires' (1996) 13 History and Philosophical Quarterly 239, 247. This view implies that desires and passions offer a natural resistance to reason.

[28] Hume (n 26) 462.

[29] ibid 125.

[30] ibid 457. See also John Leslie Mackie, *Ethics: Inventing Right and Wrong* (Penguin 1977). According to Hume, right and wrong, or good and evil, are just in the mind. Therefore, disagreements are not genuine but are about our connecting patterns, conventions, and beliefs. ibid 464.

[31] ibid 439.

cause the second kind of passions, which are impressions of pain and pleasure that we can recall, establishing relations, and developing into a habit. In this way, we build a reservoir of impressions through memories and habits. Reason shows us the causal and probable connections between objects and states of affairs in the world that will enable us to satisfy our desires and passions. Theoretical reason serves our desires, passions, and instincts. In this picture, it is uncertain and mysterious how we manage to restrain ourselves from acting upon our desires and passions. Hume talks about 'calm' passions, whereas contemporary philosophers who defend a Humean or sub-Humean model talk about 'hot' and 'cold' decisions.[32] But this language does not explain our phenomenology when we talk about right, dutiful, good, or evil decisions. Furthermore, when we deliberate, we discriminate between good and evil actions, righteous and immoral actions, and just and unjust actions.[33] We do more than just talk about how we feel and whether our desires are calm, impetuous, cold, or hot. The Humean conception appears to reduce our ethical judgements to a purely experiential dimension. The paradox is that to determine which desires are hot or cold, calm or impetuous, we need second-order desires that discriminate between hot or cold, calm or impetuous desires. But, *arguendo*, these second-order desires can themselves be cold or hot, necessitating a third-order desire to distinguish between hot and cold, calm and impetuous second-order desires *ad infinitum*. In the bifurcation thesis, the focus on desires tends to be superficial, depriving us of a rich picture of desire, its complexity, and its connection to different kinds of pleasures.[34] All is unified in one measure (see also Socrates *technē* below).

Thirdly, the only mistakes we make when we act are theoretical reasoning errors, ie beliefs about causal connections and probabilistic estimates. We cannot say that desires contradict desires because only propositions, which are the result of theoretical reasoning, can be contradictory, and as theoretical reasoning is the only kind of reasoning, then desires and passions are *beyond reason*.[35] According to Hume, motivating passions or desires are caused by feelings of pain or pleasure. These motivating passions or desires are the cause of action. As reason is merely theoretical reason or reasoning that establishes causal connections or statements of facts, reasons play no role in transforming or changing desires and passions. Desires and

[32] Lewis (n 24) 323–24.

[33] Some neo-Humean conceptions advocate the idea that moral judgements are merely projections. They accept a realm of quasi-realism; our ethical sentences are mere projections of our emotions. See Simon Blackburn, *Essays in Quasi-Realism* (OUP 1993).

[34] Elijah Milgram, 'Practical Reasoning: the Current State of Play' in Elijah Milgram (ed), *Varieties of Practical Reasoning* (MIT Press 2001) 1, 5.

[35] Hume might have space for criticism for irrational people, eg vices are criticized through the theory of sentiments. See Dale Dorsey, 'Hume's Internalism Reconsidered' (2007) 2 Journal of Ethics and Social Philosophy 1. Hume analyses vices and other irrational decisions as a projection of conventional norms, or as a reflection of how other people's vices strike us, though there is no external ideal that a person has violated with her action. See Jean Hampton, 'Does Hume Have an Instrumental Conception of Practical Reason' (1995) 21 Hume Studies 57; Hume (n 26) 581–82.

passions are inherently *passive, taking place spontaneously within us*. As a result, passions and desires are conceived outside the domain of reason,[36] and it is not possible to attribute to them predicates such as 'rational' or 'irrational'. There is, therefore, no struggle or conflict between passion and reason, which distinguishes Humeans and contemporary neo-Humean theories of action and motivation, as well as all bifurcationist theories on deliberation from Aristotle's conception of action and motivation. Conversely, we simplistically depict desire as an experience of pain and pleasure, a phenomenon within us, or a mental state.

According to Hume, theoretical knowledge cannot organize desires and passions, as they are too messy. Yet desires and passions impinge on us indirectly through the effects and causes of our actions.[37] If we calculate wrongly, we observe the results of our actions and understand that we were mistaken in our beliefs. For example, I want a chocolate mint ice cream, but I have a pistachio ice cream in front of me that I mistakenly think is chocolate mint. After tasting it, I realize that I am mistaken in my beliefs, but not in my desires.

§3.5 The Bifurcation Model and Socrates' *Technē*

We might think that the origin of the bifurcationist thesis lies in Hume's empirical conception of agency. However, there exist ancient theoretical frameworks that do not presuppose an empirical conception of agency, nor do they envision the possibility of reason altering and transforming desires, a fundamental aspect of practical reason. Thus, in this precise sense, arguably, Socrates was also a bifurcationist, though a moderate one. He believed that ignorance caused the inordination of passions and desires. *Technē* represents hope and has the potential to save our lives. Martha Nussbaum's analysis[38] of the Platonic dialogue *Protagoras*[39] highlights the contrasting perspectives put forth by Protagoras and Socrates. For the latter, the paradigm of knowledge is scientific *technē*, whereas mathematics and astronomy are the paradigms of excellence in thinking. Socrates tells us that appearances will combat the art of measurement, or scientific *technē* (*Protagoras* 356 D–E).[40] Desires and passion are in clear opposition, and the art of measurement and commensurability can unmask the deceptive nature of our desires and passions.

The bifurcation thesis is evident; by actively engaging with our theoretical thinking and carefully evaluating, assessing, and quantifying, we might uncover the truth that lies underneath superficial appearances. Socrates is not a hedonist, Nussbaum tells us, but he uses the hedonist premise to show us that we can find

36 Hume (n 26) 413.
37 ibid 459.
38 Martha Nussbaum, 'The Protagoras: A Science of Practical Reasoning' in Elijah Milgram (ed), *The Varieties of Practical Reasoning* (MIT Press 2001) 153.
39 Plato, *Protagoras* (tr Christopher C Taylor, Clarendon Press 1976).
40 ibid.

a unit of measurement to control and save our lives.[41] For Socrates to act badly is nothing more than acting in ignorance or lacking knowledge (*Protagoras* 345 B). The deep need is to eradicate messy deliberation and incommensurability, and only theoretical reasoning that emulates mathematics and science can do this. *Akrasia* is presented as an illusion of ignorance.[42] This ignorance stems from the agent's inability to master the science of measurement. With the right perspective and measurement skills, things won't look as messy as they do for the *akratic*. By contrast, Protagoras presents us with a picture where moral education and moral training are key to good citizenship. There is also a need to adjust our desires. The adjustment is not natural, but the need for it is natural.

According to Nussbaum, Protagoras's story on Prometheus suggests a deep understanding and interconnection between our sociability, the development of ethical actions, and self-understanding. However, Protagoras refuses to acknowledge a reduction to one single and unique standard, quantitative measure, or unifying virtue. The arts, abilities, and talents of a species play a crucial role in shaping their identity and, in the case of human beings, their actions. However, in order to preserve their lives, individuals may resort to a novel form of artistic expression, namely the art of science, encompassing the skills of weighing, counting, and measuring. The arts have the potential to profoundly alter human existence. If such a change were to occur, we would be justified in questioning whether these lives would still be considered 'human'. Furthermore, we would like to enquire whether, even if the transformation were to be drastic, we would still acknowledge our lives as human lives. Protagoras's thinking paves the way for Aristotelian[43] thinking on deliberation and practical reasoning, as well as its insistence on not losing sight of our ordinary and phenomenological experience of choosing and deliberating.

We cannot undervalue the legacy of the bifurcation thesis on our understanding and rejection of robust conception of practical reason in contemporary philosophy. Hume and bifurcationist theories have inspired two contemporary

[41] Nussbaum asserts: 'We will be saved only by something that will assimilate deliberation to weighing and measuring; this, in turn, requires a unit of measurement, some external end about which we can all agree, and which can render all alternatives commensurable. Pleasure enters the argument as an attractive candidate for this role: Socrates adopts it because of the science it promises, rather than for its own intrinsic plausibility.' Nussbaum (n 38) 179. As pointed out by Nussbaum, a similar need to reduce value conflicts motivates utilitarianism. It shows a distaste for the incommensurability of common-sense values. Nussbaum (n 38) 181. We should note that for some interpreters, this is all a dialectical strategy. See Hans George Gadamer, *The Idea of the Good in Platonic-Aristotelian Philosophy* (Yale UP 1986). According to Gadamer, *technē* is absurd, and Socrates aims to show this.

[42] Fears, passions, desires, and love, as we perceive them from a deliberative point of view, do not enter into this picture. Once we understand that we can measure all values against one single unity, we are able to choose with confidence and replace losses as we weigh losses and gains. From an ordinary perspective, Socrates perceives Alcibiades as irreplaceable, yet the science of measurement reveals to him that he can replace this love with any other. Nussbaum (n 38) 188.

[43] Arguably, Gadamer recognizes the continuity of the Platonic-Socratic project when one understands that the art of measurement is a component of a dialectic and presents extreme possibilities. Gadamer (n 41).

positions in the domains of ethics and moral philosophy. One is emotivism or non-cognitivism, which emphasizes ethical judgements as mere projections of our desires and passions;[44] the other is standard cognitivism, which aims to show that theoretical reasoning and beliefs are sufficient to guide us on how we should act. Debates about cognitivism and non-cognitivism in our moral judgements have garnered a significant amount of attention, potentially hindering the examination of the validity of the bifurcation thesis.

Moreover, theorists tend to employ the bifurcation thesis to illuminate contemporary research on the philosophy of action and practical reason. The bifurcation thesis reinforces itself by taking the famous Anscombian distinction between two directions of fit out of context. Based on Anscombe's views, beliefs, our theoretical reasoning, and practical reasoning substantively differ in their targets. Practical reasoning seeks to achieve a desired and envisioned state of affairs in the world. In theoretical reasoning, we aim to give a sound description of what the world looks like. If, in practical reasoning, we fail to produce what we aim to produce, we say that the mistake is in the performance,[45] but in normal circumstances, we repeat our efforts until we bring about what we intend and in the way we conceive it. However, neo-Humeans interpret this distinction between Anscombe's theoretical reasoning and practical reasoning as a conflict between beliefs and desires. The bifurcationist thesis is employed to interpret the opposition between theoretical and practical reasoning. This distinction is used to assert that a cognitive understanding of the world alone does not provide reasons for integrating our desires, tracking values, and objective reasons for action. Desires, on the other hand, simply seek to alter the world in order to achieve satisfaction. Interestingly, the Anscombian differentiation is isolated from other significant Anscombian reflections, such as practical truth and practical knowledge.[46]

Other authors, like Michael Smith, aim to preserve the key Humean insight on motivation and the key role of desires and formulate a more sophisticated conception of the role of our desires. Given the desires that I have from the first-person perspective, Smith asks how I can change and adjust them.[47] Smith rejects the

[44] See Charles L Stevenson, *Ethics and Language* (Yale UP 1994); Blackburn (n 33).

[45] Anscombe states that 'the mistake is in the performance'; she calls this 'Theophrastus's expression' and expresses it as follows: 'As when now I tell myself, "Now I press button A"—pressing button B—a thing which can certainly happen. This, I will call the *direct* falsification of what I say. And here, to use Theophrastus's expression again, the mistake is not one of judgement but one of performance. That is, we do *not* say, "What you *said* was a mistake, because it was supposed to describe what you did and you did not describe it", but "What you *did* was a mistake, because it was not in accordance with what you said."' Anscombe *Intention* (n 2) §§32–33. For a detailed explanation of Anscombe's position, see Rodríguez-Blanco (n 16) ch 3.

[46] It is common among philosophers of action and moral psychology theorists to interpret Anscombe's distinction in light of Hume's bifurcation thesis. See eg Kieran Setiya, 'Hume on Practical Reason' (2004) 18 Philosophical Perspectives 365, 375.

[47] Michael Smith, 'The Humean Theory of Motivation' (1987) 96 Mind 33; Lewis (n 24); Mackie (n 30).

strategies of Nagel[48] and McDowell[49] due to their inability to make sense of motivating reasons, and instead, he seeks an account of desire with proper content. However, by employing this argumentative strategy, he departs from Hume's perspective.[50] Smith asks how we can still preserve our intuitions and insights about the 'direction of fit'.[51] Desires play a functional role, according to Smith, and the dispositional account can explain this role. Desires are, nevertheless, conceived as states. Smith tells us nothing about the production of desires apart from telling us that they equip us with dispositions when certain conditions are satisfied. Furthermore, Smith does not explore the metaphysics of dispositions.

For the Socratic *technē*, the Humean, sub-Humean, and neo-Humean accounts are in either the cognitivist or non-cognitivist positions; there is *no* room for *akrasia*. They either reject the possibility of *akrasia* or reduce it to compulsion.[52] This is a consequence of the bifurcation thesis and the position of these accounts on practical reason.

The bifurcation thesis also imposes a restriction on what and how we can be motivated, but also on what and how we should explain action, on what and how we deliberate, and potentially whether there is such a thing as robust practical reason. It also imposes distortions and unjustified limits on our theories of responsibility and blameworthiness in cases where agency breaks down, ie when we act inadvertently and carelessly. We might conclude with Korsgaard[53] and Nagel[54] that our understanding of practical reason and deliberation is tainted by our metaphysics of action. To this, I will add that our understanding of practical reason and deliberation is determined by how we conceive of the character of belief and desire and how they eventually interact. I will show that the Aristotelian-inspired conception of practical reason and deliberation is the most plausible and sound view, grounded not only in a metaphysics of action but also in the way our practices of responsibility, belief, and desire interact.

In the next two chapters, I will advance arguments to explain the neo-Aristotelian conception of deliberation and practical reason as opposed to the 'balancing' conception of deliberation, which is the corollary of the bifurcation thesis. In Chapter 8, I will demonstrate how the bifurcation thesis can mislead us in assessing responsibility for negligent actions.

48 Ernest Nagel, *The Possibility of Altruism* (Princeton UP 1970).
49 John McDowell, 'Are Moral Requirements Hypothetical Imperatives?' (1978) 52 Proceeedings of the Aristotelian Society, Supplementary Volume 13; John McDowell, 'Virtue and Reason' (1979) 62 The Monist 331.
50 Smith (n 47) 50.
51 ibid 51.
52 See Chapter 6 for a detailed discussion on this point.
53 Christine Korsgaard, 'Scepticism about Practical Reason' (1986) 83 The Journal of Philosophy 5.
54 Nagel (n 48).

4

The Aristotelian-Inspired Model of Deliberation and Practical Reason

§4.1 Valuing and Desire: Key Distinctions

Prior to explaining a plausible Aristotelian-inspired conception of deliberation and practical reason, it is necessary to lay the groundwork by introducing some Aristotelian ethical principles into the discussion, drawing a link between them and contemporary ethical concepts.

In contemporary philosophical literature, it is widely agreed that we should distinguish between appetites and desires that are thought-dependent or judgement-sensitive.[1] Aristotle, on the other hand, uses two different terms, *epithumiai* for mere desires such as thirst or hunger[2] and *orexis* for more thoughtful desires. Consider savouring a satisfying meal, maintaining friendships, or achieving college graduation. Many philosophers allude to desires in general without making the aforementioned distinction.[3] According to Aristotle, only *orexis* is subject to transformation and practical reasoning. *Epithumiai* are natural,[4] and we want to 'get rid of them' right away.[5] Making errors about our appetites is not an ethical or practical flaw, but a pathological condition.[6] Having established these conceptual grounds, we will now proceed to advance an Aristotelian-inspired conception of deliberation and practical reason.

[1] See for example Stuart Hampshire, *Freedom of the Individual* (Princeton UP 1975) 47. Tim Scanlon, *What We Owe to Each Other* (Harvard UP 1998) ch 1; Donald Davidson, 'Actions, Reasons and Causes' (1963) 60 The Journal of Philosophy 685; Richard Moran, *Authority and Estrangement: An Essay on Self-Knowledge* (Princeton UP 2001) 115.

[2] Aristotle, *Nichomachean Ethics* (tr Sarah Broadie and Christopher Rowe, OUP 2002) 1118b10–21.

[3] Davidson (n 1). Davidson talks about desires as 'the desire to switch on the light' and plays with the ambiguity between mere appetites and judgement-sensitive or thought-dependent desires.

[4] Aristotle (n 2) 1118b9.

[5] ibid 1118b15–19. See also Hyman, who discusses this feature of 'satiability' and compares it with Russell. John Hyman, *Action, Knowledge and Will* (OUP 2015) 109.

[6] Aristotle (n 2) 1118b19. See also Young for a discussion on how temperance is a thought-dependent desire and the potential pathological nature of common appetites. Charles Young, 'Aristotle on Temperance' (1988) 97 Philosophical Review 521.

Responsibility for Negligence in Ethics and Law. Verónica Rodríguez-Blanco, Oxford University Press.
 DOI: 10.1093/9780198948193.003.0004

§4.2 Deliberation as an Inquiry: Settling an Answer to the Question *What?* Through Answering the Question *How?*

According to the Aristotelian model, practical reason consists of both practical argument and deliberation. If there is a hypothetical attribution of deliberation, we are closer to practical argumentation, where practical syllogism plays a key role.[7] Contrast this with the deliberative stance: when we act in a forward-looking manner, we are neither reconstructing past actions nor pondering what to do from a purely theoretical standpoint. Practical syllogism is typically a scheme of interpretation of future or past action, rather than something we use when we are acting.[8]

Our focus in this chapter is on deliberation, which is centred on the first-person perspective or deliberative stance. In the next chapter, we carefully scrutinize the nature of practical argumentation and show its connection to the first-person or deliberative stance.

Aristotle presents us with a uniquely innovative model that differs from the Socratic idea of deliberation as the science of measurement, in which deliberation is reducible to a skill or craft, as well as from the contemporary model of 'balancing'.[9] Aristotle aims to show that deliberation and its outcome, a rational decision—*prohairesis*[10]—are not skills or crafts but have important elements that overlap with what we understand as a skill or craft. At the same time, Aristotle shows that there is an important overlap between theoretical reasoning[11] and deliberation.

[7] John Cooper, *Reason and the Human Good in Aristotle* (Hackett 1975) 14. See also Heda Segvic, *From Protagoras to* Aristotle (Princeton UP 2008) 148–51. The practical syllogism is not true to life and, arguably, the practical syllogism truly works as an imputation or scheme of interpretation. See Elizabeth Anscombe, *Intention* (Basil Blackwell 1957, reprinted by Harvard UP 2000) §§41, 42 and Sarah Broadie, *Ethics with Aristotle* (OUP 1991). See also Chapter 6 for a detailed discussion of practical syllogism. See Broadie (this note) 226, for a criticism of the schematism of practical syllogism. Other commentators have highlighted that Aristotle's explanation of the incontinent's reasoning in the form of practical syllogism is too sketchy, see Bonnie Kent, 'Transitory Vice: Thomas Aquinas on Incontinence' (1989) 27 Journal of the History of Philosophy 199, 200.

[8] Agnes Callard, 'Aristotle on Deliberation' in Ruth Chang and Kurt Sullivan (eds), *Routledge Handbook of Practical Reason* (Routledge 2021) 126.

[9] For further exploration of the difference between the contemporary model and the Aristotelian model, see Callard (n 8) and Karen Nielsen, 'Deliberation as Inquiry: Aristotle's Alternative to the Presumption of Open Alternatives' (2011) 120 The Philosophical Review 383, 386. Nielsen also adds some interesting notes on the comparative model of Aristotle's deliberation. ibid 387.

[10] There are a variety of translations of the Aristotelian term 'prohairesis'. *Prohairesis* or rational decision, can be interpreted as the end of deliberation. Hardie advances an analysis of the *prohairesis* as an efficient cause. William Hardie, *Aristotle's Ethical Theory* (originally printed in 1968, Clarendon Press 2004) 160–65. It is not an intellectual opinion, rather, after choosing and acting, we show our character. We show, within our model, the key element of becoming or transformation. For a complete explanation of this point, see Chapter 6 of this book. According to Segvic, *prohairesis* is used only once in Plato's *Parmenides*. Segvic (n 7) 162 fn 25. Vigo distinguishes two senses of *prohairesis*. Vigo highlights that *prohairesis*—rational decision—is not a commitment but rather the end of the investigation into the basic action where the agent began the action. Aristotle (n 2) 1139a30. *Prohairesis is a result of deliberation that* combines cognitive and emotional elements. ibid 1113a10ff. Alejandro Vigo, 'Deliberación y Decisión Segun Aristóteles' (2012) 43 Tópicos: Revista de Filosofía 51.

[11] See Hardie (n 10) 225–28.

However, deliberation has a proper way of functioning. Consequently, Aristotle's explanation navigates between the Scylla of a craft and the Charybdis of theoretical reasoning,[12] aiming to show that deliberation is reducible neither to a craft nor to theoretical thinking. If Aristotle's endeavour is successful, it will reveal the possibility of practical reason. Let us then examine the similarities between craft, skill, and deliberation.

§4.2.1 The Craft or Skill Analogy

Throughout history, both in ancient times and across different societies, humans have cultivated a diverse array of crafts, spanning from the art of origami to the practice of medicine. In the contemporary world, if we are asked how a medical doctor, who is treating a patient with ovarian cancer stages II–III, deliberates to cure her patient, we will say that the medical doctor knows what she is doing because she knows *what* a healthy body is and *what* the appropriate treatment to obtain a healthy body is. In philosophical terms, we can say that the medical doctor has two representations or sets of beliefs as she practises her craft or skill. First, she has a set of beliefs about what constitutes 'health'. For instance, the patient's organs and normal abilities like speech, breathing, and mobility are functioning well. This constitutes a 'formal' set of beliefs or representation of a 'healthy human being'. On the other hand, the medical doctor also holds a more 'substantive' conception of health. Since medicine is a technical discipline, we can say that the substantive conception of health and the technical conception of health overlap. Thus, in the example of the patient who is suffering from ovarian cancer stages II–III, the doctor's goal is that the treatment results in the total elimination of the mass of abnormal cells that are currently contained within one part of the body and prevents metastasis, ie the spreading of cancerous cells into healthy organs.

For Aristotle, deliberation is an inquiry or investigation into '*what*' should I do? As we develop this concept of deliberation, it will become clearer why the agent must provide both the question and the answer. For Aristotle, the answer to the question '*What* should I do?' can be provided if I, the agent, can state *how* I should do it. Consequently, this conception dictates that the *how* determines the *what*.

This is certainly puzzling and interesting for the modern conception of deliberation that is hostage to the balancing model and its corollary, the neo-Humean bifurcationist thesis. This theory suggests that the agent must evaluate and compare alternatives. According to the latter, the *what* and the *how* are 'given', and consequently, we have multiple means to achieve different desire-based ends. There

[12] See Aristotle (n 2) 1139b18–1140a20. There is a tendency to collapse theoretical and practical reasoning. See Chapter 1 of this book.

is clarity and determinacy of the *what* and multiplicity of the *how*,[13] and therefore the task is to compare and evaluate the multiplicity of means—the *how*. In contrast, in the Aristotelian model of deliberation, the *what* remains indeterminate, while the *how* requires further thought or investigation to bring the *what* close to myself and, consequently, to my action, thereby making the action clearer to myself and enhancing my practical understanding.

This is still very cryptic, but perhaps the simile of Neurath's boat can help us explain the Aristotelian type of deliberation. If we need to repair a boat while at sea, we must do so plank by plank, because trying to rebuild it from the bottom up will almost certainly result in its sinking. As sailors, we are actively engaged in the activity of sailing. We are at sea and have no choice but to fix the boat.

Similarly, in the Aristotelian model of deliberation, we are in the world of acting, and we need to deliberate *what* we should do.[14] However, as I will suggest later in this chapter, our vision of the *what* is indeterminate and key aspects of the substantive *what* are unknown to us. This is a corollary of one key feature of deliberation, ie that it concerns only what is contingent and, therefore, particular and circumstantial.[15] Therefore, we must simultaneously hold the vague and indeterminate what, as well as the other planks of Neurath's boat, and concentrate solely on one plank at a time. Each plank represents a unique set of circumstances that support the specific *how*. As a result, the focus of deliberation is on the *how*. The *how* provides us with a clearer understanding of the *what*, allowing us to revise the *how* based on the insights we've gained from the *what*. Furthermore, this process goes backwards and forwards, ie we revise the *what* in light of what we have learned from the *how* and reconsider the *how* in light of what we have learned from the way the *what* is now presented to us, at this new stage of the deliberation. This continues until we reach a point of insight, ie we have brought the *what*, or what is now '*the end*', to ourselves. The ends impregnate and illuminate the means, and vice versa. The cycle will continue with further '*what*' and '*how*' questions in light of our deliberations and actions.[16]

Let us consider that deliberation involves the formation of the *What* based on the *How*, and conversely. This position presupposes the following:

[13] For instance, according to the internalist theorist, the deliberator is aware of his internal reasons for action, such as desires within his motivational set, and the methods to fulfil these desires. See eg Bernard Williams, 'Internal and External Reasons for Actions' in *Moral Luck* (CUP 1981) 101; Michael Smith, *The Moral Problem* (Blackwell 1994). For the externalist, the deliberator has a reason for action to the extent that the reason is a normative reason and applies to him/her. According to the externalist, the deliberator has the capacity to grasp these normative reasons and, therefore, has clarity on them, and is able to act accordingly; see Derek Parfit, 'Reasons and Motivations' (1997) 71 Proceeedings of the Aristotelian Society 94. See Chapter 5 for a detailed discussion of the balancing model.

[14] This is also central to Finnis's explanation of practical reason; see John Finnis, '"The Thing I am": Personal Identity in Aquinas and Shakespeare' (2005) 22 Social Philosophy and Policy 250.

[15] See Aristotle (n 2) 1141b14–25.

[16] For Broadie (n 7) 245, Aristotle requires the continual re-evaluation 'in the light of means, means to means, and their consequences'.

(a) The *what* of deliberation is indeterminate.
(b) Deliberation is an inquiry into the *what* to make it more specific and determinate.
(c) At the first stage, an inquiry into the *how* illuminates the *what*.
(d) The *what* is presented under a new light and, more specifically, we can then proceed to revise the *how*.
(e) This process can be iterated multiple times, even during the execution of the action.

I have previously stated that Aristotle establishes an analogy between craft or skill and deliberation. The medical doctor has a formal representation and a substantive—technical—representation of both what a healthy body looks like and the necessary technical knowledge, or 'know how', to cure patients of ovarian cancer. Thus, an objector might protest, there is no need to hold an indeterminate image of the *what* while we are considering the *how*. Furthermore, the simile of Neurath's boat does not bring any clarity to the explanation. The example of the medical doctor clearly illustrates that we do not need to hold the indeterminate *what* and work plank by plank, as we already have a precise representation, both technical and substantive, of what is required. We do not need to revise the *what* in light of the *how*, and vice versa.

But this is where the craft analogy breaks down. Aristotle's goal is to prevent deliberation from collapsing into a craft or skill. He explains that deliberation, unlike the practice of medicine, is not a skill or craft. This is because, as human beings, we hope and seek to ensure that our lives go well, and this gives us a formal *what* for seeking what we should do. However, this *does not* give us a substantive *what* which is determined, shaped, and specific, as in the case of technical knowledge like medicine.

Let us think about the following example to illustrate our point. Chapter 1 introduced the case of Alessandra, a mother of two children who, on a hot day, drives to the hockey pitch to collect her children. She leaves her dog in her vehicle while she walks to the clubhouse. The children engaged in arguments, leading to tantrums that caused a delay in her return to the car. Upon her return, she finds her dog has died of heat stroke. Alessandra wishes for her life to go well. Before starting a family, Alessandra envisioned a multitude of possibilities for her life, including having a loving family, maintaining good health, facilitating her children's educational success within their talents and capacities, securing good job opportunities for herself and her husband, achieving a harmonious work-life balance, living in a place where she and her family can flourish, residing in a country that respects human rights and civil liberties, living in a country with a consolidated democracy, cultivating meaningful friendships, and experiencing good aesthetic experiences. During her adolescent years, Alessandra, like many others, had (a formal) image or picture of what living well entailed, but she did not know in a determinate manner *what* this would look like. The *what of her life* was open to her. It would be absurd to think that we can deliberate in the abstract about (all) these goods, or that Alessandra can compare and evaluate them, or that she can know their content as if it were predetermined before engaging in deliberation and action. However, this seems to be required by certain views within the bifurcationist model and its corollary, the 'balancing' model of deliberation. The 'balancing' model of deliberation, arguably, stems from an artificiality in our understanding of our ends and the potential to achieve and comprehend their specific contents.

Aristotle's point is precisely that the only thing we can actually do in virtue of our nature, which has both an animal element and a rational aspect, is to engage in narrow deliberation. This involves deliberating about the *what* under specific circumstances, considering the perspective of our unique situation. Due to the indeterminate and opaque nature of the *what*, we must put it on hold while we determine the *how*.

True, the formal *what* of living well exists in the background, but as we live our lives and engage in narrow deliberation, the *how* takes shape.[17] In Alessandra's case, she strives to provide her children with optimal opportunities by registering them with a hockey club, and she aims to instil in them the joy of pet ownership by purchasing a dog. Nevertheless, she needs to figure out the *how* to combine both goals, ie caring for the family pet and caring for the physical health of her children. She does not know *what* this combined state of harmony of both goals looks like, nor does she fully grasp, prior to registering the children in hockey and buying the dog, the *what* of her deliberation. Becoming a mother and a pet owner are indeterminate '*whats*' that are prior to deliberating on and taking subsequent actions. But even once she has taken her decision on the basis of her deliberation, and while executing her decision, she is continually grasping and shaping her *what*, ie *what* being a mother and a pet owner entails, in light of executing the *how* that she has deliberated upon. After achieving a more specific determination of the *what*, she still needs to go to the 'deliberation drawing board' to revise her *how*[18] and subsequently continues with a new specification of the *what* which is now impregnated with and shaped by the new understanding of the *how*.

The craft analogy is of enormous help because it brings to our attention the fact that in deliberation, as well as in crafts and skills, the idea that the end—the *what*—shapes the means—the *how*—and the means—the *how*—shapes and determines

[17] Scholars have argued since Donald J Allan's *The Philosophy of Aristotle* (OUP 1952) that we must examine books 3, 6, and 7 of the *Nichomachean Ethics* in their entirety to comprehend Aristotle's practical deliberation. See also Donald J Allan, 'The Practical Syllogism' in Auguste Mansion (ed), *Autour d'Aristote* (Publications Universitaires de Louvain 1955) 325. Wiggins has also argued that there is continuity in Aristotle between the readings of books 3, 6, and 7. David Wiggins, 'Deliberation and Practical Reason in Amélie Rorty, *Essays on Aristotle's Ethics* (University of California Press 1980) 221. See also John Finnis, 'Practical Reasons's Foundations' in *Reason in Action: Collected Essays:* vol I (OUP 2011) 19.

[18] See Chapter 5.

the ends—the *what*. It also highlights the idea that deliberation is limited to transforming particulars and applying to specific situations and circumstances. In the aforementioned medical scenario, the doctor, drawing on her expertise, engages in actions to cure the patient's ovarian cancer, aiming to produce and bring about a specific state of affairs for the patient, such as the eradication of malignant cells and the restoration of overall well-being. Other crafts and skills clearly show how this practical engagement can result in the transformation of elements and materials in the world into something else. For example, a carpenter, relying on his knowledge and experience, will select the appropriate wood and design to make the best possible table as he sees it in his particular circumstances. Technical knowledge and know-how transform materials in the world towards a specific product. Most significantly, an external standard dictates the production of goods through craft or skill. For instance, an external standard determines the appropriateness of a table for a specific use, just as it determines the health and non-cancerous status of a patient. In other words, in crafts and skills, there are rules, standards, and codes of what is good or what is best. In contrast, when we engage in ethical deliberation, we make decisions and carry out actions based on our deliberations; no external standard determines the rightness or goodness of our actions. Thus, there is a formal good, ie *living well*, that receives substantive content as we deliberate, act, and live.

Aristotle, on the other hand, posits that the individual who possesses practical wisdom (*phronimos*), namely the one who excels in using their practical reason in both deliberation and practical argument, determines excellence in deliberation. This emphasizes that excellence in deliberation, practical argument, and, thus, practical reason cannot be codified or reduced to a set of *a priori* rules, but rather involves us as individuals in a process of aspirational transformation towards becoming a person of practical wisdom—*phronimos*. Chapter 5 provides a thorough explanation of the concept of *phronimos*, which will be fundamental to this work.

Persevering with the craft or skill analogy, what kind of aspirational transformation is involved in the process of deliberation? We shall claim that we act and deliberate upon our primary materials, which are our desires. We aim to transform ourselves, and the primary material upon which we work is our desires.[19] When we deliberate and act accordingly, there is no external standard, but there is a possibility of reaching an aspirational point. In aspirational transformation, reason

[19] Aristotle states, 'Virtue ensures the rightness of the end we aim at, prudence ensures the rightness of the means we adopt to gain that end.' Aristotle (n 2) 1144a8–10. Broadie's interpretation of these lines is as follows: 'Virtue ensures that whatever is aimed for is aimed for rightly at any stage and pursued only in terms of what is best. As reflection brings out new considerations, the value of O under the circumstances (its worthiness to be an end) is judged and rejudged, and the rightness of these judgements depends on character. Moral virtue is active throughout wise deliberation, not only in the form of a general thrust or readiness to discern and do the best whatever it might be, but as a plexus of specific evaluative dispositions expressed in a series of differently focused but mutually cognisant responses.' Broadie (n 7) 245–46. In other words, the rightness of those judgements depends on character all the way through. Segvic (n 7) 153 posits that one set of desires transitions to another set of desires and so on, and that desires are transformed by reasons.

operates to transform our lower desires.[20] Chapter 5 discusses further details of how this is possible.

We have been exploring Aristotle's use of the craft or skill analogy thus far. We have said that to illuminate what deliberation is, Aristotle navigates between deliberation as a craft or skill and deliberation as theoretical reasoning, and that he tries to avoid any reduction of deliberation to either. We now turn to the latter analogy—deliberation as theoretical reasoning.

§4.2.2 The Theoretical Analogy

Aristotle invites us to think about deliberation by focusing on the question of *how* we trace a geometrical figure.[21] Let us say we need to trace a parallelogram, as in Figure 4.1 below:

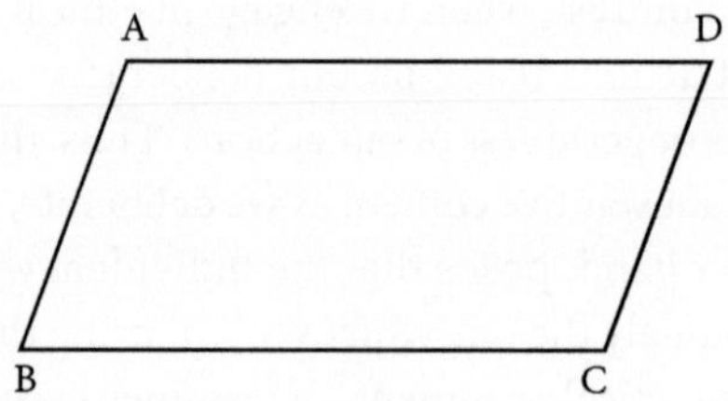

Figure 4.1 Parallelogram

We must analyse and comprehend the parallelogram's most basic parts or elements. Thus, after deliberating and investigating, we discover that it is composed of four triangles, as shown in Figure 4.2:

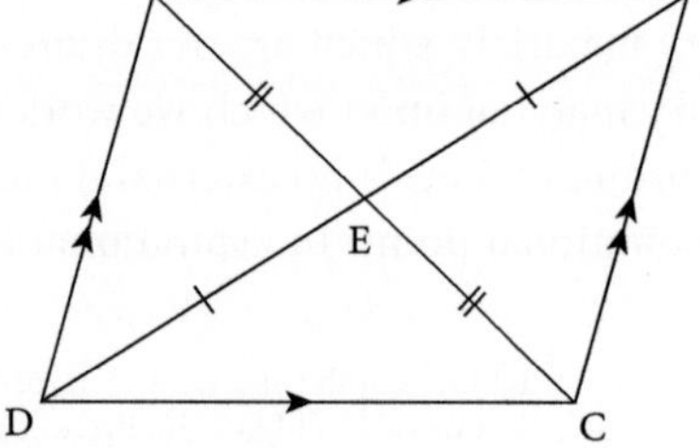

Figure 4.2 Parallelogram's composition

[20] Aristotle (n 2) 1139a20–30. Commenting on this passage, Kosman asserts that acting is a form of thinking, and at the end, deliberation is a deliberative desire. Aryeh Kosman, *Virtues of Thought* (Harvard UP 2014) 289–91. Deliberation is a process that leads to preparedness to act. Segvic (n 7) 164. Deliberation is not a mere activity of reason. If he had thought in these terms, Aristotle would have needed to accept non-deliberative volition. ibid 165.

[21] Aristotle (n 2) 1112b15–24 and 1142a23.

The diagram of the basic compositional elements of a parallelogram enables me to start tracing *from it* the parallelogram. As Aristotle puts it, 'And the last thing in the analysis would be to be the first that comes into being.'[22] In deliberation, we transform through our thinking the mean 'x' in order to achieve the end Y, which is indeterminate and unspecified, and discover that 'x' is also composed[23] of 'a' and 'b'. Upon further investigation, we ascertain that 'b' originates from a more basic mean, which is 'a_1', and we also discover that 'b' necessitates 'b_1'. Similar to our investigation into *how* to trace the parallelogram, our thought process reveals that the parallelogram consists of four triangles. In this case, our reasoning leads us to conclude that by doing 'a_1' and 'b_2', I do 'a' and 'b', and by doing 'a' and 'b', I do 'x'. We now have insight into how to achieve Y and a performance that is close to us because this is something that is possible and immediately actionable. In action, we now have a series of *hows* that will get us to the *what*. The series could take the form shown in Figure 4.3:

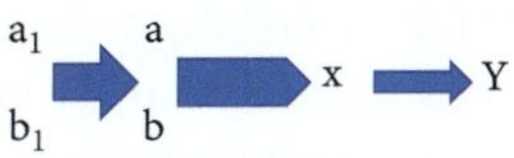

Figure 4.3 Practical reasoning's diagram

As I engage in thought, I specify and shape the series of means to do 'Y', ie to get 'a' from 'a_1', 'b' from 'b_1', 'x' from 'a' and 'b', and finally 'Y' from 'x'. It is not an *inferential process* as from premises to a conclusion, but rather a transformational thought process where 'a_1' and 'b_1' become 'a' and 'b' and 'a' and 'b' become 'x' and consequently, 'a_1', 'b_1', 'a' and 'b' and 'x' become 'Y'. However, the transformational thought process is not like production because (a) there is no product external to the agent who engages in deliberation, and (b) there is no external standard to assess the performance of the agent. The transformation and subsequent insights[24] operate through thought.

However, there is a complication with this transformational process through thinking, which is neither present in crafts or skills nor in theoretical thinking. In deliberation and rational decision—*prohairesis*—emotions and desires are involved, but they are not states or static entities. Until now, we have refrained from

[22] These lines are stated in the following context, where Aristotle introduces the analogy with a geometrical figure: 'Rather, we lay down the end, and then examine the ways and means to achieve it. If it appears that any of several means will reach it, we examine which of them will reach it most easily and most finely; and if only one means reaches it, we examine how that means will reach it, and how the means itself is reached, until we come to the first cause, the last thing to be discovered. For the deliberator would seem to inquire and analyse in the way described, as though analysing a diagram—for, apparently, all deliberation is inquiry, though not all inquiry—in mathematics, for instance—is deliberation. And the last thing in the analysis would seem to be the first that comes into being.' Aristotle (n 2) 1112b15–24.

[23] See Wiggins for a focus on decomposition. Wiggins (n 17) 224–25.

[24] Aristotle thinks that there is *nous* in practical deliberation.

using the word 'practical' when referring to 'thinking', as we are attempting to show that 'practical thinking' or 'practical reasoning' is indeed feasible. Our thinking or reasoning is practical because of two key elements. First, the emphasis is on specifying and understanding the specific details of both the *what* and the *how*. In other words, grasping my situation as a deliberator, ie '*from here*'.[25] Secondly, the fact that desires are not states or static entities. On the contrary, they evolve through our thinking about the *how*, which shapes and determines the *what*. Therefore, upon realizing that 'a' and 'b' are constituted by 'a_1' and 'b_1', I began to cultivate desires and emotions towards 'a_1' and 'b_1'. I have now also gained a perspective in relation to 'a' and 'b' that I did not have before, and this perspective transforms the quality, understanding, and depth of my desire for 'a', 'b', and 'x'.

Let us consider the case of Beatrice as an illustrative example to support our argument. Beatrice identifies 'the best possible physical health for her children' as her *what* (which she puts on hold as its specification and content will be provided by the *how*). During the early years of her children's development, she has a very vague idea of the content of this *what*. According to the Aristotelian-inspired conception, when attempting to define the *what*, we make 'stabs in the darkness'.[26] In this case, Beatrice registers her daughter for gymnastics classes. However, it quickly becomes evident that her daughter possesses an extremely competitive nature, which is amplified by gymnastics, and appears to manifest as aggression. Beatrice is reluctant to foster this aggression and begins to think she should withdraw her daughter from gymnastics lessons. As a result of deliberating and engaging in *how*, 'x', Beatrice has also grasped a new perspective on *what*, 'Y', and this leads her to have a better specification of the *what*, ie she desires physical health conceived in harmony with a balanced competitive spirit. Beatrice is developing the right desires and transforming herself in an aspirational way, such as becoming a mother who deliberates correctly and is developing the right desires concerning the best physical health for her child in the context of their particular circumstances.

Let us think about an alternative variation of the previous example. Beatrice enrols her daughter in gymnastics classes and discovers that she has great flexibility and a natural sense of rhythm. Beatrice now thinks that ballet and tap lessons will

[25] See Bernard Williams, 'Moral Luck' in *Moral Luck* (CUP 1981) 20, 35.

[26] Segvic (n 7) supplies this metaphor. See also Myles Burnyeat, who argues that the *what* is presupposed. Myles Burnyeat, 'Aristotle on Learning to be Good' in Amélie Rorty (ed), *Essays on Aristotle's Ethics* (University of California Press 1980) 69, 73. According to Wiggins' interpretation, the ends are assumed. Wiggins (n 17) 225. However, Wiggins seems to suggest that the end is indeterminate, there are no rules, and the discovery and specification of the end is an intellectual problem, but also practical in the sense that it involves practical deliberation, ie practical wisdom. ibid 230–31, 234. Wiggins seems to advance the view that practical reasoning consists in appreciating the specific situation of our practical question or search and relating it to the complex ideal that the agent tries to achieve in living well. ibid 237. Curzer puts it as follows: 'Deliberation identifies ends by clarification rather than selection.' Howard J Curzer, 'Aristotle's Practical Syllogisms' (2015) 46 The Philosophical Forum 129, 138.

help her daughter develop her natural sense of rhythm and improve her flexibility. The development of both the former and the latter will facilitate her daughter's gymnastic abilities. Beatrice has now a better grasp of *her daughter's* physical health, which in turn informs the content, quality, and 'thickness'[27] of her desire for her daughter's physical health. This involves 'x' (becoming a good gymnast) by practising 'a' and 'b' (developing rhythm and flexibility), as well as 'a_1' and 'b_2' (taking ballet and tap lessons). We will see in Chapter 5 that this is merely a simplistic depiction of the transformation of Beatrice's desires regarding her children's and family's 'living well'. For now, we only need to keep in mind that our thinking transforms and specifies desires and emotions, and that there is the possibility of a right transformation of desires and emotions, ie aspirational transformation.

We cannot overstate the psychological and logical value of engaging in deliberation with an indeterminate and unknown end. Consider the opposite viewpoint, in which there is neither a substantive nor an indeterminate end. We simply need to analyse the agent's situation so that she can make a decision. Thus, the deliberator should only focus on her particular situation, or perhaps on a set of principles and rules, to determine what to do. In the case of Alessandra, we could state that she is a human being, a mother who has beliefs about the physical health of her children, has a dog, and has registered her children in hockey lessons. How is all of this connected in a way that allows us to determine what Alessandra should do? If the agent knows everything about her situation and condition, nothing follows. We could take a more sophisticated or complex approach and state that there are rules and principles governing mothers, pet owners, and children's physical health, and that these rules or principles apply to Alessandra. However, how she perceives her particular situation will be determined by her desires and emotions, and their relationship to her specific principles and ability to guide her in *particular* circumstances are problematic. How can an answer to the question '*What* should I do?' follow from a set of principles?

In summary, practical deliberation entails investigating and searching for the fundamental elements of the performing action that are close to us at the level of possibility, as well as gaining insight into our unique particular circumstances in order to answer the question, '*What* should I do?' Thinking in this piecemeal fashion enables us to start the action, and, in this way, I bring the *what* to myself through insight into and understanding of the *how*. *This is why there is no gap between deliberation, rational decision*—prohairesis—*and performing the action. This is because the transformation of my desires has already happened when I reach the point of insight* into *what* to do, ie when I get to the basic performance of the *how*. As I decomposed and translated 'x' into 'a' and 'b', 'b' into 'b_1', and 'a' into 'a_1',

[27] This term refers to the idea that desires gain stability and endurance through thinking and deliberation, and that they evolve according to the agent's particular circumstances.

I not only engaged my reasoning and thought about the how, but also transformed my desires.

This model eliminates the famous contemporary gap that arises from the bifurcation thesis and its corollary, the 'balancing' model, in which the agent supposedly chooses between a set of open options, between external and internal reasons, between reason and desires, between reason and motivation. In this Aristotelian-inspired model, thinking reveals the fundamental elements of action in particular circumstances as experienced and perceived by the deliberator. Thinking refines the desire at each stage of the process, merging insight and desire to lead to practical action. The elements 'x', 'a' and 'b', 'a_1' and 'b_2' do not follow inferentially, like in theoretical reasoning, nor causally, like in the natural world, but this does not mean that thinking is not immersed in the natural world. It is immersed because the thinking and desire are intertwined in a special way. Thinking shapes, specifies, and determines desires.

Given our emphasis on the role of deliberation in action, is it feasible for an action to not proceed after deliberation? It is certainly possible, and many of our actions are failures to achieve what we have already deliberated upon. 'There are many slips between the cup and the lip.' We shall discuss this possibility in Chapter 6. However, the lack of performance is not due to a lack of motivation as understood in contemporary moral psychology and moral philosophy, but rather to a failure to integrate character with practical reasoning.

For now, we can say that if Beatrice deliberates and has the insight that her daughter's aggressive competitiveness is amplified by her gymnastic lessons and fails to cancel the lessons, despite her desire to develop her daughter's physical health, we will explain this as a lack of integration between her character and deliberation, and the details of this explanation are the subject of Chapter 6.

In the preceding section, we used the simile of Neurath's boat to emphasize the need to remember that the *what*, even in the case of narrow deliberation, remains indeterminate. A number of philosophers have resisted this image of an indeterminate and vague *what*, attempting to find an alternative interpretation of Aristotle's conception of deliberation. According to this alternative image, the deliberator, who engages in action from first-person perspective, can grasp the *what* as a grand end, and her deliberation is a search for means-ends that fit her vision of the grand end. This interpretation portrays our deliberation as an upward journey, connecting various means towards a grand end. Furthermore, the deliberation's content is clear, or at least the grand end is implicit and lurking in the background.[28]

[28] For the idea that the grand end is implicit, see Heda Segvic. She asserts that our conception of 'living well' is triggered by the opportunity. Segvic (n 7) 159–60. In other passages, however, she asserts that the grand end is a hypothesis or a presupposition. Segvic (n 7) 156.

I will challenge this interpretation and present several arguments to support the concept of the indeterminate and vague *what* or end, which I will refer to as the '*upward journey towards the specification of the what*'.[29]

§4.3 The 'Grand End' Versus the 'Upward Journey Towards the Specification of the *What*' View

For the balancing model, all premises are equal starting points. We infer that we have clarity on our ends—the *what* in deliberation—and that we are confronting our desires prior to deliberation.[30] There is a propensity to interpret Aristotelian deliberation in terms of both the bifurcation thesis[31] and its corollary, the balancing model. This reading leads us to the conclusion that, either explicitly or implicitly,[32] there is a substantive end—a *what*—upon which we can begin our deliberation. The formal end of 'living well' is fused with the idea of a substantive end or restricted end that guides our deliberation and actions. Aristotle's comparison with theoretical reasoning and use of the example of a geometrical figure discussed in the previous section might invite us to think that Aristotle's analogy leads to the fusion of practical deliberation and theoretical reasoning. However, the analogy between deliberation and tracing a geometrical figure focuses on something

[29] Sarah Broadie is the main advocate for this viewpoint. Broadie (n 7). I have chosen the term 'upward journey' instead of her own terminology, 'ground-level', to emphasize that there is an aspirational element, which I will defend in Chapter 5. The term 'upward journey' is indirectly connected to Dominic Scott's interpretation of Aristotle's *Nichomachean Ethics*. See Dominic Scott, *Levels of Argument* (OUP 2015) pt II. It is also inspired by the work of Katja Vogt, who emphasizes the connection between narrow deliberation and medium- and large-scale deliberation. Katja Vogt, *Desiring the Good* (2017). In some key passages, Segvic appears to accept this interpretation. For example, according to Segvic the agent's conception of a good life relies on the agent's own previous deliberations. She accepts that our conception of 'living well' is incomplete, but not that it is completely indeterminate, as Broadie suggests. Segvic (n 7) 167.

[30] Broadie (n 7) 236–37. John Cooper distinguishes between justification and explanation and says that to make sense of the former, we need the grand end view. Cooper (n 7) 10. See also Vogt (n 29) 130, fn 50. According to Cooper, we also need to endorse a hierarchy of ends, recognizing that deliberation cannot determine the ultimate end. Therefore, we need to presuppose it. Cooper (n 7) 18, 58–67. The grand end is the agent's conception of what kind of life is best. ibid 59 and 34. The thesis of a chain in deliberation, where we do not deliberate about ultimate ends but about means-ends that are constitutive of the grand end, is accepted by several Aristotelian contemporary interpreters, see Wiggins (n 17); Cooper (n 7).

[31] For criticism of this reading, see John McDowell, 'Some Issues in Aristotle's Moral Psychology' in *Mind, Value and Reality* (Harvard UP 1998) 31. See also Weinman who proposes a harmony between reason and virtue—desires. Michael Weinman, *Pleasure in Aristotle's Ethics* (Continuum 2007) 84. A few passages later, however, we see an indirect adherence to the bifurcation thesis. ibid 88.

[32] Broadie (n 7) 236. For a complete definition of the grand end view, see Cooper (n 7) 76. For a clear delineation of the view and its criticism, see McDowell (n 31) and John McDowell, 'Deliberation and Moral Development in Aristotle's Ethics' in Stephen Engstrom and Jennifer Whiting (eds), *Aristotle, Kant and the Stoics: Rethinking Happiness and Duty* (CUP 1996). McDowell calls it the 'universal blueprint'. Burnyeat appears to endorse the grand view. Burnyeat (n 26) 83, as do Terence Irwin, 'Ethics with Aristotle by Sarah Broadie' (1993) 90 The Journal of Philosophy 329 and Antony Kenny, 'The Ends of Life' in *Aristotle on the Perfect Life* (OUP 1992) 199.

different. Therefore, we must presuppose and hold the *what*, formulate the question, and articulate an answer as if we knew the *what*.[33] The analogy also enables us to understand that we decompose and translate the *what* into parts until we reach the point of insight into *how* to start acting.

§4.3.1 The Grand End View as a Necessary Postulate for the Justification of Deliberation and Rational Decision

Following on from the previous discussion of bifurcation, the grand end view holds that we need to be able to justify our deliberations and actions. The idea of a grand end provides precisely this grounding. We choose 'x' as a means to 'Y' because we consider 'Y' to be good or best. The deliberator's value judgement asserts that the end—the *what*—is valuable, so the deliberation and actions aimed at achieving it are imbued with the significance of the end.[34] However, to determine its worthiness, the deliberator cannot question whether, in this particular circumstance, this is the best way to act.[35]

In contrast, the 'upward journey towards the specification of the what' concept does not view the grounds of deliberation and rational decision as the ends, as it is the process of deliberation that unveils the ends. However, the process of unveiling, refining, discovering, and re-discovering, of the end—the *what*—involves both the

[33] Broadie (n 7) 236–37. Richard Kraut, 'In Defense of the Grand End View' (1993) 103 Ethics 361. This is also a plausible interpretation of Finnis's set of objective goods. John Finnis, *Natural Law and Natural Rights* (Clarendon Press 1980) ch 1. They remind us, and specifically judges and legislators, of the *what*. In their decisions, they need to act *as if* they know the content of the *what*. Arguably, legal principles operate in this way. Judges hold on to them and presuppose them but at the same time, they modify and refine their content as they try to determine the answer to the legal question that has been posed. We will delve deeper into this topic in Chapter 9.

[34] The importance of the role of the grand end in deliberation is emphasized in Kraut (n 33) 262. Wallace's interpretation of McDowell also offers us this picture. We can make sense of an agent's plurality of desires in terms of other desires, and what organizes this plurality is a substantive end—the grand end. Thus, a conception of 'how to live' renders the election intelligible. Jay Wallace, 'Virtue, Reason and Principle' (1991) 21 Canadian Journal of Philosophy 469, 479. McDowell believes that there is clarity at the abstract level, though further specification takes place while we are deliberating. For McDowell, the agent has a conception of doing well. McDowell (n 31) 28, 33. McDowell formulates two stages, a large-scale formal end and a medium one that is indeterminate. ibid 32–33. See also Vogt (n 29) ch 2. McDowell clearly criticizes the 'grand end view' as 'living well' but says that it is an attribute of a whole life, which might encourage a softer version of the grand end view. McDowell (n 31) 41, 43. Broadie appears to advocate a more radical view in which there is no clarity at the abstract level. Broadie (n 7). Other authors are ambiguous in relation to the grand end view. For example, Sherman thinks that commitment to the grand end can be the precondition for a long term and coherent integration of life. Character coherence becomes dependent on or constrained by how well we can integrate our multiple ends. Nancy Sherman, *The Fabric of Character* (Clarendon Press 1989) 76. A few pages later, however, she seems to advocate Broadie's view, ie perception of the particular situation is not a 'sense', but a result of an investigation. ibid 89–90. The particularism of McDowell is criticized in Vogt (n 29) 39–40. See also Martha Nussbaum, 'Virtue Ethics: A Misleading Category?' (1999) 3 The Journal of Ethics 163, 181.

[35] Broadie (n 7) 239.

transformation of desires and the performance of our intelligence and thinking. Therefore, it is always sensible to ask whether pursuing the end—the *what*—under this particular circumstance is good. Thus, to discover that 'x', 'a', 'b', 'a_1', and 'a_2' are the *how* to obtain a more determinate end—the *what*—is to pursue it now and therefore to start doing 'a_2'. However, if the end—the *what*—has been unveiled and the deliberator subsequently has a better grasp of the *what*, it always makes sense to revise it, change it, or even abandon it. In contrast, the grand end view, which conflates formal and substantive ends, precludes any questioning of these ends in principle. Furthermore, if there is a grand or substantive end, it remains unchanged and identical through the circumstances and over time. Moreover, we could codify the grand end into a set of rules and principles,[36] thereby solving the problem of guidance, to which we now turn.

§4.3.2 The Grand End View Explains the View that we Need Guidance in Acting

The grand end view's second tenet is that we require guidance in our deliberations. When we desire and pursue the grand end in isolation from specific circumstances, it must manifest as a universal, a rule, or a principle. However, Aristotle emphasized that we aim at the end—the *what*—as a particular within specific circumstances.[37] In other words, the end—the *what*—is indeterminate. As a result, the following question arises: how can an indeterminate entity, independent of specific circumstances, guide us?[38]

The Aristotelian-inspired model proposed here is far more modest. Practical deliberation involves 'stabs in the darkness' and entails deliberating and acting according to what is best, or what seems best in the eyes of the agent, in the circumstances. But how do we know what is best in the circumstances when the substantive end is indeterminate or unclear? Deliberation precisely answers the question '*What* should I do?' by addressing the '*How* do I do it?' question. We can only decompose and translate the indeterminate *what*, and understand the end by investigating, piecemeal, the *how*. There is no standard external to the deliberative process that guarantees the correctness of the answer.

Individuals are guided on the 'upward journey towards the specification of the *what*' by excellence in deliberation and the exercise of our practical reasoning—*phronesis*. We learn basic end-concepts and value-concepts from our parents and our community. We develop desiderative and cognitive capacities due to

[36] The grand end is necessary for principles. According to Cooper, to act well, we need principles. If we do not have principles, rational planning is not possible. Cooper (n 7) 82–85. We offer an alternative to rational planning, see Chapter 9.

[37] Aristotle (n 2) 1143a28–b5. See also the discussion in Broadie (n 7) 243.

[38] Brad Hooker and Margaret O Little, *Moral Particularism* (OUP 2000).

excellence in deliberation and in practical reasoning (see §5.1). *Phronesis*, or practical wisdom[39] is precisely what guides us, but it is not conceived as a given reality, a given substantive end, or a set of principles or rules, but something that we constantly exercise and cultivate towards an aspirational point.

One issue with the 'upward journey towards the specification of the *what*' view is that there is little or no integration with the formal end of 'living well'. The grand end conception integrates the formal end of 'living well' and the substantive end—the *what*—of deliberation. This is not true for the 'upward journey towards the specification of the *what*' view. In Chapter 6, I defend a view of integration that is both attainable and plausible within the latter Aristotelian interpretation.

§4.3.3 The Grand End View Presupposes that Selection of the End—the What—is Intuitive, or Implicit, and a Causal Conception of the How

For the grand end view, intelligence plays no role in selecting the end. In Chapter 6, I will analyse the practical syllogism and show that the major premise operates as the end—the *what*—that is good, while the minor premise presents the material upon which deliberation begins. The major premise is interpreted as the rule or principle of action[40] and the minor premise is the set of facts that are apprehended and can be subsumed under the rule or principle. For instance, Cooper posits that intuition grasps the substantive end of the major premise, which is the rule or principle.[41] Other authors argue that the deliberator grasps both the major and minor

[39] Broadie argues that practical wisdom refers to the combination of moral excellence and *nous*. Aristotle, therefore, refers to means *or* ends. Broadie (n 7) 242–43.

[40] See Cooper (n 7). However, some authors argue that the content of the major premise is determined by the deliberator according to what is adequate in the situation. Wiggins (n 17) 234. Some contemporary authors have developed this strand of Aristotelian ethics into a concept known as particularism. See Hooker (n 38).

[41] Other authors also advocate the 'intuitive' view regarding the end. See Wallace (n 34) 484. According to Reeve, we need rational intuition to apprehend the end. CDC Reeve, *Action, Contemplation and Happiness* (Harvard UP 2012) 161–62; 172–73. Cooper accepts that there is a 'lived' conception that lies at the centre of the person's practical thinking. However, he also quickly jumps into intuitionism and focuses on guidance as the key. Cooper (n 7) 64. Broadie rejects any 'intuitionism'. According to Broadie, the construction of the 'live' conception involves the interplay between deliberation and desire. Character is the function of that, it shows how we are living our lives. Cooper recognizes that Aristotle did not always spell out the relations of desire and intellect. Cooper (this note) 64. Hardie rejects intuitionism. Hardie (n 10) 233–34, though he supports the grand end view. ibid 233–57. See also Weinman, who advances the view that the good is underwritten by a cosmological end. Weinman (n 31) 82. Can we be parsimonious and accept that we can distinguish good deliberation from not-so-good deliberation without presupposing a cosmological end? See also Engberg-Pedersen, who endorses some kind of intuitionism. Troels Engberg-Pedersen, *Aristotle's Theory of Moral Insight* (Clarendon Press 1983). Another interpretation of the way we grasp the end will be through habits, see Jessica Moss, *Aristotle on the Apparent Good* (OUP 2012). However, this reading brings Aristotle too close to the Humean view of a bifurcation between desires and reasons. Moss defends her view against the non-Humean reading of Aristotle by authors such as Broadie (n 7) and Cooper (n 7). Moss contends that people often mistake the non-rational for the non-cognitive. However, the non-rational is a form of cognition, ie perception and *phantasia*. Moss (this note) 158. However, one might ask how close this

premise, which she does by intuition. Following this scheme, we could say that the facts or means that are the content of the minor premise are causes that lead us to the satisfaction of the principles, rules, and therefore to the substantive end of the major premise.

According to this viewpoint, the starting point of deliberation—the *how*—and the end deliberative point—the *what*—are clear and visible, or implicit, and may be discerned through reflection.[42] Furthermore, intuition apprehends the rule, principle, or substantive end, while our reasoning and intelligence play no role. The deliberation really starts with the second premise. As a result, the deliberator must engage with the necessary circumstances and facts that will satisfy the substantive end or principle. The minor premise does not impact the major premise. This view of practical syllogism is too simplistic to represent the complexity and richness of the deliberative process.

In Chapter 5, we problematize the view that the practical syllogism is an exact representation of deliberation. Furthermore, we defend the view that practical syllogism's role is to formally represent deliberation when we need to attribute responsibility or explain what has failed when executing a deliberated decision—*prohairesis*—but it does not explain the workings of deliberation and its complexity.

There are passages in Aristotle's *Nichomachean Ethics* that might seem to support the grand end view.[43] According to this view, we need something that mediates between the substantive end and the particular. Thus, there is a subtle threat of irrationality if we just desire or apprehend the substantive end—the *what*—by intuition. We need a bridge between the end—the *what*—and the particular. Principles and rules can play that role, and here we see the need to interpret the major premise as a rule or principle. The rule or principle will serve as the bridge between the substantive end and the particular and individual facts and

view is to that of intuitionists. On the other hand, she fails to explain how our appetites have a cognitive basis as 'evaluative' *phantasia*. ibid 159, 51–66. *Phantasia* seems evaluative. If evaluation is 'something I pursue', how can this be possible without thinking? See ibid 55.

[42] Broadie (n 7) 244, fn 59.

[43] Aristotle (n 2) 1142b3. Virtue guarantees the right pursuit of the desired end in the particular situation. There is a clear division of labour, where practical wisdom's role is separate from character's role. However, some authors focus on the Janus-faced aspect of this concept; see Broadie (n 7) and McDowell (n 31) where practical wisdom motivates and plays a cognitive role. My own account demonstrates that there is a transformation of desires and emotions through deliberation and that there is an aspirational model of deliberation in which reflexive perspective plays a role (see Chapter 5). Hardie also recognizes that practical wisdom is not about demonstration or deliberation in the form of a simple analysis of the practical syllogism, nor is it about principles. Hardie (n 10) 233. However, Hardie endorses the grand end view to avoid the tautology that to choose rightly and therefore virtuously, we need to be a virtuous person, ie the person who possesses practical wisdom, and at the same time, the person who possesses practical wisdom is the one who acts virtuously. Therefore, if a grand end exists, we can assert that a person with practical wisdom is one who has grasped the grand end or the *what*. ibid 236. For Hardie, the agent needs to consciously accept the substantive end. However, this view relies on guidance and justification as the key features to be explained by any theory of deliberation and practical reason.

circumstances. The principle or the rule performs all the work, leaving practical intelligence out of the picture. However, if the analogy with theoretical reasoning is kept in mind, it is possible that what Aristotle is trying to convey in this passage is that the wish for the end—the *what*—is only provisional. I have similarly tried to demonstrate that the *what* is indeterminate and revealed over time; the clarity of the *what* is obtained after engaging in deliberation.

The focus is on the intelligibility of particulars attained via the exercise of thinking and investigating in contingent and constantly varying circumstances. In the previous example of Beatrice, Beatrice grasps 'x' by 'doing a, b, $a_{1,}$ and b_1', and thus Beatrice cannot say that 'x is the right thing to do, but I am ignorant about what x is'.[44] We will discuss this significant conclusion and its important implications in Chapters 5 and 8, where we will consider potential solutions for the problem of negligence and responsibility for inadvertent actions.

If 'the upward journey towards the specification of the *what*' view rejects the grand end view, how can we explain the role of principles and rules in our lives? Is it counter-intuitive to say that they do not play any role in our deliberations? The 'upward journey towards the specification of the *what*' view holds that the starting point of deliberation is indeterminate, as shown in the analogy between deliberation and tracing a geometrical figure. However, this is no impediment to the development of choices that might become rules or principles.[45] By contrast, according to the grand end view, we form our choices based on pre-existing standards, principles, and rules. Consequently, the 'upward journey towards the specification of the what' view leads to the establishment of a substantive end, principles, or rules, which are grasped and clarified during or after the deliberation process.

One key feature of the 'upward journey towards the specification of the *what*' view is the idea that, using the example of Beatrice, a_1 and b_1 represent her insight on registering her daughter in ballet and tap lessons to improve her daughter's skills of flexibility and rhythm for gymnastics, which is very close to perception. There is an important body of literature on what we perceive, and what we perceive to be salient,[46] which seeks to capture the role of perception in our practical reasoning and deliberation. We will discuss this role further in Chapter 5. The general lesson is that we can only grasp the universal through action, and within what is particular and circumstantial.

Furthermore, if deliberation and rational decision—*prohairesis*—are conceived as deliberation directed towards a grand end, then the role of character and its transformation are unclear. Arguably, reflective policies for decision-making will also follow a determinate substantive end—or *what*. For instance, Beatrice has a

[44] Broadie (n 7) 255.
[45] Broadie (n 7) 254.
[46] See Iris Murdoch, 'The Sublime and the Good' in Peter Conradi (ed), *Existentialists and Mystics* (Penguin 1950) 205.

clear vision of her daughter's physical health and will implement reflective policies, or perhaps a life plan,[47] that will help her to actualize what she has in mind. However, this is problematic, as this view presupposes that there is no connection between our intelligence and our lower desires and emotions. This view might indicate that there is, or should be, a connection between our desires and plans.[48] However, such theories, both in the contemporary version of the grand end view and in Aristotle's interpretation, fail to explain the way desires and our intelligence interact. For the grand end view, deliberation and rational decision—*prohairesis*—cannot connect to lower desires unless principles and rules are established.[49] As a result, rational decision—*prohairesis*—collapses into rational justification. Consequently, according to this view, we need to resort to principles, codes, or rules to guide us, and allow us to descend to our lower desires.

§4.3.4 A Rejection of the Idea that Justification is the Key to Deliberation

Arguably, the bifurcation thesis and its corollary, the balancing model,[50] tend to focus on the justification of the action. This means that, as deliberators, we need to focus on our connections between reasons for actions, internal or external, our means, and their connection to other means and certain ends, to make sense of, and justify our actions.[51] One of the strongest elements of the 'upward journey towards the specification of the *what*' view is the proposal that we are thrown into the world,[52] and have no choice but to deliberate and decide. This means that we are forced to make salient certain particularities of the world and grasp our circumstances, what I have also called our position *from here*.[53] The grand end view

[47] See Michael Bratman, *Intention, Plans and Practical* Reason (CUP 1987).

[48] These theories tend to obscure the connection between our intelligence and desires by using terms such as 'commitments' or 'normative commitments'.

[49] For a criticism, see Sherman (n 34) 81. Sherman also accepts that the grand end is revised by another grand end, but then this makes it closer to Broadie's view, see Broadie (n 7).

[50] See Sherman (n 34) 80 and Callard, who highlight the view that Aristotelian deliberation does not involve the evaluation of alternatives. Callard (n 8). Sherman tries to show that deliberation involves specification of the end. It is not only the business of ends-means coherence. Sherman (this note) 71.

[51] Kraut insists that we need to give a justification and presses for clarification of the stage at which the justification can be given. Kraut (n 33) 367. This is the role given to practical argument and practical syllogism. Arguably, within the grand end view, there is some circularity in the conception of practical wisdom as the determining factor of the grand end. If the standard is the man of practical wisdom, how can we determine the rightness of the grand end if we reject the intuitionist explanation? See ibid 368. Practical wisdom seems to include the grand end, and vice versa. According to Broadie, we obtain practical wisdom as we exercise intelligence and integrate it with our desires and passions. Broadie (n 7). MacIntyre defends the grand end view and argues that it is key for the legislators and judges who are the audience of *Nichomachean Ethics*, see Alasdair MacIntyre, 'Rival Aristotles: Aristotle against Some Modern Aristotelians' in MacIntyre, *Ethics and Politics: Selected Essays* (CUP 2006) 22, 24–25.

[52] See Raz for an interesting approach on 'being in the world'. Joseph Raz, 'Being in the World' (2010) 23 Ratio 422.

[53] Williams (n 25) 20.

theorist assumes that everything that matters is in the substantive end—the *what*. However, Broadie's interpretative point on Aristotle is that he wants us to focus on the particular and contingent as the objects of deliberation. We need a deliberative process that connects desires and emotions to intelligence and reasoning to truly grasp the complexity and richness of the particular.[54]

Starting the deliberation from the abstract, universal, given, and known, and then applying it to the particular instance, bypasses the process of truly understanding the particular as unique. Therefore, in the case of Beatrice, the 'grand end view' assumes that Beatrice already understands the significance of her daughter's physical health, which includes her daughter's harmonious personality development and the recognition of her skills, such as flexibility and rhythm. The question that arises concerns the source or origin, or perhaps the mechanism, of this particular piece of knowledge. Aristotle argues that we can only acquire this knowledge through experience, specifically the unique process of deliberating and thinking about our actions. The general idea of the *what* is easy. However, the challenge lies in defining the '*what*' in our own lives, given our unique capacities, limitations, skills, and unique circumstances.

Justification necessitates framing our actions from the observer's or third-person point of view as we engage in the details of our actions. In other words, it presupposes that the deliberator needs to see her action primarily from the third-person perspective (see Chapter 1) rather than the first-person or deliberative point of view. But this is difficult to imagine psychologically. It presumes that I don't perceive the world, its values, or the essential elements of the '*what*' when I'm immersed in it. Rather, it demands that I am constantly detached and assumes that intelligence in deliberation is mainly justificatory. The 'upward journey towards the specification of the *what*' view, on the other hand, rejects the idea that this forms the core of deliberation. Instead, it presents a more psychologically realistic depiction of our immersion in the world and the resulting pressure to deliberate.

§4.3.5 A Rejection of the View that we Need a Rational Intuition of the Grand End

If we follow Kraut in his defence of the grand end view, we can conclude that the grand end is clear for the deliberator. One claimed advantage of this view is that the end is clear, which guides us in our action. However, the ambiguity of the idea that intuition grasps the grand end or that the grand end is in the background while we deliberate and perform actions limits the clarity of how this guidance operates. The challenge arises because the guidance needs to be within the particular's

[54] See Reeve (n 41) 186–89. There is no change in the conception of happiness. Rather, the change is in the agent.

complexity and richness. The concept of rational intuition, or the substantive end, seems too passive and contemplative to explain how we can break down the understanding of the grand end, like Beatrice's daughter's physical health, into the individual components of 'x', 'a', 'b', 'a1', and 'b1' while also aligning our desires and passions with these components. Finally, a close examination of our phenomenology during deliberation reveals that we are constantly revising, transforming, and changing ourselves and our projects, or the '*what*'. However, given the special status of the substantive end, is it possible to abandon the '*what*'? The grand end view portrays us as obsessive and dogmatic characters who pursue the '*what*', regardless of our circumstances, talents, skills, or limitations.[55] Nonetheless, our experience tells us something else.

Furthermore, we have stated that the guidance perspective, when considering the grand end, must establish principles that serve as a bridge between our lower desires and the grand end. Nevertheless, it remains unclear how these principles, if they emerge from reflection, will be connected to our lower desires. Conversely, if these principles stem from our experience and we endorse them and follow them, it indicates that we have likely already acquired the desires that we need to perform the correct or right actions, rendering principles or rules unnecessary for guidance. The role of principles or rules is justificatory only, and they play no role in guiding our deliberation and action. The 'upward journey towards the specification of the *what*' view necessitates that we undergo a transformative process, elevating our desires and emotions as we engage in intelligent thinking about our actions. Kraut and MacIntyre, two key defenders of the grand end view, underestimate Aristotle's contribution to the idea of deliberation as a process of transformation through reason and thinking about *how* towards the *what*, while we strive to align our emotions and desires.[56]

§4.3.6 A Focus on the Idea that the Exercise of a Capacity Produces Right Answers as Opposed to a 'Recognition' Capacity that Recognizes When a Procedure Has Produced the Right Answers

In Chapter 8, we discuss the 'capacity view' of responsibility for negligence. The contemporary conception of capacity suggests that we have the ability to reach the right answer on *what* we should do, but also need to recognize and understand this process. Thus, we have the capacity to establish a procedure to teach a foreign language to a child. For instance, we begin with teaching the alphabet, basic grammar,

[55] See Kraut (n 33) 366.

[56] MacIntyre's view on ranking values and deductive reasoning misses the Aristotelian point of deliberation, though he recognizes that the deductive model is only applicable retrospectively. MacIntyre (n 51) 33–36.

vocabulary, and listening skills. However, at a later stage, it becomes imperative to recognize that this is the correct procedure that equips the child with the necessary skills to learn a foreign language. The process of exercising capacity encompasses both the development of the procedure and its subsequent recognition. Following Alessandra's previous example, she deliberates and discovers that 'x' is composed of 'a', 'b', 'a_1', and 'b_2'. She now engages with a and b, which are the actions closest to her. However, for the grand end view theorist, an additional step is required; Alessandra needs to recognize that this procedure is the correct one, and the grand end or substantive end will be the final indicator to 'recognize' that doing x, a, b, $a_{1,}$ and b_2 will lead to the substantive end—the *what*—which she has intuitively grasped. By contrast, for the 'upward journey towards the specification of the *what*' theorist, there is no need for the latter stage of 'recognition' of a procedure. Beatrice exercises her capacity for decomposing or translating 'x' into a set of feasible actions. There is no need to recognize or validate the procedure for correctness. Does this mean that there is no reflection on the *what* and the *how*? Does this mean that there is no process of recognition? In Chapter 5, we will demonstrate how recognition can occur within the 'upward journey towards specification of *what*' perspective.

The 'upward journey towards the specification of the *what*' admits that while we are exercising our capacity, we are also perceiving, learning to perceive, and acquiring insights, and that the quality of this learning depends on the quality of deliberation and rational decision—*prohairesis*. Furthermore, the particulars of the action are the essence of the action as opposed to a product.[57] The particulars can only be seen from the deliberative perspective, and the 'seen' can be improved through reflection. Chapter 5 will elaborate on this point.

[57] See Broadie (n 7) 209.

5

Becoming Good

Reflection and Ways of Inhabiting the Deliberative-Aspirational Perspective

§5.1 Language-Games, Aspects, and Learning to 'See': Some Preliminaries

In the previous chapter, we explicitly stated that value arises from a change in the subject. We asserted that the subject develops different ways of 'seeing' things, ie perspectives, through both deliberation and bringing the *what* of the action closer to the *how*. This necessarily entails a process of transforming desires. The craft analogy effectively highlights this point, as both in crafts and deliberation, the action is the object, and the person is the subject. Thus, we can illustrate how performing a craft transforms us as follows:

(a) 'My knitting causes dexterity in my hands'.
(b) 'My playing the flute causes the refinement of my musical abilities'.

But can we find a similarity in the way deliberative thinking and changes in desires transform the subject? We can express the following statement, for example:

(c) 'My deliberation on *how* to attain my daughter's physical health has led to a change in my perspective on *how* to achieve my daughter's physical health and *what* constitutes her physical health.'

We saw that the craft analogy breaks down in deliberation. In Chapter 4, I explained that, in deliberation, the transformation operates on the entire self or person. The transformation extends beyond physical aspects, such as the hands I use when knitting. Thus, the only standard is internal to the action's circumstances and particularities. In contrast, the standard of excellence in crafts is external; we have a clear understanding of what constitutes excellence in knitting. Therefore, in the example of Beatrice, her desires undergo a transformation, which in turn alters her perspective on the physical health of her daughter, ultimately leading to a change in her entire self. The forthcoming part will provide a more comprehensive analysis of this transformative element.

Responsibility for Negligence in Ethics and Law. Verónica Rodríguez-Blanco, Oxford University Press.
 DOI: 10.1093/9780198948193.003.0005

This part examines our interaction with the world and how, as a result of this interaction, we develop and learn valuing, transform ourselves, and engage with what is right and good. Therefore, the proposed Aristotelian-inspired conception of deliberation suggests that valuing does not stem from a decision or commitment made at a specific moment in space and time, nor does it stem from the agent's desire to pursue the object. On the contrary, we learn value-concepts and end-concepts through our interactions with our environment and through facing the demands of its particularities. In a way, the particulars are the essence of the action.[1]

The idea of language-games illuminates how we learn about values and concepts and shows us that concept-values and concept-ends are in the background of our engagement with *how* and *what* when we deliberate.

Wittgenstein starts his *Philosophical Investigations*[2] by unleashing the details of the fantasy that we learn language through ostensive definitions that refer to representations or images in our mind. Thus, every word has a meaning, and the meaning appears in our mind or mental states. St Agustine's view of language, which he criticizes, presupposes this image: we learn words, specifically nouns, as labels or names to constitute a language. To learn this language, one must retain the memory of the representation or image that corresponds to the object and its corresponding label. But this idea of language makes a clear vision of what language is impossible.[3] Naming is not an occult process.[4] From the start, Wittgenstein advances his main thesis, ie that particular training and teaching make possible the functioning of even primitive languages. The meaning is not revealed in images, rather 'children are brought up to perform *these* actions, to use *these* words as they do, and to react in *this* way to the words of others'.[5] The learning and training are done in *this specific* way. When language and action are interwoven, Wittgenstein tells us, we speak of language-games, and we can recognize that there are primitive language-games.[6] These language-games shape the world in distinct ways, and we perceive the world through their lens.

The idea of language-games is a powerful concept, as it also suggests that speaking a language is an activity and, therefore, is a form of life.[7] Wittgenstein argues that it is incorrect to believe that there was a time when we lacked 'language' or 'meaning'. We learn new language-games when we already have a language and with other language-games in the background, and during our childhoods,

[1] Sarah Broadie, *Ethics with Aristotle* (OUP 1991) 209.
[2] Ludwig Wittgenstein, *Philosophical Investigations* (originally published in 1953, Blackwell 2009) §1.
[3] ibid §5.
[4] ibid §38.
[5] ibid §5.
[6] ibid §7.
[7] ibid §23.

playing language-games is the way we carve our world. St Augustine's conception of language begins with the idea that we learn words as children coming to a strange country where images and words need to be stuck together, and that there is no previous way of thinking and seeing the world that builds on what we have learned.[8]

Wittgenstein does not deny that there are inner processes and inner experiences, but his thesis implies that reflection, including self-reflection or philosophizing about language, does not require looking into our mental state. There are no agreements, commitments, acceptances, or opinions, but rather ways of carving the world, of engaging with it, of making distinctions, of establishing internal meaningful relations with the words and concepts we have, and this is agreement in our forms of life.[9]

If conformity or non-conformity is only a matter of practice, the question of understanding disappears. Initially, we may learn love through resentment and intimidation, but as we mature, we may come to understand that this conception or perception of love is limited. We may discover alternative forms of love, such as selfless giving and forgiveness, which build upon our initial understanding. Just as we learn the value of 'love' through language-games, we also learn all other values. Parents and guardians teach the word or concept 'good' as a container for a myriad of other value-concepts. For example, we learn about temperance, patience, humility, generosity, and concepts related to values like right, just, and duty. Different contexts teach us this multiplicity of value-concepts, which intertwine with our activities and interactions with the world. Understanding is developed and revealed through the complex forms of life.

Similar to values, understanding entails a complex and thick practice that encompasses a variety of language-games. As Cavell observes, *learning and maturation* are not too different.[10] Our deliberations and experiences enable us to mature into the depths of our values. But at some point in our lives, we also become teachers, and we need to take responsibility for this.[11] Our experiences unveil new layers and deepen our understanding of forms of life where charity, benevolence, and justice play a key role. However, we gain knowledge about greed, ambition, resentment, and hatred, and these negative properties and traits reveal their depth as part of our different experiences. Identifying errors involves taking a fresh look at ourselves through our activities, deliberations, thinking, and engagement with the world, whether we choose to avoid or embrace them. The direction we take in

[8] ibid §32.
[9] ibid §241.
[10] Stanley Cavell, *The Claim of Reason: Wittgenstein, Scepticism, Morality and Tragedy* (OUP 1979) 171.
[11] ibid 178.

our deliberations is crucial, and this chapter addresses how it is possible to inhabit a deliberative-aspirational perspective.

However, as Chapter 4 demonstrates, this does not imply that the deliberator is working toward an explicit or implicit grand end.[12] The focus on language-games helps us see that some things gain salience from our interactions with others and our environment. Through language-games, we inherit salient features that shape the world, and this serves as the backdrop for our deliberations. We develop a 'form of life', which is the background against which transformation operates.[13]

Can we say that language-games lie in the background of our deliberations, playing the role of the formal end? It gives us a general idea of what 'living well' means while we try to determine through our lives what we should do. We have learned from the dispute between theorists who advocate the 'grand end' and those who favour the 'upward journey towards the specification of the *what*' (see §4.3) that if the latter has the upper hand in the discussion, then the *what* as a general conception of living well cannot be the starting point of deliberation, but rather is the pre-condition of deliberation.

Concept-ends and concept-values are learned through language-games, and engagement with them reveals a multiplicity of ways of looking at them, considering them, and learning them. Forms of life shape our evaluative outlook. There is no passivity; there is activity as long as there is thought, because when we deliberate, we engage with the particular circumstances that demand action, and thought is required to see and settle *what* we need to do.

If I ask the question 'What shall I do?' as if there were a unique, correct end or value, or grand vision that can be grasped as an image, then the language-game is dragged out.[14] This is precisely what Wittgenstein warns against. The language-game of deliberation, both immersive and aspirational, can only be shown. The teaching and learning never end. In evaluative judgements and deliberation, we are builders, but in science, we aim at representation. When I settle the question, *What* ought I to do? or *What* shall I do?, the settling is what happens. There is no misrepresentation or misidentification. Of course, there can be *akrasia* but, as we will explain in Chapter 6, this is due to a lack of transformation and integration of character and thought.

One important lesson of the language-games approach is that the external/internal or inner/outer dichotomy is a metaphor that, if taken seriously, leads to philosophical confusion. Through our forms of life and language-games, we realize

[12] Williams describes the 'grand end' or 'grand vision' view as representing 'one's life as a rectangle, so to speak, presented all at once and to be optimally filled in'. Bernard Williams, 'Moral Luck' in Williams, *Moral Luck* (CUP 1981) 20, 33.

[13] See Katja Vogt, *Desiring the Good* (2017) 15 and Elizabeth Anscombe, 'On Brute Facts' (1958) 18 Analysis 69. For a discussion of background and 'forms of life' in law, see my paper, Verónica Rodríguez-Blanco and Pilar Zambrano, 'The Myth of the Classical Natural Law Theory: Reflecting on the "Thin" View of Legal Positivism' (2018) 31 Ratio Juris 9.

[14] Wittgenstein (n 2) §370.

that one aspect of an experience conceals other aspects. *To learn means displacing one aspect of an experience to let another in.* The result is not a simple replacement but an enrichment of what we could see before; it is also the connection between two aspects of an experience.

In the first chapter, we were presented with the case of Alessandra, who, on a hot day, drove to collect her children from a hockey lesson. Regrettably, she forgot that her dog had been in the hot car for a prolonged duration, resulting in its death, for which she was ultimately responsible. Alessandra neither infers what happened from the facts nor does she conjure or hypothesize what happened. She knows what happened because she is the one who engaged in deliberation and action, and she knows why she put her dog in the vehicle. She also knows where the errors of her actions lie. Her errors dawn on her because a new layer or facet of her own character has been revealed in the action. In Chapter 6, we will argue that Alessandra failed to inhabit a deliberative-aspirational perspective, and in the next section, we will explain it is possible to inhabit a deliberative-aspirational perspective.

§5.2 Becoming Good: Potential Responses

In the previous chapter, we showed that desires are the work of intelligence, indicating a process of thinking and transformation. When we make judgements about responsibility, we often concentrate on the reasons for action and our rational capacities, while also considering desires and beliefs as the mental states of the individual performing the action. We have learned that in the balancing model, reasons for actions, desires, or beliefs happen at a specific moment. Action is a snapshot of what the deliberator experiences at any given moment. The standard model of deliberation, the balancing model, focuses on desires as given states and beliefs that make the necessary connection with either normative reasons or desires within the so-called motivational set. The Aristotelian-inspired model of deliberation, in contrast, explains how thinking transforms our desires.

Burnyeat has highlighted the integration of the *what* and the *why* in Aristotle's philosophy. He calls it the 'because' of the deliberation. In our example of Beatrice, we focused on how she learned about *what* to do through her reasoning of the *how*; her thoughts on 'Y' led her to 'x', which in turn led her to 'a' and 'b', and thus to 'a1' and 'b2'. Arguably, the *what*, 'Y', gradually became clearer for her. We could say that Beatrice now better understands that ensuring her daughter's physical health includes becoming less competitive, developing gymnastic abilities, achieving harmony with her body, and so on. However, in order to answer the question *why* 'Y', Beatrice would need to engage in reflection, locating her newly acquired view of her daughter's physical health within a larger picture of goals, desires, meanings, and ends for herself and her daughter. Arguably, what we called the narrow deliberation presented in Chapter 4 cannot answer the question *why in terms of a wider perspective of our lives;*[15] it can only answer the *why* within narrow deliberation. Thus, Beatrice chooses ballet lessons *in order* for her daughter to develop rhythm, and the development of rhythm is chosen *in order to* obtain physical health. However, this narrow 'in order to' approach fails to encompass broader goals, values, and ends. Furthermore, we have rejected the 'grand end' view, and, therefore, the possibility of a grand end that can encompass narrow deliberation becomes doubtful. In the previous chapter, we learned that deliberation involves the transformation of *how* to achieve the end in terms of digestible particulars, the *how*, for the *what*. This conception is primarily immersive[16] or substandard.[17] It might be asserted that narrow deliberation is the empirical surrogate of animal movement and that, consequently, as a surrogate, narrow deliberation is not properly empirical but emulates the empirical world and the way animals pursue their goals. This view emphasizes the immersive and empirical-like nature of deliberation, as well as its Aristotelian roots.

In contrast, our everyday experience of deliberation shows us another face or aspect of deliberation. Reflecting on our own lives, we can discern that we have larger goals, values, or ends. We can also see the failure of some of our projects, as well as the success of others. Looking into the future, we envisage a number of medium- and long-term projects. The former might include, for example, refurbishing the house, landscaping the garden, or travelling to an unfamiliar part of the world; and the latter could include, for example, pursuing a Master's degree at university, getting married, having children, writing a book, learning to play an instrument, committing oneself to a noble cause, or practising a religion. Medium- and long-term ends are, like narrow deliberation ends, also uncertain, indeterminate, or unknown in terms of their specific features or components.

I have tried to show that thoughts and intelligence are crucial for action. In the following chapters, I demonstrate how this way of understanding intelligence and thoughts is key to determining judgements of responsibility. Therefore, if thought leaves us, it is more likely that our actions will be judged as compulsive. On the other hand, confusion in thought can result in irrational actions or *akrasia* (Chapter 6 will provide a detailed explanation of both possibilities).

[15] See my book, Verónica Rodríguez-Blanco, *Law and Authority Under the Guise of the Good* (Hart/Bloomsbury 2014), where I attempt to show that the question *why* in Anscombe's theory of intention applies to the structure of practical reason and law. The book employs the question *why*? to unveil the deliberative structure of an intentional action, demonstrating how this understanding of practical reason sheds light on legal authority. Following Myles Burnyeat, my focus here is on 'why?' along the lines of Aristotelian deliberation and the way that narrow deliberation is connected to wider goals, good and right. Myles Burnyeat, 'Aristotle on Learning to be Good' in Amélie Rorty (ed), *Essays on Aristotle's Ethics* (University of California Press 1980) 69. In Chapter 9, I apply this to the key role of negligence law.

[16] Agnes Callard, 'Aristotle on Deliberation' in Ruth Chang and Kurt Sullivan (eds), *Routledge Handbook of Practical Reason* (Routledge 2021) 19.

[17] Karen Nielsen, 'Deliberation as Inquiry: Aristotle's Alternative to the Presumption of Open Alternatives' (2011) 120 The Philosophical Review 383, 403.

The problem that now arises is the following: if thinking in terms of narrow deliberation is immersed or substandard, how can we correct our thoughts within an immersed vision? Furthermore, I've demonstrated that thoughts transform our desires and character. Therefore, we must ensure that our thoughts are directed towards what is right or correct, which will guide our desires[18] and enable us to strive for excellence in character.[19] We seem, nevertheless, trapped within the limited vision of our own narrow deliberations. In the previous chapter, we discussed Neurath's boat metaphor and said that we would need to put in brackets the question of whether the end was good while deliberating. Alternatively, we take as a hypothesis that the end to be pursued is good and pursue the *how* as we repair one plank at a time whilst navigating rough seas. The remaining planks remain untouched and stable, and in a similar fashion, the conception of the end as good remains stable. However, we see ourselves not only immersed in short term goals, for example whether to register our daughter in ballet, gymnastics, or tap lessons, but in medium- and long-term projects, goals, and plans. Using Neurath's boat as a metaphor, we can envision ourselves standing at the shoreline, observing the entire boat, witnessing its dismantling, and then witnessing its full repair and admiration.

It is not only a matter of establishing a bridge between digestible particulars and more abstract rules or principles (we will reject this way of conceiving deliberation and practical reason in Chapter 6). It is rather how the 'upward journey towards the specification of the *what*' can involve medium- and longer-term projects and plans without losing the acquired practical knowledge and insights of narrow deliberation and replicating the depth of that *knowledge* on a larger scale.

One potential answer is to say that we need to reflect on our medium- and long-term goals. We could present the modern conception of reflection as a potential answer.[20] But how should we understand reflection without losing the immersed perspective?[21] At this point, we should address a complication to the issue of reconciling reflection and immersion. When I ask myself the question 'What shall

[18] If practical truth is the function of practical reason, and practical truth is 'right desires', how can we obtain 'right desires'? It is not correct to think of practical truth as related to theoretical truth. Practical truth is clarity and coherence in choice, and we should emphasize the disanalogy with theoretical truth. Broadie (n 1) 226–27, 230.

[19] This will be the character of the *phronimos*.

[20] The problematic character of reflection in the Aristotelian corpus is recognized by McDowell. See John McDowell, 'Some Issues in Aristotle's Moral Psychology' in *Mind, Value and Reality* (Harvard UP 1998) 3. According to McDowell, our values are subject to reflection. Reflection, however, does not mean 'stepping outside'. See also Bernard Williams, *Ethics and the Limits of Philosophy* (Fontana Press 1993). One key concept is the concept of practical wisdom–*phronesis*. For McDowell, for example, the state of motivational propensities is a reflectively adjusted form. There is an indeterminacy of end. McDowell (this note).

[21] Some contemporary authors, like Bernard Williams, do not think this is possible. He sees reflection as detachment, the 'view from nowhere'. Therefore, it entails that the deliberator does not grasp the particularity that characterizes Aristotelian models of deliberation. Williams, *Ethics and the Limits of Philosophy* (n 20).

I do?' and engage in narrow deliberation that has continuity in time, both the object of my consideration and I undergo transformation. Not only do my reasons and thought about what to do undergo change, but also my desires and, therefore, character[22] and emotions.[23] Certain authors see this trajectory as a 'seamless' journey of deliberation. They claim that intelligibility serves as the intermediary between ethics, ie actions that are good and/or right, and physical actions.[24] However, the main concern is how we transit from intelligibility to goodness or rightfulness, or more precisely, how we are learners, and ultimately whether 'becoming good' is even feasible. Therefore, the uncritical or unethical person also engages in a transformation of herself. As a result, the narrow deliberation account does not say much about the direction of the journey, or the trajectory to becoming good.[25]

Virtues of character and desires are active throughout wise deliberation as a nexus of evaluative dispositions expressed in focused responses.[26] Stage by stage, characters and desires shape and reveal themselves.[27] According to the 'grand end' interpretation of Aristotelian deliberation, the virtuous person can grasp the major premise and successfully apply it to the facts of the circumstances, as represented by the minor premise. Action, therefore, should be successfully ensured. However, the issue with rules and principles lies in the assumption of a gap between the agent's knowledge of her position, such as Beatrice's endeavours to ensure her child's physical health, and the practical conclusion that she should

[22] Virtue ethics is devoted to understanding the role of virtue in our ethical lives; we cannot understand the role of virtue and character in our ethical lives, if we do not provide a sound explanation of how practical reason and deliberation operates. This book focuses on deliberation and practical reason as preliminary to any consideration of virtue. Virtue should not be understood in isolation from complex questions related to thinking in practical terms. Commenting on Aristotle's notion of virtues, Broadie asserts: 'Virtue ensures that whatever is aimed for is aimed for rightly at any stage and pursued only in terms on which pursuit is best. As reflection brings out new relevant considerations, the value of O under the circumstances (its worthiness to be an end) is judged and rejudged and the rightness of these judgements depends on character. Moral virtue is active throughout wise deliberation, not only in the form of a general thrust or readiness to discern and do the best whatever it might be, but as a plexus of evaluative dispositions expressed in series of differently focused by mutually cognisant responses. Virtue is involved in selecting means to O.' Broadie (n 1) 245–46. In this stage-by-stage presence, character is shaped and revealed. Narrow ends and values are a common concern. For a criticism of virtue ethics, see Martha Nussbaum, 'Virtue Ethics: A Misleading Category?' (1999) 3 The Journal of Ethics 163.

[23] Nussbaum remarks that Aristotle's project is highly rationalistic. We can accept that emotions undergo transformations. Reasons can be upward or downward. 'Emotions and desires are not simply mindless pushes, but complex forms of intentionality infused with object directed thought. They can be significantly shaped by reasoning about the good.' Nussbaum (n 22) 199.

[24] Kevin Flannery, *Action and Character According to Aristotle* (The Catholic University of America 2013).

[25] The complexity of thinking towards a transformation of excellence in character virtue and the connection between these two components is highlighted by Aristotelian commentators as unclear. See William Hardie, *Aristotle's Ethical Theory* (Clarendon Press 2004, originally printed in 1968) 238–39.

[26] Broadie (n 1) 245.

[27] Kosman interprets key passages of Aristotle as stating that choice is a form of cognition, an ability to act, and a form of thought. Aryeh Kosman, *Virtues of Thought* (Harvard UP 2014) 291.

enrol her daughter in both ballet and tap lessons (see Chapter 4). The principle or rule 'Mothers should pursue the physical health of their children when possible' bridges the gap between her position and the practical conclusion. Therefore, the rational generation of the conclusion stems from the existence of a justificatory principle or rule.

However, we have already rejected the 'grand end' view and the possibility of a major premise from which we can infer a conclusion. In Chapter 6, I advance further criticism of the schematism of practical syllogism as the paradigm of practical reason.

The problem emerges at an earlier stage, when the deliberator is attempting to change her character and desires, but she has not yet achieved virtue. The challenge is how we learn to be virtuous and act according to what is right and good. The fundamental question is how we become good.

At the lower level and within the domain of narrow deliberation, the realization of the good becomes clearer. If you do not know what to do, you really do not have knowledge of the circumstances.[28] Furthermore, after narrow deliberation and rational choice, the impulse to pursue 'Y' coincides with the thought that 'Y' needs to be done. In other words, we need to understand the way in which we acquire the knowledge that will direct us towards not only our narrow goals but also our medium- and long-term goals. In the next section, we will explore some potential answers and show their deficiencies. In the final section, I will show some weaknesses of the contemporary model of reflection and demonstrate that learning to become good entails bringing attention to ourselves.[29] I argue that this is possible without losing the knowledge gained through the immersion perspective.

This picture is nevertheless still too vague. In the following sections, our goal is to offer a more precise account of how we are actually learners and identify some of the conditions that enable us to become good.

§5.3 Becoming Good: Further Responses

The fact that we focus on deliberation in a narrow way does not mean that there is no vision of human goodness, though it is not always formulated universally, or, furthermore, that a universal formulation will be of no help in action.

Deliberation is an activity, a seeking of desire and thought[30] to settle the question, *What shall I do?* Thought transforms desires and character until they are in harmony. Many Aristotelian theorists see the limits of the 'immersed' conception of narrow deliberation and search for further evidence of something closer to a

[28] Broadie (n 1) 249.
[29] ibid 253.
[30] ibid 217.

reflective stance. For example, Cooper[31] focuses on models of deliberation and justification. Segvic recognizes that practical goods are dependent on human perspective[32] but says that '*practical reason gives unity to our various pursuits by introducing the standpoint of a life as a whole. Specific goods do not lose their independence when seen from this standpoint. Their full value is, however, determined by the place they occupy in this larger context, and how they interact with other goods.*'[33] Thus, Segvic asserts that critical reflection is key for Aristotle.[34]

Vogt recognizes that deliberation is not sufficient to attain integration between character, practical reason, and happiness.[35] She argues that Anscombe, like most contemporary action theorists, focuses narrowly on small- or medium-term actions, but that this approach is wrong. It offers a narrow reading of ancient philosophy and, more specifically, ignores Book I of Aristotle's *Nichomachean Ethics.* Conceptions of life declare something to be central, and our actions, small- and medium-term, need to accommodate this key feature. In other words, according to Vogt, it is a mistake to separate ethics and theories of action because human agency is about the human good.[36] Human good is about 'living well' which inevitably involves long-term goals and ends.

The motive behind the grand-end view is concern about the integration between narrow deliberation and medium- and long-term goals. According to Vogt, McDowell presents a textual defence of the 'grand end' view.[37] However, Vogt herself attempts to steer clear of this solution. Vogt tells us that reflecting on living well is part of our agency. Nevertheless, *deliberation on living well is not possible.* Conceptions of living well are too abstract for deliberation, although they serve as guidance. Unfortunately, her book does not explain how to transform lower desires, and integrate long-term goals or ends, and narrow deliberation.[38] Vogt dismisses the 'grand end' solution,[39] yet does not specify the way that narrow deliberation can be integrated with long-term goals, ends, and projects. Nevertheless, the significance of her interpretation and work lies in demonstrating the key role of Book I of Aristotle's *Nichomachean Ethics*, as well as the importance of conceptions of living well, and highlighting the insufficiency of deliberation alone.

Annas[40] highlights that virtue is the drive to aspire, not a static or natural state. It is something we gain through self-direction and the drive to improve.[41] The craft analogy is merely an analogy, and we should resist the temptation to reduce

[31] John Cooper, *Reason and the Human Good in Aristotle* (Hackett 1975).
[32] Heda Segvic, *From Protagoras to Aristotle* (Princeton UP 2008) 98–106.
[33] ibid 105.
[34] ibid 160, 168.
[35] Vogt (n 13) ch 2.
[36] ibid 144.
[37] ibid 130–32.
[38] ibid 136–37, 147.
[39] ibid 129–32.
[40] Julia Annas, *Intelligent Virtue* (OUP 2011) 25.
[41] ibid 27.

the idea of virtue to a craft. There are differences between the two, and practice alone will not enable us to become virtuous individuals. Virtue necessitates understanding and engaging with reasons.[42] But how do non-immersive or aspirational reasons become part of our deliberations? It is not sufficient to emphasize the synchronic aspect of our learning to be virtuous; we also need to show how aspirational reasons enter into our practical, immersed reasoning or deliberation.

A strategy among Aristotelian commentators is to advance a developmental conception of character that can lead us to an apprehension of what is good and, arguably, to an apprehension of the good for medium- and long-term ends. The focus of these developmental conceptions is diverse. Some Aristotelian commentators concentrate on pleasure;[43] others take sections of the *Nichomachean Ethics* that focus on habituation and learning by doing;[44] others pay attention to intentional guidance;[45] and for other commentators, inculcated feelings also play a predominant part.[46] Kosman's conclusion, for example, is that emotions are action-dependent. Thus, moral education tells us about wrong and right ways of feeling. Actions that aim to actualize desires are under one's control, while habits instil right feelings. We can engage in actions that make us feel in a certain way. Does this imply that we do not choose our feelings? Kosman contends that Aristotle affirms the choice of feelings.[47] Feelings are indirectly transformed by *prohairesis*. The state of character is the key condition of action.[48] However, in this case, we are talking again about *prohairesis* and, consequently, deliberation in a narrow sense. How are the medium- and long-term ends integrated? Some authors advance a combination of all these elements. The noble is acquired by learning rules and habits of pleasure.[49] Broadie emphasizes that virtues need to be acquired[50] and that moral virtues are defined in terms of *prohairesis*.[51]

The development approach is subject to two criticisms. First, there is ambiguity regarding the consequences of habituation.[52] Secondly, habituation occurs for reasons.[53] However, here, reason does not influence desire, either at the start or at

[42] ibid 26.

[43] Burnyeat (n 15). For a development of Burnyeat's view on pleasure and shame, see Marta Jimenez, *Aristotle on Shame and Learning to be Good* (OUP 2020). See also Sauvé Meyer and Olfert for a discussion on pleasure and emotions at the core of learning to become good. Susan Sauvé Meyer, 'Living for the Sake of an Ultimate End' in Jon Miller, *Aristotle's Nichomachean Ethics: A Critical Guide* (CUP 2011) 47. Christiana Olfert, *Aristotle on Practical Truth* (OUP 2017) 190–97.

[44] Gavin Lawrence, 'Acquiring Character: Becoming Grown Up' in *Moral Psychology and Human Action in Aristotle* (OUP 2011) 233, 272–79.

[45] ibid 250.

[46] Kosman (n 27) 69, 72–73

[47] ibid 76–77.

[48] ibid.

[49] Kosman (n 27) 264–66.

[50] Broadie (n 1) 75–80.

[51] ibid 78–84.

[52] Lawrence (n 44) 276.

[53] ibid 277.

the end. *Phronesis* and reason are just added, and there is no integration between desire and reason. Consequently, the stages of habituation and development are unclear.

The development approach is rich and interesting and tells us that the possibility of a correct trajectory towards our transformation depends on contingencies such as habituation, the development of pleasure, and so on. This is illuminating, as it explains human ways of becoming good. It also embraces the fact that we share features with other creatures in the animal kingdom. It explains the process of becoming good within the context of empirical features. The developmental account gives a rich and active conception of our empirical features. However, the question of trajectory and direction of transformation poses a question about the role of intelligent thinking, and how our intelligent thinking shapes our rich empirical features, such as our desires and character, and shapes the journey towards good and/or right. Similarly, we need a better way to understand how our character and desires shape our practical thinking and intelligence. In other words, we need a better explanation of how our intelligent thinking interacts with our empirical selves.

Aristotelian-inspired rational choice—*prohairesis*—is the bridge between character and the empirical features that are relevant for choice, such as desires, pleasure, and habit.[54] Nevertheless, in developmental accounts, the phenomenology of choice disappears; the self or person is not the master of what happens. It is a training process. For example, in the case of Alessandra, we would say that she left her dog in the vehicle because her children were engaging in an argument. However, her character's tendency to be hasty and easily distracted did not cause the action. The problem that emerges is why she is responsible for her character if her character emerges as a result of contingencies, ie training practices. Furthermore, our everyday judgements and experiences lead us to believe that Alessandra's entire self, not just her ethical character, is the cause of what happens.

§5.4 The Deliberative-Aspirational Perspective and Other Perspectives

We need to provide a sound explanation of 'the upward journey to the specification of the *what*' that embraces our medium- and long-term goals and is able to retain the acquired practical knowledge of immersed or narrow deliberation.

I have already mentioned that contemporary philosophy tends to focus on reflection and that one difficulty that arises when thinking about reflection in the practical domain is that we are both object and subject. This means that we must pay attention and, therefore, think intelligently about our actions before, during,

[54] Kosman (n 27) 284, 292–96.

and after acting. When faced with the question of what we should do, we must investigate the particulars and circumstances of the action to determine the *what* through the *how*. At the same time, we are objects of our actions because, while investigating and deliberating what to do, we transform our desires and character, and these desires and character change our vision of the *what*. We are not only subjects of our actions but also objects.

Furthermore, Aristotle emphasized that in ethical matters and *praxis*, unlike in crafts or *technē*, our transformation can either be in the right or wrong direction. Consequently, the development of 'right' desires[55] can either occur or not occur, leading to the contortion of one's own being. In ethical matters, there is no direct or intuitive knowledge; when we get it wrong, there is only contortion and deformation. For instance, we can demonstrate our knowledge of grammar by purportedly making errors, and the more subtle the errors, the more proficiently the grammar expert demonstrates her knowledge. An engineer can demonstrate her proficiency in applied physics and bridge construction by constructing a defective bridge, yet this does not diminish her knowledge. On the other hand, when we make mistakes in our actions, our character and desires undergo changes, leading to a transformation of our entire self.[56]

The challenge lies in the correct understanding of reflection while simultaneously becoming the subject and object of our actions. Self-knowledge is necessary for world adjustment, making it inevitable and imperative. We need to know our current desires and beliefs so that we can adjust.[57]

Reflection can be understood as detachment, subject to a variety of interpretations. First, we can conceptualize it as an observational or perceptual stance. The perceptual model of self-reflection and self-knowledge presupposes that we can look inside at our states, desires, intentions, and character and determine their nature. This perceptual knowledge of our desires and character can assist us in our actions and in determining what we are going to do.[58] By contrast, the outward-looking model of self-reflection and self-knowledge establishes that you need to engage with the world and its features in order to determine what to do.[59] It presupposes the transparency conception of self-knowledge and rejects the idea that

[55] In the vicinity of this issue is what is called practical truth. Aristotle, *Nichomachean Ethics* (tr Sarah Broadie and Christopher Rowe, OUP 2002) 1139a29–31. For a detailed analysis of the nature of practical truth in Aristotle, see Olfert (n 43).

[56] Aristotle, *Eudemian Ethics* (tr Harris Rackham, Harvard UP, Loeb Classical Library 1989) 1046a26–1246b13. For a discussion of *Eudemian Ethics'* passages on contortion as a result of defective practical reasoning, see Flannery (n 24) ch 7.

[57] Christopher Bobonich, 'Plato and Akrasia and Knowing Our Own Mind' in Christopher Bobonich and Pierre Destrée (eds), *Akrasia in Greek Philosophy: From Socrates to Plotinus* (Brill 2007) 41.

[58] On perceptual reflection, see David Armstrong, *A Materialist Theory of Mind* (Routledge 1968). cf Sydney Shoemaker, 'Self-Knowledge and the Inner Sense' (1994) 54 Philosophy and Phenomenological Research 249. See also Richard Moran, *Authority and Estrangement: An Essay on Self-Knowledge* (Princeton UP 2001).

[59] This has an ancient pedigree, see eg Plato, *Charmides* (Harvard UP, Loeb Classical Library 1927).

we can perceive our own mental states (which can eventually generate knowledge). Thus, there is a paradox when I say 'p, but I do not believe it' or 'not p, but I believe it'. The paradox emerges[60] because these sentences seem to show us that we are able to settle our mental states, desires, beliefs, and intentions without perceiving them or having an interior view of them. Should someone inquire, 'Do you believe p?' I do not need to look at my mental state in order to decide whether I should believe 'p' or believe 'not-p'. On the contrary, I need to investigate and decide whether p is true or not. In other words, I need to engage with the content of the belief to assess whether I should actually believe 'p'.

Similarly, if I am asked whether I desire the *what*, 'Y', I do not look at my mental state to determine whether I should desire 'Y'. I need to engage in the *how* to determine the *what* and see whether I should continue desiring the *what* or rather to let it go. Furthermore, the perceptual stance requires that, in order to observe myself, I, as a subject, inevitably become the object. Some authors tend to reject this view because what we learn about ourselves is purely based on our empirical nature.[61] For instance, I can identify certain psychological traits such as ambition and impatience. However, this model does not answer the question of what I am going to do. Do I take into account these psychological features, or do I ignore them? Shall I transform them, and if so, how do I go about doing so? Moreover, it fails to provide us with any directionality or guidance towards achieving goodness. In conclusion, interpreting the detached view as an observational or perceptual stance leads to a deficient and incomplete understanding of ourselves as both the subject of our actions and the object of transformation through action.

Let us examine another conception of reflection, one that emphasizes looking at features of our relationships with others, looking carefully at our desires and aims over time, and examining how shifts in our thinking alter our view of the subject matter, such as our relationships, the characteristics of others, and our perceptions of good and right. Although our thinking and vision have changed, there is no action that reflects these changes. Iris Murdoch has advanced this model. She illustrates it with her well-known example of the mother-in-law, whose thinking about her daughter-in-law changes with time, though there is no external action that reflects her thinking. Let me quote the example, as its detail will become crucial in our analysis:

> A mother, whom I shall call M, feels hostility to her daughter-in-law, whom I shall call D. M finds D quite a good-hearted girl, but while not exactly common yet certainly unpolished and lacking in dignity and refinement. D is inclined to be pert

[60] See George E Moore, 'Moore's Paradox' in Tom Baldwin (ed), *G.E. Moore: Selected Writings* (Routledge 1993) 207; Wittgenstein (n 2) pt II, s X, 162–64; Moran, *Authority and Estrangement* (n 58); Iris Murdoch, 'The Idea of Perfection' in *Existentialists and Mystics* (Penguin 1950) 299.

[61] See Moran, *Authority and Estrangement* (n 58).

> and familiar, insufficiently ceremonious, brusque, sometimes positively rude, always tiresomely juvenile. M does not like D's accent or the way D dresses. M feels that her son has married beneath him. Let us assume for the purposes of the example that the mother, who is a very 'correct' person, behaves beautifully to the girl throughout, not allowing her real opinion to appear in any way. We might underline this aspect of the example by supposing that the young couple have emigrated or that D is now dead: the point being to ensure that whatever is in question as *happening* happens entirely in M's mind. Thus much for M's first thoughts about D. Time passes, and it could be that M settles down with a hardened sense of grievance and a fixed picture of D, imprisoned (if I may use a question-begging word) by the cliché: my poor son has married a silly vulgar girl. However, the M of the example is an intelligent and well-intentioned person, capable of self-criticism, capable of giving careful and just *attention* to an object which confronts her. M tells herself: 'I am old-fashioned and conventional. I may be prejudiced and narrow-minded. I may be snobbish. I am certainly jealous. Let me look again.' Here I assume that M observes D or at least reflects deliberately about D, until gradually her vision of D alters. If we take D to be now absent or dead this can make it clear that the change is not in D's behaviour but in M's mind. D is discovered to be not vulgar but refreshingly simple, not undignified but spontaneous, not noisy but gay, not tiresomely juvenile but delightfully youthful, and so on. And as I say, *ex hypothesi*, M's outward behaviour, beautiful from the start, in no way alters.[62]

Murdoch shares our belief that language-games provide the framework for our ends, values, and experiences and that words acquire their meaning through context.[63] Nevertheless, the way we experience language and describe matters enriches and modifies our shareable concepts. The concept '*does not give us an experience with an immediately self-contained, unambiguous sense*.'[64] However, we can describe values, ends, desires, and sensations in countless ways, and our multiple descriptions shape the meaning that context and our language-games initially give.[65] Our thoughts depend on our concepts, and we can think because we have learned concepts; however, contrary to some interpretations of Wittgenstein's criticism of

62 Murdoch 'The Idea of Perfection' (n 60) 312–13.

63 For a more detailed explanation of this, see §5.1

64 Iris Murdoch, 'Nostalgia for the Particular' in Peter Conradi (ed), *Existentialists and Mystics* (Penguin 1950) 43, 54. Murdoch also shows us that between 'everything is public' and 'everything is an internal event', there is an intermediate position. Iris Murdoch, 'Vision and Choice in Morality' in *Existentialists and Mystics* (this note) 76. Our thoughts work with concepts as mediators of reality, but our own perspectives, which constantly change and provide us with a vision and clarity on the matter at hand, are independent of our behavior or how we interpret the behaviour of others. This is what the example of the mother and daughter-in-law aims to show. She also refers to forms of life, see Murdoch 'Vision and Choice in Morality' (this note) 97. According to Murdoch, 'living is making distinctions and indicating order and pattern'. Iris Murdoch, *Metaphysics as a Guide to Morals* (Penguin 1993) 327.

65 Murdoch, 'Nostalgia for the Particular' (n 64) 44–46. See also the discussion in Chapter 1.

private language, this does not mean that thoughts and our inner life do not exist. It is rather that, if we follow a reading of Wittgenstein's arguments against private language, our psychological concepts like desire, beliefs, intentions, thoughts, or imagining do not refer to an internal state or private event. On the contrary, they need to find their expression in a language-game. Privileged access does not capture the phenomenon of privacy. There is no substantive and particular event that constitutes the reference to our psychological concepts. There is, however, a thinking that we engage with, where our learned and shareable concepts acquire shape, texture, colour, and depth.

The example of the changes that the mother-in-law experiences in relation to her daughter-in-law are elaborations and re-elaborations of her thoughts;[66] the attitudes, actions, and general behaviour of the daughter-in-law have not changed. What has changed is the way the mother-in-law describes and re-describes her thinking about her. Thus, changes in our thinking are characterized by three key features. First, there is no correspondence with a substantive or empirical reality, a referent that determines the shape of our thoughts. Thus, the daughter-in-law has not changed her behaviour or attitude, everything remains the same. The changes are at the level of thinking and perspective of the mother-in-law.

Secondly, the variations in the mother-in-law's descriptions and re-descriptions of her daughter-in-law cannot be explained by an act of will. The descriptions and re-descriptions of her daughter-in-law are somehow imposed upon us. We merge the language and the object. One could argue that the object we encounter is transparent, and the meaning and the event are inseparable. Language-games are intermediaries that define our experiences' contours, but our elaborations and descriptions give them shape. Simultaneously, the object, such as the character and attitudes of the daughter-in-law, undergoes changes due to shifts in our perception, focus, and appreciation. The more we focus on the object and think about it, the sharper our vision becomes, and we obtain clarity on the object. In parallel, the concept becomes more exact.[67] If we focus on the empirical matter only or the essential properties of the world—what Murdoch calls the substance of the world[68]—then we stop being reflective, and Murdoch conceives reflectivity as this process of describing, re-describing, elaborating, and re-elaborating our own thoughts on the matter. According to Murdoch, reflection is not detachment, as in the perceptual model of self-knowledge and self-reflection. Rather, reflection is looking carefully and paying attention (with all our conceptual apparatus and language resources) to the content of our beliefs, desires, and thinking. In this way, we exercise

[66] Murdoch calls it 'inner experiences' to emphasize that it does not depend on our will nor on the conduct that we manifest outwardly. It's all an internal process of elaboration and re-elaboration.

[67] Murdoch 'Nostalgia for the Particular' (n 64) 53.

[68] Iris Murdoch, 'Metaphysics and Ethics' in Peter Conradi (ed), *Existentialists and Mystics* (Penguin 1950) 59, 66. Murdoch reiterates that moral concepts do not move about within a hard world separated by science and logic. Murdoch, 'The Idea of Perfection' (n 60).

our freedom and learn to see the world differently.[69] Our thinking, not confined to a specific time or space, exhibits its own changes, leading us to see things and relationships in unique and different ways.

Thirdly, Murdoch emphasizes a stance of respecting the truth and avoiding fantasy that distorts our thinking; we need to give careful attention to the object in question. Fantasy is opposed to imagination.[70] Fantasy is characterized by its resistance to changes in thought and its resistance to attention. It could be said that fantasy focuses on our experiences for our experiences' sake, and consequently, while fantasizing our attention is removed from the object. The object of fantasy is our sensations or inner thoughts. Fantasy, as opposed to imagination, is a 'barrier to our seeing "what is really there"'.[71] By contrast, the object of our imagination is outside us, it is the subject matter of our attention. We direct ourselves towards the object and are open to its features and different presentations of it.[72] 'To be a human being is to know more than one can prove, to conceive of a reality that goes "beyond the facts" in these familiar and natural ways.'[73]

Imaginative thinking means going beyond the facts, but it also means being close to the subject matter through its consideration, description, and re-description. Changes in our thinking, through careful and proper attention to the subject matter and our imaginative thinking, generate new moral visions and concepts.[74] Consequently, we minimize the notion of choice as the determination and exercise of the will.[75] Ethical differences and ethical disagreements are presented as differences and disagreements in visions and perspectives.[76]

To conclude, according to Murdoch, reflection entails seeing beyond mere facts and the substance of the subject matter. Ethical reality is not there for every

[69] Murdoch, 'Metaphysics and Ethics' (n 68) 70–73.

[70] 'Imagination is a type of reflection on people's events.' Murdoch defines imagination as follows: 'Imagination as restoration of freedom, cognition, the effortful ability to see what lies before one clearly, more justly, to consider new possibilities, and to respond to good attachments and desires.' Murdoch, 'Metaphysics as a Guide to Morals' (n 64) 322. 'The particular can be brutalised, not respected, and absorbed into private fantasy.' ibid 340.

[71] Iris Murdoch, 'The Darkness of Practical Reason' in Peter Conradi (ed), *Existentialists and Mystics* (Penguin 1950) 193, 199.

[72] This openness is characteristic of the human power of indefinite and extended rational capacity. Iris Murdoch, 'The Sublime and the Good' in Peter Conradi (ed), *Existentialists and Mystics* (Penguin 1950) 205. She also claims that love is knowledge of the individual. Murdoch 'The Idea of Perfection' (n 60). One way to interpret this is to argue that, for example, through narrow deliberation, I grasp the specific end and learn to see all the different features of this end. If we continue to develop our understanding of its particularities through both our thinking and deliberation, this knowledge becomes love.

[73] Murdoch, 'The Darkness of Practical Reason' (n 71) 199.

[74] For Murdoch advances in ethics are insights generated by thinking. Murdoch, 'Vision and Choice in Morality' (n 64) 83.

[75] Murdoch criticizes Kant's notion of the will and also the notions of the will of existentialists, like Sartre. For a criticism of her interpretation of Kant, see Carla Bagnoli, 'Respect and Loving Attention' (2003) 33 Canadian Journal of Philosophy 483. For a criticism of her interpretation of Sartre's existentialism, see Richard Moran, 'Iris Murdoch and Existentialism' in *The Philosophical Imagination: Selected Essays* (OUP 2017) 169.

[76] Murdoch, 'Vision and Choice in Morality' (n 64) 93.

observer to determine its nature.[77] Neither it is an inner mental state that is projected onto the world, nor an inner shadow of our thinking,[78] our describing, elaborations, and re-elaborations.[79] Ethics is a matter of thinking clearly, and this entails shifting our perspective and vision. Ethical action does not entail moving our will away from our thinking as an independent reality. Murdoch presents us with the possibility that our thoughts and imaginative thinking will change, despite the fact that there is no external manifestation of these changes.

Murdoch is right in saying that our perspectives of others change and that there are *open and closed ways of seeing others*, and what changes is not the ethical reality as if our language can capture it. However, *it is implausible*, or so I will argue, that our intelligent, imaginative, and open thinking about matters, including the people in our lives, and their visions of goals, ends, and desires, has no repercussion for our actions. Let us go back to the example of the mother-in-law's changing attitudes towards her daughter-in-law. The example presents several issues. The illustration begins by telling us that M behaves beautifully towards the daughter-in-law, keeping her thoughts hidden. If this is the case, then the example is not truly realistic and believable. From our own experiences of relationships with in-laws, it is more likely that at the start of the relationship—when the mother-in-law thinks that the girl is vulgar, lacks dignity, and is unpolished—there will be some manifestation of her attitude. It is true that the mother-in-law can behave beautifully. However, there is always a wrong gaze, a guarded conversation, a long silence, and cues that betray our best possible intentions and efforts. The mother-in-law, inevitably, becomes reserved or on guard in her conversations and interactions with her daughter-in-law. When she changes her opinion and sees her as gay and delightfully youthful, then something in her conduct must have changed—some openness and being less guarded in her conversations and interactions with her daughter-in-law must be visible.

Furthermore, the setup of the example begs the question. Murdoch tells us that for the example to work better, we can imagine that the young couple have emigrated or D has died. However, this last requirement is puzzling because the purpose of the example is to demonstrate that our actions and interactions with others do not affect our thinking about them. However, the example instructs us to assume the absence of any interactions. The example works only if we isolate the mother-in-law from the daughter-in-law. Murdoch's point is important, but it

[77] The example is powerful and illustrates this. M's thinking is an activity, but there are no observers. The activity is hard to characterize, not because reality is hazy, but because it is moral. Murdoch, 'The Idea of Perfection' (n 60) 317. In this context, M is striving to determine what is justifiable and loving. M's activity is perfectible as she is engaged in an endless task. For Plato and Aristotle, thinking is activity. Kosman (n 27).

[78] Murdoch rejects the idea that the inner is a shadow of the outer. Murdoch, 'The Idea of Perfection' (n 60) 315–16. This is reminiscent of Wittgenstein's private language criticism.

[79] ibid 304.

needs softening; our thinking and perspectives towards others change, but our actions and interactions with them are not irrelevant.

Murdoch highlights that our intelligent and open thinking changes our visions and perspectives, leading to changes in both our attitudes towards other people and who they are. We can extend this analysis to desires and, hence, the cultivation of our character. In order to decide what to do, it is necessary to settle on what to desire and what to believe. However, we do not look at our psychological concepts, ie beliefs or desires, as if they were internal events. On the contrary, it is essential to look at the features of the world and pay careful attention to goals, ends, values, and other people, together with their unique moral vision, as they are presented in particular contexts and circumstances.

True, we do change perspectives and our ways of thinking about a specific matter. It also appears inevitable that we act based on the knowledge we have gained from our thoughts. We direct our thoughts in specific directions, and we either pay attention to or ignore subjects that may later become part of our narrow deliberations. The changes in our thinking are important and might lead to action. Murdoch's point is that action does not immediately follow thoughts. It can be argued that our thinking and changes in our thinking are an integral part of our narrow deliberation, and they can influence it at any stage of the process. Thus, imagine that the couple in Murdoch's example did leave town ten years ago and that the mother-in-law meets the daughter-in-law in her new home after all these years and after the death of her son. She sees her now as gay, delightful, and dignified. She engages in narrow deliberation and puts careful thought into making a delicious meal, making the encounter a special moment for her daughter-in-law. We now comprehend that these actions stem from shifts in her perception of her daughter-in-law's qualities.

Let us recall that our original difficulty was how to preserve the insights of our immersed or narrow deliberation while also locating ourselves within a wider perspective that encompasses medium- and long-term goals, ends, values, projects, and plans. Nevertheless, we recognize that they are indeterminate and uncertain. Furthermore, we confront the challenge of firmly grasping medium- and long-term goals, ends, and values and become good while maintaining the immersed perspective that shapes our empirical reality and our deliberative process. As a corollary of this, the question that arises is whether we can engage in deliberation that is non-immersed while nevertheless maintaining the immersed perspective.

I will show that it is possible to grasp medium- and long-term ends and values and become good while maintaining an immersed perspective. However, we can also engage in non-immersive deliberation. We need a deliberative-aspirational perspective to learn about the good and right, I will argue. Hence, this will suffice to show that there is a possible trajectory towards the 'specification of the *what*' that embraces medium- and long-term ends and values.

I have already shown that our thinking can change, leading to a shift in perspective and thinking about the subject matter, including the content of our desires, goals, beliefs, and other psychological concepts. For Murdoch, the mother-in-law is a well-intentioned person, and this seems to be sufficient for us to occupy a critical space for our thoughts. There is no internal mental event that we are trying to grasp, represent, or refer to (correctly) when we think about the content of our attitudes or desires; rather, it is *our perspective or vision* of the subject that changes. However, it is difficult to believe that people are self-critical and self-reflective in paradigmatic examples. Furthermore, in her example, Murdoch downplays the role of time, the fact that the mother-in-law has become more mature, which has aided in the transformation of her desires and character. Possibly, she has had experiences—for example, meeting other couples and young people—that have caused a change in her views. After her son's marriage, she has probably seen positive changes in him. It's possible that her role as a grandmother has influenced her perception of her daughter-in-law, or she may have experienced health issues or other hardships that have prompted a change in her perspective. We pay attention to the subject matter and look carefully, but this might not be sufficient. There is an element of richness missing from the experience. Furthermore, fantasy, distractions, and self-deceptions can all hinder our vision and intelligent thinking.

We recognize that in Murdoch's example, the mother-in-law has been active in her thinking, but not infallible. Murdoch tells us that she is self-critical and that she returns to the matter of her daughter-in-law to give it her full and careful attention, '*I am old-fashioned and conventional. I may be prejudiced and narrow-minded. I may be snobbish. I am certainly jealous. Let me look again.*' The question that arises is precisely how the mother-in-law can see herself as 'old-fashioned, narrow-minded, snobbish and jealous'. This is an important question that Murdoch does not address. Perhaps other experiences have made her reflect on the person that she is. For example, prior to changing her views concerning her daughter-in-law, she developed a friendship with a young person and paid attention to how she interacted with her and how the young lady acted with others. Through this friendship, she learned that her way of looking at life is rather old-fashioned and narrow-minded. She has also become friends with people of a different social status who have made remarks about her snobbish attitudes. In general, my point is that her shift in perspective doesn't happen solely through thought. There are experiences and relationships that the mother-in-law has engaged in that have forced her to 'look again' at her views on her daughter-in-law.[80]

I will argue that the interplay between narrow or immersed deliberation and self-reflection on our narrow deliberations illuminates both the path for transforming our thinking, desires, and character, as well as how we engage with our

[80] Murdoch, 'Metaphysics as a Guide to Morals' (n 64) 331. Murdoch recognizes that the 'outward initiates the change'.

medium- and long-term goals and projects. In my transparent self-knowledge and reflection, I focus on the features of the subject matter and try to understand its particularities. In the example of Beatrice (see §4.2), she tries to determine the way rhythm, balanced competitiveness, and harmony are all key components of physical health, and when considering how to achieve the physical health of her daughter, she engages with the *how* to determine the *what*. At every step, she engages in specifying the *what* and what constitutes physical health *for* her daughter. She comes to this realization as a result of her immersed or narrow deliberation. She can continue paying attention to the features of her daughter's physical health. At the same time, she learns through her interactions with other mothers that worrying excessively about her daughter's physical health can undermine her daughter's self-confidence. She now begins to recognize that her excessive focus on her daughter's physical health is a sign of an obsessive mother. She has now gained a perspective that she did not have prior to engaging in the narrow deliberation of maintaining her daughter's physical health. Furthermore, her interactions with other mothers, as well as her own deliberations and interactions with others, have resulted in an additional layer of thinking. Beatrice now values her daughter's physical health more deeply and profoundly than she did previously.

I will argue that Beatrice is now inhabiting a 'deliberative-aspirational perspective'. She recognizes features of herself, not as merely empirical or as an object, but as something that she needs to take into account in future deliberations. Indeed, she can either avoid certain features, such as the obsession with her daughter's physical health, or she can recognize and improve them. She is compelled to adopt a particular perspective in order to learn. The emphasis is on the fact that deliberation occurs not only when the *how* determines the *what* but also when we experience relationships, think about others, and consider their myriad ways of thinking and acting, thereby gaining knowledge and enriching our interactions. Humans engage in this process. As we deliberate and interact with others, we also learn to see and think about ourselves, making it critical to understand what happens between each discrete, narrow, or immersed deliberation. It is also practical reasoning, as it focuses on (a) particularities and (b) evolving desires.

Cavell's examination of the slave owner effectively illustrates how we occupy different perspectives, whether we recognize and inhabit them through narrow or aspirational thinking and deliberation, or whether we avoid or stop inhabiting them.[81]

Cavell interprets the denial of the fantasy of private language in Wittgenstein's *Philosophical Investigations* as denying the existence of mental events or when we use psychological concepts like desire, belief, intention, imagining, and so on. However, he tells us, this denial does not entail that there are no inner thoughts.

[81] Cavell (n 10) 376–78.

Inner thoughts take on a distinct identity, and if we reject the concept of a 'mental event' or 'referent' model, then what does the inner thought truly represent? According to Cavell, inner thoughts revolve *around perspectives and their various layers.* Let me explain. When I say, 'I am in pain', I demonstrate that I want to tell you something about my soul and body. However, I am also presenting myself, telling you something about myself. The fantasy of private language is pernicious because it leads to a conception of mysterious mental events and mental entities. As a result, we may be confused, thinking that there is something unique about your pain that I cannot grasp; something mysterious that will always be inscrutable for me, the other.

Cavell demonstrates that scepticism of other minds, ie the idea that there is something inscrutable and incomprehensible in how others use psychological expressions, concepts, and words, is not possible, and his argument is crucial to demonstrating his point on perspectives. The argument is complex but can be summarized as follows. In the case of scepticism about our knowledge of things and objects, we can imagine that there is a demon who plays with how things appear to us. Thus, the demon is able to deceive me about, for example, whether the desk in front of me is really there, and this leads me to question whether the desk is truly real or only appears to be real. For this kind of sceptical argument to work, the demon needs to know more than me because she needs to produce the illusion of appearance as well as understand the difference between what is real and what merely appears to be real. In other words, the demon is in a better epistemic position than me.

Scepticism about other minds, on the other hand, cannot work because we have immediate knowledge of our desires, values, intentions, and so on. In our example, Beatrice *knows* that she intends to register her daughter for ballet lessons, and she knows why. Could Beatrice doubt her intentions? Because she has answered the question, 'What shall I do?', she knows what she is doing and why. She has gained this knowledge, and for the demon to undermine it, it would require a deeper understanding of her intentions than she has. The demon needs to know what Beatrice's real intention is, as well as her apparent intention. But if intention is the result of engagement with the world and settling the question 'What shall I do?', and reflects *why* and *how* Beatrice sees a matter, then the demon *cannot* have more knowledge than Beatrice about her own intentions. Similarly, when someone tells me about Beatrice's desires or intentions, what I hear is her own perspective on the matter, and I cannot be sceptical about what she desires or intends. I cannot have more knowledge about her or deny that she does not really know what she desires and intends. I can't establish that there is a true and hidden desire or intention that she does not know. However, this seems to contradict our daily experiences. There are many occasions in which we act according to what we think our desires are, only to later discover, usually with surprise, that we actually had different desires. Similarly, friends tell us what they intend, or desire, and we might later discover that they truly had another intention or desire. The temptation is to think that our psychological words refer to a mental reality or refer to something, and, therefore, changes in or discoveries of desires are conceived as the 'discovery' of hidden desires or intentions, ie mental states that were always there, but that now can be brought to light. This can lead to a sense of scepticism towards the minds of others, as they appear truly mysterious. They have intentions and desires that we really do not know with certainty and probably will never know.

But if we deny the fantasy of the private language account, the fact that I express another desire or intention after deliberating and acting reveals simply a change in perspective in my deliberations or actions, or perhaps both. For example, Murdoch's mother-in-law can now see that her daughter-in-law is not as undignified as she previously thought. On the contrary, she now sees her daughter-in-law as gay and polite. There is no new mental state present for her, nor is there a unique referent that corresponds to her past or current thoughts. The mother-in-law has changed perspective.

Imagine that I am a very close friend of the mother-in-law (let us call her Sylvia) and that I knew her prior to her changed perspective. Sylvia tells me about the ways her views of her daughter-in-law have changed. It would be wrong to infer that others are inscrutable to us or that there are mysterious mental events that I need to interpret and reinterpret in light of others' actions and my interactions with them. Rather, from our conversations and Sylvia's actions, I assume that Sylvia is struggling to take the right perspective and that she is trying to make herself intelligible both to herself and to me.

More interestingly, like Sylvia, we often struggle to maintain coherent perspectives and may avoid or recognize certain perspectives or visions that are in conflict with our other perspectives or visions. Cavell's example of the slave owner clearly illustrates these shifts in perspectives or visions, as well as their recognition or avoidance.[82] The example follows, but I have slightly modified it to emphasize my point. Imagine a slave owner who allows his slaves to eat with him, who goes hunting with them, who lets his children play with those of the slave, and who allows his slaves to call him by a nickname. This pleases the slaves. For the slave owner, the slave is a good man, a good hunter, a good father, and a humorous person; however, the only space that he does not recognize in his slave is the space of justice. He thinks that it is right that his slave does not have freedom or autonomy.[83] What Cavell emphasizes is the capacity to make connections. We do not share inner thoughts; rather we share connections embedded in language-games. Imagine that this relationship between the slave and slave owner occurred at the end of the nineteenth century in a certain country, and that Parliament has enacted a new statute abolishing slavery. Furthermore, abolitionist movements have for some time articulated their views

[82] ibid 376–78.
[83] ibid 353.

and propagated them to this country's population. Our slave owners may remain unmoved by their arguments. However, Cavell asks for how long he can continue to avoid taking a new perspective and depriving his slave of the space of justice. How consistent is this with his other perspectives and thoughts about his slaves, such as being a good man, a good father, and a humorous human being? Can he still deny him justice and dignity?

I have also tried to show that the deliberative-aspirational perspective is key. We learn about the possibility of a deliberative perspective both through others and by engaging in immersed deliberation. For example, when our inadvertent actions cause harm to others. In the first chapter, we presented the case of Alessandra, who left her dog in her vehicle on a scorching day. Upon her return from a hockey game with her children, she tragically found that her dog had perished. Alessandra does not learn about the tragedy through a process of inference, such as inferring from the factual premises that it is hot, the dog is not breathing, it has not moved for twenty minutes, and it has passed away. *Nor does she interpret* what she sees and attribute responsibility to herself for what has happened. On the contrary, prior to acting, she deliberated and determined the *what* through the *how*. She registered her children for hockey lessons and encouraged participation in hockey games to instil in them a sense of teamwork and a healthy lifestyle. She did not know *what* the unique qualities and essential elements of this good would be, such as fostering a sense of team spirit and promoting a healthy life, but she discovered that hockey is a good by deliberating on *how* to achieve this end. She also bought a pet for the children, hoping that they would learn to care for animals. Alessandra must combine being a mother, who strives to cultivate a team spirit in her children and being a good pet owner. Prior to collecting the children at the hockey game, she deliberated on whether to bring the dog; she desired for the dog to have fresh air and engage in playtime with the children after the game. Some of these deliberations took place prior to the fatal moment of the accident. When Alessandra returns from the hockey field and sees her dog dead, she immediately understands what has happened. Similar to the duck-rabbit example, the tragedy dawns on Alessandra, causing her to perceive an *aspect of her own actions and thinking*. As argued in §5.1, aspects are hidden by other aspects, and experiences transform us, revealing different aspects of the particularities of our actions. Because she has constructed her thoughts on the subject matter through narrow deliberation, she does not require any process of inference or interpretation. She knows the content of her deliberations, her thinking, and the ways, I will argue, she avoided inhabiting the deliberative-aspirational perspective.

Let us assume that Alessandra has already heard about the high temperatures, and her friends have mentioned her tendency to juggle too many things, her tendency to do everything and refuse to accept her limitations. Alessandra could take the perspective of the aspirational-deliberator and transform her desires and character. For example, she could buy a pet for the children only when they are able to take care of it, when they are able to walk home from hockey, and when they can take responsibility for the animal.

Avoidance might lead to fantasy and a lack of attention. However, recognition allows us to inhabit the deliberative-aspirational perspective. Once we recognize a particular feature in its uniqueness, we can think about it and change our views on it, transforming our emotions and desires as this recognition and thinking become part of our deliberations. Beatrice, for example, recognizes her obsession with her daughter's physical health and must now decide whether to continue paying for ballet lessons or not. She can give up her pursuit of her daughter's physical health and 'let it go'. Her thinking about herself as 'obsessive' has now altered her desires and deliberations. The key is that this movement, in either direction—recognition or avoidance—is of the entire self. The transformation encompasses our emotions and desires and, as a result, has an impact on our character's development. Nevertheless, these transformations are not *solely* the result of training our desires, emotions, and character; they also result from adopting a perspective, which involves either thinking about and acknowledging the subject matter or avoiding it and not thinking about or examining it. Training may still play a role, but not because of action repetition, but because we get used to inhabiting a perspective multiple times and learn its depth and complexity.

However, how does inhabiting this deliberative-aspirational perspective enable us to also engage with medium- and long-term goals and ends while remaining in the immersed or narrow deliberative perspective? We have learned that changing our perspectives through both thinking and experience does not involve contemplating our inner experiences and thoughts as if they were mere events or objects. I reject the idea that we can be impartial or detached from our experiences, as inevitably we lose something vital. I also reject the perception model of self-reflection and self-objectification. I advocate for a transparent model of self-reflection, where the agent not only addresses the question 'What shall I do?', but also engages with careful consideration of the subject matter, including relationships, what is good, and what is right. When the agent looks outward to the world and discovers deficiencies in her interactions with others, recognition of this can be taken on as material for further narrow deliberations. When we are confronted with others through relationships and experiences, we are invited to either avoid or recognize, and when we pay careful attention to features of the world and our relationships, we are able to aspire to medium- and long-term goals and ends within the narrow or immersed deliberative perspective. The depth and richness of the latter enable us to better understand if or how our current position is lacking. In our previous example, Beatrice's recognition of herself as an 'obsessed mother' forces her to see her medium- and long-term goals and ends. Grasping these goals is possible because there is a trajectory from the immersed perspective to inhabiting the deliberative-aspirational perspective. Nonetheless, Beatrice's grasp of medium- and long-term goals remains within the confines of the immersed perspective, having absorbed the wisdom acquired through her deliberations. The medium- and long-term goals and ends are uncertain, but they can form part of future-immersed or narrow deliberations. Beatrice can engage with the good of internal peace, attend yoga lessons, or develop a new sport that will challenge her existing thinking.

We have said that we can occupy or inhabit a higher ethical position—the deliberative-aspirational perspective—if we think of our current position as deprived or lacking. This is one of the roles that regret and shame play in our lives. They make us aware of our deprived or lacking position. In Alessandra's case, she feels regret for her actions and the tragic death of her dog. Once she pays attention and carefully examines her narrow deliberations, it becomes clear to her that she had, and perhaps still has, a deprived or lacking perspective. Regret and shame force us into another perspective. We can either avoid or recognize the particularity of the *what* and our failure to achieve it, with all the thinking, including our thoughts on our emotions, shame, and regret. If Alessandra acknowledges her perspective of deprivation, she can inhabit the deliberative-aspirational perspective and transform her emotions. She is invited to rethink her goals, ends, values, and desires.

In Chapter 9, I will argue that regret and shame can work as proleptic emotions—emotions that are anticipated and are part of our narrow or immersed deliberation, allowing us changes to our perspective. The deliberative-aspirational perspective is a potential perspective. Thus, we transform our thinking, including thinking about our emotions, desires, and character, which in turn leads to changes in our desires and emotions. These transformed desires and emotions will, at the same time, shape our thinking and the way we pay attention to particularities in the world, as well as our actions.

In Chapter 9, I also argue that legal directives, principles, and norms that impose a duty of care on citizens play the role of proleptic thoughts, ie anticipated thoughts that are integral part of the immersed deliberation of the citizens when they engage in different activities; for instance, a medical doctor operating on a patient. Legal rules and directives impose duties of care, signalling to the citizen that they must consider this duty in their deliberations. This means that they need to pay attention and think carefully about how the *specification* of the *how* can determine the *what*, and think and pay attention to their own thoughts about the specific subject matter.

If we take the denial of the fantasy of private language and extend it to our deliberations and thoughts on what is good, worthwhile engaging with, or right, we see that there cannot be a private vision of the good. We cannot have a private space where our reference to the good is only intelligible to us and inscrutable to others. If I feel, through shame and regret, that my perspective is deprived or lacking, I cannot find refuge in a special notion of good or right, which I myself only inhabit.

The 'balancing' model of deliberation presents reasons as fully grasped, with no role for learning, cultivation, and transformation of our thinking, emotions, and desires. There is no diachronicity, and we can interpret the moment of choice as an evaluation of various reasons, internal or external, that provide the best answer to the question, 'What shall I do?' The defective execution of an action, like in cases of negligence or inadvertence, becomes problematic and puzzling. Non-sceptical strategies attempt to show that there was a moment of choice at some point—ie the so-called 'tracing strategy'—or some ability or capacity to choose, or the executed action was within the domain of rational competence of the agent, or the agent should have thought harder and discharged her epistemic duties, or the agent exposed others to an unreasonable risk and should have seen it, or perhaps a combination of all these different non-sceptical strategies. We will discuss in detail these different solutions to the sceptical problem of negligence in ethics (Chapter 8) and law (Chapter 7). At this point, however, I only want to highlight that all these strategies presuppose that the 'balancing model' of deliberation is the correct one and, therefore, their explanation of negligence in both ethics and law is not satisfactory.

6

Taking *Akrasia* Seriously

§6.1 Preliminary Reflections

Multiple interpretations and ambivalences plague the concept of *akrasia*, making it seem less helpful. Moreover, in addition to the complexity of interpreting Socratic and Aristotelian technical notions, contemporary and ancient understandings of *akrasia* differ. This discrepancy arises from the disparity between ancient and contemporary understandings of practical reason and deliberation, as discussed in earlier sections. Consequently, *akrasia* appears to be an elusive and inscrutable phenomenon.

Let us recall that in Chapter 2 we discussed Rosen's scepticism about responsibility for negligent actions. His position is that there cannot be responsibility for negligence unless we show that we have failed to discharge our procedural epistemic duties, leading to an infinite regression. In order to stop the regression, we need to identify an intentional action that shows a failure to discharge our epistemic duties. In this way, negligence either collapses into intentional action or leads to infinite regress. Alternatively, Rosen tells us, we could show that the negligent action is *akratic* because the agent considers 'a' to be a better choice than 'b'. Nevertheless, the agent performs 'b'. Rosen's criticism targets 'clear-eyed *akrasia*'[1] and states that it cannot be a potential solution to stop the infinite regress for responsibility for inadvertent acts. If we are aware of or have a 'clear eye' on the wrongness of the act and, in spite of this, perform the action, then the action is either reckless or intentional.[2] Furthermore, he also believes that *akrasia* is a cryptic

[1] There are different interpretations as to whether Aristotle allows 'clear-eyed' *akrasia*. Among the authors who argue that Aristotle allows it is Bradley's interpretation of Dahl's explanation of *akrasia*, where the failure is in acting according to the conclusion of the practical syllogism. Dennis Bradley, 'Thomas Aquinas on Weakness of the Will' in Tobias Hoffman (ed), *Weakness of Will from Plato to Present* (The Catholic University of America Press 2008) 82, 92. See also Norman Dahl, *Practical Reason, Aristotle, and Weakness of the Will* (University of Minnesota Press 1984). For a similar proposal, see David Charles, *Aristotle's Philosophy of Action* (Cornell UP 1984). See also Richard Robinson, 'L'Acrasie, selon Aristote' (1955) 145 Revue Philosophique de la France et de l'Etranger 261, 266–71 and Anthony Kenny, 'The Practical Syllogism and Incontinence' (1966) 11 Phronesis 163, 184. Other authors argue that Aristotle does not allow it, see James Walsh, *Aristotle's Conception of Moral Weakness* (Columbia UP 1963) 120–22. See also David Wiggins, 'Deliberation and Practical Reason' in Amélie Rorty, *Essays on Aristotle's Ethics* (University of California Press 1980) 221. Arguably, for Aristotle, there is no clear-eyed *akrasia* because there is a blurring of our knowledge. But the difficulty is to explain how this blurred vision/knowledge occurs without becoming a compulsive or intentional action.

[2] In my view, Husak successfully argues that we should understand recklessness as clear-eyed *akrasia*. Douglas Husak, *Ignorance of Law* (OUP 2016) 174–75. This should be distinguished from

Responsibility for Negligence in Ethics and Law. Verónica Rodríguez-Blanco, Oxford University Press.
 DOI: 10.1093/9780198948193.003.0006

and obscure concept and therefore cannot illuminate our judgements of responsibility for negligence. *Contra* Rosen, I will show that our interpretation of acting *akratically* explains how we can act inadvertently, and still be ethically, and legally, blameworthy, and responsible.

In §6.1, I distinguish the modern conception of *akrasia* from the view advocated by Socrates and Aristotle and discuss how some contemporary models of acting *akratically* are either deflationary or change the subject. Additionally, I advance the view that the Aristotelian practical syllogism is problematic as an explanation of how we act *akratically*. When we focus on how deliberation works, we consider the diachronic structure of practical agency; by contrast, practical syllogisms serve as practical arguments after the action has been performed, but they are unable to elucidate the actual workings of deliberation.[3] Practical syllogisms provide the structure of the agent's practical argument when justifications are at stake, or when the agent or observer is reconstructing the action. *Practical syllogisms, on the other hand, do not represent what happens to the agent when she engages in acting akratically.* To put the point differently, it falls short of providing a true and compelling explanation because it ignores the dynamic and complex aspects of deliberation. It has an unsettling artificiality and schematic quality about it.[4] Arguably, to fully grasp the agent's deliberative process and exercise of practical reason, we need to understand the diachronic structure of the first-person perspective.[5] This is at the core of a sound explanation of acting *akratically*.

In §6.2, I show how we can fail to integrate thinking and desire and how we can inhabit the deliberative-aspirational perspective. This is the core of a sound explanation of acting *akratically*, which shows the underpinning structure of acting negligently. This chapter establishes the foundations for the discussion of responsibility for negligent action, deliberation, and diachronic agency, which takes place in the following three chapters of the book.

§6.2 Socrates and Aristotle on *Akrasia*

In Plato's *Protagoras*[6] Socrates denies the feasibility and/or stability of the *akratic* position, stating that *akrasia* is not possible as it leads to a contradiction.

cases that are called by Sarch 'broad sense of willful ignorance', in which the person subconsciously remains ignorant of her act, or the risk involved in her action. Alex Sarch, *Criminally Ignorant* (OUP 2019) 19.

[3] Heda Segvic, *From Protagoras to Aristotle* (Princeton UP 2008).

[4] Sarah Broadie, *Ethics with Aristotle* (OUP 1991); Kenny (n 1); Elizabeth Anscombe, *Intention* (Basil Blackwell 1957, reprinted by Harvard UP 2000).

[5] Walsh, for example, emphasizes the importance of an explanation of *akrasia* in light of the wider context of Aristotelian concepts, ie practical reason and deliberation. Walsh (n 1) 118.

[6] Plato, *Protagoras* (tr Christopher C Taylor, Clarendon Press 1976).

In *Protagoras*, the *akratic* position is the so-called majority view. According to *Protagoras*, the position of the majority is that when an agent acts against her deliberation and rational decision, something stronger, such as pleasure or the pleasant, overrides her knowledge of the good. Imagine the following example: at a party, a driver is aware that consuming a large glass of wine can elevate her blood alcohol level beyond the legal limit. In spite of this knowledge, she decides to have a glass of wine and, after that, a second glass. She becomes tipsy and, on the way home, collides with another vehicle, causing injury to herself and the other driver. What is a sound account of her practical reasoning? The majority view in *Protagoras* will assert that her knowledge[7] was overcome by pleasure. This means she knew what she should do, but her knowledge was submitted to pleasure. For Socrates, this position is incoherent. According to Socrates, knowledge can never be overcome by what is pleasant or less good, making this position an absurd or 'ridiculous' position.[8] Socrates would argue that the driver could resist the temptation to consume a glass of wine if she possessed the specific knowledge about the 'art of measurement', which involves balancing what is pleasant and good against what is painful and evil instead of following appearances.[9] Her knowledge would enable her to recognize that the pain of getting drunk, colliding with another vehicle, and injuring herself and another driver surpasses the pain of abstaining from alcohol. This knowledge is for Socrates the 'art of measurement', which, like any skill (and virtues conceived as skills), can be taught. For Socrates, the majority view ends up with the following absurd assertion: 'Knowledge of what is good was overcome by what is less good', or, if you adhere to hedonism, 'Knowledge of what is pleasant was overcome by what is less pleasant'.

The Socratic position sheds light on Watson's demarcation between compulsion and *akrasia*. For Watson[10] we cannot clearly distinguish between *akrasia* and compulsion. If our desires are sufficiently strong and can bend our judgements then there is nothing we could have done, and it is a compulsive act. Watson poses the question of whether we can hold ourselves accountable for compulsive acts that fit this description, to which he responds negatively.

Socrates would embrace Watson's potential sceptical conclusion, ie that we cannot truly distinguish between *akrasia* and compulsion, and we could infer that

[7] The focus of Socrates in Plato's *Protagoras* is knowledge, not belief, see Terence Irwin, 'Aristotle Reads the Protagoras' in Tobias Hoffman (ed), *Weakness of Will from Plato to the Present* (The Catholic Univesity of America Press 2008) 22.

[8] Plato (n 6) 355a–357e.

[9] Callard defends a puzzling Socratic position. She argues that Socrates denies *akrasia*, but she also says that Socrates is not defending *akrasia*-immunity. For Socrates, she tells us, *akrasia* refers to something less than belief, and obviously something less than knowledge. She calls it 'simulacrum'. *Akratics* dismiss their beliefs and also their 'simulacrum'. Therefore, they are ignorant of their 'cognitive make-up'. Agnes Callard, 'Ignorance and Akrasia-Denial in the Protagoras' in Brad Inwood (ed), *Oxford Studies in Ancient Philosophy* (OUP 2014) 31.

[10] Gary Watson, 'Scepticism About Weakness of the Will' in *Agency and Answerability: Selected Essays* (OUP 2004) 123.

as Socrates denies *akrasia*, he would, arguably, have no problem saying that *akrasia* is just compulsion.[11] If *akrasia*, the underpinning phenomenon of negligent acts, is indistinguishable from compulsion, then we cannot distinguish between negligence and compulsion. Judgements of responsibility for compulsion and negligence refer to the same phenomenon and, arguably, are inappropriate because the agent has no knowledge of what is happening. Desire or passion, in a pathological sense, takes over the thinking and knowledge, and the latter is 'dragged as a slave' by passion and desire. What the offender needs is treatment, not a judgement of responsibility. Alternatively, we could say that the driver acted ignorantly, and she is responsible for not learning what everyone else can learn through the teachings of the 'art of measurement'. Following Socrates, we would argue that the driver lacked the 'art of measurement' because she succumbed to appearances, such as the immediate pleasure of drinking a second glass of wine. But is it true that we can all learn the 'art of measurement'? Is it true that to truly understand what is good, pleasant, and right, we simply need the 'art of measurement'?

In previous chapters, I defended a view of deliberation and practical reason that differed from the 'art of measurement'. Furthermore, I resisted the notion that we can learn to become good simply by teaching, balancing, or weighing reasons, values, or desires. In Chapter 3, I argued that there is a vestige of the 'balance' view of deliberation in the Socratic position of the 'art of measurement'. In Chapters 4 and 5, I tried to demonstrate that desires and emotions are a key part of both immersed or narrow deliberation and the deliberative-aspirational perspective. I claimed that in narrow or immersed deliberation, we are uncertain about the *what* and, therefore, we need to bring it closer to us and our actions through the *how*. I also explained that our thinking transforms our desires, particularly our desires for the *what*. The modified *what* also has a transformative effect on our desires. Furthermore, I demonstrated that our experiences and thoughts on a particular subject matter shape our desires, and this knowledge can inform our subsequent deliberations. As we inhabit different perspectives, including the deliberative-aspirational perspective, our experiences and thinking change.

I should also mention that in this model, like in the Aristotelian account, pleasure is internal to our conception of 'living well', and this is a crucial feature of *akrasia*. Immersed deliberation is in continuity with medium- and long-term ends and goals, and our thoughts and conceptions of ends and goals shape our experiences of pleasure.[12] Note that up until now, we have argued thoughts can realize the

[11] Arguably, since for Socrates, self-knowledge and self-awareness are necessary for pleasure, the pleasure that takes over the agent without any cognitive apparatus is just mere compulsion or a pathology. Christopher Moore, *Socrates and Self-Knowledge* (OUP 2015) 198–200.

[12] Julia Annas, *Intelligent Virtue* (OUP 2011); Mark Sultana, *Self-Deception and Akrasia* (Editrice Pontificia Universitá Gregoriana 2006) 269; and Amélie Rorty, 'Akrasia and Pleasure: Nichomachean Ethics Book 7' in Amélie Rorty (ed), *Essays on Aristotle's Ethics* (University of California Press 1980) 267.

good, the pleasant, and so on forth as ends, and that our thoughts on the pleasant will shape the way we realize our ends.[13]

According to the Aristotelian-inspired model that I have defended, purely thinking or cognitive skill, à la Socrates, is not sufficient to combat the strength of desires. The latter needs to be transformed. What happens before the action is crucial to what happens later, at the moment of performing the action. MacIntyre rightly observes: '*here is a scary thought, what determined the final stage of my reasoning on some particular occasion may or may have not occurred immediately beforehand*.'[14]

While engaging with judgements of responsibility and blameworthiness in negligence, we need to consider the diachronicity of the deliberation and the subsequent actions. But prior to advancing a defence of *akrasia* as the underpinning phenomenon of ethical and legal negligence, I will both expand on the Socratic position and scrutinize some interpretations of the Aristotelian position of *akrasia*. This analysis will shed light on the idea that the Aristotelian position is a refinement of the Socratic view instead of a rejection. I will also show that the modern view of *akrasia* deflates the phenomenon and impoverishes our understanding of deliberation and learning to become good.

Let us go back to the majority view in Plato's *Protagoras*. If desires, passions, and emotions can randomly overtake knowledge, we are likely unmotivated to better understand our actions, or worse, the idea of becoming good is unintelligible to us.[15] In this case, *contra* Socrates, knowledge cannot save us. According to this picture, not only do desires and emotions dominate us, but it is also uncertain when they will appear in our deliberations or actions. Note that *akrasia* occurs when we cannot restrain our desires and passions while failing to integrate them with our reasoning. It is not true that passions can never overcome us. If passions are so strong that they overcome or bypass anyone's reasoning, then we are clearly in the realm of compulsion.[16] The *akratic* is not a woman who fails to be heroic; rather, *her failure is weakness*. This model overlooks perspective and its crucial role in our transformational process.

Let us go back to Chapter 4's example of Beatrice. Beatrice is deliberating whether to enrol her daughter in gymnastics, aware that this action is necessary to achieve her daughter's physical health and foster physical and spiritual harmony. After deliberation, Beatrice decides to enrol her daughter in gymnastics and to pay for the registration. She transfers the money from her savings account into her current account. However, prior to making the payment, she starts to look at beautiful coats on a popular website, and her desire to buy an expensive coat overtakes her.

[13] Broadie (n 4) 84–185.

[14] Alasdair MacIntyre, 'Conflicts of Desire' in Tobias Hoffman (ed), *Weakness of Will From Plato to the Present* (The Catholic University of America Press 2008) 276, 290.

[15] Plato (n 6) 357e2–4.

[16] Aristotle, *Nichomachean Ethics* (tr Sarah Broadie and Christopher Rowe, OUP 2002) 1150b6–14.

She envisions herself purchasing a stunning and costly coat with the funds she had set aside for her daughter's gym/ballet fees. The 'majority' view in *Protagoras* will tell us that this is a common pattern; it happens to Beatrice, to you, to myself, and to everyone. There is nothing mysterious; we are subjects to our passions and desires. Furthermore, we have no control over our actions, and even worse, we may come to the conclusion that we are incapable of improving ourselves or our circumstances. Nevertheless, we know that some people *can* avoid temptation; how is this possible? The majority view will probably say that the strength of desires in each particular individual is the key factor. The majority view, however, does not present a coherent picture of our aspirational transformation or is sceptical about this possibility, as desires and passions can always dominate us.

Contrast this position with modern and contemporary views that put forward an explanation of this phenomenon of 'avoiding temptation' in terms of particular conceptions of the 'will'. This perspective portrays *akrasia* as a battle of the 'will', emphasizing the importance of self-control in resisting temptation. We will engage with this explanation in Chapter 8. We will discuss another contemporary view, which emphasizes the conditionality of our judgements, in the next section. For now, we aim to address the question of *akrasia* within the intellectual apparatus of Socrates, Aristotle, and their interpreters.

Socrates' solution relies on three key elements. First, the 'art of measurement' can save our lives, as well as, no doubt, Beatrice's existence. Beatrice should learn the skill of weighing pleasure, which includes the short-term joy of her luxurious coat and the long-term joy of witnessing her daughter's physical and mental growth, as well as the skill of weighing pain, which includes the short-term pain of not having a new coat and the long-term pain of her daughter's laziness and lack of physical health. This knowledge possesses strength[17] and will enable her to master her desires and emotions. Furthermore, anomalies in her deliberation and performance will reflect a lack of knowledge, and *akrasia* is nothing but a symptom of a lack of unity within the self.[18]

True, the Socratic explanation focuses on knowledge, skill, and the 'art of measurement', but it also has a second key element, which is an emphasis on diachronicity. Evaluation of a performance does not only occur when we form an intention and deliberate on it. We need to resist reading the action as a mental event, ie intention, belief, or desire, which precedes and causes the bodily movements. Within this model, we conceptualize the latter as effects, which occur in the world independently of our mental events. Once I initiate an action, it becomes solely a matter of determining its effects and outcomes.

[17] Plato (n 6) 356e8–357a1.

[18] Christopher Shield, 'Unified Agency and Akrasia in Plato's Republic' in Christopher Bobonich and Pierre Destrée (eds), *Akrasia in Greek Philosophy: From Socrates to Plotinus* (Brill 2007) 61.

Secondly, the Socratic diachronic understanding of action focuses on the thinking and deliberative exercise of weighing prior to the execution of the action. But the act of thinking projects itself beyond the simple world of effects and facts and beyond the particular result and its respective appearance. It invites us to think about our actions and results beyond the present moment of execution. The question, 'What shall I do in light of my knowledge of pleasure and pain?' prompts Beatrice to contemplate and balance her various beliefs and desires. This is why, arguably, Socrates rejects *akrasia*, as it only conceptualizes action in its synchronic dimension. *Akratic* action is located at a particular time, confined to the facts and appearances that randomly strike the agent. By contrast, knowledge as the 'art of measurement' is essentially diachronic.[19] As a result, knowledge neutralizes passions, and the agent gains her rational structure in acting.

A third key element is that for Socrates, the problem lies not in the thing to obtain or action to perform but in the *agent's perspective*. A correct perspective is a stance on the truth that empowers the agent to destroy appearances. Furthermore, for the agent who possesses moral knowledge, strong irrational pleasures and desires do not compel belief.[20] According to Socrates, it is key that the agent can recognize their own attitude towards knowledge. In the last chapter of this book, we explore this idea further.

Aristotle agrees with Socrates that desires and emotions cannot bend knowledge. However, Aristotle believes that *akrasia* is not an absurd and incoherent phenomenon.[21] He proposes a refinement of the Socratic proposal, establishing that knowledge is not sufficient and considerations of character and development are key. Aristotle's explanation is complex and focuses on three different kinds of character, ie self-indulgent (*akolastos*), weak (*akratic*), and self-controlled (*enkratic*). The *akolastos* engages in vicious acts and develops a character that pursues excesses in pleasure. They are self-indulgent out of principle rather than being weak. Their conception of what is pleasant is mistaken. The *akolastos* does not understand the good of each activity and concentrates on their own pleasures.[22] In contrast to the *akrates*, whose moral choices and deliberations (*prohairesis*) are sound,[23] the *akolastos* does not preserve their moral knowledge.[24] The *akratic* individual deliberates correctly and makes a rational choice, but acts contrary to their own deliberations and rational choice. Ultimately, the *enkratic* individual correctly deliberates

[19] Christopher Bobonich, 'Plato and Akrasia and Knowing Our Own Mind' in Christopher Bobonich and Pierre Destrée (eds), *Akrasia in Greek Philosophy: From Socrates to Plotinus* (Brill 2007) 41.

[20] Thomas Brickhouse and Nicholas Smith, 'Socrates on Akrasia' in Christopher Bobonich and Pierre Destrée (eds), *Akrasia in Greek Philosophy: From Socrates to Plotinus* (Brill 2007) 1.

[21] Aristotle categorically rejected Socrates' denial of *akrasia* and suggested it is a phenomenon of our lives. 'To say this is to say something at odds with what patently appears the case.' Aristotle (n 16) 1145b27–28. However, he agrees with Socrates that *akrasia* is lack of knowledge. ibid 1147b13–17.

[22] Aristotle (n 16) 1117b22–1119b18. See also Rorty (n 12) 272.

[23] Aristotle (n 16) 1152a15–17.

[24] ibid 1151a11–25. The *akrates* acts against her own choice and deliberation (*prohairesis*). She is not twisted. ibid 1246b12–15.

and makes a rational choice when attempting to settle an answer to the question, 'What shall I do?' Although they are attracted by vicious or less good or pleasant choices they are able to resist them.[25] A correct understanding of the process of practical reasoning of the *enkratic* is key because it shows that the knowledge that shields us from error and saves our lives is neither theoretical or epistemic knowledge nor ethical strength but reflects thinking about the subject matter, the transformation of desires and emotions, and an attempt to inhabit the deliberative-aspirational perspective.[26]

Although these types of characters are ideal, there are nuanced and borderline cases, as well as plenty of room for impurity and mixed cases.[27] In addition to these three types of characters, we also have the woman and man of virtue, who are also referred to as *phronimos*. She or he (a) engages in an action with the knowledge of *what* and *how* they are doing what they are doing, (b) does the action for its own sake,[28] and (c) possesses a stable character. Arguably, only the *phronimos* has a stable character and the actions of the less-than-*phronimos* type probably oscillate between the self-indulgent, *akratic*, and *enkratic*.[29]

[25] ibid 1151b30–35.

[26] Dorion has argued that *enkrateia* or self-control concerning appetites and pleasures in Plato's Socrates and Xenophone's Socrates in *Memorabilia* is not proper knowledge nor the making of thought as the standard measure, which is *sophrosuné* (*temperance*), but rather what enables the development of virtue and knowledge. However, he argues that Plato has not much interest in *enkrateia* as prior to the *Republic* the term does not occur. Dorion gives this as evidence of Plato's and Socrates' denial of *akrasia*. Affirming *akrasia* entails the affirmation that knowledge is not sufficient and necessary for virtue, and, therefore, that we need something else if we want to master ourselves and control our pleasures and passions. Louis-André Dorion, 'Plato and Enkrateia' in Christopher Bobonich and Pierre Destrée (eds), *Akrasia in Greek Philosophy: From Socrates to Plotinus* (Brill 2007) 119, 123–26. The Aristotelian position seems very different. For example, Aristotle in the *Eudemian Ethics* states that *enkrateia* is a virtue. Aristotle, *Eudemian Ethics* (tr Harris Rackham, Harvard UP, Loeb Classical Library 1989) 1223b12. For a discussion on the Aristotelian position, see Agnes Callard, 'The Enkrates Phronimos' (2017) 99 Archiv für Geschichte der Philosophie 31 and Carol Gould, 'A Puzzle About the Possibility of Aristotelian Enkrateia' (1994) 39 Phronesis 174. Gould emphasizes that for Aristotle the *enkratic* is the cure for *akrasia* and that the *enkratic* is in a developmental stage in her journey towards a virtuous life.

[27] Callard, The Enkrates Phronimos' (n 26).

[28] This implies that the agent's description of the action encompasses what she performs and forms the essence of the action itself. For example, if I say that I play the piano for its own sake, the act of playing serves to explain my actions. On the other hand, if I take a spoon and someone asks me what I'm doing, and I respond, 'I'm adding sugar to my tea to drink it', then my action of taking the spoon is not for its own sake. Therefore, when we consider *eudaimonia* as the ultimate goal, we don't view it as something external that requires promotion. McDowell criticizes Irwin for interpreting *eudaimonia* as something external that we need to 'promote'. McDowell puts this as follows: 'Talking of actions as promoting *eudaimonia* precludes taking with the proper seriousness Aristotle's insistence that *eudaimonia* is the doings (undertaken for their own sake) that make up the good life, not some further aim that one who lives the good life has in view.' John McDowell, 'Comments on Irwin's "Some Rational Aspects of Incontinence"' (1989) 27 The Southern Journal of Philosophy 49, 91. See also Terence Irwin, 'Some Rational Aspects of Incontinence' (1988) 27 The Southern Journal of Philosophy 49.

[29] Aristotle tells us that the *akratic* does not have practical wisdom. Aristotle (n 16) 1152a16–17. Despite his ability to deliberate and make correct choices, he fails to act accordingly, as the acquisition of *phronesis* is contingent upon virtue. ibid 1144a20–b1.

According to Aristotle, there is a process of learning to become good for both the *akratic* and the *enkratic*, which is the key issue.[30] However, within our Aristotelian-inspired model of deliberation, this process does not depend on knowledge of the 'art of measurement', as Socrates proposes. It depends on our thinking about the subject matter, our character development, and the transformation of our desires, as they will determine our 'seeing' and perspective of what is good, pleasant, right, evil, or vicious. To put the point in a different way, the knowledge that shields us from acting in error is not only the kind of knowledge that is obtained through thinking, ie deliberation and rational choice, but is the alignment of our non-rational part, ie desires and emotions, with deliberation and rational choice. We need to explain how emotions and desires develop and interact with our deliberation and rational choice, as well as how they are able to *integrate* with our rational choice. The Aristotelian insight also invites us to recognize that there is agency in transition towards the virtuous agent or *phronimos* type of character. Thus, understanding the *enkratic* is key to this explanation.

In order to explain *akrasia*, Aristotle uses the notion of 'practical syllogism'. Interpreters of Aristotle's *Nichomachean Ethics* advance three different explanations concerning what goes wrong with the *akratic*'s practical reasoning via her practical syllogism. These explanations are:

1) The *akratic* recognizes the major premise of the practical syllogism, which establishes a good or an end but fails to identify the minor premise.[31] This is interpreted in different ways. For example, according to Rorty,[32] we forget what kind of person we are. The sources of initial pleasure are in the body, but there are also other goods such as wealth, victory, and honour, and the

[30] Myles Burnyeat, 'Aristotle on Learning to be Good' in Amélie Rorty (ed), *Essays on Aristotle's Ethics* (University of California Press 1980) 69.

[31] Aristotle (n 16) 1147a31–b17. She does not possess knowledge of the particular premise. ibid 1146b35–1147a10.

[32] Rorty (n 12) 273. Note that Rorty's interpretation adds to the minor premise the following explanation: in the minor premise, one forgets who one is. Character is embedded in one's ends. Let us think about our example of Alessandra, who leaves her dog locked in her vehicle on a hot day and it subsequently dies. The major premise will be something along the following lines: 'Some people make mistakes when they are in a rush.' The minor premise will be 'I am the kind of person who makes mistakes when I am in a rush'; the conclusion will be 'I should be more careful when I am in a rush'. But Rorty moves quickly out of the purely somatic account to advocate a 'capacity' view: 'Even when moved by pleasures they (akratics) react rather than act, they actively have all the traits and capacity that could have led them to act otherwise (NE 1113b3–1115a6)'. Rorty (n 12) 280. And then she adds: 'But if one is the sort of person whose character is capable of self-determination, then one is responsible for having the sort of character one develops, because one has, by hypothesis, the sorts of traits that can determine the ends one adopts and how one acts from them.' Rorty (this note) 280. Rorty's initial explanation is more somatic, focusing on the relationship between pain and pleasure. She surmises and accepts that, for Aristotle, the problem has an intellectual dimension, as Socrates aims to demonstrate. However, she disagrees with Socrates, arguing that *akrasia* is not an intellectual error. Rorty (this note) 281. Consequently, a 'capacity' view seems to be a compromise between somatic and intellectual interpretations. For further developments of the 'capacity' view, see Chapter 8.

pleasures change according to the intentional description.[33] One can mislead a person to derive pleasure from an inappropriate aspect of the activity. Rorty concludes that the *akratic* acts are based on her reactions and emphasizes the need for self-knowledge to prevent this, while also reminding us that Socrates failed to remember the pleasures.[34] For other authors, the *akratic* substitutes the minor premise[35] with a permissive premise that reflects her conception of what is pleasant but not what is good.[36] Thus, following the Aristotelian example, the major premise is as follows: 'All tasting of sweets is forbidden', and the minor premise is 'This is sweet'. The conclusion is specific and action-oriented, yet the *akratic* fails to act in accordance with it. This is because, according to this interpretation, they replace the minor premise with a combined premise that includes a permissive proposition. Therefore, the *akratic*'s minor premise would be a combined one as follows: 'Everything sweet is pleasant, and this is sweet'. The *akratic*'s strong appetite causes changes in her deliberations. As a result, she inadvertently introduces a permissible premise that contradicts the main premise. The permissible premise is an opinion about what is pleasant, not about what is good.[37] According to this interpretation, the *akratic* fails to 'see' the good on this particular occasion. The major premise represents the conception of the good.

However, practical reason does revolve around mere propositions. I have tried to argue that this way of thinking is confusing because who I am will be shaped by how I deliberate. Presenting practical reason and deliberation to the agent as a practical syllogism maintains the integrity of the major premise containing the principles or universals.[38] This presupposes the 'grand end' view, which we have challenged because it cannot be the basis for practical reasoning and deliberation. In Chapter 4, I show that the 'grand end' view assumes that we have clarity on the features that constitute our ends and that there is no transformation of our desires. The practical syllogism is only a

[33] Aristotle (n 16) 1173b25–1174a1.

[34] Rorty (n 12) 278.

[35] Some commentators also criticize the understanding of *akrasia* in terms of practical syllogism because they claim that *protasis* should not be translated as a premise. Thus, Aristotle does not talk about propositions. Jennifer Whitting, 'Human Nature and Intellectualism in Aristotle' (1986) 68 Archiv für Geschichte der Philosophie 70.

[36] Aristotle (n 16) 1147a26–32. A potential interpretation of this passage is that there are two different syllogisms; the syllogism of desire and the syllogism of reason. ibid 1147a32. The *akratic* has formed a good syllogism (ibid 1147a25–28) but follows the bad syllogism based on desire or appetite. ibid 1142b18–20.

[37] See Walsh (n 1) 106–12.

[38] See eg Irwin, 'Some Rational Aspects of Incontinence' (n 28) 53, who considers that 'the inferential process described in the practical syllogism (1147a25–31) must be part of the process of deliberation'. See also Price, who argues that the seeking in deliberation involves establishing a deduction between means and ends. Anthony Price, 'The Practical Syllogism: A New Interpretation' (2008) 11 History of Philosophy and Logical Analysis 151.

snapshot of one point in the deliberation and does not explain the complex and rich process of both narrow and medium- and long-term deliberation.

2) The *akratic* knows the major premise and the minor premise, but fails to combine both. Instead of being ignorant of the particular premise, the *akratic* commits a logical error when they fail to integrate the universal with the particular. This interpretation relies on a comparison between *Nichomachean Ethics* and the *Analytica Posteriora* (71a21).[39] Joachim asserts that the incontinent desire suppresses the prohibition or universal premise and substitutes the knowledge of this particular case.[40] In other words, the *akrates* fails in his task of *combining* the major and minor premises of the practical syllogism.
3) The *akratic* cannot arrive at the correct conclusion of the practical syllogism.[41] This would depend on a reinterpretation of the practical syllogism, as well as whether the conclusion of the practical syllogism is the action itself.[42] Charles has attempted to demonstrate that the practical syllogism's conclusion is not an action but a proposition, and that the *akratic* fails to act according to the correct conclusion, which is a normative statement.[43] This view presupposes a gap between judgement and choice. The negative effect of pleasure is an empirical cause, acting as an impediment. There is no ignorance or intellectual error in this model. Although the agent has reasoned correctly, pleasure impedes the action and, consequently, the execution of the deliberated actions.

Hardie rejects the view that practical syllogism is equivalent to deliberation and argues that it refers to a rule that applies in particular circumstances.[44] However, he also insists that Aristotle's explanation of *akrasia* in terms of practical syllogism and in terms of pleasures and carnal temptation is a poor approximation to the complexity of our lives; 'these appetites rarely operate alone; the threat to virtue comes not so much from their intensity as from their fusion with more subtle satisfactions'.[45]

We should note that all interpretations of how the practical syllogism explains *akrasia* face challenges.[46] Furthermore, if the practical syllogism interprets the loss

[39] Saarinen attributes this interpretation to Averroes. Risto Saarinen, 'Walter Burley on *Akrasia*: Second Thoughts' (1999) 37 Vivarium 60, 65, fn 23.

[40] Harold Joachim, *Aristotle, The Nichomachean Ethics, A Commentary* (Clarendon Press 1951) 224–28.

[41] Charles (n 1) 117–21. cf Aristotle (n 16) 1146b35–1147a10, 1147a24–31. These passages refer to action as the conclusion of the practical syllogism.

[42] ibid 1147a25–30. See also Kenny (n 1).

[43] Charles (n 1) 113, 148. See also Jonathan Dancy, *Practical Shape: A Theory of Practical Reasoning* (OUP 2018).

[44] William FR Hardie, *Aristotle's Ethical Theory* (originally printed in 1968, Clarendon Press 2004) 225–28. See Segvic, who sees it as a third-person attribute. Segvic (n 3). See also Chapter 5.

[45] Hardie (n 44) 261.

[46] Bradley (n 1) 90.

of understanding as a desire-induced loss of the particular premise, it becomes unclear how to differentiate between compulsion and *akrasia*. Austin charges Aristotle with a confusing loss of control and succumbing to temptation.[47] The latter characterizes the *akratic*. Let us also remind ourselves that Watson[48] has similarly argued that if desires undermine practical reasoning due to the force of desire, then the distinction between *akrasia* and compulsion is unclear. Compulsion is more physiological, whereas desire, represented as something that just happens to us, is passive and physiological. The idea that the *akratic* loses knowledge, the knowledge of the particular premise, due to her desires does not shed light on the distinction between the compulsive and *akratic* agent and why the latter is within the domain of responsible agency.

Aristotle's distinction between *use and knowledge*[49] might shed light on how *akrasia* operates. Rorty,[50] for example, asserts that the distinction between active and unused knowledge reflects the position of the *akratic*. The *akratic* finds herself in a situation where she cannot use her knowledge. These, however, are *simple re-descriptions of the phenomena* without any further explanation. They constitute the primary material that enables us to fully explain *akrasia*, but we also need to use Aristotle's conception of deliberation and practical reason to completely illuminate *akrasia*. Therefore, we need to scrutinize the phenomenology of *akrasia* in light of the results obtained in Chapters 3, 4, and 5, where I propose an Aristotelian-inspired model of practical reasoning.

Arguably, the potentiality/actuality distinction[51] does little to illuminate *akrasia* and tends to obscure our understanding of the development of desires and emotions, as well as the way deliberation operates. If the *akratic* has 'knowledge' of what she should do in a particular circumstance but does not use it, then it means she has not deliberated correctly, or so I will try to argue.[52] In other words, we can say

[47] John Austin, 'A Plea for Excuses' in John L Austin, Geoffrey J Warnock, and James O Urmson (eds), *Philosophical Papers* (OUP 1979) 175, 198.

[48] Watson (n 10).

[49] Aristotle (n 16) 1146b31–35. Interestingly, Broadie asserts that Aristotle uses standard examples of theoretical knowledge to shed light on the distinction between 'merely having' and 'having and using one's knowledge'. It does not mean that the theorist has all the principles clearly in front of her; rather, when she uses her knowledge, she only undertakes 'an endeavour to explore or understand further by means of them or to uncover underlying principles. But the practical equivalent of the scientist's appropriate use of scientific knowledge is appropriate use of practical knowledge; and this is not holding it clearly in mind, but acting in accordance with it.' Broadie (n 4) 296.

[50] Rorty (n 12).

[51] Pickavé and Whiting elucidate the concepts of first and second potentiality in the context of possessing and utilizing knowledge. Martin Pickavé and Jennifer Whiting, 'Nichomachean Ethics 7.3 on Akratic Ignorance' in David Sedley (ed), *Oxford Studies in Ancient Philosophy* (OUP 2008) 323.

[52] Broadie seems to agree with this view. 'Aristotle recognises him (the akratic) first, comparing his state to madness and drunkenness (1147a10–16) and then notes other possibilities. What we have been calling "clearheadness", Aristotle sees in terms of being able to say what one is supposed to do: "The fact that men use the language that flows from language proves nothing [i.e., it does not prove that they are not ignorant]" (1147a18–19). He is not claiming that the agent can utter the words as meaningless noises (what would be the point of that claim?) but that the saying does not express what it should, i.e.,

that she has *potential* knowledge of what she should do but not *actual* knowledge as she does not use it. This means that she has not truly brought the *how* closer to the *what*. If we go back to our example of Beatrice, we will say, in light of the knowledge/use distinction, that after deliberating on the physical health of her daughter, Beatrice should register her daughter in gymnastic lessons. If she had deliberated correctly, she would have brought the *how* closer to the *what* and would have also transformed her initial desire for her daughter's physical health to a closer specification, ie harmony of body and soul.[53]

We also stated that this transformation encompasses the entire self.[54] But how can we now assert that the agent possesses the 'knowledge' of what she should do, but is unable to 'use' this knowledge? One possibility is to say that Beatrice only contemplated the choices, for example registering her daughter in different activities to achieve physical health, *without truly thinking about* the *how*, or, in other words, without actually engaging her desires and transforming them. We could compare this to purely theoretical thinking, akin to aesthetic contemplation. Consider observing the elegance of a geometric shape on a whiteboard. It does not lead to any action. However, this would mean Beatrice's practical reason was irrelevant. This cannot explain *akrasia*. In the phenomenon of *akrasia*, the agent deliberates and therefore actually engages in practical reasoning; her thoughts look at the particularity of her actions with the purpose of acting. However, the *akratic* deliberator fails to execute her deliberation. If we are saying that this is due to the deliberator having knowledge but not using it, it would be like saying that she contemplates the issue but fails to 'apply' her knowledge. If our Aristotelian-inspired model of deliberation is sound, this would not be possible. Practical reason as constituted by deliberation requires seeing the *what* through the *how* and transforming our initial desires for what appears good, valuable, right, or pleasant. In a nutshell, it is argued the *akratic*'s failure stems from her inability to sufficiently transform herself, encompassing her emotions, desires, and passions, thereby preventing her from embracing the deliberative-aspirational perspective. Desires, passions, and emotions do undergo transformation, but not to the required standard of excellence that allows the deliberator to inhabit the deliberative-aspirational standpoint.

the actively serious purpose, which is the grasp of practical truth. This incontinent is like the student who can tell you that Plato's Theory of the Forms leads to an infinite regress but without being able to explain why. It is not that the incontinent does not understand what he knows, but that he and the philosophy student alike fall short of the goals of reason, practical and theoretical respectively. Aristotle also makes a comparison with actors speaking their lines. He may have in mind the sort of case where what the incontinent person knows he should do seems to have no connection with *him*.' Broadie (n 4) 296.

[53] See Chapter 4.

[54] Aristotle states that attaining truth at the practical level is a task for the intellect but also involves *right desire*. Aristotle (n 16) 1139a29–31. Virtues act in cooperation with reason. ibid 1152a15–17.

§6.3 The Contemporary Conception of *Akrasia*

The contemporary conception of *akrasia* differs substantially from the ancient and medieval conception. Davidson[55] believes that Aquinas got it wrong and advances the view that *akrasia* is present when the deliberator has given less than sincere assent. Many authors praise Davidson for managing to separate the question of the weakness of the will from morality. Others aim to vindicate the importance of moral assessment in better understanding *akrasia*. They contend that the narrow definition of the problem obscures the phenomenon of character and evaluative assessment.[56]

If Davidson is right and *akrasia* simply refers to a less than sincere assent,[57] meaning that the *akratic* engages with a *prima facie* judgement or conditional judgement of what is best, all things considered, but acts based on what she thinks is best on the basis of her unconditional judgement, then two issues arise. First, it would be irrational and unjustifiable for the *akratic* to feel regret or shame upon performing the action and either realizing, or not realizing, the result of her performance. It would be puzzling to explain why the driver feels regret in our previous example. If there were no consequences and the driver avoided hitting another car, an agent might feel ashamed about how she drove home drunk.

In Chapter 1, I also explained the 'aspect dawning' of agents who act negligently and therefore *akratically*. In our example from Chapter 1, Alessandra left her dog in her vehicle and went to collect her children at the hockey pitch. The children argued, and it took her longer than expected to return to her vehicle. As a result, her dog died of heat stroke. When she initially left the dog in the vehicle, she did not 'see' or 'foresee' what would happen; it was only after her return that her action 'dawned on her'. She could 'see' what *she* had caused.

When we act based on our unconditional judgement the results of our acting *do not* dawn on us. Because the action is an unconditional judgement, we know what we are doing. One could object to the fact that I am begging the question. This chapter aims to show that *akrasia* is the underpinning structure that explains inadvertent or negligent action, but using this example as a counterfactual to Davidson's explanation of *akrasia* is question-begging.

I need to provide a paradigmatic example of *akrasia* and see whether Davidson's explanation is satisfactory. Let us think about the following example. An agent has decided to go on a diet and not to eat chocolates; after a long day of work, however,

[55] Donald Davidson, 'How is Weakness of the Will Possible?' in *Essays on Actions and Events* (first published in 1969, Clarendon Press 2001) 21.

[56] Thomas Hill, 'Weakness of Will and Character' (1986) 14 Philosophical Topics 93, 94.

[57] Davidson narrows the problem of *akrasia* to a problem of 'belief'. If Davidson is saying that diachronic belief *akrasia* is possible and that what occurs in the *akratic* is merely a switch in beliefs, then this is not the issue that arises in Plato's *Protagoras*. Aristotle poses the Socratic issue as knowledge, insisting that the degree of conviction has no bearing on *akrasia*. Aristotle (n 16) 1145b36–1146a4, 1146a35–b5. See also Bobonich (n 19).

she walks by a shop and decides to buy chocolates contrary to her all-things-considered judgement. Davidson would explain the example as follows. The agent formulated a conditional judgement that, all things considered, she will not eat chocolates; however, as she passes the shop, she changes her mind and judges that it would be better if, on this particular occasion, she eats some chocolates. Davidson cannot explain why the agent, after eating the chocolate, feels regret. Similarly, both Alessandra and the driver will feel experience feelings of shame and regret, and their actions 'dawn' on them, yet Davidson fails to provide an explanation for this crucial aspect of the phenomenology of *akrasia*.

Secondly, we could say that the Davidsonian account of *akrasia* is false if the bifurcation account and its corollary are also false. These ideas involve seeing deliberation as a 'balancing' process in which the agent faces a number of choices.[58] However, as we have demonstrated, it is not conceivable that an agent is able to see all the reasons for her actions in a determined or certain and clear way, and her only task is simply to choose the ones that she judges 'best'.[59]

The Davidsonian approach's legacy has further obscured the way we understand what Aristotle calls 'inverse *akrasia*'[60] In 'inverse *akrasia*', the agent acts against her initial wrong evaluative judgement, and the result is a good or right action. In contrast to *akrasia*, inverse *akrasia* is ethically praiseworthy. The issue of 'inverse *akrasia*' underscores the possibility of separating rationality and ethical praiseworthiness. However, Aristotle warns us that we should not confuse this case with *akrasia*. In *akrasia*, as described by Aristotle, the agent acts against her correct deliberation and rational decision—*prohairesis*. Arpaly[61] argues, however, that the case of Huck Finn shows that we can act against our best judgement, though it might be a wrong judgement, and the consequence of the act will be ethically right or good. In *The Adventures of Huckleberry Finn* by Mark Twain, the character Huck deliberates and decides to turn Jim in. It is his best judgement. '*But along comes a perfect opportunity for him to turn Jim in, and he finds himself psychologically unable to do it. He accuses himself to be a weak-willed boy, who has not the "spunk of a rabbit" and cannot bring himself to do the right thing, and eventually shrugs and decides to remain a bad boy*'.[62] Arpaly argues that Huck is morally praiseworthy and tells us that he has experienced a shift in his perception.[63] Despite his deliberate or official racism, his visceral experience contradicts his conscious stance. Arpaly

[58] See Chapter 3.

[59] Davidson's account also contradicts Aristotle's position in the *Nichomachean Ethics* that an opinion can be as firm as knowledge. Aristotle (n 16) 1145b32–1146a4, 1146b24–30. How can there be less of a sincere assent to a moral principle? The modern view seems to emphasize a kind of irresolution in which one cannot make up one's mind. See Richard Holton, *Willing, Wanting and Waiting* (OUP 2009). But this is not the core of Aristotle's concern for *akrasia*. In *akrasia*, the puzzle lies in the agent's deliberate and knowledge-based actions, which become blurred at the moment of action.

[60] Aristotle (n 16) 1146a18–22; 1151b17–23.

[61] Naomi Arpaly, *Unprincipled Virtue* (OUP 2003) 75–79.

[62] ibid 75–76.

[63] ibid 76.

maintains that Huck's interactions with Jim provide him with evidence that Jim is a person, yet he does not *reflect on these facts*. She asserts that this could be due to a 'non conscious awareness' that remains unconscious,[64] despite of plenty of awareness of the ostensibly correct actions; when Huck behaves morally and chooses not to turn Jim in, these reasons are 'not even in his head'.[65] There is no correlation between the motivations behind Huck's actions and the positive aspects of them.

Arpaly's reasoning reflects the Davidsonian legacy. If the weakness of the will is related to beliefs and potential conflicts between them, and since it is unclear how our beliefs can track our values or right desires, we can separate our rationality, thinking, and what is good or virtuous. However, Arpaly does not arrive at the Davidsonian conclusion that Huck acts based on his unconditional judgement, as she believes that Huck lacks conscious awareness of his reasons for actions. Arpaly's reasoning is under the spell of the bifurcation model. On the one hand, we have reasons for action, and on the other, desires emerge through experiences (eg Huck's interactions with Jim), but desires and beliefs *do not* interact. Non-conscious experiences persist, and they do not align with our thinking or intelligence. This is a mistaken conception of practical reasoning; it is too easy to think that Huck's action happens because there is an obscure angle, non-conscious experiences, or a *locus* that escapes our reasoning, and that this mechanism explains weak-will.[66]

The agent's thinking about desires and passions in particular cases, as well as the possibility of inhabiting a deliberative-aspirational perspective, sheds light on how *akrasia* operates. In the case of Jim, as with Murdoch's mother-in-law, we can conclude that Huck's experiences and interactions with him are thought-dependent. Huck is trying to learn how to think about Jim and whether, say, Jim's superstitions are similar to his own. He can either recognize or avoid giving Jim personhood. When Huck does not turn him in, he places Jim in this space of personhood, but there is no need for an abstract or conscious formulation; it suffices to say that he did so because he recognizes Jim as a person. Huck, as a learner, may not be able to formulate it right away, but if he continues to acquire the right desires and perform the right actions, he will be able to formulate why he did not turn Jim in. My point is that there is no *locus* for a non-conscious domain that remains obscure or unknown to us. On the contrary, our actions are the result of our transformations and, more specifically, *the transformation of our perspectives*. There is no mysterious place or mystical realm where our thoughts hide; there are no private or non-conscious thoughts as mental occurrences.[67]

64 ibid 77.
65 ibid.
66 See Chapter 8.
67 See Chapter 5.

Hare also proposes a deflationary conception. *Akrasia*, Hare tells us, is not a matter of ignorance or knowledge but of a lack of sincerity. He cannot distinguish between the weak-minded and the *akratic*. Hare asserts that engaging in evaluative judgements compels one to act, as normative judgements entail an 'ought', and it appears impossible to act against one's evaluative judgements.[68]

Holton[69] believes that the phenomenon of *akrasia* is just a matter of changing our resolutions. Thus, there is no failure of performance or practical reasoning. Holton's conception of *akrasia* also fails to explain regret. Williams[70] also believes that *akrasia* should be interpreted as a resolution because of the problem of evaluation, but not because it is intrinsically a resolution.[71]

Holton and Davidson construct *akrasia* as closer to theoretical knowledge, overlooking the complexity of practical reason.

§6.4 *Akrasia* as a Failure to Transform and Integrate Desires, Emotions, and Thinking Towards the Aspirational-Deliberative Perspective

In the contemporary account of *akrasia*, the control part of the action occurs during the formation of the intention or deliberation. Contemporary scholars overlook the diachronicity of action, the temporality of deliberation, and the progress of actions. This diachronicity is the key to recognizing that the agent, in her deliberations, is trying to give an answer to the question, 'What shall I do?' She undergoes transformations and is a learner. Consequently, some of these transformations are uneven and defective, while others are successful due to her adoption of the deliberative-aspirational perspective. But while she is learning, her error is 'not here', 'not there', but rather *in the entire process*.

Contemporary conceptions of negligence, both in law and ethics, mirror this conception of agency, in which everything happens at a specific *locus* and at a specific time. What the agent controls happens before the performance. We assert that the agent should have known or foreseen it. Our assumption is that the agent 'should have' or 'could have' identified her performance error at a specific time. This question of how knowledge of the *akratic* has come to be absent[72] invites us to look for a specific *locus* or *time* when the error is identifiable and isolated. When

[68] Richard Hare, *The Language of Morals* (Clarendon Press 1952); Richard Hare, 'Weakness of Will' in Lawrence Becker and Charlotte Becker (eds), *The Encyclopaedia of Ethics* (Routledge 2001) 1789.

[69] Holton (n 59).

[70] Bernard Williams, 'Voluntary Acts and Responsible Agents' in *Making Sense of Humanity* (CUP 1995) 22–34, 24.

[71] Segvic (n 3). She emphasizes that changes of belief or judgement are not what Socrates is after, as named *akrasia* in the *Protagoras*. *Prohairesis* is, she tells us, a firm practical commitment, and the *akratic* acts against it. Segvic (this note) 71–72, 72, fn 33.

[72] WD Ross, *Aristotle* (Routledge 1949) 140.

Aristotle tells us that *akrasia* is more like Empedocles' speech, where we can utter words without full understanding,[73] or a drunkard or someone falling sleep,[74] we succumb to the intellectual temptation of searching for a *specific* locus *or psychological event* that formed this state, attempting to trace the initial choice that caused this state or occurrence.

Other interpreters of Aristotle's *Nichomachean Ethics* ask whether *akrasia* is more like relaxing one's grip on a golf club when told not to do so.[75] Listening to this metaphor, we are tempted to look for the mechanism that caused the loss of grip.[76] Other interpretations present *akrasia* as a *locus* of error, eg lack of awareness or attention.[77] However, I argue that there is no mechanism, *locus*, or specific psychological event whose absence or presence explains *akrasia. Akrasia* is a process of learning through deliberation, experiences, thinking about the subject matter, and inhabiting perspectives. This is the underpinning phenomenon of negligence or inadvertence in action. *Lack of awareness and/or attention, or awareness and attention, are symptoms of either failure or excellence in this process, respectively.* Furthermore, the *akratic* act and, therefore, the negligent act manifest conflict, which is revealed in feelings such as shame and regret, ie the *akratic* regrets what she has done[78] and feels shame precisely because her ethical development is uneven and her errors in action and performance make her aware of it.

The question that emerges is why the *akratic* agent did not take action, even though she had access to relevant knowledge. Thus far, we have established that access to this knowledge occurs through deliberation and the adoption of a deliberative-aspirational perspective. Chapter 9 will focus on how this knowledge, in the context of negligence law, is accessible to the agent who performs a negligent or inadvertent act.

Contemporary conceptions of *akrasia* dissolve the Socratic question, ie whether thinking (*logos*) can determine good or right action, as well as the role of desire and perspective. The question of good or right connected to action is dissolved and only deflationary conceptions, focusing on the epistemic condition, are emphasized.[79]

The problem of knowledge and ignorance in the practical realm, including practical reason as constituted by deliberation, involves a question about the perspectives that are present. The agent's perspectives from a first-person deliberative stance are multiple, potentially embracing a deliberative-aspirational perspective. In addition, the process of deliberation and inhabiting perspectives involves and

[73] Aristotle (n 16) 1147a20.

[74] ibid 1147a12–15.

[75] William Hardie, 'Aristotle on Moral Weakness' in GW Mortimore (ed), *Weakness of Will* (Macmillan 1971) 69, 94.

[76] See Chapter 8 for a criticism of this way of thinking about *akrasia.*

[77] Segvic (n 3) 69.

[78] Aristotle (n 16) 1150b28–30.

[79] This perspective views the question of ignorance as solely epistemic. For recent discussions, see Phillip Robichaud and Jan Willem Wieland, *Responsibility: The Epistemic Condition* (OUP 2017).

transforms the entire self, ie not only cognitive abilities but also desires and emotions. As a result, the question of desire's strength or weakness cannot be asked in isolation from the question of engagement with deliberation and inhabiting of multiple perspectives.

We can summarize by saying that there are three explanations for *akrasia* in ancient and modern conceptions of agency. One explanation presents *akrasia* as a struggle in which regret plays a crucial role. This struggle is represented in an analysis of the deliberator's practical syllogism. Thus, the *akratic* understands the major premise that provides the universal or general principle of action, but she fails to grasp the particular premise that characterizes her current situation. She allows herself to be temporarily led by temptation or passion and succumbs to a permissible premise that substitutes the general principle or the universal premise of action. For example, the agent knows that she should not be kissing her neighbour's husband or being unfaithful to her husband. However, when she is alone at home and her neighbour pays her a visit, she lets the permissible premise 'to kiss a man is pleasant' as opposed to 'one should not be unfaithful' play the guiding role in her action. This view respects the phenomenological feature of the *akrates* as a struggle. However, Davidson's explanation of *akrasia* minimizes this conflict or struggle, leading to a deflation of this key element. For Davidson, the agent advances a conditional judgement and, therefore, she has not really decided what to do yet. In the example above, she only asserts 'I should not be with this man, who is my neighbour's husband, all things considered'. But this judgement is not her actual judgement, it is only a *prima facie* judgement. When she acts and kisses her neighbour's husband, her actual reasoning has been something along the following lines: 'I prefer to kiss my neighbour's husband than to sit and watch TV'. Therefore, there is no conflict between her *prima facie* and actual judgement. What Davidson ignores, as MacIntyre emphasizes, is the nature of our struggle,[80] ie the fact that both judgements occur within a period of time. Both my model and the voluntarist conception focus on revision and the struggle of becoming, including the transformational process to inhabit the deliberative-aspirational perspective. However, I reject the voluntarist view that attributes this task to 'the will' (see Chapter 8 for my criticism of voluntarism). Rather, my focus is on perspectives and on how our perspectives change through knowledge and its interaction with our desires and passions.

The agent's practical syllogism represents a diagnosis that explains a lack of knowledge in various ways. However, this approach closely follows the Aristotelian

[80] MacIntyre argues that Davidson ignores the temporal aspect of practical reasoning, where struggles, doubts, and revision are part of the process of deciding what one ought to do. Thus, for MacIntyre, Davidson's criticism of Aquinas misses the entire point of the struggle in practical reasoning, where we are in dialogue with ourselves. This struggle is a key feature of Aquinas's and Aristotle's models of deliberation. See MacIntyre (n 14) 289. Furthermore, MacIntyre also emphasizes, rightly in my view, the necessary dialogue with others. MacIntyre (this note) 290. See also Chapter 5.

explanation of practical syllogism, to the detriment of understanding the *akratic* in the context of Aristotle's explanation of deliberation and character development.

Finally, our own explanation shows the importance of the deliberative process, including the role of desires and emotions. We have advanced the view that deliberation operates within perspectives, specifically the deliberative-aspirational perspective, to shed light on where the *akratic* agent makes errors.

Our account does not embrace the view that there is a gap between deliberation and execution because the former is already involved in execution via transforming desires and emotions. If the agent engages in sound deliberation at both levels—immersed deliberation and inhabiting the deliberative-aspirational perspective—sound performance is in continuity with thought, the right desires, and emotions. It is, nevertheless, a continuous process of self-transformation towards inhabiting the deliberative-aspirational perspective of the particular action.

In contrast, the view that *akrasia* stems from a 'struggle of the will' or a lack of knowledge within an Aristotelian understanding of practical syllogism, which makes subtle distinctions between: using knowledge and 'having' knowledge; a lack of perception or a lack of sound perception of particulars; and between knowledge of the general without the particular, knowledge of the particular without knowledge of the general, or the failure to merge the general and the particular at the moment of judgement, reflects the anxiety of identifying a *unique locus or specific psychological event* that would reveal the *akratic*'s error.

We can say that there is 'fiction or myth of a particular *locus of error or specific psychological event*' when we try to put forward a sound account of *akrasia*. Different accounts that emphasize how perception can remain static, as if we could better observe or understand empirical conditions to prevent intellectual errors, intensify our anxiety. The belief is that the correct conception of 'attention' or 'awareness' will, consequently, enable us to make a clear demarcation between *akratic* and non-*akratic* performance of an action.

If *akrasia* is the key structural feature that underpins inadvertent or negligent acts and is therefore important for understanding who is responsible and blameworthy for negligent or inadvertent acts, then identifying a *locus* or *specific psychological event* will help to differentiate between negligent and purely compulsive acts. The myth states that there is such a *locus*. Theorists perpetuate this myth, contending that *akrasia* causes the agent to succumb to desires and emotions. Unsurprisingly, this gives rise to scepticism about the possibility of explaining inadvertent actions.[81]

In our account, by contrast, the agent who acts compulsively has neither thoughts nor desires involving thoughts. The compulsive agent neither deliberates nor gives thought to the specific subject matter in a way that constitutes further

[81] See discussion in Chapter 2.

deliberation. The agent operates through physical forces, and neurological explanations or pathologies, such as psychosis or pathological addictions, provide a more accurate explanation for her actions.

According to the explanation that we aim to advance here, the *akratic* deliberates soundly and makes a rational choice. However, because she fails to inhabit the deliberative-aspirational perspective, as well as to integrate knowledge with desires and emotions, the *akratic* gives us an incomplete representation of what could have been. Worse, she presents an upside-down version of *her entire self.* There is a mistake happening in the world, but she is also a contortion of herself.

Another important point emerges from the idea that *akrasia* is the structural feature that underpins judgements of responsibility and blameworthiness for inadvertent or negligent actions. The performer of an *akratic* act is on the opposite end of the spectrum from a performer who inhabits the deliberative-aspirational perspective. Following legal directives, rules, and principles plays a key role in the possibility of citizens inhabiting the deliberative-aspirational perspective and, consequently, becoming good. This will be the theme of the book's final chapter.

PART III

THE LEGAL PROPOSAL. WAYS OF BECOMING A CITIZEN

TRANSFORMATION AND MATURITY

This part of the book demonstrates that there is an internal structure in negligence law that expands and embraces what is good, rightful, and dutiful. This does not mean that the law engages with 'external' ends or values that are not properly juridical. On the contrary, the argument posits that courts' decisions enable us to have a better grasp of what is valuable, rightful, and dutiful in the concrete particularities of the subject matter through legal pronouncements. Consequently, different doctrinal aspects of negligence embody what we deem good, rightful, and dutiful. In contrast to corrective theories of tort law, I maintain that the law of negligence not only focuses on backward-looking reasoning in terms of rights and duties but also is involved in forward-looking reasoning, where the citizen's deliberative stance and engagement with descriptions and re-description of values are at the core.

If it is true that *akrasia* is the underpinning phenomenon of negligence law, then how does negligence law operate so that citizens are able to avoid *akrasia*? I contend that courts' decisions advance *proleptic* reasons, which are integral to citizens' practical reasoning. *Proleptic* in this context means that, as reasoners, you can anticipate thoughts and ways of valuing that will help you to move forward, so to speak, and transform yourself through deliberating and acting. Negligence law invites the citizen to inhabit an aspirational-deliberative point of view, describing and re-describing the relevant values presented in particulars. In a similar vein, I argue that there is also a backward-looking perspective where judges attribute rights and duties, but they are in continuity with what is valuable and good, and the forward-looking perspective.

This part also explores the various theories of tort law that purport to elucidate negligence. I contend that none of them successfully demonstrates how negligence law has an internal structure that engages with particular values rather than just abstract notions such as rights and duties. Some of these theories also fail to show how negligence law enables us to guide our actions and deter us from acting negligently in a way that engages the citizens' practical reasoning.

Finally, this section of the book engages with theories of negligence in ethics. It demonstrates that contemporary theories of negligence in ethics assume that the bifurcation thesis is true. There are theories that take the agent's temporal dimension seriously, as well as the idea of controlling one's action through knowledge or belief. However, these theories merely aim to establish the moment at which the agent forms a belief or ought to have acted in a certain way to avoid the negligent or inadvertent action. They assume the existence of a *locus* of responsibility, thereby reducing the agent's extended temporal dimension to this *locus*. The underlying premise of these positions is that there is a bifurcation between desires and beliefs, construed as mental states. Beliefs are 'absent' while we are acting negligently or inadvertently, and the only relevant question seems to centre on how this 'absence' might have happened.

Other theories either minimize or obliterate the agent's temporal dimension, encompassing the idea that we are responsible for negligent or inadvertent actions because these actions manifest underlying patterns of evaluative judgement or unreflective patterns of awareness. These theories present us with a picture that is akin to a 'black box', where the input consists of the agent's evaluative judgements, along with the emotions and desires that are part of the evaluative judgements. On the other hand, we have the respective output, the expressions or manifestations of these evaluative judgements via unreflective patterns of awareness, and the potential demands from either the third-person or second-person perspective. These accounts miss something important, our *becoming*. Responsibility plays a crucial role in our *becoming*, possible by inhabiting aspirational perspectives. When we demand responses from others and express moral criticism, we express our reactive attitude. However, we also *intend for the agent to be able to inhabit a different perspective* regarding her actions, judgements, emotions, and desires, and incorporate this new perspective into her future actions. We also desire that the agent reassess her entire self and explore new ways of looking at her actions and conduct.

7

Legal Theory and the Law of Negligence

Reclaiming Practical Reasoning and Valuing in the Domain of Law

§7.1 Preliminary Reflections

In this chapter, we will show that current general theories of tort law fail to address one or more of the four key challenges that arise from the phenomenology of negligent action. First, *the abstract challenge* shows that all theories that focus on the right/duty pair in the law of negligence engage with an abstract conception of action, thereby obscuring the question of responsibility or blameworthiness for negligent action at the level of agency and deliberation.[1] Secondly, *the particularity challenge* conveys the idea that engagement with a negligent action on the part of law's addressees cannot be from the point of view of general rules, directives, or principles. Nor can it engage with ways of thinking and concepts that are alien to our deliberative stance, for example risk,[2] probability, etc. Thirdly, *the deterrence challenge* shows that we should not conceive of deterrence as an empirical engagement with action, such as pure coercion, or in terms of an intelligible connection to risk. Ripstein, for example, tells us that negligence always involves the realization of a specific risk to the plaintiff created by the defendant.[3] He emphasizes the entire sequence that goes from the risk to the defendant's injury, but because his approach is attributive or from the third-person perspective, it fails to explain the law's role concerning deterrence when the citizen is engaged in a specific action or is deliberating about the action, ie the forward-looking perspective. Fourthly, *the guidance challenge* establishes that an adequate theory of negligence needs to explain the way the law engages with the addressee's practical reasoning.

[1] This challenge takes seriously Goldberg's and Zipursky's view that we need a concept of 'duty of care' that is ordinary, but non-moralistic. See John Goldberg and Benjamin Zipursky, 'Seeing Tort Law From the Internal Point of View: Holmes and Hart on Legal Duties' (2006) 75 Fordham Law Review 1563.

[2] Notably, Oberdiek advances a moral conception of risk. However, this view fails to meet both the particularity and guidance challenges, and it cannot contribute to the forward-looking function of the law of negligence. John Oberdiek, *Imposing Risk: A Normative Framework* (OUP 2017). See Chapter 9 for further discussion on this point.

[3] Arthur Ripstein, *Private Wrongs* (Harvard UP 2016) 87.

Responsibility for Negligence in Ethics and Law. Verónica Rodríguez-Blanco, Oxford University Press.
 DOI: 10.1093/9780198948193.003.0007

In this chapter, I will provide an explanation of these theories and give detailed arguments about why the different theories that ground the law of negligence provide a deficient answer to one or more of these challenges.

There is a vast literature that aims to provide a theoretical grounding of tort law in general and, in particular, of the law of negligence and acts of negligence in order to either describe or justify our attributions of legal responsibility for inadvertent actions. We can divide the literature into three categories. First, we have theories that concentrate on our interactions with others and their justification or permissibility. I call them *person-centred theories* because their responses focus on what we can or cannot do to others and why this is so. The emphasis is on our nature as persons, and they appeal to our free and rational agency, including the means available to us to realize our aims or goals and the way interactions are permissible or not. A corollary of this focus is that within the context of these theories, relationality, or the interactions between people, provides the predominant perspective. Person-centred theories include theories of corrective justice,[4] the civil recourse theory of tort law,[5] and theories that are grounded on the idea of *ex-ante* omnilateral duties or a contractualist theory of tort law.[6] Secondly, aim-centred theories that aim to identify and achieve the goals that our institutions such as private law should achieve,[7] while third, there are theories that advocate a 'continuity' between legal and our ethical and moral agency.[8] We will discuss the latter two in §§7.4–7.9.

[4] Ernest Weinrib, *The Idea of Private Law* (OUP 2012) and Ripstein, *Private Wrongs* (n 3). See also Jules L Coleman, *Risks and Wrongs* (CUP 1993).

[5] John Goldberg and Benjamin Zipursky, *Recognizing Wrongs* (Harvard UP 2020).

[6] Gregory Keating, 'The Priority of Respect Over Repair' (2012) 18 Legal Theory 293; Gregory Keating and Dilan Esper, 'Putting Duty in Its Place: A Reply to Professor Goldberg and Zipursky' (2008) 41 Loyola-Los Angeles Review 1225 and John Oberdiek, 'Structure and Justification in Contractualist Tort Theory' in John Oberdiek (ed), *Philosophical Foundations of the Law of Torts* (OUP 2014) 103. Some authors recognize the importance of rights as the primary norm of tort law but also want to acknowledge the role played by the deliberative or internal perspective that is mainly forward-looking. See Paul Miller and Jeffrey Pojanowski, 'The Internal Point of View in Private Law' (2022) 67 American Journal of Jurisprudence 247.

[7] Richard Posner, 'A Theory of Negligence' (1972) 1 The Journal of Legal Studies 29.

[8] Tony Honoré, *Responsibility and Fault* (Hart 1999); Stephen Perry, 'The Moral Foundations of Tort Law' (1992) 77 Iowa Law Review 449; John Gardner, 'What is Tort Law For?' (2011) 30 Law and Philosophy 1; John Gardner, 'Obligations and Outcomes in the Law of Torts' in Peter Cane and John Gardner (eds), *Relating to Responsibility: Essays in Honour of Tony Honoré on His 80th Birthday* (Hart/Bloomsbury 2001); John Gardner, *From Personal Life to Private Law* (OUP 2018). Diego Papayannis has observed that Gardner's theory of tort law should be considered a person-centred theory instead of a third category. However, though it is true that Gardner recognizes the key role that personal relationships and interactions between persons play in tort law, his position has additional layers of complexity and shows that there should be a continuity between ethical and legal thinking on this matter. It includes his view of responsibility as answerability and the importance of recognizing the outcome of our actions as part of our personal identity.

§7.2 Person-Centred Theories of Negligence Law

§7.2.1 Weinrib's Corrective Justice Theory

Person-centred theories argue that the law of negligence defines the boundaries and limits of our permissible interactions with other persons. In tort law, the law of negligence establishes the legal framework or legal conceptual apparatus that judges use to attribute blameworthiness or responsibility for the committed negligent act. Kant's conception of external freedom and an interpretation of Aristotle's conception of corrective justice inspire theories of corrective justice. For example, according to Weinrib, the Aristotelian conception of corrective justice[9] establishes that when someone commits harm to another person by acting negligently and causing injury to a victim, the latter has suffered a loss, and the former has accrued a gain. There is an *arithmetic* asymmetry, something has been taken from the victim while the injurer has obtained what has been subtracted. On the victim's side, there is a minus or subtraction, and on the injurer's side, there is a plus or addition. On the victim's side, there is passivity, while on the injurer's side, there is activity.[10] However, Weinrib explains that these are normative losses and gains, not factual losses and gains, linking plaintiff and defendant in a '*single and coherent justificatory structure*'.[11] The role of private law is to restore the equality in these relational[12] or bipolar transactions.[13] Aristotle's formulation of corrective justice, Weinrib tells us, is also conceptual, as it does not refer to anything in the empirical world but rather to concepts through which we understand relationships between persons. It is the mode by which we organize and order the world of interactions

[9] Commentators on Aristotelian conceptions of corrective justice disagree on the correct interpretation of the term. The standard view asserts that it is a matter of compensation, that there is no normative element, and that it is purely descriptive. Others believe that Aristotle advances a punitive conception, which is mainly normative. See Thomas Brickhouse, 'Aristotle on Corrective Justice' (2014) 18 Journal of Ethics 187. Weinrib seems to advocate the descriptive account, whereby compensation is the central notion. Weinrib (n 4). However, Weinrib recognizes different stages of corrective justice. ibid 76–83. There are three stages: (a) the mere understanding of the doctrinal concepts of private law, (b) understanding the Aristotelian notion of corrective justice as compensation and realizing that compensation is the underlying structure of the doctrinal conception, and finally, (c) fully understanding the deep structure of private law as the Kantian normative correlativity conception of rights and duties. Arguably, according to Weinrib, the fully normative structure of private law occurs only at the latter stage. However, no explanation exists for why the injured should receive compensation, as Perry has noted. Only punishment can annul the wrongness of the negligent act. Perry relies on Kant himself to advance this critique. See Perry (n 8) 480. See also Martin Stone, 'The Significance of Doing and Suffering' in Gerald Postema (ed), *Philosophy and the Law of Torts* (CUP 2001) 131. For further discussion on the 'internal logic' of the law of negligence, see Chapter 9.

[10] Weinrib (n 4) 64, 73.

[11] ibid 57.

[12] This is the preferred term of some authors, see Goldberg and Zipursky, *Recognizing Wrongs* (n 5) and Perry (n 8).

[13] 'Corrective justice requires the actor to restore to the victim the amount representing the actor's self-enrichment at the victim's expense.' Weinrib (n 4) 63, fn 23, quoting Aristotle's *Nichomachean Ethics* 1132a32–b5). See also Weinrib (this note) 65.

with others.[14] Combining different modes of orders, such as corrective and distributive justice, undermines the justificatory force and the unifying intelligibility of each. In other words, it leads to incoherence because there are two different and mutually exclusive modes of understanding; corrective justice excludes the comparative mode of distributive justice, and the latter excludes the bipolarity of the former.[15]

According to Weinrib, this thinking in terms of loss and gain is the key underlying structure of the law of negligence, but Aristotle does not explain the substantive aspect of the bipolar equality between the plaintiff and defendant.[16] In this way, Weinrib explains that the Kantian correlativity thesis of rights and duties provides the ultimate normative structure of private law,[17] including the law of negligence. Therefore, it is mirrored in doctrinal concepts, ie a duty of care, an objective standard, causation,[18] remoteness of damage. The equality of corrective justice is the abstract equality of two persons *whose free will is presupposed*.

According to Weinrib, self-determining agency, ie agency that reflects our capacity to choose our ends and deliberate on our means to achieve our ends, has a juridical manifestation, which is the concept of 'right'. 'Right' abstracts from the agent's *particular circumstances*.[19] Law is a manifestation[20] or embodiment[21] of this normative structure.

According to the Kantian conception of external freedom,[22] interaction between persons necessitates that one person's free choice can coexist with another's freedom. The formal relationship of will-to-will becomes the framework for the correlativity of rights and duties. Weinrib extends this framework from contract, property, and criminal law to the law of negligence, and he reaffirms that the nature of these acts is 'externally recognizable acts'[23] and *that motivation and internal practical reason play no role*.[24]

Weinrib states that this framework is (a) internal, (b) immanent, and (c) formal. This framework's internal structure stems from its understanding within the boundaries of legal doctrine and legal and juridical thought processes. Thus,

[14] Weinrib (n 4) 70–72.

[15] ibid 73, 78–79. Honoré attempts to mix both views. See Honoré (n 8) 80–81. Other authors argue that corrective justice is subordinate to distributive justice. Corrective justice requires economic theories of law—what I call here aim-centred theories of tort law. See Richard Posner, 'The Concept of Corrective Justice in Recent Theories of Tort Law' (1981) 10 Journal of Legal Studies 187.

[16] Weinrib (n 4) 57–58.

[17] ibid 19.

[18] ibid 12.

[19] ibid 81.

[20] ibid XVI.

[21] ibid 104.

[22] Immanuel Kant, *Metaphysics of Morals* (originally published in 1797, tr Mary Gregor, CUP 2017).

[23] Weinrib (n 4) 104.

[24] Weinrib points out: 'Interaction between free wills engages the external aspect of practical reason, which requires that each actor treats the other's personal and proprietary embodiments in a manner that does not violate their *formal equality* as free wills.' ibid 104. The emphasis is mine.

private law is *both* a mode of reasoning and the subject matter that we elucidate when we engage with the idea of reason *qua* private law.[25] Like love or friendship,[26] the practice has its internal thinking and justification, and, therefore, explaining and understanding it is only achieved if we engage with the idea of reasoning *qua* love or friendship. The explanation of love as a series of chemical reactions renders the practice of love incomprehensible, just as the reduction of private law to objectives like wealth maximization or economic incentives renders private law incomprehensible.

Weinrib also states that private law is immanent[27] because it aims at understanding legal material, legal norms, and legal concepts, and the subject in its understanding cannot transcend the legal subject matter and the legal formal structure itself. Furthermore, it can be argued that, unlike love or friendship, the structure of reasoning is justificatory, encompassing all the reasons and justificatory space, and leaving no room for description.[28] Hence, it aims at comprehensive coherence[29] and the articulation and order of justificatory or normative reasons. Due to our exercise of practical reason, as defined by Weinrib and following Kant,[30] as purposive activity, we are able to produce norms, but in the sphere of private law, we impose these norms from within in the form of legality. Private law is therefore normative by nature, and '*no norm external to purposive activity could be relevant to it*'.[31] Private law inextricably links normativity and immanence. Private law is also formal because it has a form dictated by the structure of legal thinking, and therefore this form can only be grasped in its abstract[32] mode. It cannot be grasped by empirical reality, for example social reality and social problems such as accidents,[33] that law as an institution aims to resolve, nor by subjective particularities such as the motivation of agents and participants in a practice, for example victims' sentiments of revenge,[34] or by the motives due to the character of judges and legal participants.

[25] ibid 92.

[26] ibid 6 and 19. See also Ripstein, *Private Wrongs* (n 3) 22–23.

[27] Weinrib (n 4) XIV.

[28] ibid XVIII and XIX.

[29] I do not rely much on the coherence argument advanced by Weinrib as it is unclear what his account of coherence is. For a persuasive criticism of this point, see Dennis Patterson, 'The Metaphysics of Formalism' (1992) 77 Iowa Law Review 741.

[30] Weinrib (n 4) 88–94.

[31] ibid 94.

[32] The abstract character of corrective justice is emphasized in Weinrib's *The Idea of Private Law* in the following terms: 'Equality and the abstraction from particulars go hand in hand, because particulars are factors that might differentiate individuals and make them unequal. Similarly, abstraction from particulars and the sheer correlativity of doing and suffering go together, because when doing and suffering are each considered solely in relation to the other, the qualities particular to the doer or to the sufferer as individuals are irrelevant'. ibid 81. This is puzzling, how can there be suffering without particularity, without grasping the person in her particularity? Further discussion of this point is developed in Chapter 9.

[33] See Guido Calabresi, *The Cost of Accidents* (Yale UP 1970).

[34] See Scott Herschovitz, 'Tort as a Substitute for Revenge' in John Oberdiek (ed), *Philosophical Foundations of the Law of Torts* (OUP 2014) 86.

Thus, while the abstract form elucidates the ordering of legal relationships,[35] it is unable to engage with substantive matters and the particularities of the respective agency and actions, including inadvertent acts. There is doing and suffering,[36] but both are understood within the normative Kantian framework of correlativity and interactions under the conditions of external freedoms. The doer and sufferer can recognize their self-determining natures, ie noumenal selves.[37] Weinrib[38] quotes Kant's *Metaphysics of Morals* (6:230)[39] to advance the idea that agents are duty-bound under the idea of freedom and reason, and that positive law embodies this idea of freedom and reason. In the quoted passage of the *Metaphysics of Morals*, Kant tells us that, like the wooden head in the Phraedrus fable, a doctrine of right in empirical terms is empty, it has no brain. Right and duty are correlative because (i) there is a practical and external relation of actions as deeds between two persons, and (ii) one person's choice is in relation to another person's choice—it is not just wishes, desires, or passive happenings; and (iii) in this reciprocal relationship of choice, no account at all is taken of the subject matter of choice. '*All that is in question is the form in the relation of choice on the part of both, insofar as choice is regarded as merely free, and whether the action of one can be united with the freedom of the other in accordance with a universal law*.'[40]

§7.2.2 Ripstein's Theory of Corrective Justice

Ripstein also uses Kantian grounding for his theory of corrective justice, but he emphasizes the importance of access to means as a fundamental right.[41] Ripstein defends Weinrib's conclusion, ie wrongs in private law are violations of rights,[42] but aims to show that his proposed route is sounder. Ripstein begins with the notion

[35] Weinrib (n 4) XIII.
[36] This 'doing and 'suffering' are abstract. For a criticism of this abstract 'doing' and 'suffering', see Stone (n 9). For a further development of Stone's criticism, see Chapter 9.
[37] Weinrib (n 4) 82.
[38] ibid 82, fn 57.
[39] Kant (n 22).
[40] ibid 6:230.
[41] Ripstein states that the law of negligence 'protects the means that you already have against the side effects of other people's use of their means. The basic case of a damage-based tort is the case of a completed wrong, that is, the case in which one person damages what belongs to another through the use of means in ways that characteristically cause that type of damage. As always, the wrong arises when the defendant's actions conflict with the plaintiff's rights.' Ripstein, *Private Wrongs* (n 3) 87. This passage emphasizes that Ripstein's corrective justice account is backward-looking, from the third-person perspective, and attributive. Some authors, like Ripstein, have focused on agents' normative relationships with others to explain responsibility for negligence. Pavlakos, for example, describes the normative relation that governs responsibility for negligence as an instance of the legal relationship. However, this view also prioritizes the backward-looking perspective over the first-person deliberative view. George Pavlakos, 'Agent-Relativity without Control: Grounding Negligence on Normative Relations' in Verónica Rodríguez-Blanco and George Pavlakos (eds), *Agency, Negligence and Responsibility* (CUP 2021) 118.
[42] Ripstein, *Private Wrongs* (n 3) 6.

that we are self-determining and autonomous individuals and that the exercise of this capacity should not be illegitimately hindered; 'no person is in charge of another'.[43] As a result, private law and its various types reflect this moral idea in multiple ways. Finally, he aims to demonstrate that a violation of a right does not equate to its annulment. The right *continues*, thus necessitating a duty that arises to remedy the situation with the antecedent factual situation. 'The right survives its own violation.'[44] The norm is based on the idea that since all autonomous individuals are entitled to pursue their aims and access their means, our use of means must be consistent with the use of means by other individuals. However, the act of negligence, which violates the norm, persists in its effects. Let me explain.

The core argument starts by acknowledging that persons have aims and ends that they can only accomplish through access to means. Similarly, the exercise of our right to property and our rights over our own bodies are part of our realization of aims and ends. It is unjustifiable for someone to obstruct another person's ability to exercise their own choices, including access to means. Ripstein, like Kant in his work 'Doctrine of Right',[45] looks at our external interactions with other human beings and the way any obstruction to, or harm to, our access to means is illegitimate and coercive.[46] The interaction is limited to the external manifestation of our will or choice. '*You are allowed to use your means however you see fit, and you have no obligation to use them in a way that enables your neighbor to use his or her means in the way that she wishes to*.'[47]

However, risk also plays a key role in Ripstein's analysis. If you expose others to a minimal or small risk, then a system of rights will permit you to use your means in this way; otherwise, there will be an unjustifiable limitation of your freedom inconsistent with your independence.[48] However, Ripstein cautions that assuming a 'safe' risk or realizing a 'reasonable' risk is not a purely quantitative exercise. Legal courts assess risks based on 'dangerousness', for example, and require a contextual judgement to determine whether an activity or action is *too* dangerous. The question is whether 'you have been careful enough', not whether there is a continuum between slightly dangerous, dangerous, and too dangerous. Ripstein reiterates, however, that the question of whether the defendant is aware is irrelevant.[49] Risk contemplation is formulated in ordinary and familiar terms, both as particulars and *abstract archetypes*.[50] As a result, the prevalence of external freedom, where

[43] ibid.
[44] ibid 13.
[45] Kant (n 22).
[46] Corrective justice theorists consider external freedom and its relationship to practical reason straightforward. At no point do they problematize this relationship, and this is precisely one of the weakest points of the theory. For an expansion on the problematic relationship between external freedom and practical reason, see Chapter 9.
[47] Ripstein, *Private Wrongs* (n 3) 10.
[48] ibid 103.
[49] ibid 104.
[50] ibid 107.

the focus is on whether engaging in an activity and taking a risk will affect others, and the function of attribution are reasserted.[51]

One can argue that the strength of Ripstein's and Weinrib's arguments is in showing that the 'bad conduct' argument and the subsequent matter of moral luck do not play a key role in our attributions of responsibility for negligence[52] According to the 'bad conduct' argument, the defendant's bad conduct justifies the application of negligence law. However, we can see that on some occasions, two people behave equally badly, but only one causes harm, and therefore, only one is responsible. Consequently, in both cases, causation is arbitrary, and luck seems to play a role in determining responsibility. Let us now take a closer look at the problem of moral luck in the context of negligence law and corrective justice theory.

§7.2.3 The Problem of Moral Luck and the Relationality Thesis of Corrective Justice

Bernard Williams and Thomas Nagel first introduced the puzzle of moral luck in contemporary philosophy, and Jeremy Waldron later applied it to tort law. In response to Williams' paper 'Moral Luck',[53] Nagel[54] asks whether we are responsible for actions that are beyond our control, for example circumstances, opportunities, capacities, temperament, and contingencies in the world. According to Nagel, the success or failure of our actions depends on what is happening in the world when we act. Williams refers to this as 'moral luck'. The idea of the agent losing control of her actions due to contingencies in the world, including who we are and how we are constituted, undermines any standard notion of responsibility and moral judgement. As Nagel puts it, '*the self which acts and is the object of moral judgment is threatened with dissolution by the absorption of its acts and impulses into the class of events*'.[55] However, Nagel insists that a moral judgement is *not* what happens, it is not about a state of affairs but rather about an active self. In his piece on moral luck, he merely outlines the idea of the active self, but he provides a clearer idea in *The Possibility of Altruism*[56] and *The View from Nowhere*.[57] The active self is capable of identifying and distinguishing between what belongs to us when we engage in choice and rational deliberation and what is simply happening. Thus, we cannot take a purely external evaluative view of ourselves, and understanding our

[51] ibid 105–06.
[52] ibid 84.
[53] Bernard Williams, 'Moral Luck' in *Moral Luck* (CUP 1981) 20.
[54] Thomas Nagel, 'Moral Luck' (1976) 50 Proceedings of the Aristotelian Society 137.
[55] ibid 148.
[56] Thomas Nagel, *The Possibility of Altruism* (Princeton UP 1970).
[57] Thomas Nagel, *The View From Nowhere* (OUP 1986).

actions is key to shaping the contours and borders of what we have done as opposed to what is merely happening in the world. We cannot, Nagel tells us, operate and make ourselves intelligible if we operate as causes in the empirical and contingent world.

Contrast Nagel's position with Williams' view on the matter. Williams focuses on rebutting the view that we are immune to moral luck and that the agent's reflective assessment and justification of her own actions are not subject to luck.[58]

The example of the painter Gauguin illustrates Williams' point. The painter abandons his wife and children to pursue a painting career. We cannot separate his success as a painter from any justification of his actions, which includes leaving a unique artistic legacy and defining the meaning of human existence. However, neither Gauguin nor anyone else could have foreseen his success at *the moment of his actions*. If Gauguin fails, he has made a mistake; if he succeeds, his actions may find justification.[59] Of course, this justification is not moral, but it is part of a life that adheres to certain values, ie a life that is meaningful through aesthetic experience. Williams acknowledges that this justification is not directed towards others, meaning the children will still be subject to criticism, but rather it operates retrospectively. Williams' point is that, *at the moment of the action*, Gauguin cannot act in light of all the relevant rational considerations that apply to him[60] because much of the justification of his actions will depend on his talents, deliberative capacity,[61] and character, and how *he* successfully develops these talents.

This is what Williams calls 'intrinsic luck'.[62] He tells us: '*the locus of intrinsic luck, largely lies in him—which is not to say, of course, that they depend on his will, though some may*'.[63] Nevertheless, he recognizes that the *locus* of intrinsic luck can lie outside the agent. Williams seems to hint at the idea that agency continues once we have performed our actions; when we look back and ponder over the consequences of our actions,[64] we can see these consequences as part of our actions, *in spite of the fact that we may have had no knowledge of the action and did not intend it*. According to Williams, we would expect that the lorry driver, who runs over a child by accident, harbours specific emotions about the incident. These feelings, or emotions, are difficult to dismiss by arguing that what happened was not his fault. The lorry driver recognizes that his act of driving the lorry has resulted in the child's death.[65] According to Williams, it would be an insane conception of rationality if we expected people not to feel they own the consequences of their actions,

[58] Williams (n 53) 22.
[59] ibid 23.
[60] ibid 24.
[61] ibid 25.
[62] ibid 26.
[63] ibid.
[64] For a way of understanding this retrospective reflection of our own actions, see Chapter 1.
[65] Williams (n 53) 28.

or if we expected them to detach themselves from the unintended aspects of their actions.[66]

However, let us recall that for Williams, this evaluation is not in terms of moral blameworthiness, since one cannot make clear judgements of liability and moral blameworthiness. The latter, in principle, requires control, but in cases of non-intentional action, there is no control.[67] He concludes that contingencies in the world cannot purify agency, and, therefore, any sound account of rationality and responsibility needs to consider this impure conception of the self. Furthermore, he underscores that we do not solely evaluate and justify actions from a moral perspective, which separates actions and consequences, as Nagel attempts to demonstrate.

Let us now analyse how these ideas have been examined in tort law. Honoré and Gardner,[68] inspired by Von Wright's philosophy of action and norms,[69] outline an alternative conception that navigates between Nagel's and Williams' positions. Gardner, following Honoré's argument that responsibility in the law of negligence is about outcome-responsibility, establishes a distinction between results and consequences. Therefore, results are part of the action description and what agents do and bring to the world. By contrast, consequences are outside the scope of the action and are merely 'happenings'.[70]

Waldron[71] also takes up Williams' points on moral luck to establish a case for the replacement of negligent liability for a scheme where losses and gains are distributed in terms of adequate models of fairness and justice. Waldron aims to demonstrate that the law of negligence is fundamentally unjust. He argues that we cannot justify liability in negligence for the alleged harm the plaintiff has suffered due to the defendant's action, given that others may have acted in a similarly morally wrong manner but were fortunate enough not to injure or cause any loss to anyone. With the following example, Waldron effectively illustrates his argument:

> Two drivers, named Fate and Fortunate, were on a city street one morning in their automobiles. Both were driving at or near the speed limit, Fortune a little ahead of Fate. As they passed through a shopping district, each took his eyes off the road, turning his head for a moment to look at the bargains advertised in a storefront window. In Fortunate's case, this momentary distraction passed

[66] ibid 29.

[67] For a discussion of the sceptical position of negligence and the question of control, see Chapter 2.

[68] Gardner, 'From Personal Life to Private Law' (n 8) 58–64.

[69] Georg Von Wright, *Norm and Action* (Routledge and Kegan 1963) 39–41.

[70] Gardner uses his conception of action to establish that the duty of care in negligence law is only a duty to try, not a result-requiring duty. Gardner, 'From Personal Life to Private Law' (n 8) 64. However, he recognizes that success is primary, see ibid 134. 'My succeeding by trying', ibid 139. Trying is necessary but not sufficient: 'Obligation not to fail for want of trying', ibid 123.

[71] Jeremy Waldron, 'Moments of Careless and Massive Loss' in David Owen (ed), *Philosophical Foundations of Tort Law* (OUP 1995) 387.

> without event. The road was straight, the traffic in front of him was proceeding smoothly, and after few seconds he returned his eyes to his driving and completed his journey without accident. Fate, however, was not so fortunate. Distracted by the bargain advertised in the shoe store, he failed to notice that the traffic ahead of him had slowed down. His car ploughed into a motorcycle ridden by a Mr. Hurt. Hurt was flung from the motorcycle and gravely injured. His back was broken so badly that he would spend the rest of his life in a wheelchair. Fate stopped immediately to summon help, and when the police arrived he readily admitted that he had been driving carelessly.[72]

Like in Williams' case of the painter Gauguin, Waldron invites us to reflect on the complexity of action and its connection to blame and responsibility. If our actions inevitably merge with world contingencies, it becomes challenging to justify from the *moral standpoint* that we are responsible for negligence, as moral luck seems to permeate our tortious actions. Similarly, if liability in negligence is grounded in our conduct and blameworthy action, it becomes challenging to argue that Fate bears responsibility while Fortunate does not. This example challenges Nagel's defence of the moral viewpoint. Fate and Fortunate conducted themselves in exactly the same way, and there is no rationale for blaming Fate and demanding $5 million in compensation for Hurt, a decision that ultimately leads to his financial ruin. Neither Fate nor Fortunate *chose* to act in the way they did.

Williams and Waldron present a simplistic and inaccurate conception of action. The formation of an intention, which includes desires and beliefs, is on one side, while unrelated events are on the other. Between the formation of beliefs and desires and the outcome of the action, nothing seems to happen. Moreover, time T1 presents the formation of beliefs and desires as a singular instance, while time T2 presents the outcome as a distinct event. However, we have learned, through narrow and aspirational deliberation, that the formation of beliefs and desires does not happen all at once at time T1. According to Williams and Waldron's model, what happens in the world seems arbitrary and is independent of our thinking about the matter and our transformed desires. Not surprisingly, the law of negligence seems unjustified.

Understanding why legal courts intervene when the defendant violates a duty and the plaintiff's right to use her property and person, as well as her access to means to achieve her goals necessitates Ripstein and Weinrib's focus on relationality. However, this does not imply that the law is uninterested in the citizens' actions and conduct. In Chapter 9, we will demonstrate the ways in which the law engages with citizens' conduct.

[72] ibid 387.

We must examine the law of negligence from a dual perspective, considering how these two perspectives interact. The first perspective is backward-looking, which means that judges attribute rights and duties and assess violations of these rights and duties. The second perspective is forward-looking, which scrutinizes how the law engages the citizen's practical reasoning in her deliberative perspective, ensuring civic maturity and an aspirational perspective via which the citizens engage with rights and duties.

Goldberg and Zipursky's civil recourse theory of tort law, which is grounded in our current practices, criticizes the formal and abstract nature of Weinrib's and Ripstein's correlativity thesis. It also emphasizes the courts' role in determining the content of the right/duty pair. We now turn to this theory to shed further light on the nature of the right/duty pair.

§7.2.4 Goldberg's and Zipursky's Civil Recourse Theory

Similar to corrective justice theorists, Goldberg and Zipursky[73] argue that the relationality or correlativity thesis is key to understanding and providing an intelligible unity to the complexity of torts or wrongs that are part of current common laws. Torts such as defamation, nuisance, product liability, negligence, and privacy find a common core in the idea that a wrong has been committed and, therefore, a breach of a duty has occurred, which corresponds to the right of the defendant not to be injured or suffer loss. Unlike corrective justice theorists, however, Goldberg and Zipursky do not rely on the Kantian framework of rights and duties, conceptions of personhood, or rational agency.[74] Goldberg and Zipursky *ground rights and duties on the emergence of practice-based directives*. We will refer to this perspective as the 'directive-based relationality thesis'.

In addition to the directive-based relationality thesis, Goldberg and Zipursky put forward the idea that theorists should also consider the courts' role in intervening to solve disputes regarding rights and duties. Goldberg and Zipursky strive to demonstrate how the law of torts empowers the plaintiff to seek redress for the wrong they have suffered through civil recourse.[75] It is an 'empowerment' because the plaintiff instigates the claim and can decide at any moment to abandon it. This additional feature further elucidates the directive-based relationality thesis within tortious relations. Therefore, tort law is not a matter of a moral right that

[73] Goldberg and Zipursky, *Recognizing Wrongs* (n 5) 4, 13, 26, 89, 181. On p 82, Goldberg and Zipursky refer to the idea of rules as generators of relational wrongs. They explain how relational legal directives give rise to legal rights and duties. Goldberg and Zipursky, *Recognizing Wrongs* (n 5) 92–98.

[74] See Weinrib (n 4) chs 4 and 5 and Arthur Ripstein, *Equality, Responsibility and the Law* (CUP 2012) ch 3.

[75] Goldberg and Zipursky, *Recognizing Wrongs* (n 5) 13, 15, 29, 30–37, 42, 52, 72, 80, 91, 113, 115, 163–65. They make a distinction between narrow and wider civil redress. The former refers to the right to redress legal wrongs, as in tort law, whereas the latter refers to the private right of action. ibid 124.

has been violated by the defendant's conduct and the corresponding moral right of remedy. It is a matter of *legal empowerment through a civil recourse* conferred on the plaintiff by the law.

In philosophical terms, this theory addresses the question of the normative and justificatory force of tort law, which is specifically legal rather than moral. The normative and justificatory aspects rely on the directive-based relationality thesis. However, the normative force of the directive-based relationality thesis emerges as a combination of legal practices and self-understanding of these legal practices.[76] According to Goldberg and Zipursky, we do not need to advance a Kantian framework of political and moral philosophy in order to give content to the relationality thesis and, consequently, justify the state's intervention, nor do we need to use the Kantian framework to demonstrate the immanent formal features displayed in the correlation between a duty and a right in tort law. Furthermore, there is no need to rely on an empirical reality, such as vengeance,[77] to explain the courts' characteristic normative language,[78] nor to advance an Archimedean conception of objective morality and moral truths. Goldberg and Zipursky insist, nonetheless, that there is an immanence and an inner normativity of law,[79] but that it is always *legal* in character, as provided by the empowerment of the law,[80] and by the fact that the courts elucidate the content of the right and duty.

§7.2.5 Keating's Contractualist Theory[81]

Keating distinguishes between reasonableness and rationality. When people act reasonably, they aim to reconcile the conflicting aims and interests '*of different people on terms that each could acknowledge as legitimate if they were to change places with those burdened by the pursuits of their ends*'.[82] In contrast, rationality only requires acting according to instrumental reasons to pursue one's ends, yet this rational pursuit may be unreasonable. Rationally speaking, an agent could effectively pursue her interests while failing to show respect for the interests of others, making her unreasonable. Keating conflates rational thinking with rational decision-making in economic theory, ie maximizing benefits while minimizing costs. Keating argues that the duty of care in negligence law requires us to act

[76] ibid 15.
[77] ibid 65 and 121–22.
[78] ibid 6 and 12.
[79] ibid 61–62, 190–91. Goldberg and Zipursky insist that torts are wrongs, not construed as blameworthy acts but as violations of the plaintiff's right not to be injured. They also argue in favour of taking at face value the normative language of law and the fact that there is an inner normativity of law. ibid 211, 252–53.
[80] ibid 2, 4, 86–89.
[81] Gregory Keating, 'Reasonableness and Rationality in Negligence Tort Theory' (1996) 48 Stanford Law Review 311.
[82] ibid 312.

according to principles of reasonableness rather than principles of rationality. This implies that the duty of care imposes demands on citizens, ie the pursuit of their aims while respecting others' legitimate interests. Therefore, the law of negligence frames risk imposition[83] in terms of equal freedom and mutual benefit, and the language of the law of negligence is clearly cast in terms of reasonableness and not rationality.

Keating also claims that Fried's and Fletcher's reciprocity theory is incomplete and, furthermore, does not shed light on the idea of duty of care. The failure is due to two reasons. First, there is no benchmark for, or permissible level of, the benefits and burdens of risk imposition. Secondly, there is no clarity on the appropriate level of reciprocal risk imposition. Keating argues that we must precisely define the contours of permissible risk imposition, as reciprocity is the only way to find the idea of equal freedom. The imposition of permissible risk is essential to pursuing our ends and flourishing as human beings. However, the idea of reciprocity gives no guidance on where, how, or why the benefits and burden should lie. As his own example illustrates, non-negligent road risks are equally reciprocal, regardless of the speed limit. Keating contends that we require deep moral philosophical foundations that ground reciprocity and suggests that Kantian contract theory, as advanced by Rawls' theory of justice,[84] can provide the necessary foundations.

The incommensurability of goods and the incompatibility of ends are the starting points for emerging principles of justice, which require us to strike a balance between the right to impose risks and the duty to take precautions. However, due to the nature of private interactions, we cannot directly apply Rawls' theory of justice, which is based on equal basic liberties, to negligence law. But, according to Keating, '*a fuller understanding of the concepts of freedom of action and security will enable us to develop the benchmarks of comparison necessary for determining which accidental risks imposition are reasonable and what behaviour constitutes due care*'.[85]

The contractualist theory of tort law views harms caused by negligent action as a threat to our self-determining agency, recognizing our agency and capacity to self-determine our ends as fundamental. As a result, freedom and our ability to exercise free choice predominate over other powers or capacities. We cannot trade off our agency against the overall interests and aims of society in general. Against this background, our liberties compete, and we must strike a balance to ensure that each person has equal freedom. It refers to the balance between equal freedom of action and freedom from accidental injury, ie freedom of security, in the context of negligence law. Keating asserts that risk imposition is unreasonable when it fails

[83] Keating relies on the normative foundation of the idea of reciprocity and risk imposition advanced by Charles Fried, *An Anatomy of Values: Problems of Personal and Social Choice*. Cambridge (Harvard UP 1970) and George P Fletcher, 'Fairness and Utility in Tort Law' (1972) 85 Harvard Law Review 537.
[84] John Rawls, *A Theory of Justice* (originally published in 1971, Harvard UP 1999).
[85] Keating, 'Reasonableness and Rationality' (n 81) 321.

the test of mutual benefit; '*they fail that test when they burden freedom of action more than they benefit security, and vice-versa*.'[86] Interestingly, Keating accepts that freedom of action and security are yardsticks of well-being, though very *abstract* ones.[87]

In later works, Keating criticizes corrective justice theory because it is backward-looking. It focuses on remedies and does guide the citizen in terms of her primary duties and the tort law's primary norms. By contrast, early formulations of the contractualist theory of negligence law do not seem to focus much on primary norms or duties. Once the right has been violated and the duty of care has not been met, contractualist reasoning comes into play, or at least in the specific way that courts have thought about it in their decisions. Prior to the accident or harm, the formulation is too abstract to enter into the agent's practical reasoning (see the next section for further discussion on this).

In his subsequent work, Keating also contends that the primary norm and its breach should be the focus of any tort theory. He argues that we have omnilateral obligations to others,[88] and that tort's primary rights and duties are an expression of these obligations. Tort law articulates our obligations to others.[89] However, unlike his earlier work, Keating does not base this approach on moral or political philosophy. He regrets that corrective justice is so focused on remedies.[90] Nevertheless, his analysis is based on Coleman's work,[91] as explicitly acknowledged by him. He presents Coleman's writing as his primary example of a corrective justice theory that focuses on remedies, implying that Weinrib's perspective does not focus solely on remedies. Keating expresses this as follows: '*Weinrib's conception of tort as being about "wrongs", not "wrongful losses", places his view closer to the view of this paper. On the other hand, his development of that idea mistakenly (in my view) tries to reverse engineer the wrongs out of the remedies*.'[92] This is certainly not a charitable reading of Weinrib's book *The Idea of Private Law*,[93] in which Weinrib dedicates an entire chapter to explaining how Kantian external freedom provides the grounding for what Keating calls 'the primary norm', ie the duty of the plaintiff and the right of the defendant in tort law. Reducing the principle of external freedom to the idea of '*reverse engineer(ing) the wrongs out of the remedies*' is uncharitable.

Keating is right, nonetheless, to bring to our attention the need to explain the obligations that we have towards others prior to any breach or violation of a right or duty. Thus, tort law and, more specifically, negligence law emphasize the idea

[86] ibid 325.
[87] ibid 325.
[88] Keating, 'The Priority of Respect Over Repair' (n 6) 308.
[89] ibid 318.
[90] ibid 295, 297.
[91] Jules L Coleman, *The Practice of Principle* (OUP 2003); Jules L Coleman, 'The Practice of Corrective Justice' in David Owen (ed), *Philosophical Foundations of Tort Law* (OUP 1995).
[92] Keating, 'The Priority of Respect Over Repair' (n 6) 302, fn 19.
[93] Weinrib (n 4).

that citizens should not breach their duties of care towards others. Claiming that the law of negligence only reveals these obligations, rights, and duties in the event of a breach would be absurd. As Keating underlined, the law of negligence pertains to rights and duties, and the violation of these rights gives rise to a secondary duty to repair. The law of negligence exists largely to ensure that we comply with it, engage with its values and ends, and prevent wrongdoing. As a result, we have a duty to discharge our obligations and duties while also respecting others' rights to be free from injury or harm.

In the next section, we will discuss the challenges that these theories confront and demonstrate how they provide deficient answers to one or more of these challenges.

§7.3 The Abstract Challenge and Person-Centred Theories

The abstract challenge establishes that the correlativity or bidirectional form of right/duty as *directionality to the addressee* of the legal norm obscures the nature of agency and the manner in which an agent engages with actions, resulting in a negligent action. It makes no difference how we carve the theoretical space to explain the grounds, scope, or domain of rights and duties in negligence law, whether through Kant's external freedom or morality and reasonableness principles. This is because Weinrib, Ripstein, and Keating obliterate agency and its key component, the deliberative perspective. Consequently, agency becomes so abstract that we are unable to understand the character and nature of the duty/right pair in relation to our practical reasoning.

We must begin to question Ripstein's or Weinrib's views on the 'internal' aspect of corrective justice theories. However, we have no explanation for why, according to Ripstein and Weinrib, the relationship must be internal as they characterize it, namely in relational or correlative terms. I provide the following diagnosis. According to Ripstein, it is internal in terms of the interactions between persons since people require the means to achieve their aims or goals, and choice can only be appreciated and known internally, implying free agency. Weinrib believes that *it is internal to judicial and/or legal thinking*, and that the latter should be arranged in terms of correlativity because this is the defining feature of the structure of thinking. '*Liability consists in a finding that the parties are situated correlatively to each other as doer and sufferer of the same injustice*.'[94]

Liability aims to correct this injustice. Interestingly, we see here that the internal structure of the thinking in corrective justice theories is in terms of *attribution* for the purposes of liability.[95] Following *Kant's Metaphysics of Morals*, Weinrib also

[94] Weinrib (n 4).

[95] Weinrib asserts: 'Aristotle, however, was the first to point to the distinctive features of this process: its bipolarity, its constrained standard of relevance, and *its relationship to adjudication*.' ibid

teaches us to abstract the correlativity between doer and sufferer from the matter of choice, focusing only on the interaction or form of the choice when both actions and deeds are *regarded* as free.[96]

Right only delineates the contours of permissibility, and negligent concepts guide judges in determining what is permissible and not. However, abstract rights cannot guide the citizen if the model of deliberation advanced in Chapters 4, 5, and 6 is sound. It would be illogical and against common sense to state that the citizen has a right only when this right is violated, namely in the context of negligence law only when 'doing' and 'suffering' are united. Prior to the violation of the plaintiff's right being violated, the defendant has a duty of care, though the plaintiff's abstract right cannot guide the citizen. The abstract right *qua* abstract cannot be translated or formulated as a value-based mean or end that engages the citizen's narrow and aspirational deliberation. Arguably, the abstract right only guides the citizen's action when it translates into what is particularly good, right, or worthy to pursue through deliberation.

Unfortunately, Weinrib explains reason through the lens of theoretical reason that come into being through '*the operation of the will*'.[97] In the first chapter, we demonstrated that some authors conflate the first-person or deliberative stance with the third-person perspective, and the backward-looking with the forward-looking perspectives. Weinrib, despite his efforts to engage with practical reason as choice, if only as external freedom, is not immune to the criticism of conflation. Actions are viewed as deeds that may be understood through concepts, and hence law is the domain of *right*. His theory only focuses on the third-person perspective and backward-looking stance. Values and the will's *substantive content* cannot play any role because the theory focuses on the external manifestation of the deliberators' actions and the space they occupy regarding each other.[98]

56, the emphasis is mine. 'The agent of this rectification is the judge. Aristotle connects adjudication to the bipolarity of corrective justice by deriving the word for judge (dikastes) from *dicha*, split into two . . . A controversy in corrective justice involves an allegation that the defendant has disturbed the equality pertaining to transactions. For Aristotle, the judge is the living representative of the quantitative equality between the parties.' ibid 65. See also ibid 84, where Weinrib states: 'The involvement of the judge means that corrective justice, although it deals with the interaction of two parties, involves an impartial and disinterested third party in assessing and enforcing the legal consequence of that interaction. In Kantian legal theory, the presence of the judge is not merely a phenomenologically observed element of private law but is conceptually necessitated by the mutual externality of the interacting agents.'

[96] Kant (n 22) 6:230.

[97] Weinrib (n 4) 87–88.

[98] Ripstein's and Weinrib's interpretations of Kant's Doctrine of Right are based on a narrow reading of the distinction between internal and external freedom. If Kant's conception of the realm of ends serves as the common normative source for his categorical imperative and the Doctrine of Right, then Ripstein's and Weinrib's exclusive focus on external freedom lacks justification. See Pauer-Studer, who advances an argument for this reading of Kant's *Groundwork of the Metaphysics of Morals* (n 22). Herlinde Pauer-Studer, '"A Community of Rational Beings". Kant's Realm of Ends and the Distinction Between Internal and External Freedom' (2016) 107 Kant Studien 125. Guyer has also posited the possibility of a shared origin between the principle of right and the moral law. Paul Guyer,

Both Ripstein's and Weinrib's theories of negligence law reduce the richness of deliberation to an abstract single point, where the agent experiencing suffering, harm, or loss meets the deed. They are united in an abstract interaction defined by *right*. Contrary to this conflation, which, from the point of view of the right theorist, seems inevitable, I have argued that there is an asymmetry between the first-person and third-person perspectives, and, more importantly, a recalcitrant asymmetry between the backward-looking and forward-looking perspectives. In the final chapter, we will demonstrate that a theoretical analysis of negligence law ignores this at its peril.

When an agent engages in a negligent action, her choice or practical deliberation is characterized differently when she views her action from a backward-looking perspective, as opposed to when she is deliberating and acting from a forward-looking perspective.[99] However, when we comprehend the relationship between the backward-looking and forward-looking perspectives, we understand that attributions of past events may involve a defective exercise of our practical reasoning. Consider the case of Alessandra,[100] who went to collect her children from hockey, but left her dog in the car, resulting in her dog's death. When Alessandra looks back at her action, the errors and mistakes in her practical reasoning 'dawn' on her, and there is a new 'seeing' of an aspect or layer of her own action that was not 'seen' before. She can now see the two aspects of her action: the forward-looking and the backward-looking. She can now also 'see' clearly her own mistakes and errors. We demonstrated in Chapters 4, 5, and 6 that deliberation is substandard or narrow. This implies that the agent establishes the *what* by examining the *how*, which in turn shapes her desires and passions, and vice versa. However, we have also shown

'Kant's Deductions of the Principles of Right' in *Kant's Metaphysics of Morals: Interpretative Essays* (Clarendon Press 2022) 23. See also Katrin Flikschuh, 'The Morality of External Freedom' in *Kant and Modern Political Philosophy* (CUP 2000) 80, who recognizes the role of desires in Kant's Doctrine of Right, but argues that these desires are constrained by reasons. See also Hills, who explores the possibility of deriving the principle of right from Kant's Formula of Humanity by interpreting key passages in Kant. Alison Hills, 'The Principle of Right: Practical Reason and Justification in Kant's Ethical and Political Philosophy' (2007) 3 Politics and Ethics Review 24. See also Kant (n 22) 6:239–40. After discussing the key difference between the moral law and the principle of right (the latter justifies coercion whereas coercion for the former is impermissible and even useless), Hills asserts that 'the moral law may require each individual herself to follow the principle of right, even if it does not support its coercive enforcement'. Hills (this note) 28. This implies that, despite acknowledging the inability to derive the principle of right from the Formula of Humanity, judges and legislators should strive to balance the moral law with the principle of right. However, coercion is legitimate only on the basis of the right principle. cf Allan Wood, 'The Final Form of Kant's Practical Philosophy' in Mark Timmons, *Kant's Metaphysics of Morals: Interpretative Essays* (Clarendon Press 2002) 1 and Marie Newhouse, 'The Legislative Authority' (2019) 24 Kantian Review 531.

[99] Note that Weinrib points out that Kant connects corrective justice to 'his obscure but powerful analysis of the process of willing'. Weinrib (n 4) 84. However, the connection between *willingness or choice* and corrective justice remains unexplored. Since the mode of thinking in corrective justice is mainly attributive, the willingness or choice is either given or presupposed. Thus, there is no analysis or attempt to connect justice and choice.

[100] See Chapter 1.

that it is possible to inhabit an aspirational perspective—'the upward journey to the specification of the *what*'—where we are able to integrate our narrow deliberation into medium- and longer-term goals and inhabit a new perspective, a more aspirational or cultivated view.

In Chapter 9, we will see that the law demands that we take this aspirational perspective, and that the aim of the legal reasoning underlying legal judgements is precisely to connect to the citizen's practical reasoning. The citizen actively participates in actions and activities, thereby adopting a forward-looking perspective. When we need to attribute responsibility for an action, we take a third-person perspective and resort to doctrinal concepts, for example duty of care, objective standard of care, causation, and remoteness of damage. Nonetheless, this is not how citizens engage with deliberation from the first-person perspective. The citizen's position is forward-looking towards the action, including acting negligently. Theorists ignore or confuse other internal perspectives, such as the deliberative stance and the aspirational stance, when they solely concentrate on the negligent action as an event.

Ripstein and Weinrib could argue that the predominant third-person perspective is precisely the judging perspective. Legal liability imposes this perspective on us as necessary or inevitable. The law embodies the abstraction of free choice between individuals, which *we need to regard as such or presupposed.* It requires that we look back at actions *as events or deeds* and attribute responsibility. The Kantian conception of external freedom gives us the precise grounds to engage with attribution. It abstracts from the practical reasoning or deliberative perspective of the agent; it abstracts from the matter of choice; it abstracts from the aims of the agent who engages in choosing and acting, considering only the space of interaction between two persons. Like billiard balls invading each other's space, the aim is to determine how one person's space has invaded another's and whether this is permissible if we assume that both agents are free. As a result, we require abstraction from both the first-person or deliberative perspective and the forward-looking perspective. However, in this book, we have demonstrated that actions as deeds or events, actions as abstractions from aims, and the subject matter of choice are deficient, incomplete, and even unintelligible. If we fail to address the fundamental question of the relationship between the backward- and forward-looking perspectives in action and negligence law, we risk misinterpreting the doctrinal aspects of negligence law and going astray on the grounds of responsibility for negligent acts in both law and ethics. The sceptical positions discussed in Chapter 2 will have an upper hand in the discussion.

In Chapter 9, I will show that the relationship between external freedom and practical reason is not as straightforward as presented by corrective justice theorists. I will also show that in order to connect to the citizen's practical reasoning, judges engage in both forward-looking and backward-looking perspectives. This becomes clear if we examine an inadvertent action. The structure of practical reasoning and, therefore, the nature of the action only become intelligible when we look at both the forward-looking and backward-looking perspectives.

The problem is not that abstract rights cannot encapsulate particularity as an empirical matter; nor is it that the idea of abstract rights is flawed because agents cannot interact, as agents' purposeful nature only exists as a potential.[101] Furthermore, we acknowledge the clear connection between the primary duty of 'you should not act wrongly and harm others' and the secondary duty of compensation that the injurer owes to the victim. Weinrib argues that the capacity to abstract is a necessary but not sufficient condition of free, purposeful agency.[102] Thus, Weinrib tells us that actualizing this capacity is key to understanding purposeful activity. Ripstein also recognizes that the conceptual structure of private wrongs is abstract and that there is a need for determination and consistency in particularity.[103]

Therefore, our objection does *not revolve around the challenge of transitioning from abstraction to particularity*. Our objection is that this abstraction is not present *at all* in the agent when she occupies the first-person or deliberative perspective, both in narrow or substandard and aspirational deliberations. Therefore, when the judges attribute a negligent act, their use of abstract doctrinal concepts cannot illuminate *what*, *how*, and *why* the agent engages with the world and its values. The purpose of the law of negligence is not for citizens to breach it, but for them to comply with it and have flourishing lives. The law of negligence and attributions of responsibility need to show how citizens engage with the law and how, when they fail to do so, they are responsible.

Corrective justice theorists might contest my stance, contending that the agent's narrow and aspirational deliberations are too particular, intricate, and complex to take into account when judgements of corrective justice are demanded in courts. Furthermore, judges need abstract doctrinal concepts that provide a justification for the attribution of responsibility for negligent actions. This, however, is a paradoxical way of thinking about the matter. The judge, through doctrinal concepts, establishes that a specific interaction between persons is not permissible, ie the negligent act falls below the standard of care and results in injury. The judge also establishes that the defendant's careless conduct violates the plaintiff's right not to be harmed, and that the plaintiff owes a duty of care to the defendant, in addition to a duty not to cause a loss. Therefore, conceptualizing this impermissible action in terms of duty of care and breach of the objective standard of care is the best possible approach. However, attribution is not the only purpose of negligence law. It also aims to prevent accidents and engage citizens to avoid them.

[101] Weinrib seems to think that this is the core critique of Perry (n 8). See also Weinrib (n 4) 126–27 and Jules L Coleman, 'Property, Wrongfulness and the Duty to Compensate' (1987) 63 Chicago-Kent LR 451.

[102] Weinrib (n 4) 127.

[103] Ripstein, *Private Wrongs* (n 3) 13.

However, if deliberation functions as both narrow and aspirational, then the citizen or addressee does not engage in the aforementioned mode of deliberation. This means that the idea of potential plaintiffs' rights and her own duty towards potential plaintiffs does not enter into the citizen's practical reasoning. He or she *does not choose in this abstract way* because this would presuppose that when she acts, she takes the third-person perspective of attributing *to herself an action*. In Alessandra's case, we would assert that she did foresee her dog's death from heat stroke while she was parking her vehicle at the hockey pitch, but she still left her dog in the vehicle. Here, negligent actions collapse into either reckless or intentional action. Or, more plausibly, if we wish to preserve the phenomenology of 'pure' negligence, assume she had no idea the dog would die of heat stroke or that she would have to stay longer than intended at the hockey pitch. We would argue that she 'should have foreseen' that keeping the dog in the vehicle with the temperature so high would violate her duty of care to the dog. The problem is that this perspective fails to provide insight into Alessandra's engagement with her duties, her thoughts, her own actions, potential ways to improve or become less negligent in the future, or how the law might shape her views. In other words, her 'doing' and 'becoming' cannot be grasped. Of course, we will not say that if Alessandra is careful and takes her dog with her to the hockey pitch, then she is conscientious about her duty of care because she has a legal duty of care towards her dog. We would instead say that in a healthy legal system, specific legal decisions and judges' reasoning show ways of engaging with values and ways of occupying a deliberative-aspirational perspective. In Chapter 9, we will show how the law provides *proleptic* thoughts and ways of thinking for our deliberations. My point here is that abstract formulaic sentences such as 'She should have foreseen it', 'It was foreseeable', 'She has taken a substantive and foreseeable risk', or 'She should have contemplated her duty of care' cannot enter into Alessandra's practical reasoning *while* she is acting.[104] Furthermore, formulaic or abstract reasoning cannot be part of her practical reason.

On the contrary, when the citizen engages in practical reasoning, she does not perceive herself as having a 'duty of care', nor does she understand the 'objective standard of care' or 'what a reasonable person ought to do' in terms of principles or rules. How can we expect her to interact with these concepts in such an abstract manner as to avoid causing the defendant harm? When she engages in her forward-looking action and adopts a first-person or deliberative stance, she is not considering the plaintiff's right to access the means to achieve her ends or the possibility that careless actions could deprive the plaintiff of these means. Such

[104] Not surprisingly, sceptics argue that the concept of negligence collapses into either recklessness or compulsion. Gary Watson, 'Scepticism About Weakness of the Will' in *Agency and Answerability: Selected Essays* (OUP 2004) 123 and Larry Alexander, Kim Ferzan, and Stephen Morse, *Crime and Culpability* (CUP 2009). See the discussion in Chapters 2 and 4.

doctrinal concepts that embody a moral idea are *abstract*, and at no stage of practical reasoning can the citizen engage with them. Nor can the citizen engage with doctrinal concepts at the stage of narrow deliberation or in the more reflexive stage of aspirational perspective. We have shown that to inhabit the aspirational perspective is also an exercise in grasping the particular, avoiding or recognizing a specific situation and values within determining circumstances. In Alessandra's case, she can 'see' the value of sports for her children and the importance of caring for a pet. She is attempting to balance both roles, as a mother who encourages her children to participate in sports and as a responsible pet owner, all while engaging in the world and carrying out her daily activities. Given that negligent actions revolve around the concept of doing and suffering, it is crucial for courts to understand how citizens exercise their practical reasoning, which fundamentally revolves around the act of doing.

If corrective justice principles were to enter into her practical reasoning, then the only value that would be salient in her deliberation would be something along the following lines: 'You need to respect the freedom of others' and/or 'You need to respect the autonomy of the people you interact with'. However, as we have seen in Chapters 4, 5, and 6, this value does not help or guide her actions. External freedom only establishes prohibitions, limits, and enforcement requirements. However, as demonstrated in previous chapters, both narrow and aspirational deliberations necessitate specific engagement with the values manifested in the action.

Ripstein is not totally indifferent to the importance of guiding the citizen through the law and that the law of negligence requires the citizen to care to avoid injuring others. Ripstein tells us: '*It is a qualified duty of non-injury; it does not simply tell you either that you ought to be careful or not to injure others, but rather instructs you not to injure them in certain ways*.'[105] Ripstein rejects the idea that it is a matter of character or concern for others.[106] This position effectively fences off moral luck arguments, but it does so at the cost of disregarding the perspective of the deliberating citizen. By contrast, it seeks an abstract viewpoint, such as *right*, which cannot be part of the citizen's practical reasoning. Ripstein asserts: '*the plaintiff's right explains why the defendant must be careful*.'[107]

However, this explanation is only attributive and backward-looking; it is only relevant once the violation of the right has happened. In other words, my point is that grasping this qualified duty is only possible if we engage in deliberation, both narrow and aspirational, and the 'seeing' is only possible if a certain transformation takes place.

In Chapter 9, I will expand on this point and argue that courts' decisions advance *proleptic thoughts and reasoning* for the citizens and addressees of legal

[105] Ripstein, *Private Wrongs* (n 3) 117.
[106] ibid 116.
[107] ibid 118.

norms. Judges use practical reasoning to engage citizens, incorporating legal principles and rules as values into their *proleptic* thoughts during both narrow and aspirational deliberations. I will also show that legal principles and rules do not appear *qua* principles and rules, but *qua* values in the citizens' practical reasoning, and that good judges know this. Thus, the law, in the form of legal decisions, is an invitation for the citizen to inhabit the deliberative-aspirational perspective and integrate it with their character.

In this way, the proposal for a theoretical foundation of the law of negligence advances a version of the 'continuity' thesis in which ethical thinking is in continuity with legal thinking. However, we arrive at this conclusion from very different premises than those advanced by theorists who defend the 'continuity' thesis. Our conception is based on a sound, psychologically realistic, and complex framework of deliberation, action, practical reason, and negligent action.

Nor does Keating's contractualist theory provide a satisfactory answer to the *abstract challenge*. As previously stated, he recognizes that freedom of action and security are the yardsticks of well-being that should determine the principle of reciprocity in negligence law. He relies on Rawls's theory of justice[108] to provide the normative grounding for the idea of reciprocity. This means that our agency as self-determining individuals pursuing our ends, as well as the need to avoid impermissible or illegitimate conflicts due to the incommensurability of goods, require a balance of freedom and security. However, Keating recognizes that the balance required between freedom of action and security is *abstract*. As a result, it is unclear how they can be an integral part of the citizen's practical reasoning, seeking to pursue her ends and have a flourishing life. Of course, we would need a more precise account of action and practical reason that would explain how this balanced view of reciprocity can enter into the citizen's practical reason. We might need to flesh out an account that combines Kant's external and internal practical reason. Otherwise, Keating's account remains incomplete and mysterious. However, if the model of deliberation and practical reason that I defend is sound, the citizen's practical reasoning cannot incorporate notions such as rights, duties, and omnilateral rights unless they can be articulated in terms of what is good, valuable, or worthy in the particular circumstances, such as the right of security, which is articulated as the protection of one's physical integrity, for instance, in the specific case of driving a vehicle.

In later work, Keating criticizes corrective justice theory because it is (merely) backward-looking; it focuses on remedies and does not serve to guide the citizen in terms of her primary duties and the primary norms. He asserts that common law legal decisions not only bind us retrospectively but also prospectively on '*all who fall within its scope. They obligate indefinite classes of potential wrongdoers and*

[108] Rawls (n 84).

protect indefinite classes of potential victims going forward indefinitely.'[109] This is an important thought, but it is incomplete because Keating does not explain how citizens can engage with their obligations. I will offer an explanation of how citizens engage with their obligations and duties in Chapter 9 of this book.

Goldberg and Zipursky appear to overcome the abstract challenge by arguing that our legal practices and self-understanding determine the content of the legal structure of the right/duty pair. They do less well, however, when we think about the *particularity challenge*. Goldberg and Zipursky's conception of action as applied to the law of negligence is in tension with the idea that the directive-based relationality thesis is central. If the defendant's action and conduct are central to explaining the tort of negligence, then their theory cannot respond to the *challenge of particularity*. I shall address this criticism in the following section.

§7.4 Person-Centred Theories and the Particularity Challenge

The *particularity challenge* is a corollary of the *abstract challenge*, conveying the idea that engagement with, or avoidance of, a negligent action on the part of the law's addressees cannot be from the point of view of general and abstract rules, directives, or principles, such as rights or respect for others.[110] We should engage with, or avoid, a negligent action through narrow or substandard and aspirational deliberation, viewing the latter as continuous with the former. As shown in Chapters 4, 5, and 6, the legal rules' and principles' addressee cannot engage in modes of thinking and concepts that are alien to her deliberative stance, such as risk, probability, and foreseeability. Nor can the addressee engage with directives or norms that emerge from our social practices alone, as Goldberg and Zipursky aim to demonstrate. It is unclear how to transition from social practice to directives or norms, which are characteristically normative. This normative element can be expressed as follows: the social practice itself offers a self-understanding of the law of negligence, based on the relevant directives and norms. According to Goldberg and Zipursky, this self-understanding is based on the right/duty pair. However, in normative terms, this emergence of the right/duty pair seems arbitrary because it

[109] Keating, 'The Priority of Respect Over Right' (n 6) 322.

[110] Weinrib seems to justify liability for the inadvertent imposition of a risk, as the injurer would have failed to demonstrate respect for the persons who are within the domain of the risk. However, this would fail to address the particularity challenge. Perry raises another important challenge to Weinrib's position. He argues that failure to respect others who are within the risk domain will result in responsibility regardless of harm. Therefore, the obvious punishment is criminal punishment, not reparation. However, the law of negligence only assigns responsibility when harm occurs. In other words, as expressed by Perry, 'Weinrib states that "takings are wrongs that constitute general denials of the validity of right," but surely this denial is present whether or not the attempt to assert dominion succeeds. According to Weinrib, liability in tort juridically nullifies the denial, but liability presupposes harm and so cannot serve as a general mode of nullification. The remedy that naturally serves this role is, again, criminal punishment.' Perry (n 8) 487.

is the result of social practices alone, and there is no guarantee that an alternative legal framework would not have emerged.

Goldberg and Zipursky aim to show that the defendant's conduct cannot be separated from the plaintiff's loss or injury and that this non-separation between conduct and loss is the correct conception of action. Goldberg and Zipursky offer no explanation or further argumentation to support this notion. Goldberg and Zipursky's directive-based relationality thesis appears to be the source of their methodological approach to action. Nothing suggests this is a valid explanation of action. Goldberg and Zipursky argue that the directive-based relationality thesis is the result of our social practices. Furthermore, their theory concludes that the directives' addressees do not need to engage with the values or the structure of thinking underlying the directive or rules. But this argument appears question-begging. Moreover, Goldberg and Zipursky fail to explain how negligence law is forward-looking. However, let us suppose that they were to adopt the idea that there is citizens' engagement with the law of negligence via directives and rules that emerge from social practice. The courts' decisions and doctrinal concepts articulate these rules and principles. However, if the model of deliberation that we have defended is sound, Goldberg and Zipursky's theory cannot explain how citizens exercise their practical reasoning, as this requires engagement with values. Rules and principles cannot enter into a citizen's practical reasoning.

For Goldberg and Zipursky, the conduct or action, including how the defendant conceived her action or the knowledge that she had when she was engaged in the negligent action, plays no role in the justification and explanation[111] of the law of negligence.[112] Goldberg and Zipursky point out that the correct description that identifies a negligent act is 'x negligently injured y' and *not* 'x acted carelessly, and y suffered a setback because of x's careless act'. They assert:

> To ground a claim for negligence, the plaintiff's injury must ordinarily be a *realization of the aspects of the defendant's behavior*[113] that rendered it careless: the plaintiff's injury must be capable of being cogently described as being *immanent within the defendant's carelessness.*[114] Negligence, in other words, contains a directive that enjoins careless injuring, not careless conduct itself, nor even harm caused (in any manner) by careless conduct.

[111] Goldberg and Zipursky, *Recognizing Wrongs* (n 5) 248–49.

[112] There is a specific conception of 'wrong' advocated by Goldberg and Zipursky that is not related to blameworthiness or conduct. See ibid 187–99. A conduct is 'wrong' when it is attributed as such by the courts in their interpretation of the legal material. ibid 106, 182. The argument underlying the view that conduct is irrelevant in negligence is that there is an objective standard of care, which is defined according to what a reasonable person would do in the specific circumstances. See ibid 104, 107. Assessment of liability is in terms of what the defendant ought to have done, not what they actually do. See ibid 191–92.

[113] The emphasis is mine.

[114] The emphasis is mine. Goldberg and Zipursky, *Recognizing Wrongs* (n 5) 248–49.

The legal directive establishes the nexus between the injury and the careless conduct, but the nexus is not in terms of an evaluation of the conduct; it is in virtue of the right/duty pair and the directive-based relationality thesis.

This is a paradoxical position because the role of the different criteria to evaluate conduct is now unclear. For instance, in English law, foreseeability, proximity, and the reasonable person[115] are the standard of care; in the US, it is reasonable risk. It is unclear how we can determine and assess negligent conduct from a philosophical perspective, as Goldberg and Zipursky do not provide a detailed and justified theory of action to evaluate conduct or action in general. The philosophical and conceptual implications of phrases in this paragraph such as, '*the plaintiff's injury must ordinarily be the realization of the aspects of the defendant's behavior*' or '*the plaintiff's injury must be capable of being cogently described as being immanent within the defendant's carelessness*' are unclear. What do 'being *immanent*' and '*realization*' mean here? This conception of action is too weak to justify the attribution of responsibility for negligence.

For Goldberg and Zipursky, the core view that explains and justifies the tort of negligence is the directive-relationality thesis, which emphasizes the plaintiff's right not to be injured or suffer loss, as well as defendant's duties, which the courts elucidate through practice-based directives of the law of negligence. The state confers an empowerment in the form of a civil recourse on the plaintiff, shaping the special relationship between the plaintiff and the defendant. Consequently, according to this view, questions regarding the defendant's subjective understanding and description of her action, or whether the defendant was a proximate cause of injury or loss suffered by the plaintiff, are not at the core of the justificatory and/or explanatory framework of the law of negligence. The knowledge and conduct of the defendant and *whether it was foreseeable that the action of the defendant would cause harm seem irrelevant*.[116] The directive-based relationality thesis seems to do all the required work because the right/duty pair defines what kind of action is a negligent one.

[115] The English case *Blyth v Birmingham* establishes the principle of the reasonable person as the standard of care in the law of negligence. 'Negligence is the omission to do something that a reasonable man, *guided upon those considerations which ordinarily regulate the conduct of human affairs*, would do, or doing something which a prudent and reasonable man would not do' (the emphasis is mine). *Blyth v Birmingham Waterworks Company* (1856) 11 Ex Ch 781. In Chapter 9, I contend that only narrow and aspirational deliberations can settle these considerations that 'ordinarily regulate the conduct of human affairs'. I show that courts' decisions advance proleptic thoughts grounded on descriptions and re-descriptions of values, either aspirational or less aspirational, so that they enter into the citizens' practical reason. In this way, my account gives content to the reasonableness and ordinariness of our legal duties. See Benjamin Zipursky, 'Sleight of Hand' (2007) 48 William and Mary Law Review 2033 for a discussion of the ideas of 'ordinariness' and 'reasonable person' in the law of negligence.

[116] For a full development of my criticism of Goldberg's and Zipursky's civil recourse tort law theory, see my article, Verónica Rodríguez-Blanco, 'The Law of Negligence, Blameworthy Action and the Relationality Thesis: A Dilemma for Goldberg and Zipursky's Civil Recourse of Tort Law' (2021) 41 Law and Philosophy 63. For Goldberg's and Zipursky's replies to my views, see Richard Goldberg and Benjamin Zipursky, 'Replies to Commentators' (2021) 41 Law and Philosophy 127.

The result of this reasoning is that Goldberg's and Zipursky's theory of civil recourse cannot explain how practices and the legal practised-emerging right/duty pair are connected to the citizen's practical reasoning. In Goldberg's and Zipursky's theories, the issue of the particularity of the legal judgment that engages the citizen's practical reasoning remains unclear. They advance the idea that social practices play a crucial role in understanding the right/duty pair. However, they fail to explain how the citizen's practical reasoning, *through* the particularity of a legal judgment, enables them to comply with the law of negligence.

§7.5 Aim-Centred Theories of Negligence Law

Aim-centred theories focus on our aims or goals. The role of our institutions is to identify the most efficient way to achieve these aims or goals. If these goals and aims cannot be achieved, then the social institution, specifically the private law of negligence, can be discarded. These theories prioritize what we can and should achieve, while downplaying the significance of the character and nature of individuals and their relationships, resulting in an aim-centred approach. These theories suggest that once we have a clear understanding of what and how we should achieve them, the nature of agency and action, along with institutions like law, become a function of what and how we should achieve our aims and goals. Consequently, these theories tend to oversimplify our agency and the nature of our actions, which in turn oversimplifies the principles of negligence in law in particular and private law in general. We alternatively refer to these theories as functionalist or instrumentalist theories of tort law.

Because the purpose of these theories is to advance social goals, it is inevitable to conduct a comparative analysis between persons. For example, when evaluating the standard of care, it is necessary to conduct a comparative analysis. This can be done using the Learned Hand Formula in *Carroll Towing*.[117] This approach involves assessing the probability that an event will occur and comparing it against the gravity of the harm, as well as the cost or burden of the precautions to avoid the risk. However, Posner[118] extends the Learned Hand Formula and contends that it is actually an economic test. In other words, the test establishes whether the defendant has taken an effective level of precautions by balancing the cost of precautions against the cost of harm, while considering the probability of harm occurring. As a result, the question concerns the cost of taking precautions against an accident. If the safety measure's cost is less than the benefit derived from the activity, society will be better off. However, if the cost of taking precautions outweighs the

[117] *United States v Carroll Towing Co*, 159 F.2d 169–73 (2d Cir 1947). See *Paris v Stephney Borough Council* [1950] UKHL 3 for an English case that uses the Learned Hand Formula.

[118] Posner, 'A Theory of Negligence' (n 7).

benefits of the activity, society will be worse off. The focus of this analysis is on harm rather than wrongdoing.

§7.6 Aim-Centred Theories of Negligence and the Deterrence Challenge

Corrective justice proponents justify the use of deterrence as a form of coercion because it acts as a barrier to freedom, preventing one person's freedom from infringing upon another's.[119]

The citizen does not need to engage with their respective duties or incorporate the law into their practical reasoning. There is no need to locate one's practical reasoning in the normative world of law. Weinrib tells us:

> Since the point of right is to hold the external aspect of action to the external demands of practical reason, law must posit an external force capable of determining the actor's will, that is, capable of acting as a *deterrent*.[120] The prospect of external coercion complements the prospectivity of legal duty, by giving potential violators notice of the consequences attending any violation.[121]

Ripstein's analysis starts with the risk that has already materialized due to the defendant's wrongful conduct, which involved a negligent use of her means and resulted in the plaintiff's injury. No global assessment of risk from the defendant is contemplated, and whether the conduct of the defendant was bad or not is relevant[122] *only* when attribution in the courts takes place. Ripstein explains that the foreseeability requirement in the law of negligence is merely a formal constraint. Therefore, the law does not require you to consider factors that are beyond your control, and this is precisely what makes something unforeseeable.[123]

One way of interpreting this view is as follows; the judge makes an attribution of responsibility for negligence only for what is foreseeable, because this is what can be required or demanded from the defendant. However, if the role of the law primarily plays an attributive role unrelated to the defendant's conduct, *it remains unclear why the judge should refer to the defendant's conduct* and the actions the defendant ought to or could have taken.

In other words, we could describe the stance of Ripstein and Weinrib as both paradoxical *and incomplete*. It is paradoxical because it implies that the judge's

[119] Weinrib (n 4) 108 and Kant (n 22) 6:307.
[120] The emphasis is mine.
[121] Weinrib (n 4) 108.
[122] Ripstein, *Private Wrongs* (n 3) 88.
[123] ibid 89.

practical reasoning is the only one that holds significance. The citizen is subjected to coercion, and as a form of coercion, deterrence functions as an empirical reality within the citizen. Empirical reality, as described by Kant using the analogy of Phaedrus' wooden head, is empty, yet it inevitably resurfaces in the form of coercion as a means of deterrence. It is justified from the point of view of *right*, the judge, and the law; yet it may not be justified from the citizen's point of view. The reasoning behind the law's reference to foreseeability as a crucial aspect of the defendant's conduct renders it incomplete.

Advocates of aim-centred theories contend that they have an advantage over corrective justice theories in terms of deterrence. They effectively interact with citizens by offering incentives. However, for aim-centred theories, incentives are mainly empirical, ie they focus on the pain that the agent would suffer as a result of paying compensation without considering the citizen's practical reasoning. Their focus is on motivation as conceived empirically. Their conception of action aligns more closely with the Humean view on agency, in which the bifurcation thesis, as elucidated in Chapter 3, is dominant. Desires are separated from reasons or beliefs. The latter determines the means to achieve desires or desire-based ends, but the former are merely determined empirically by our passions and impulses, for example the inclination to avoid the pain of paying compensation. There is no further intelligible connection whereby reasons transform desires, other than the causal connection between means and ends.

Legal incentives function based on citizens' desires and impulses, while deterrence relies on this conception of agency. Judges employ a cost-benefit analysis to both impose a specific conduct on the citizen and achieve a specific social goal, eg maximization of wealth, with the expectation of deterring citizens from acting in certain ways in the future. The citizen's primary motivation is to shield herself from the courts' legal obligation to provide compensation. In this way, the courts shape the citizens' conduct. According to this picture, the citizen depicted appears to prioritize avoiding the pain of the cost of compensation rather than engaging with reasons or values. As a corollary, the law's guidance will be limited, focusing solely on *avoiding or affirming the conduct in purely empirical terms*. We will now turn to this analysis.

§7.7 Aim-Centred Theories of Negligence and the Guidance Challenge

If action is understood solely in empirical terms, such as motivations, impulses, and incentives, it becomes challenging to envision how citizens might effectively engage with the principles and rules advanced by legal courts, as well as the embedded values that legal principles and rules presuppose. The core motivation for the citizen to align with the social aims of courts, such as taking necessary precautions to avoid a specific harm, would be to avoid the cost or pain of paying compensation. Her own apprehension and calculation of the pain she would experience from paying the appropriate compensation will determine the self-correction of her conduct. The potential alignment of her conduct with social aims will not be the result of her own reasoning. She will be alienated from the law, perceiving it as the result of judges and legislators who are focused on achieving social aims, specifically by calculating costs to reflect compensation to address the harm caused by her negligent action. Her actions will be limited to avoiding the pain that results from negligent conduct, such as the financial consequences of compensating for the harm caused by her negligence. As a result, there will be a disassociation between the citizen's motivations and the judges' legal reasoning.

Judges' reasoning based on standards of care and reasonableness will not resonate with her, as her primary focus is on avoiding or minimizing the costs resulting from her actions. For example, the employer in a chemical factory asks his employees to wear protective equipment only in order to avoid paying compensation for potential accidents. Injuries suffered by his employees and the value of physical integrity play no motivational role in his thinking. The employer will act for the 'wrong kind of reasons',[124] and her action will be alienated from the value embedded in the legal rule, ie employees should wear protective equipment to avoid injury and preserve their physical integrity.

Aim-centred theories accept that the wrongness of causing something, such as blindness or a mutilated arm, has no resonance in the employer's practical reasoning. Worse, the practical reasoning of the employer is not involved when the law establishes responsibility for negligence. Furthermore, they strip the law of all ethical or normative force. Thus, aim-centred theories provide an answer to the guidance challenge of negligence, *but at the cost of losing agency as we understand it.* Neither laymen nor legal practitioners, such as lawyers, judges, and legislators, can recognize the reasoning framework of aim-centred theories. These theories say the law would be better without moral language. According to these theories, the law would do better if all moral language in it disappeared.[125]

[124] See Rabinowicz and Ronnow-Rasmussen for a discussion on moral philosophy on the 'wrong kind reasons'. This term refers to an evaluation that does not fit the acting. As opposed to the wrong kind of reasons, there are right kinds of reasons that fit the object and provide the grounds for action. Wlodek Rabinowicz and Toni Ronnow-Rasmussen, 'The Strike of the Demon: On Fitting Pro-Attitudes and Values' (2004) 114 Ethics 391. Arguably, in the case of the employer who acts to avoid the cost of paying compensation, we would say that she misses the correct grounds for action, ie protecting the physical integrity and lives of his employees.

[125] Richard Posner, 'The Path Away from the Law' (1997) 110 Harvard Law Review 1039, 1041.

§7.8 The Legal and Moral Continuity Conception of Negligence Law

Finally, there are theories that argue that there is a continuity between the specific features of our agency, personhood, action, and our aims and goals. Agency, personhood, and action are neither a function of our aims and goals nor vice versa. They reject the reductionism of aim-centred theories as well as argue that permissible interactions should not be the only focus of our agency and action. As a result, the outcome of our actions should play a role in describing our actions and in determining responsibility. We intimately connect our outcomes to our moral and ethical goals and aims. The law of negligence reflects the continuity between our agency, the structure of our legal thinking, and, on the other hand, our ethical and moral agency. These theorists advance the so-called 'continuity' conception of negligence law.

Honoré has argued that we are responsible not only for our intentional actions but also for extensions of our agency, such as luck-resultant outcomes, which he refers to as 'outcome responsibility'.[126] The objective standard of care is the defining standard because we are responsible for the outcomes of our actions, even if we believe we are acting soundly and are following the correct standard. If we did not act according to the objective standard and caused harm, we would be responsible.

The objective standard demands that the citizen act as a reasonable person[127] would act in a similar circumstance or situation. Therefore, we expect citizens to model their actions after those of a diligent, careful, and thoughtful person engaging in the relevant activity. For instance, consider a reasonable father tending to a sick child, a reasonable pilot descending in an emergency, a reasonable employer handling chemicals, a reasonable doctor assisting a cancer patient, and a reasonable solicitor drafting a will for a terminally ill patient.

The objective standard will disregard features of one's character such as laziness, lack of concentration, impatience, volatility, and so on. It will also disregard our current skills, for example poor parenting skills or unsatisfactory medical training, and demand that we engage in the respective activity as if we were a reasonable person, for example a reasonable father, doctor, pilot, or solicitor. According to Honoré, when we act in the world, we produce things that we intend, but we can also cause harm that we did not intend. We sometimes, pleasantly, produce things that we do not intend. This is because we are constituted in certain ways, and we find ourselves in specific circumstances that we do not always control.[128] Furthermore, the principle of risk distribution, Honoré tells us, establishes precisely this. The following passage is illustrative of his point: '*We cannot take the*

[126] Honoré (n 8) 14.
[127] ibid 17.
[128] ibid 9.

credit without the discredit, since that would be to violate the principle of taking the rough with the smooth—a principle that possesses moral force and perhaps can be regarded as a form of distributive justice (risk-distributive justice).'[129] Thus, we reap the benefits of our good luck. However, Honoré's use of the metaphor of a wager reminds us that we also bear the responsibility for our bad luck, which stems from our actions. Because this attribution of action outcomes defines us and our character.[130]

However, Honoré fails to explain how the outcome of our actions, even those that are outside of our awareness, knowledge, attention, and control, might contribute to our sense of self, namely our identity and character formation. Honoré advances the notion that general capacity[131] is the primary determinant of control. While it does not provide complete control, it does offer a certain degree of control. Consequently, we are held responsible for negligence since we possess the ability to successfully perform the action that we have failed to accomplish.[132] Honoré seems to struggle with his own proposal when we read the following two contradictory sentences. In one key passage Honoré tells us that, since '*people do not have complete control over what they do, human action always involves risk-taking, and one of the risks we take when we act is that of incurring blame or liability because we fall short of our normal level of achievement*'.[133] Honoré aims to explain blame or liability, but he now tells us that when we act, we take the risk of incurring blame or liability. Nevertheless, the premise of action and risk supposedly establishes why we are blameworthy. However, in the same paragraph, he tells us that '*it is not easy to say why moral blame should be affected by the agent's relative capacity and freedom*'. Freedom and capacity appear to be the essential factors in unlocking blame and maybe liability. At other points, Honoré appears to suggest that we can reconcile both perspectives: the notion that both good and bad luck play a role in the outcomes of our interventions in the world, and the idea that we are in control over our actions due to our freedom and general capacity. This is because (a) we need to attribute responsibility for inadvertent actions to foster individual and social well-being, maintain social order, and encourage us to do well; and (b) it is the condition that enables the development of our personal character and identity, which holds value for its own sake.[134] Nevertheless, the text fails to provide an elucidation of how legal directives, norms, rules, and principles can enter into our practical reasoning, enabling us to do well and shaping our personal character and identity.

[129] ibid.
[130] ibid 10, 15, 76–77.
[131] Several authors in legal ethics and legal philosophy develop this 'capacity' view. For a discussion and criticism of this view, see §8.3.4.
[132] Honoré (n 8) 11–12, 29. He sometimes refers to this capacity as 'minimum capacity for choosing and acting', see ibid 14–15.
[133] ibid 12.
[134] ibid 10, 125.

Furthermore, the sceptical concerns raised in Chapter 2 resurface in this discussion. If we lack the ability to control our actions, and, as Honoré acknowledges, the agent does not know the circumstances of her actions, and the knowledge of her own incompetence seems to go hand in hand with her ignorance or lack of knowledge, then how can we conclude that she is at fault? Where is the wrong in her action? Moreover, if any fault of character seems impossible to correct within the given timeframe, how can we attribute responsibility on the basis of a negligent act that manifests fault or wrongness?[135]

Honoré seems to endorse a radical conception of action. On the one hand, we have a general capacity to choose, but once we choose and start the action, we cannot fully control what happens, and, therefore, we are subject to either good or bad luck.[136] Honoré tells us: '*The person concerned, though he cannot be sure what the outcome of his action will be, has chosen to act in the knowledge that he will be credited or debited with whatever it turns out to be*.'[137]

This model of action justifies his view of responsibility as outcome-based. However, there is no explanation or argument to support this model of action. Worse, it seems that the model does not fit our everyday ethical and moral experiences.

As demonstrated in Chapters 4, 5, and 6, we have short, medium-, and long-term plans, and if we deliberate and work on our character and passions, we tend to succeed in doing what we aim for. It would be strange to say, 'I intend to make coffee this morning, but I am not sure whether I will succeed', or 'I intend to marry my fiancé Thomas tomorrow, but I do not know whether I will succeed'. Imagine a medical student stating, 'I intend to study medicine at the University of London and have received an offer to study there, but I do not know whether I will succeed in becoming a doctor'. In this case, we assume that the student has taken the necessary admissions exams, has achieved the A-Level requirements, has the correct temperament and vocation to study medicine, and that the University of London has given her an unconditional offer. If she does not succeed, it is because she does not have the skills, endurance, vocation, or fortitude to succeed in her plan to study medicine. This means that she failed in both her narrow and aspirational deliberations (see Chapters 4, 5, and 6). However, for Honoré, it seems that we choose, and this means that I say to myself, 'I will do x' and from that point on, it is all random or arbitrary whether the agent will succeed or not. Furthermore, the role of law in building and shaping our practical reasoning becomes totally mysterious, and his statement that law 'encourages us to do well' collapses.

Moreover, Honoré's assertion that the justification for outcome responsibility stems from its connection to our personal identity and character is also flawed.

[135] ibid 18–19.
[136] ibid 31.
[137] ibid 31.

According to Honoré, the ownership of my action is due to my 'choosing', but after that, nothing that I do changes what I do. As a result, many of the actions' results or outcomes may not feel like they are 'ours'. We have not contributed to producing what has come about in the world. Let us go back to the example of the person making coffee. She might express, 'I plan to prepare coffee this morning, but I'm uncertain about my chances of success.' This means that she is only responsible for choosing; her personal identity is connected to her choosing, but not for bad or good results. Let us suppose that the coffee machine breaks, and the agent fails to succeed. Why would she be responsible for not making coffee? Let us suppose that she succeeds and makes coffee. If Honoré's action model is sound, this means that the agent feels responsible for her actions. However, she might also believe that her actions are random or arbitrary, as this is one of Honoré's premises. After choosing to act, it is arbitrary whether she will succeed or not. Her choices must, at least in part, determine her sense of identity, as a manifestation of who she is in the world. Since she cannot control the outcome, it is unclear why Honoré thinks that the attribution of responsibility will be connected to the agent's identity, given that the results and outcomes are just random or arbitrary.[138] One possible response is to say that 'we take responsibility' for what we do when we choose to engage in an activity, even if the outcomes are due to bad luck. Nevertheless, it is unclear what this 'taking of responsibility' means. Honoré presents it as an inevitable and necessary outcome of the distributive justice principle of risks. Because our actions and situations are uncertain, we need to distribute the risks of our activities, which means that we must 'take responsibility' for good and bad outcomes.

The problem with this solution is that it commits a *petitio principii* fallacy. Outcome responsibility would be explained by the obscure notion of 'taking responsibility',[139] but we do not yet know what responsibility is. Furthermore, this model no longer relies on individual responsibility, but rather on the concept of 'taking responsibility', which takes into account the randomness or arbitrariness of the results and our actions' uncertainties. This model relies on an implausible conception of action, in which the agent chooses to act, and the results are arbitrary. Directives, norms, rules, and principles do not assist us in choosing. If we follow Honoré's model of action, once we choose, the law plays no role in shaping our action. These results contradict Honoré's conclusions and put pressure on his model of action and legal responsibility.

Gardner advances two key arguments to provide further sophistication and philosophical support for Honoré's position. First, Gardner defends the idea that responsibility involves being answerable for the outcomes of our actions and giving

[138] Honoré suggests that we *implicitly* choose the outcomes, good or bad, when we act. Honoré (n 8) 77. However, it remains unclear why he holds this view, and there is no additional justification or clarification of what 'implicitly' means in this particular context.

[139] See Chapter 9 for further discussions on the issue of 'taking responsibility'.

reasons to ourselves and others.[140] He asserts that outcome responsibility is an aspect of responsibility as answerability. Secondly, Gardner uses Von Wright's theory of action[141] to defend the view that one should not separate actions from their outcomes. According to Von Wright, actions are specified by their effects, namely outcomes, rather than by end states, ie their results. Thus, the open window could be the result of an intentional action of opening the window or of someone who hinders another's action of closing the window. In Von Wright's *Norm and Action*,[142] the author establishes a distinction between action and behavior. In a normal *façon de parler*, we say that the former has an inner component that is characterized as the intentionality of the action. However, he also aims to demonstrate that there are neither inner nor outer aspects, as these would suggest an internal process occurring within the agent, and an external process mirroring the inner process. According to Von Wright, the connection between intention and bodily movement is a *logical* connection. Intention is not a mental event but rather a description of what the agent does when she is doing it. Let us suppose that I say, 'I will make a cappuccino this morning', but I have an espresso instead. We would say then that either I changed my mind, ie I decided to make an espresso instead, or something went wrong, or there was an error or mistake in producing my intentional action.

However, like Honoré, if Gardner relies on Von Wright's conception of action, it appears that he is simply stating what we need to explain. We need to explain *why* we are responsible for the outcome of our actions when we fall short of meeting the objective standard of care, even if these failures are not the result of our intentional or deliberate actions. According to Von Wright's action model, we cannot refer to what our actions create in the world if they are unintentional. Perhaps Gardner has in mind a more extensive meaning of the term 'intentional action'. This would include what we bring about through our intentional action, as well as desired and undesirable states of affairs. Let us suppose, following the example in Chapter 1, that Alessandra states she will take her dog for a promenade in the car and collect her children at the hockey pitch. However, if the outcome of her action is that 'she killed her dog as she left it in her vehicle', we would say that she either changed her mind and went to kill her dog, or something went wrong with her intentional action. Gardner's reliance on Von Wright's conception of action, which describes actions based on their outcome, raises questions about why our responsibility assessments do not actually stop at the descriptions of the agent as not knowing or not paying the required attention. Sceptical approaches will have the upper hand

[140] John Gardner, 'The Mark of Responsibility' (2003) 23 Oxford Journal of Legal Studies 157 and Gardner 'From Personal Life to Private Law' (n 8) 75. In tort law, Herschovitz also advocates for an answerability model of responsibility. See Scott Herschovitz, 'Harry Potter and the Trouble with Tort Theory' (2010) 63 Stanford Law Review 67. For a further critique of this model in law and ethics, see §8.3.1 and §8.3.2.

[141] Gardner focuses on Von Wright, see Von Wright (n 69). See Gardner, 'From Personal Life to Private Law' (n 8) 59, fn 2.

[142] Von Wright (n 69).

precisely because their point is that the agent did not know what she was doing, and therefore we cannot attribute responsibility. The third-person perspective and attributions of responsibility differ significantly from the agent's own description of her action.

Gardner's second idea, which posits that we should describe our actions in terms of their outcomes, is premised on the idea that we are accountable for the results of our actions. Gardner articulates this reasoning in the following formulation:

> *In assessing how we did, how we fared, we cannot but think of ourselves (and others) as the agents of outcomes. This goes with us wherever we go. In language I favoured elsewhere, our outcome responsibility is an aspect of our basic responsibility. Our basic responsibility is our ability and propensity, as rational beings, to explain ourselves (including our actions as well as our intentions, beliefs, desires, emotions, etc.) by giving reasons.*[143]

This view seems to put the cart before the horse. The idea that we are responsible for the outcomes of our actions, even when we do not intend them, is based on the premise that we are rational and therefore answerable beings. But again, why would I be answerable for something that I did not intend? Answerability precisely tells us that we accept some outcomes as ours, while we should reject other states of affairs as not produced by us. Moral philosophers have developed this idea of responsibility as answerability based on a theory of action connected to evaluative judgements, which can be extrapolated to explain responsibility for negligence. In Chapter 8, I will demonstrate responsibility, as answerability also fails to explain negligent action.

If Von Wright's characterization of action is sound, we need an explanation of *why the description of the action as outcome is the correct one* and why responsibility as answerability is the correct account of responsibility for negligent actions. The former cannot be the premise for the second idea because it would mean 'whatever we are answerable for, then we are also responsible for'. This understanding of responsibility in negligence as answerability deflates our understanding of responsibility and agency for negligent acts. Chapter 8 demonstrates this in detail. Additionally, we need to explain what happens when the agent performs an action that *deviates* from the description of what she intended to do. Furthermore, we need to address the challenges raised by the sceptical positions discussed in Chapter 2. Sceptics have argued that we cannot be responsible for an action concerning which we do not know the specific circumstances. For example, if were distracted, forgetful, or not attentive, and therefore, we *did not intend* the action.

[143] Gardner, 'From Personal Life to Private Law' (n 8) 75 and see also Gardner, 'The Mark of Responsibility' (n 140).

Perry also relies on Honoré's notion of outcome responsibility to advance a foundational conception of the law of negligence. However, he asserts that outcome responsibility is about the backward-looking perspective that has been explored by Nagel[144] and Williams.[145] This means that the normative aspect of outcome responsibility lies in the evaluative perspective of the action in relation to the agent's previous actions.[146] Outcome responsibility is agency-orientated, but it is also about the way we see our own actions, ie through the outcomes of our agency. Perry tells us that even though we cannot blame the agent for the action, it is appropriate for her to feel regret if she reflects on her action.[147] Thus, according to Perry, Honoré omits to mention that the regret is not only for the outcome *but also for the action*. It also affects how others evaluate our actions, and outcomes are an integral part of this evaluation. When faced with bad outcomes, we often evaluate them harshly, such as deeming attempted murder less culpable than actual murder. However, for example, attempted murder and high-speed driving—even it does not produce harm—are wrong, and therefore the outcome of our action is just one element in the evaluation of actions. Perry aims to connect the agent's capacity to choose and the outcome of her action, stating that, somehow, she feels that the action is hers even though the outcome is undesirable and not what she intended.[148] Perry grounds this on the experiential notion of agency, where we need to live with what happens to us, and perhaps this takes us back to Williams' idea of agent-regret.

However, because there is no elaboration of the idea of action or the specific notion of agency that he has in mind, the notion of capacity to choose, together with the idea of outcome, faces the same challenge formulated against Honoré. If the action is conceived at the point of choice and the outcome is a matter of something random or arbitrary, it is unclear why the agent's feelings of regret are justified. Simply stating that the agent experiences regret does not justify attributing to her ownership of the outcomes, including the undesirable ones. We need an explanation of why we experience regret, why this is a *justified feeling*, and why we tend to own or disown certain outcomes.

Perry does not explain the mechanism by which we sometimes own our actions, such as when I drive at a high speed and run over a child, or why I sometimes disown actions, such as when I am sleepwalking and break your expensive vase. Perry only states what needs to be explained, ie that agents experience regret and that on specific occasions we own the outcomes of our actions, even if we did not foresee the outcome of the action.

[144] Nagel, 'Moral Luck' (n 54).
[145] Williams (n 53).
[146] Perry (n 8) 492.
[147] ibid 493.
[148] ibid 497.

§7.9 Legal and Moral Continuity Conception of the Negligence Law and the Particularity Challenge

The continuity conception of negligence law does not provide a satisfactory response to the *particularity challenge.* The notion of risk has a central role in both Honoré's and Perry's models of the 'continuity' thesis. However, the concept of risk does not play any role in citizens' practical reasoning because it is a necessary social imposition.[149] Furthermore, Perry develops his continuity thesis between moral and legal responsibility for negligence, arguing that responsibility based on outcome relies on the backward-looking perspective. However, the particularity challenge asserts that the law shapes the citizens' practical reasoning based on particular descriptions of the action and engaging in a forward-looking perspective. I argue that the law accomplishes this not through principles, rules, or abstract notions like risk, but rather by valuing what is good or worthy.

Gardner's focus is on the details of our answerability practices when we need to give reasons for why we did what we did, but he fails to connect this insight with the way the law engages with the particularities of action. Thus, he seems to recognize that the law will impose outcome-responsibility authoritatively, '*when the assignment of outcome-responsibility is a bone of contention*'.[150] This implies that rules will be established ahead of time to determine who should be considered the agent of each outcome. He also recognizes that the law regulates via general rules and that indeterminacy generates a threat to people's freedom; therefore, we should avoid indeterminacies.[151] This reflects a naïve and simplistic conception of our agency and practical reason, though common among philosophers and jurists. The idea is that only precise rules can indicate what we ought to do, and that somehow these rules will enter into our practical reasoning as the '*law exists to improve how people (including its own officials) will act*'.[152]

§7.10 Legal and Moral Continuity Conception of Negligence Law and the Guidance Challenge

The 'continuity' conception of negligence law either misconstrues or rejects the guidance challenge.

Perry rejects the view that the law of negligence can provide any guidance, at least when citizens engage with the objective standard of care[153] as this would require responsibility only when the citizen can foresee the action and act according

[149] Perry (n 8).
[150] Gardner, 'From Personal Life to Private Law' (n 8) 75.
[151] ibid 77.
[152] ibid 77.
[153] Perry (n 8) 512.

to the objective standard of care. However, we see that this is not what the courts presuppose.[154] Judgements of responsibility are attributions in terms of capacities, outcomes, and risk distribution. Therefore, Perry only considers the backward-looking perspective of judgements in negligence. Furthermore, according to Perry, there are no general norms that can guide the actions of citizens to avoid negligent acts. He asserts at various points that moral intuition is necessary.[155]

Gardner's continuity analysis has also established that the law requires me to exercise care not only to avoid causing you any loss but also to avoid causing the loss carelessly. Therefore, according to Gardner, the duty of care in negligence requires the duty to succeed by trying.[156] This implies that you must succeed in your endeavours and activities to ensure that you carry out your activities with care and do not fall below the standard of care. However, one question arises: how can the law guarantee this?[157]

The continuity thesis, due to its own theory of action, cannot respond to the guidance challenge. Gardner's conception, following Von Wright, interlinks action and outcomes, but fails to explain the relationship between the movements of our bodies, our thoughts and reasoning, our desires and passions, and the subsequent outcomes of our actions.

In the next chapter, we will advance a number of criticisms of the different theories of negligence in the domain of ethics and show that they are unsatisfactory because they fail to explain the basic features of the phenomenology of negligent action.

[154] See Lord Atkin's foreseeability test in *Donoghue v Stevenson* [1932] AC 562 and the two-staged test in *Anns v Merton BC* [1978] AC 728. For a further application of foreseeability see *Top v London Country Bus* [1993] 1 WLR 976 and *Home Office v Dorset Yacht Co Ltd* [1970] AC 1004.

[155] Perry (n 8) 512.

[156] Gardner, 'From Personal Life to Private Law' (n 8) 63. Gardner, 'What is Tort Law For?' (n 8). cf Ori Herstein, 'Responsibility in Negligence: Discussion of "From Normativity to Responsibility"' (2013) 8 *Jerusalem Review of Legal Studies* 16; Ori Herstein, 'Nobody's Perfect: Moral Responsibility in Negligence' (2019) 32 *Canadian Journal of Law and Jurisprudence* 109; Ori Herstein, 'Reasons to Try' in Haris Psarras and Sandy Steel (eds), *Private Law and Practical Reason: Essays on John Gardner's Private Law Theory* (OUP 2023); Haris Psarras, 'Corrective Justice, the Continuity Thesis, and the Duty of Care in Negligence: Lessons from John Gardner's "From Personal Life to Private Law"' (2019) 19 *Jerusalem Review of Legal Studies* 34.

[157] See Chapter 9 for further discussion.

8

Rival Conceptions of Responsibility for Negligence in Ethics

Limits and Lessons to Learn

§8.1 The Myth of the Locus of Responsibility and the Bifurcation Thesis

In Chapter 3, I advanced the view that in contemporary philosophy there is a persistent conception that scrutinizes action, decision-making processes, and deliberation in terms of a bifurcation of beliefs and desires, while presupposing that they neither interact nor merge. In this way, the analysis of reasons for actions, motivation in action theory, and theories of rationality generates a narrow and artificial bifurcation of desires and beliefs, motives and reasons, or internal and external reasons. I also argued that, as a corollary of this narrow conception, we have a theory of deliberation that assumes that while acting, we have clarity on our beliefs and/or desires, or at least that they are 'given' to us, and hence, our only task is *to balance and select* which desires we will pursue and how our beliefs will match these desires. In some cases, theorists present normative or external reasons for actions, as well as telling us that our task is to try to understand these normative or external reasons. This line of research focuses on the *way* we engage with reasons for actions.

The bifurcation thesis is, therefore, equally present among internalist and externalist theorists of reasons for action, among motive-based and reason-based theories of rationality, among intellectualist theories of rationality à la Socrates, and among decision-making theories that aim to reduce practical reason to an exercise of probability. In the same chapter, we analyse a corollary of the bifurcation thesis: the balancing model of deliberation. In all versions of the balancing model of deliberation, values, desires, and beliefs are presented to us; they are 'given'. There is no conversion, change, or transformation that the agent needs to engage with.

To undermine this conception and offer an alternative picture of practical reason and deliberation, I have sought to advocate for a concept of agency in which deliberation operates at a substandard or immersive level where settling the question, 'What shall I do?' is crucial. This entails engaging with and understanding the values involved in the particularity of our actions, as well as inhabiting a

Responsibility for Negligence in Ethics and Law. Verónica Rodríguez-Blanco, Oxford University Press.
 DOI: 10.1093/9780198948193.003.0008

deliberative-aspirational perspective through thinking, imagination, and the recognition of deliberative-aspirational perspectives.

In this model of deliberation, which we have called '*the upward journey towards the determination of the what*', the agent begins from an indeterminate point and transforms herself by grasping the values and ends, resulting in a transformation of her desires and character. Desires and beliefs interact constantly and are continually revised and transformed. The idea of balancing, such as comparing desires and/or beliefs, is misleading as it relies on *the illusion of desires and beliefs being given, ie representing a normative reality that needs to be grasped (the content of our beliefs) or an internal state that pushes us to act (the content of our desires).* By contrast, what we actually do is both take and change perspectives, taking into account what we have learned in previous deliberations while aiming to occupy a deliberative-aspirational perspective that has also absorbed the substandard or immersed perspective of deliberation. Finally, I defended the view that *akrasia* is a symptom of the unequal integration of our thinking and character. Hence, this is the underlying structure when an agent commits a negligent act.

However, how have other theorists analysed responsibility for negligence? What are their responses to sceptical positions, and how does our model of deliberation provide a more compelling explanation than competing conceptions of responsibility for negligence? In this chapter, I will address these three questions and highlight the common criticism that all potential solutions to the problem of responsibility for negligence lie in either one, or both, of two key ideas. First, some of these solutions presuppose that there is a *locus* of responsibility. This *locus* can be characterized in different ways; for instance, a determinate or identifiable *time* where the agent *knew* what she was doing, or a specific determinate *point* at which the agent exercised or did not *exercise her will* to carry out a particular action.

Secondly, some of these solutions solely concentrate on the backward-looking perspective of responsibility, neglecting the forward-looking perspective and naively merging the two into one. Consequently, they not only oversimplify or lose the agent's reasoning but also overlook key constitutive features of the agency's responsibility for negligence.

The view that there is a *locus* of responsibility has its roots, arguably, in the Aristotelian description of responsibility in connection to voluntariness.[1] At the beginning of Book III of *Nichomachean Ethics*, Aristotle tells us that only voluntary actions are subject to praise and blame, and, therefore, in order to understand praise and blame, we need to be able to demarcate between voluntary and involuntary actions. Aristotle asserts that actions become involuntary when they occur either (i) under compulsion, or (ii) through ignorance. In the former case, we are passive, and the origin of the action is outside us. In the latter case, we do not know

[1] Aristotle, *Nichomachean Ethics* (trs Sarah Broadie and Christopher Rowe, OUP 2002) 1109b–10a4.

the particular circumstances of our action, for example the object or the means. For example, when Oedipus killed his father (Laius), he did not know that Laius was his father. Therefore, he can be blamed for the 'killing of a man' but not for 'parricide'. In a narrow interpretation, Aristotle's view on responsibility is simple; it is a theory of excuses and is unmetaphysical, ethical, and juridical.[2] Unless ignorance or coercion excuses us, we are responsible for performing our actions. The contemporary literature on responsibility paradoxically reinterprets two conditions in more metaphysical terms, ie 'absence of coercion' becomes the 'free will condition' and 'absence of ignorance' becomes 'the epistemic condition'.[3]

The epistemic condition focuses on the beliefs that the agent had when she was acting. The majority of the theories on responsibility for negligence that focus on the temporality of agency aim to identify and explain the epistemic condition to shed light on responsibility for negligence. In this way, whether the agent had the relevant beliefs, ie the *locus of responsibility, whereby* we can determine or identify responsibility, becomes the crucial aspect of the inquiry. The temporal structure of the agency plays a crucial role in identifying the *locus of responsibility* based on the agent's beliefs. This concept posits that the effective cause of negligent action is the formation, or lack thereof, of relevant beliefs.

However, I have indirectly demonstrated that we cannot analyse Aristotle's account of responsibility for praise and blame independently of his view on practical reason and deliberation. Furthermore, some contemporary commentators are unsatisfied with the narrow reading of Aristotle's theory of responsibility since it does not explain why children are not held responsible for certain actions, namely that they sometimes act knowing the particularities and circumstances of their actions and are not coerced, though we do not deem them responsible. They act voluntarily, without deliberation or *prohairesis*.[4] Thus, to remedy Aristotle's unsatisfactory theory, Terence Irwin, for example, expands on Aristotle's theory of responsibility and introduces a third requirement of responsibility. Irwin argues that we also need to give a positive account of Aristotle's idea of responsibility relying on his other doctrines, ie practical reason and deliberation, and he calls this the Aristotelian 'complex theory' of responsibility as opposed to the Aristotelian 'simple theory' of responsibility.[5]

[2] ibid 1109b34.

[3] Phillip Robichaud and Jan Willens Wieland, *Responsibility: The Epistemic Condition* (OUP 2017) 7; Georg Sher, *Who Knew* (OUP 2009) 73–77.

[4] Aristotle (n 1) 1111a24–26. Irwin asserts that Aristotle assumes that children are not subject to legal and moral sanctions. Furthermore, even if we restrict Aristotle's simple theory to 'normal adults', according to Irwin, this will not suffice as we need to explain why we impose this restriction. Terence Irwin, 'Reason and Responsibility in Aristotle' in Amélie Rorty (ed), *Essays in Aristotle's Ethics* (University of California Press 1980) 117, 125. Note that the *Eudemian Ethics*, unlike the *Nichomachean Ethics,* does not explicitly acknowledge that children act voluntarily. Aristotle, *Eudemian Ethics* (tr H Rackham, Harvard UP, Loeb Classical Library 1989).

[5] Irwin (n 4) 117–18.

According to Irwin,[6] following an interpretation of Aristotle, one key missing ingredient is the knowledge that the agent has of the action that also explains the action. This knowledge is in terms of both beliefs and desires that interact (deliberative desires or thinking desires)[7] and this means that *prohairesis*, or deliberation, is at the core of Aristotle's complex theory of responsibility. In other words, responsibility revolves around a paradigmatic case where the agent acts based on his deliberation and succeeds, as well as cases where there is deliberation but something at the executive level renders it defective, namely *akrasia*. Furthermore, it might also include cases in which the agent could have deliberated but did not.[8] According to Irwin, the crucial point for Aristotle is that as human agents, we bear responsibility because we do something about our desires; we act upon them as long as these desires are not so strong that no human being could resist them, such as in cases of a neurological pre-condition. Thus, *we can change and transform the content of our desires*, and, as a result, indirectly change their strength.[9] We now have a more precise account of what a 'normal adult' is, as well as the paradigmatic case of responsible agency. In other words, the Aristotelian 'complex theory' of responsibility connects praise and blame to deliberation (*prohairesis*).

I have shown in earlier chapters that deliberation transforms character, ie passions and emotions, and that, therefore, we are also responsible when we act based on our character. We are responsible for whatever we can affect by our deliberation. However, my view does not depend on specific capacities or a *locus* of decision or deliberation. We have shown the dynamism and transformative power of deliberation, either in immersed or substandard form, or in inhabiting a deliberative-aspirational perspective.

In the following sections, I will scrutinize the different solutions proposed concerning the idea of responsibility for negligence and argue that they either rely on the *locus* of responsibility that seems artificial or focus on the backward-looking perspective, neglecting the forward-looking view of responsibility.

We divide the different theories into two camps. First, those who advocate the temporality of agency and the identification of the *locus of responsibility*. Secondly, those conceptions that recognize the difficulties of identifying a *locus of responsibility* and wish to have a more expansive account of responsibility whereby emotions, character, and evaluative judgements play a key role.

[6] Williams also seems to advocate Irwin's perspective. Bernard Williams, 'Voluntary Acts and Responsible Agents' in *Making Sense of Humanity* (CUP 1995) 22, 25–30. However, Williams partially rejects Irwin's view that reasons can control desires but agrees that we can formulate a weaker conception of 'normal' or 'mature' agency.

[7] Aristotle (n 1) 1139a23, b4.

[8] Irwin (n 4) 132.

[9] ibid 131.

§8.2 Theories of Responsibility that Focus on the Temporality of Agency

This set of theories recognizes the importance of the temporality of agency for any account of responsibility and the need to identify the key condition(s) within the temporal structure of agency that effectively cause the action. Within this view, we find two key solutions to the problem of the responsibility of negligence, and it is to this that we now turn.

§8.2.1 Theories that Defend the 'Tracing Strategy'

Some theories that defend responsibility for negligence aim to show that at some point, the agent had control[10] of her action prior to executing the inadvertent action[11] because she decided to perform an action that can be causally connected to the inadvertent action. According to this set of theories, responsibility is attributed if the agent is capable of controlling her action. Control is possible because the agent is aware and has knowledge of what she is doing. This specific mental state is characterized by her beliefs while acting.[12] Therefore, we need to identify the point at which she had knowledge of what she was doing. The following example might illustrate the argument: Jane is at a party and drinks more than 2 units of alcohol, knowing that if she drives home that night, she will be over the legal limit for driving. Nevertheless, she drives her vehicle while being tipsy. As a result of her impaired driving, her vehicle collides with another vehicle. Jane did not

[10] Husak acknowledges that control is difficult to define. However, he argues that beliefs, desires, and actions are subject to guidance by reason, and are therefore under our control. Nevertheless, he does not elaborate further on his position and seems to rely on a capacity account, as advanced by Hart. Douglas Husak, 'Negligence, Belief, Blame and Criminal Liability: The Special Case of Forgetting' (2011) 5 Criminal Law and Philosophy 199, 204–05. For a discussion of the capacity account, see §8.3.4. As Simester points out, the proposition 'one is culpable because one has chosen the act and therefore one is in control of one's action' does not imply that 'one is not culpable if one does not choose to act'. Andrew Simester, 'Responsibility for Inadvertent Acts' (2005) 2 Ohio State Journal of Criminal Law 601, 603.

[11] Note that 'inadvertent action' is different from a 'benighting act' which is discussed in Holly Smith's 'Culpable Ignorance' (2003) 92 Philosophical Review 61. Benighting acts are acts that are performed by an agent in spite of knowing that the act is wrong. A benighting act is, therefore, in principle, a reckless act. See also Zimmerman, who notes that in Smith's discussion, a benighting act requires belief in the wrongness of the action. Mark Zimmerman, 'Moral Responsibility and Ignorance' (1997) 107 Ethics 410, 417, fn 12. See also Matthew Talbert, 'Akrasia, Awareness and Blameworthiness' in Phillip Robichaud and Jan Willem Wieland (eds), *Responsibility: The Epistemic Condition* (OUP 2017) 47.

[12] Duff gives a good characterization of the 'choice account': 'But choice requires belief: I choose to do only what I believe I am doing . . . We are responsible only for our voluntary actions. But actions are voluntary only in so far as they are chosen: it is through my choice that I exercise my will, and thus define myself as an agent. What I choose to do I do freely, in that my choice determines whether I do it or not: it is also what is properly mine as an agent, in that it expresses my own will; I make myself responsible for it.' Anthony Duff, *Intention, Agency and Criminal Liability* (Blackwell 1990) 153. Others connect beliefs as mental states, rationality, and internal pro-attitudes to control. Neil Levy, 'Culpable Ignorance and Moral Responsibility: A Reply to Fitzpatrick' (2009) 119 Ethics 729, 735–37.

intentionally cause the accident. However, Jane will be responsible for her action, namely driving while being tipsy, and the consequences and losses that result from performing the action, namely damaged vehicles. In other words, the tracing account searches for the *locus* at which the agent is not ignorant of her action, which, in Jane's case, is when she began to drink her third unit of alcohol. For this account to work, there must be a strong cognitive connection between the events;[13] for example, drinking the third unit of alcohol, impaired driving, and the collision of the vehicles.[14] We can trace the original action, which involves advertence and belief, when Jane was having her first or second unit of alcohol and establish the cognitive connection between this advertence and subsequent actions.

In Chapter 2, I analysed the sceptical positions that argue that this tracing strategy leads to either infinite regress or clear-eyed *akrasia*. For the sceptic, belief formation is a passive matter.[15] Foreseeability, foresight,[16] attention, and awareness[17] are mental states that we have or do not have. There is no developmental explanation for how we are able to acquire them. Sceptical positions tell us that they are either present or not, and our epistemic obligations are discharged if the agent engages with the correct beliefs regarding the action while acting accordingly.

Others do not share this level of scepticism. However, by distinguishing between recklessness and negligence, they highlight the intractable difficulties of responsibility for negligence, offering a complex spectrum that takes us from recklessness to 'pure' negligence. They do not assert that tracing choices as beliefs is the key to understanding responsibility for negligence, but rather they advocate the view that tracing *beliefs are dispositions* and maintain that understanding the complex nature of beliefs might lead us to a better understanding of negligence and responsibility for closely related phenomena. For example, Husak discusses negligence in the context of criminal law and, following a Strawsonian turn, emphasizes that

[13] Zimmerman (n 11) 420. Furthermore, Zimmerman argues that cognitive connection might not be enough to attribute responsibility in cases of ignorance/negligence, but it seems also necessary that the agent must advert to the character of the action and what she is doing. The reason for this is that 'a belief is not occurrent when one cannot act either with the intention to heed the belief or with the intention not to heed it'. Zimmerman (n 11). We see Zimmerman clearly endorsing the bifurcation thesis and the balancing view of decision-making. We engage in *beliefs about what to do, and beliefs about what to pay attention to or not.*

[14] Chapter 7 discusses how this strong connection is presented in law.

[15] Gideon Rosen, 'Scepticism About Moral Responsibility' (2004) 18 Philosophical Perspectives 295, 302.

[16] Zimmerman, for example, focuses on foresight instead of foreseeability, as only foresight guarantees enhanced control of the action. Zimmerman (n 11) 421.

[17] Husak emphasizes that understanding responsibility for negligence requires a better understanding of the awareness's nature and character. He seems to understand awareness in relation to dispositional beliefs. Husak (n 10) 207–10. See also Gideon Rosen, 'The Problem of Pure Negligence' in Verónica Rodríguez-Blanco and George Pavlakos (eds), *Agency, Negligence and Responsibility* (CUP 2022) 15. Recent work bases responsibility for negligence on the defendant's failure to *form a belief* (the emphasis is mine) that suggests there was a *specific* risk in connection to her behaviour. See Finlay Stark, *Culpable Carelessness: Recklessness and Negligence in the Criminal Law* (CUP 2016). Our criticism of the myth of the *locus* of responsibility extends to this kind of explanation.

we should not focus on the conditions of negligent agency as committing a wrong or on the negligent act's wrongness and breach of duty, but rather on whether and in what circumstances persons are to blame for their wrongs or breaches of duty. The focus should be *on blame* and not on conduct. Cases of 'pure' negligence, according to these authors, are those in which *it never occurred to the agent* that they created a risk to another person.[18] These cases contrast with cases of forgetfulness, which, according to Husak, are closer to recklessness. Husak argues that awareness appears to be the key to unlocking responsibility for negligence, while advocating a conception of beliefs as dispositional to clarify awareness. In the famous example of a baby who is left in the bathtub,[19] and consequently drowns, we would say that the forgetful parent has a belief in a dispositional form. According to Husak, therefore, the parent is responsible for recklessness instead of pure negligence. Somehow, the parent 'knows' that there is a risk in leaving the child in the bathtub. Contrast this case with the case in *State v Williams*, where the poorly educated native American parent was ignorant of the son's gangrenous infection as signalled by fever, and since they did not seek medical advice, the son died. For Husak, *Williams* satisfies no dispositional test; the parent had no belief, dispositional, actual, or occurrent, that he was putting his son at risk. Hence, Mr Williams is not liable for negligence. Husak tells us, '*the blame of a given defendant is reduced to the extent that his beliefs are more distant from the occurrent beliefs. As beliefs become further from actual consciousness, persons have greater difficulty bringing them to bear on their practical reasoning*.'[20]

Husak's analysis perpetuates the myth of the *locus* of responsibility. According to his view, we need to *locate* the belief and its eventual formation. This belief may be absent or actual. If it is absent, then we can explore whether it could be dispositional, because this is the best explanation of our practices, intuitions, and knowledge of the social environment of the agent. In the case of *Williams*, we can infer that there were no dispositional beliefs as the native American parents were poorly educated and immersed in practices and social norms that could not give them access to any knowledge of what a gangrenous infection is. However, there is no explanation of how these beliefs as dispositions can be triggered and become occurrent. This conception also presupposes that the agent is passive towards these beliefs as dispositions. This implies that they manifest naturally or effortlessly when the agent is immersed in certain social norms and conditions. By contrast, they are completely absent, even as dispositions in other people. It seems, therefore, arbitrary how some people have these beliefs as dispositions and others

[18] The paradigmatic example provided by Husak is *State v Williams*, 484 P.2d 1167 (Wash App 1971). Husak (n 10). In this case, poorly educated native American parents failed to seek medical attention in spite of their son having a high fever and suffering from a gangrenous infection. See also discussion of the *Adomako* case in Rosen, 'The Problem of Pure Negligence' (n 17). *R v Adomako* [1995] 1 AC 171.

[19] Larry Alexander, Kim Ferzan, and Stephen Morse, *Crime and Culpability* (CUP 2009) 77–81.

[20] Husak (n 10) 215–16.

do not. For example, if the native American parents were exposed to some degree of education in biology or access to television programmes on science, would their beliefs become 'dispositional' at this point? For Husak, there is always, arguably, a *locus of responsibility*. If the beliefs (occurrent or dispositional) are completely absent, like in the case of *Williams*, then there *cannot* be responsibility for negligence. If there are beliefs in a dispositional form, like in the case of the parent who forgets for a few minutes that they have put a baby in the bathtub, or if we can find actual or occurrent beliefs in the agent, then we can say that there is responsibility for negligence.

This way of thinking relies on the idea of finding a precise moment of formation or lack of formation of the beliefs and consequently distorts the way that reasons and desires interact, and therefore beliefs and desires merge. According to our Aristotelian-inspired model, there is dynamism and constant interaction between desires and beliefs and between reasons and motivations. Hence, the picture is more complex, realistic, and rich. Engaging with both immersed and aspirational deliberations transforms the agent's beliefs and desires. Using Husak's case of *Williams*, we could say that exposure to criticism or knowledge via more educated friends or strangers, or perhaps having access to biological or pharmacological knowledge on the part of the native American parents, should suffice to interpret it as an opportunity to recognize a deliberative-aspirational perspective. Other questions are also raised in terms of the immersed or narrow deliberative perspective; for instance, what happened in the past when the child was sick or had episodes of fever and no medical advice was pursued?

Vargas[21] criticizes the tracing account, advancing counter-examples in which (a) our intuitions show that the agent is morally responsible, and (b) we cannot trace back the agent's knowledge or advertence of what she was doing. Let me mention two of these counter-examples. The first example is Jeff the Jerk; he is unreflective about his behaviour and is a ruthless employer who laid off his employees without any consideration for their feelings or situations. Vargas tells us that, at the age of fifteen, Jeff the Jerk felt frustrated by his failure with women and decided to become a ruthless jerk as a way to become more attractive to women and succeed in dating them. At the age of fifteen, he could not foresee, could not know, and it was not foreseeable to him that one day he would become the manager of a company, and that due to the attitudes he developed when he was a teen, he would engage in ruthless and unconsidered behaviour towards others. At the age of fifteen, he develops a type of character without being aware of the key features of his character or the consequences that his type of character will have for his future actions. Vargas asks: 'Is Jeff the Jerk responsible for the laying off of his employees in an insensitive manner?'

[21] Manuel Vargas, 'The Trouble with Tracing' (2005) 29 Midwest Studies in Philosophy 269.

In the second counter-example provided by Vargas, Ruben the Unfortunate is a fan of the American football team, the Miami Dolphins. At a match that Ruben attended, the Miami Dolphins won, and he enjoyed a few celebratory beers afterwards. When he gets home, his four-year-old niece is visiting the house, and, as is customary for him, he picks her up and throws her in the air with more enthusiasm than usual due to the alcohol he has consumed. He fails to catch her, and she falls to the ground. Is Ruben responsible for dropping his niece? According to Vargas, our intuitions suggest that both Jeff and Ruben are responsible for their negligent actions. Specifically, Jeff bears responsibility for his insensitive behaviour when he laid off his employees, while Ruben is responsible for dropping his niece while playing with her. However, it is difficult, Vargas argues, to establish the required condition for which Jeff and Ruben are responsible. In both cases, there is a '*disposition, character trait, habit or non-deliberative aspect of the agent*'.[22] Vargas establishes the distinction between deliberative and non-deliberative cases. In the former, the agent knows, adverts to, or foresees the consequences of her action. In non-deliberative cases, like those of Jeff and Ruben, the agent does not have knowledge, advertence, or foreseeability regarding her actions. Dispositions, character, or habits, according to Vargas, are the sources of the action, but the agent could not have reasonably foreseen the consequences of these dispositions, characters, or habits. He portrays the development of the wrong character in Jeff in the following fashion:

> When Jeff was 15, he realized that he was having much less success with members of the opposite sex than he wanted to have. Over time, and through the usual *fallible mechanisms of belief acquisition*, he came to believe that the only males that consistently had success at gaining the attention of female classmates were those at least we might describe as jerks . . . This putative insight, coupled with a somewhat enterprising disposition that later served him modestly well in the business world, led him to *adopt a plan*[23] for self-improvement. To the extent to which he was able, he inculcated in himself all the behaviours and attitudes that we would perceive to be jerk-like.[24]

Vargas tells us that Jeff deliberated about becoming a jerk. He *took the decision* and *implemented a plan* to adopt attitudes that are jerk-like. His social context favoured this, and he received positive feedback on his attitudes from friends at school. He also had great success in attracting girls. Vargas denies that Jeff could conceive that his personal plan of acting like a jerk when he was fifteen years old would include the consequence of acting in a despicable fashion when laying off

[22] ibid 275.
[23] The emphasis is mine.
[24] Vargas (n 21) 275.

people later in life. Vargas concludes that Jeff does not satisfy the knowledge condition of tracing. The tracing condition imposes the view that the agent has to have, at *some point in the past*, knowledge, advertence, or foreseeability of the future action. However, in the case of Jeff, there is no point in the past that we can identify as the *locus* of knowledge, advertence, or foreseeability. However, Vargas does not aim to defend the position that due to our characters we are responsible for our actions. The formation of character at T1 cannot establish Jeff's knowledge or foreseeability in acting at T2. The deliberation concerning the formation of his character at an early stage of his life and his acting in a rude and unconsidered manner later in his life are too far apart.

Vargas appears to rely excessively on the idea that deliberation is due to engagement with beliefs only, while our desires and passions play no role in either deliberation or the formation of character. He relies on the bifurcation thesis and the balancing view of deliberation. For Jeff, there was deliberation on what to do to become more appealing to girls; however, there is no connection between this deliberation and past or future actions. There was a *locus* at which he decided to become a jerk; there was a plan on how to become more appealing to girls and behave in a jerk-like fashion. Jeff's character development originates in the past; he becomes a jerk, but there is no deliberation when he acts according to his character. One can infer from Vargas's discussion that desires and emotions have no direction and no significant relation to beliefs. In Vargas's paper, there is no explanation of what a character is. However, we can infer that character is a set of settled desires, passions, and emotions. They are inherent in everything that Jeff does, and therefore, according to Vargas, they have a different status than the process of deliberation, in which our beliefs, knowledge, advertence, and foreseeability are involved. Nevertheless, our proposal rejects this bifurcation and its corollary, the balancing view. In our model of narrow and aspirational deliberation, Jeff, at fifteen years old, would have engaged with the value of friendship, kindness, and feelings for others due to his narrow deliberations, ie deliberating what he should do when he sees his friends bullying another boy in the playground. When his parents, grandparents, or siblings inform him about his insensitive behaviour towards others, they are actually inviting him to take a deliberative-aspirational perspective. It could be argued that, similar to the slave owner discussed in Chapter 5, who avoids taking the deliberative-aspirational perspective that will lead him to provide justice and freedom for his slave, Jeff avoids taking the deliberative-aspirational perspective. When he becomes a manager, criticism from friends or family and probably collective narratives invite him to take a deliberative-aspirational perspective. The invitations involve the need to describe and re-describe his own thoughts about the subject matter, his own actions, and his perspective towards his employees and others. His avoidance of this deliberative-aspirational perspective is palpable, as manifested when he lays off his employees in an insensitive and unconsidered manner.

We agree with Vargas that the knowledge condition fails for the given counter-example. However, this is not because there is a distinction between deliberative and non-deliberative action, and actions that fall under the latter category cannot satisfy the knowledge condition. My argument is that the model of bifurcation is flawed and leads to a simplistic distinction between deliberative and non-deliberative actions. According to the bifurcation model, actions are deliberative because we have knowledge, beliefs, advertence, or foreseeability. In the latter case, there is an absence of knowledge, beliefs, advertence, or foreseeability, and we act because of our settled dispositions, emotions, desires, and passions. By contrast, my argument is that in the counter-example, the knowledge condition fails because deliberation is more complex and richer than the way Vargas, and authors who advocate the tracing condition,[25] have delineated it. Fisher and Tognazzi, for example, argue that Jeff *could have foreseen* at the age of fifteen that if he continued to act in a jerk-like fashion, then he would treat people poorly as a result of his jerk-like character. However, this foreseeability condition seems to be presented as merely a belief that will, should, or perhaps *ought to happen to* Jeff. Fisher and Tognazzi think it is 'reasonable' to expect Jeff's younger self to have known the outcomes of the development of his character; they appear to think that what was 'foreseeable' should have been apparent to him. In my view, however, it is unclear how or why foreseeability should be apparent to Jeff. In other words, there is a crucial condition, namely a belief in terms of foreseeability, that should or might have been apparent to the agent. It is unclear how this belief would manifest in him. Fisher and Tognazzi do not explain how this is possible.

The case of Ruben can be explained within the model that I have proposed in Chapters 4, 5, and 6. Thus, it is a case of negligence in which deliberation is conducted in a substandard or narrow way. This means that Ruben has deliberated and engaged on many occasions before the day of the fateful accident with the values of enjoying sports, friendship, playfulness and children. He could have inhabited a deliberative-aspirational perspective either before having too many beers at the football match or when he entered the house and started to play with his niece. Prior thoughts, descriptions, and re-descriptions on *what* and *how to* play with children can transform our desires and emotions, and the sharpening of the latter can also shape our thinking and descriptions. Let us now turn to the second proposal that aims to explain negligent action: the 'reasonable expectations' view.

[25] Passages in Aristotle's *Nichomachean Ethics* have been used to demonstrate the tracing strategy. In these passages, however, Aristotle is talking about acting while being ignorant, as opposed to acting through ignorance (ignorance of the particularities of the action). Aristotle (n 1) 1113b30–1114a10. He is merely emphasizing the two ways of acting wrongly when ignorance is involved.

§8.2.2 The 'Reasonable Expectations' Solution

Fitzpatrick defends the view that what we need to identify is the *normative* element of the action within the temporality of the agency instead of the *cognitive* aspect of this same temporality. Fitzpatrick asserts that unlocking responsibility for negligence necessitates understanding what agents are reasonably expected to do prior to acting in order to rectify or remedy their normative ignorance. In many cases of alleged pure negligence, in which the act's wrongness is not present for the agent, the agent's immersion in a moral outlook or vision keeps him ignorant of any moral or normative knowledge regarding the action in question. In other words, the agent has no opportunities to improve his moral position. For instance, young people educated under the *Hitler-Jugend* programme were morally ignorant of the value of tolerance or love for other races and other human beings who are different; the son of a dictator in a totalitarian regime is morally ignorant concerning others' freedom of speech; and a woman educated under the Taliban regime, a society characterized by repression, is ignorant of women's rights. These are all examples of people immersed and educated in a narrow normative landscape. According to Fitzpatrick, we cannot reasonably expect them to do something to remedy their moral ignorance. If they act due to their moral ignorance, we cannot expect them to act in a different way, and, therefore, they are not responsible.

Fitzpatrick, in my view, rightly rejects Rosen's sceptical position, arguing that it involves a strong requirement of a knowing act or omission within the causal history of the agent. Fitzpatrick argues that all we need to establish is that the agent could have *reasonably* been expected to do something to rectify or remedy his moral or normative ignorance. In this way, we could have reasonably expected her to act differently from the way she did. The example provided by Fitzpatrick illustrates his point. Mr Potter is a successful businessman and a ruthless capitalist. Although he received a poor moral education, his life was otherwise normal. He has normal capacities and has been exposed to normal social and intellectual development and opportunities to learn about moral visions that oppose his own. There have been plenty of opportunities for him to learn about better ways of behaving and appreciate other moral perspectives. Potter, however, engages in negligent actions that are harmful to his employees. Unlike the case of the young Nazi, the son of the dictator, or the women brought up under the Taliban regime, we can reasonably expect him to do something to remedy his moral ignorance. Nevertheless, Mr Potter did not take these opportunities, and as a result, his behaviour shows vices. Fitzpatrick tells us that Mr Potter is responsible for these vices because we could reasonably expect people to take advantage of the given opportunities and acquire moral knowledge. He should have remedied his moral or normative ignorance. Note, however, that these vices are conceived as epistemic vices that might or might not result from vices of character.

In Chapter 3, we discussed the Socratic view of *technē* or skills, as the key constitutive feature for acquiring moral knowledge. I argued that the bifurcation thesis and its corollary, the balancing view, are also present in ancient conceptions of agency like the Socratic view. The focus of change and transformation is true beliefs and, more specifically, the acquisition of true moral beliefs and, therefore, moral knowledge. The 'art of measurement' is a skill that can save us, and Socrates believes that this art can be taught. Aristotle thought that reason and moral knowledge play a key part in learning to be good, but he also emphasized that we need to transform our character, desires, and passions. My account of *akrasia* as the uneven integration of character and thinking aims to explain the deep structure of negligent action on the basis of a more realistic psychological portrait of the agent. However, Fitzpatrick offers us a *non-realist* psychological picture of learning and becoming good. Mr Potter's development into a vicious character is due to his lack of engagement with opportunities *to learn moral propositions or true moral beliefs.* This depicts a conception of agency far from our own experience and the phenomenology of learning to be good. One potential interpretation of Fitzpatrick's view would be that it is through the *will* that we choose or decide to engage or not with moral truth and acquire the required cognitive and moral knowledge. He states: '*I will defend an alternative view that appeals instead to facts about personal capabilities, social opportunities for acquiring knowledge, and the role of voluntary exercises of vices in certain failures to fulfil epistemic obligations.*'[26] This is a voluntarist position towards vices and virtues.[27] The problem with any voluntarist explanation is a simplification of the process of deliberation and practical reason. Beliefs inform the will, yet it possesses its own force. Virtue can be taught as we teach skills, but our 'will' also needs to engage with moral truth and knowledge to replace moral ignorance with moral knowledge. This proposal does not seem to consider the role that Mr Potter's passions and desires play in Mr Potter overlooking the opportunities that could have saved him from his moral ignorance. For instance, Mr Potter's greed and the description of his own actions from his deliberative perspective. Fitzpatrick recognizes that Mr Potter's epistemic vices[28] might have led him astray

[26] William Fitzpatrick, 'Moral Responsibility and Normative Ignorance: Answering a New Skeptical Challenge' (2008) 118 Ethics 589, 590.

[27] Fitzpatrick asserts that character traits are the result of our choices from the point of maturity onwards. ibid 608.

[28] Fitzpatrick resorts to Aquinas, who attributes responsibility for negligence when the person does not consider what she ought to consider. Fitzpatrick, 'Moral Responsibility and Normative Ignorance' (n 26) 605, fn 34. Aquinas distinguishes between 'acting in wrongly choosing' and 'ignorance of right principles', and for Aquinas, both cases are cases of negligence. The cited text in Aquinas states: 'It is present when a person does not actually attend to what he could and should consider; the technical term is "ignorance in wrongly choosing", and it may result from passion or a settled attitude. Or again, a person may have made no effort to acquaint himself with the proper notions; the technical term is "ignorance of right principles". It is voluntary as not knowing what one should know and as resulting from negligence.' Thomas Aquinas, *Summa Theologica* (tr Thomas Gilby, CUP 2006) I-II, Q6, art 8. Fitzpatrick acknowledges that the negligent agent commits intellectual or epistemic vices, which are voluntary. It might be unclear whether these intellectual vices have led the agent to either 'wrongly choose' or 'ignorance the right principles'. However, since the former would most likely involve

from moral knowledge, but he does not recognize that other passions and desires play a transformative role in our thinking and practical knowledge.

We have discovered in the voluntarist reading of Fitzpatrick the idea that it is a matter of finding a *locus* within the temporality of the agency, namely the point(s) at which Mr Potter refused to take on others' moral outlooks and learn from them, to determine and attribute the agent's responsibility for negligence. However, Fitzpatrick insists that his strategy does not involve tracing, and, arguably, there is no such *locus* of responsibility. The agent is responsible because of his epistemically debilitating choices, not '*because he was even earlier responsible for something else that led to them*'.[29] In Mr Potter's case, he is acting in light of his epistemically debilitating choices. However, arguably, we can only assess the 'reasonability' of expectations if we look at his past life and past choices, if we search for a *locus* within the temporality of Mr Potter's agency. Responsibility can still be direct, and we do not need to assert that Mr Potter's failure to seek moral knowledge and engage in changing his moral outlook *effectively causes* and is closely connected to his derivative responsibility of acting due to his epistemically debilitating view. Contrast this seeking for a *locus of responsibility* with our characterization of immersed and aspirational deliberation. If our account of deliberation is sound, the temporal history of Mr Potter's agency and development becomes more complex but also richer and more appealing from the point of view of psychological realism, ie the way we experience the phenomenology of becoming good (what I have called 'inhabiting the deliberative-aspirational perspective') and of negligence and our attributions of responsibility.

Furthermore, Fitzpatrick's view may not escape scepticism and could lead to the fallacy of infinite regress. Since he argues that Mr Potter is responsible for his negligence due to his epistemic vices, which are voluntary, we need a clear notion of what voluntariness entails, and the only way to clarify this notion might be through either 'choice' or the idea of 'clear-eyed *akrasia*'. Fitzpatrick rejects both strategies and aims to cease attributing responsibility to a prior choice or knowing sin (clear-eyed *akrasia*). Fitzpatrick argues that it is reasonable for us to expect that Mr Potter will not exercise vicious or debilitating epistemic choices given 'his capabilities and culturally available opportunities'.[30] There is, therefore, for Fitzpatrick, neither clear-eyed *akrasia* nor choice, but only our 'reasonable' expectations due to the agent's normal capacities and social environment. For Fitzpatrick, there are, arguably, two conditions of responsibility for negligence, which are: (a) our reasonable

non-clear-eyed *akrasia*, we can infer that he aims to adhere to an account of negligence in which the agent fails to act according to the right principles. Therefore, Mr Potter is ignorant of the right principles. In Chapters 5 and 6, however, I problematized the idea that we access 'right principles' through our deliberations and practical reason.

[29] Fitzpatrick, 'Moral Responsibility and Normative Ignorance' (n 26) 609.
[30] ibid 606.

expectations, and (b) the capabilities and appropriate environment of the agent. We will criticize the capacities or capabilities in §8.3.4, but for now, I will address the idea of 'reasonable expectations'.

It appears that the 'reasonableness' of our expectations hinges on whether agents in general *can and do* behave as Fitzpatrick believes. If the model of deliberation and practical reason is closer to what has been presented in this investigation, then the characterization of agency offered by Fitzpatrick is insufficient and lacks psychological realism. Epistemic virtues seem insufficient to guarantee that we will engage in acting negligently due to confusion about the content of the values connected to the action or due to the unequal development and transformation of our desires. To be fair, Fitzpatrick maintains that Mr Potter has undergone normal socialization and has the ability to extend his financial knowledge and critical thinking to morality.[31] However, our concern is that if this were to happen, Mr Potter's epistemic engagement with the right principles would not be sufficient. I have argued that we need to understand how we choose, deliberate, and engage with values at the immersive level, as well as how we can engage with aspirational conceptions that transform our lower-level desires into more sophisticated desires. For instance, Mr Potter's life revolves around the significance of money, its accumulation, and its role. Fitzpatrick appears to advocate the bifurcation thesis, which separates desires and beliefs. He also advocates its corollary, what I have called 'the balancing' view of deliberation. Hence, he has not provided an explanation for how the interaction between desires and beliefs could function.[32] Beliefs, according to Fitzpatrick, have a key role in acting virtuously and rightly and the agent's becoming good. According to this view, our defective engagement and responsibility for wrong actions are '*where there is ignorance of balance of reasons against it*'.[33]

Elizabeth Harman has also argued that Fitzpatrick's portrait of the moral agent as learner is implausible.[34] According to Harman, Fitzpatrick's claim that Mr Potter is *not* a hard case and, therefore, that we could reasonably expect him to manage his beliefs is mistaken. For Harman, *all cases are hard cases*; it does not matter if the subject is government ethics, business ethics, or the case of young people indoctrinated under the *Hitler-Jugend* programme. Thus, she aims to demonstrate that there are many cases in which the agent has false moral beliefs without mismanagement of her beliefs; '*they have thought long and seriously about the relevant*

[31] ibid 607–08.

[32] In a recent reply to Harman, Fitzpatrick states that Potter can think seriously and reflect on his moral outlook, but would reach the same false conclusions if he continued to act on the basis of his vices. William Fitzpatrick, 'Unwitting Wrongdoing, Reasonable Expectations, and Blameworthiness' in Phillip Robichaud and Jan Willem Wieland (eds), *Responsibility:The Epistemic Condition* (OUP 2017) 29, 44. However, this view does not explain how our desires and passions transform our beliefs and vice versa.

[33] Fitzpatrick, 'Moral Responsibility and Normative Ignorance' (n 26) 609.

[34] Elizabeth Harman, 'Does Moral Ignorance Exculpate?' (2011) 24 Ratio 443, 454.

moral question, have considered opposing views, and have come to false moral beliefs.'[35] They have not violated any procedural epistemic norms. Harman gives the example of a businessman who justifies his reprehensible, ruthless behaviour as permissible within the practices of competitive business. His brother criticizes his behaviour, and, after reflection, he comes to the view that his behaviour is justified by the needs of the economy. If his business maximizes profits, the economy will benefit. This case also extends to, for example, people brought up in a Mafiosi family, a sexist society, or under the dominance of an inner-city gang, in which extremely selfish and discriminatory practices are predominant. Harman argues that these agents have 'implicit' moral beliefs that, in their view, justify their actions and make them permissible. Harman points out that these agents are morally responsible because they '*have violated some moral norms that apply to beliefs themselves, not to the management of one's beliefs*'.[36] Thus, she tells us that we are morally obligated to believe moral truths. The *locus* of our moral responsibility is the false moral belief[37] and she endorses the view that our beliefs need to connect to truth, caring attitudes, and actions that link to what is morally true. However, Harman does not explain how we can achieve this, how this operates within the framework of a psychologically realistic picture of agency, or whether it is even possible to do so. Her thoughts on the importance of tracking moral truth and values are sound. However, since she appears to work within the bifurcation model and its corollary, the mere balancing of 'beliefs', she is anxious to show that there is a *locus* of responsibility and that beliefs are present in the agent, though in the form of 'implicit' moral beliefs. Her reliance on mere beliefs as a *locus* of responsibility leads her to ignore the role of desires and emotions, as well as the way thinking shapes them, and *vice versa*. Furthermore, her complaint that Rosen's view of the agent as a learner of moral truths is implausible, also applies to her proposal. Let me explain.

Let us analyse closely Harman's example of the businessman who has 'long and seriously' thought about his moral beliefs and the permissibility of his ruthless and aggressive behaviour. Harman tells us, expanding on her example of the businessman, that the businessman's brother has criticized him and that, after reflection, he thinks that it is better for the economy if his business practices focus on maximizing profit. As a result, aggressively competitive and ruthless behaviour helps to optimize business and the prosperity of the economy. In Chapter 4, we discussed how agents engage with values when they deliberate at a substandard or narrow level. Let us see how this proposal applies to Harman's businessman; let us call him Mr Potter II. Mr Potter II owns a car dealership that sells used vehicles. A few years ago, he decided that the company and its employees negotiating

[35] ibid 456.
[36] ibid 459.
[37] ibid.

with clients have no duty of disclosure. For example, when a car has been damaged.[38] Mr Potter II and his employees have developed a number of tactics and strategies to avoid disclosing the defects of the cars they are selling. When Mr Potter II started his business, he engaged in business practices that overvalued competitive behaviour and success to the detriment of transparency and honesty. When his brother criticizes him, Potter reflects on this but comes to the conclusion that his brother ignores the importance of strong profits for the prosperity of the economy. In Chapter 5, we argued that we can transition from narrow or substandard deliberation through our thoughts about our relationships with others. We used Murdoch's example of a mother-in-law whose view of her daughter-in-law changed as an illustrative case in which thoughts, descriptions, and re-descriptions can change our moral vision. However, we also argued that through our relationships with others, through either avoidance or recognition, we can eschew a deliberative-aspirational perspective. This entails not only changing our beliefs through imagination, descriptions, and re-descriptions of our particular circumstances and embedded values, but it also entails the change, transformation, and becoming of our entire self, including our desires and emotions, towards a different perspective.

Imagine another businessman, Mr Potter III, who deliberated in a different way than Mr Potter II. He created a policy of complete disclosure (in compliance with the legal duty to disclose) and informed himself of his legal duties, but he and his employees also engaged with the value of understanding why it is important to adhere to legal duties and to follow the respective values on this matter. Through this engagement, they learned the values of honesty, transparency, and trust in dealing with their clients. After a few years of doing business, the company has a fantastic reputation for being reliable, trustworthy, and honest, and the staff who work there pride themselves on this. They feel empowered by working for a company that not only makes a strong profit but is also honest.

Our proposal rejects the idea that there is a *locus* of responsibility or that our task as philosophers of responsibility is to identify and explain it. On the contrary, the idea presented here is that changes in the self are due to emotions, desires, and beliefs, and how these interact when we engage in both narrow and aspirational deliberation. Unlike Harman's and Fitzpatrick's proposals, we explain agency in cases of alleged ignorance in a psychologically realistic manner. The deliberations and performances of Mr Potter II and Mr Potter III are temporally located, presenting their engagement with values and perspectives in a complex and rich manner. If there is responsibility for negligence, it is not because we can identify the *locus* at which Mr Potter II or Mr Potter III disregarded their epistemic duties or, as Harman sustains, despite thinking long and hard, nevertheless developed *implicit*

[38] In the example, I will isolate Mr Potter's moral duties from his legal duties. A discussion of legal duties will be the focus of Chapter 9.

or explicit false moral beliefs. On the contrary, we argue that Mr Potter II acts negligently because there is an uneven development of character and thinking due to the incorrect interaction of beliefs and desires. There is, consequently, *akrasia*, an uneven development of character and thinking in practical reason, and this makes itself palpable in the failure to inhabit a deliberative-aspirational perspective. Mr Potter II does not *choose* to ignore the guidelines on disclosure because, if this is the case, his action is either intentional or reckless (clear-eyed *akrasia*). Nor is it the case that only his beliefs guide his actions, or that his beliefs are just something that happens to him. My central argument is that Mr Potter II determines the answer to the question, 'What shall I do?'. His general ends are indeterminate, and he cannot know what shape they will take prior to engaging in both substandard or narrow deliberation and deliberative-aspirational deliberation. When Mr Potter II tries to settle the question, 'What shall I do?' in the context of creating a policy on disclosing damaged and defective vehicles, he establishes that the value of maximizing profit is more important than the value of fair dealing and transparency. However, this ethical outlook has already been shaped through past substandard or narrow deliberations, namely engaging with misconceptions of wealth and greed, or perhaps avoiding engagement with different values and inhabiting a deliberative-aspirational perspective, namely the importance of truth, transparency, and honest business practices. Mr Potter II's actions are negligent and involve ignorance, but a more complex story that includes an understanding of deliberation and practical reason is required.

Mr Potter II's negligence is due to changes and transformation, but not to his beliefs alone, either passive or active, namely the active duty to discharge his epistemic duties. The transformation of his desires stems from his thinking and engagement with the respective values. Simultaneously, his vision and understanding of the respective values are revised in light of the re-described desires. For instance, Mr Potter II desires to maximize profit and accrue wealth before the age of forty in an easy manner, though this is still an indeterminate end. According to his thinking, seeing truth as a matter of 'degrees' will be the *how of maximizing profit soon*. He develops the thought that truth comes in degrees and that omitting to say the truth is justifiable when negotiating in business. In light of his engagement with or avoidance of values, Mr Potter thinks that disclosing details of the accidents that his cars have been in is not necessary. The value of truth is avoided, and, as he sees it, it is the purchaser's duty to ask for all the relevant information when negotiating the purchase of a vehicle. The purchaser bears the responsibility of taking all reasonable steps to ascertain whether the car has previously been involved in an accident or sustained damage. As he sees it, he has no obligation to disclose to future purchasers. The *What?*—What I shall do?, ie become wealthy—is determined by his answer to the question *how?*, ie become wealthy through the value, as he sees it, of truth as a simple matter of degrees and imposing a duty on the purchaser. Mr Potter II does not act intentionally; he does not 'choose' to lie in order to deceive his clients, maximize profit, and become wealthy. The moral psychological profile of Mr Potter II is different. I think this is what Harman wishes to emphasize. Mr Potter II is truthful in other spheres of his life; he is transparent in his relationships with his friends, family, and relatives, and in other matters too, he is an honest man and decent human being. It is only in the sphere of business practices that he endorses the policy of non-disclosure to his clients. He slips into this thinking of 'by degrees' approach to truth, driven by his desire to become wealthy at a young age without too much effort. Contrast Mr Potter II with Mr Potter III, who reaches exactly the opposite conclusion, but the process is a similar one, ie an interaction of beliefs and desires and the transformation of his thinking. However, Mr Potter III engages in changing and transforming his beliefs and desires towards a deliberative-aspirational perspective. Our proposal can explain the multiplicity of changes and transformations through a realistic picture of the phenomenology of our moral experiences and the changes in our moral vision. But let's now examine Fitzpatrick's 'reasonable expectations' account again.

Levy[39] advances a potential objection that Fitzpatrick himself raises against his own view on responsibility for negligence as reasonable expectations. The objection is as follows: Mr Potter's early upbringing has determined his later choices. He cannot revise and change his moral outlook due to his background and beliefs.[40] According to Levy, the objection turns into a question about *what is rational for Mr Potter to do.* Given his background and beliefs, as well as the fact that culpability and reasonable expectations are a function of our actual capacities, we cannot reasonably expect Mr Potter to do something that is beyond his actual capacities. He tells us: '*Potter, I argue, could not rationally have taken advantage of the opportunities for moral improvement that were (in some sense) available to him.*'[41] For Levy, internalism of reasons should prevail when we are dealing with blameworthy action, and, therefore, when Mr Potter considers alternative choices, he conceives them from his internal standpoint, ie beliefs and desires (what Levy calls pro-attitudes). Mr Potter III sees himself as managing his reasons and beliefs well. Levy asserts that what is rational for me to do *is settled by my mental states.* Only if I believe that p-ing is rational, do I have a reason to do so. However, Levy remains neutral on whether these reasons are motivating and emphasizes that they are actual representations and pro-attitudes. He acknowledges that a moral outlook is more than a set of beliefs, it also includes what he calls a 'moral world'.[42] Nevertheless, Levy does not expand on this and states that this moral world is the perspective from which we 'assess moral claims'. From Levy's view that internal reasons are representations and that what is rational to do is the settling of mental states, we

[39] Levy, 'Culpable Ignorance and Moral Responsibility' (n 12).
[40] ibid 734.
[41] ibid 735.
[42] ibid 737.

can infer that the moral world is mainly about *representations*. Due to his representations, ie beliefs, Mr Potter is unable to access alternative ways of assessing his own actions, which consequently prevents him from changing or transforming his moral world. '*The opportunities of moral improvements that he encounters—say, editorials by Paul Krugman in the New York Times—are seen as the whining of socialists or sissies*.'[43] Fitzpatrick, on the other hand, asserts that we could reasonably expect Mr Potter to seize these opportunities.

The dispute reflects the predominance of the bifurcation model and its corollary, the balancing view on deliberation. According to Levy, there are only internal reasons characterized predominantly by beliefs that we weigh against other beliefs,[44] but these beliefs are our own representations and we cannot change them. For Fitzpatrick, by contrast, it is a matter of vices, but his argumentation involves the implicit assumption that vices are chosen and that we can transform our false moral beliefs by simply learning other moral outlooks and taking the opportunities to revise, modify, and change our false moral beliefs. If we refuse to do so, it is because our will 'hangs on', so to speak, to vices, mainly epistemic vices; for example, arrogance, overconfidence in what we can achieve, and so on. Fitzpatrick also assumes that the bifurcation thesis and its corollary are true. Beliefs and vices are presented to us. In our deliberations, we choose or reject vices and engage with our beliefs alone. The process of deliberation itself does not account for any transformation or change. If our account is the sound model of deliberation, then it is evident that the dispute between Levy and Fitzpatrick relies on mistaken premises about how we engage with values, beliefs, and desires in our deliberations.

Talbert, unlike Levy, believes that Fitzpatrick's arguments are part of the character account of vices. Mr Potter's moral ignorance stems from his own vices. If he could have avoided exercising his vices the way he did, he could have avoided his moral ignorance.[45] However, Talbert rejects the view that alternative choices are a 'live option' for Mr Potter. Talbert asserts that we need to trace back the bad character of Mr Potter to early choices and to bad starting points, though '*a bad starting point is not something that one can reasonably be expected to avoid*'.[46] It is, therefore, not reasonable to expect him to change his moral outlook or moral vision. Talbert argues that Mr Potter's potential responsibility can be explained in terms of an attributionist theory of responsibility. We now turn to the different and complex theories that are called 'attributionist'.

[43] ibid 737.

[44] 'Our moral views are constitutive of our outlook: we assess evidence in terms of our views. We weigh the evidence in ways that are a function of these views; moreover, we give different sources of evidence different weight in ways that are responsive to our views (eg dismissing critics as motivated by the "politics of envy").' Levy, 'Culpable Ignorance and Moral Responsibility' (n 12) 738.

[45] Talbert (n 11) 51.

[46] ibid 52.

§8.3 Theories of Responsibility for Negligence that Ignore or Minimize the Temporality of Agency

Some authors point out the difficulties of focusing on mere beliefs, knowledge, and control as the source of responsibility for negligence. They see the idea of control as problematic and inadequate to explain the phenomenology of responsibility, which includes a wide range of judgements of responsibility, for example when the actor is 'forgetful', 'unaware', or expressing her emotions and what matters to her in her acting. The idea of knowledge, awareness, and control establishes that in these cases, the actor is not in control. Therefore, a judgement of responsibility cannot be established unless we follow the tracing strategy. Consequently, authors who follow this line of thought tend to minimize and, sometimes, eliminate the role of awareness or knowledge from the first-person perspective as central to responsibility judgements. Instead, they focus on the attribution of responsibility: the third- or second-person perspective when interpreting the agent's actions. For example, Smith[47] aims to show that the idea of control is not essential for our judgements of responsibility and advances the view that we should focus on attributions of responsibility that extend to forgetfulness, careless actions, and emotions, or agency that reflects evaluative judgements. Smith and others like her want to show that we are also responsible for our attitudes, commitments, characters, and emotions because they are connected to underlying evaluative judgements. Watson[48] has proposed that we are responsible for how we express our values and, therefore, what we attribute to others in terms of our evaluative judgements.

Scanlon[49] has proposed an attributionism that focuses on both unconscious and conscious judgement-sensitive patterns. Shoemaker[50] has put forward a pluralistic view of responsibility that considers attribution a sentiment, but also attribution as answerability.

These authors put forward complex and multi-layered sets of claims, but the common threads among their different views are: (a) a criticism of the idea of control and the temporality of agency, and (b) their focus on attribution as an inference from underlying evaluative judgements or value systems. I will reconstruct each position to scrutinize whether these accounts on 'attributability' of responsibility could apply to responsibility for negligence, including responsibility for negligence due to moral ignorance. I demonstrate that the problem with all kinds of attributionist accounts of responsibility is that they rely on the backward-looking perspective and the third-person point of view. The third-person point of view implies that the observer or third person looks at patterns or actions as signs or

[47] Angela Smith, 'Attitudes, Tracing and Control' (2015) 32 Journal of Applied Philosophy 115.

[48] Gary Watson, 'Free Agency' in *Agency and Answerability: Selected Essays* (Clarendon Press 2004) 13.

[49] Tim Scanlon, *What We Owe to Each Other* (Harvard UP 1998) 267–94.

[50] David Shoemaker, *Responsbility from the Margins* (OUP 2015).

expressions of what the agent intends, believes, desires, feels, or values. As a result, these theorists overlook the agent's process of learning and maturation, as well as the genuine, complex, and rich interaction between values, beliefs, desires, and emotions from the first-person or deliberative perspective. This interaction occurs when the agent engages in thinking to settle the question 'What shall I do?' and then executes the corresponding series of actions.

However, attributionists are not alone in their efforts to minimize agency's temporality and control. The rational capacity-focused conception also aims to establish that responsibility should be grounded in rational capacities and that the condition of control is not necessary to establish responsibility for negligence. The capacity-focused conception is basic and general, and it can be accepted by some attributionists. Finally, character-based responsibility relies on physiological and psychological features to minimize or reduce the role of our intelligent thinking. The latter view will be explained in §8.3.3 and the capacity-focused view will be discussed in §8.3.4.

§8.3.1 Aretaic Attributivism

In his paper 'Free Agency', Watson endorses the Platonic view of agency. According to this view, reason determines what has value, and therefore, to want something is to come to value it through reasoning. When we place value on something, we also judge that it should be pursued or achieved, leading to the origin of action-related evaluations in our reasoning.[51] What I most want is what I most value, not what I most desire, *stricto sensu*. For example, let us suppose that I want to become a good lawyer because I value justice and have the value of being a just person. However, paradoxically, I also have a desire to be unjust when it serves my self-interest. In this situation, what I want is to be just because it aligns with my values. I do not want to be unjust; I just simply desire to be unjust in 'particular circumstances', ie when it satisfies my self-interest, but this is not what I really want. In this way, our values and desires can be in conflict.

In the example, a man may perceive his sexual desires as a manifestation of the evil inside him. He does not value these sexual desires, and, as in the case of other basic desires like hunger or thirst, he just wants to 'get rid' of them. In many cases, the belief is that our rational side and our judgements are capable of correcting these conflicts. Watson distinguishes between the valuational system, which originates our 'all things considered judgements' and our motivational system, which is what moves us to act. According to Watson, the valuational system needs to have some grip on our motivational system in order to take effective action. When both

[51] Watson, 'Free Agency' (n 48) 17.

systems are in harmony, our actions are free. This means that we *can translate our values into actions.* When the motivational system is in severe conflict with the valuational system, we are acting unfreely. This means that there is no evaluative standpoint for the agent.[52]

From this conception, two key ideas emerge. First, our real selves identify with our rational evaluative part, the one that engages with values and *what we really want.* Secondly, when we act according to what we value, we manifest our evaluations through the performance of our actions. In other words, we manifest our valuational system through our deeds and, therefore, indirectly, through our real selves, or 'self-disclosure view'.[53] By contrast, when I act contrary to my evaluations, due to my unreasoned desires, I do not manifest my real self. Interestingly, not only is it the case that when we act, we show our values, it is also the case that when we do not act, forget to say or do something, ignore important things, overlook matters, or say the wrong thing without intention, we manifest our valuational system. These premises ground the aretaic 'attributionist' conception of responsibility. Thus, if someone needs to assess my conduct, she can track what I value through my actions, omissions, ways of talking, and doing things. My values reflect not my desires, *stricto sensu,* but rather my thinking on the subject matter and evaluations. This kind of responsibility, known as *aretaic,* focuses on our values as we act, do, say, or omit. Our judgements of value reflect whether we have a sound understanding of the respective value, ie whether it will show virtue or vices. If we have a distorted understanding of the respective value, it will reveal a vicious perspective. Although Watson introduces the idea of 'aretaic' appraisal, he never refers to character, passions, and emotions as integral parts of our reasoning in his work. On the contrary, he endorses an interpretation of the Platonic view, according to which passions and emotions are irrational. Thus, the conflict between values and desires stems from the fact that the latter belong to the non-rational part of the soul. He tells us, '*it is intrinsic to the appetite and passions that appetitive and passionate beings can be motivated in spite of themselves. It is because desires such as these arise independently of the person's judgement and values that the ancients located the emotions and passions in the irrational part of the soul.*'[54] For Watson, desires are persistently independent of one's values, and he gives us this metaphor: '*it is rather like jumping from an airplane*'.[55]

However, Watson recognizes that Plato poses a third part of the soul, which is partly rational to explain emotions that depend on beliefs and evaluations, but he does not explain this point further. The lack of exploration of this third part leads to a lack of understanding of the complexity of the interaction between desires and

[52] ibid 26.
[53] Gary Watson, 'Two Faces of Responsibility' in *Agency and Answerability: Selected Essays* (Clarendon Press 2004) 260, 261.
[54] Watson, 'Free Agency' (n 48) 21.
[55] ibid 21, fn 7.

beliefs, or, in Watson's terminology, between the valuational and motivational systems. It appears that we are dealing with a Socratic type of bifurcation between beliefs and desires. If we act according to our desires, to the extent that they are conceived as irrational impulses or something that 'we need to get rid of', then we are acting against our valuational system, and our action is unfree. Consequently, we cannot attribute the respective action to the agent in the aretaic sense. In the example of the man who regards his sexual desires as acts of the devil and not harmonious with his valuational system, we will say that responsibility cannot be attributed to him in the aretaic sense for his sexual desires and the corresponding acts. His sexual actions are not the manifestation of his values or his real self. Rather, arguably, his acts are impulses, and, as a result, his action is compulsive. According to Watson's conception of responsibility, we either have beliefs and corresponding values, or we have desires that are either in harmony with or in conflict with our values. In the latter case, we cannot be responsible in the aretaic sense.

However, I have argued against this bifurcation analysis of the self that sets the valuational system against the motivational system, reason-based actions against motive-based actions, and beliefs against desires. I have attempted to demonstrate how desires are engaged in values and the particular, often through narrow or substandard deliberation. Furthermore, I have also tried to demonstrate that aspirational deliberation that considers our engagement with and learning from others and their different values is possible. The result is that our Aristotelian-inspired model is more realistic from the psychological standpoint and *can account for intermediate stages when we are still learners, but there is no complete harmony between the valuational and motivational systems.*

However, the differences between Watson's Socratic-Platonic model and my Aristotelian-inspired proposal of practical reason should not be exaggerated. As I mentioned in Chapter 6, Aristotle partly agrees that the view of the majority in *Protagoras* concerning the phenomenon of *akrasia* is mistaken, and, therefore, Aristotle agrees with Socrates that the woman who knows what is good cannot be *akratic*, and, therefore, *akrasia* is a matter of ignorance rather than a matter of desires that take over our acting and deeds. On the other hand, Aristotle also wants to give an account of *akrasia* as part of our phenomenological experience of desire. I have defended the view that in *akrasia* there is a lack of integration between reason, or what we most value, and our desires, involving the failure to occupy a deliberative-aspirational perspective. However, the relationship between our valuational and motivational systems is more complex, and its interaction is richer than the one presented in Watson's Socratic-Platonic model.

A difficulty arises with the idea that we can attribute responsibility based on actions that manifest our valuing. This position privileges the backward-looking perspective to the detriment of the forward-looking and first-person perspective. Watson's aretaic conception of responsibility aims to show the importance of our reasoning and values in action and the problematic nature of desires that might not harmonize with our valuational system. However, paradoxically, the idea of responsibility via aretaic attribution focuses neither on the struggles and complexity of the deliberation nor on the agent's practical reasoning. We grasp this complexity by closely examining both the first-person or deliberative point of view and the forward-looking perspective. However, aretaic responsibility focuses on the backward-looking and third-person point of view.

The result is that the action is seen and understood as *an attribution of a performance*, closer to an event, rather than something that the agent develops over time. The performance is an event that reflects the valuational system of the agent at that particular point, and it is merely an attribution. As a result, it is questionable whether it truly reflects the complexity of the agent's action and its description as it develops or unfolds over time. Let me explain.

We have learned that practical reasoning entails that the agent is located within a temporality, and there is a learning to be good, a becoming that involves grasping complex values in the particularity of the action. This aspect is not fully appreciated in the conception of responsibility via aretaic attribution. Let us closely examine Watson's example regarding the man who believes his sexual desires are evil. It might be that, with time, he learns to develop a more harmonious view of himself. For instance, he now has a partner whom he loves, and he has learned to appreciate sexual pleasure and the beauty of intimacy. However, it is also true that at times he feels guilty, and his previous beliefs about his sexual desires come to mind. As a result, he suffers anxiety and has the tendency to reject this aspect of himself. He feels the need to 'get rid' of his sexual desires. He is an agent who is learning a different perspective regarding the value of playfulness and sexual desire, though he is struggling and is not in harmony with his evaluations and reasoning. We can say that his agency is 'in transition' because he is learning new values in the uniqueness and particularity of the experience. The attribution of aretaic responsibility in this case is more complex. His conduct is not compulsive, but it is not in harmony with his valuational system. In certain contexts and particular circumstances, his conduct can be considered *akratic*.

Responsibility in terms of aretaic attribution is lacking as it focuses on the backward-looking perspective, ignoring the struggles, complexity, and psychological realism of the deliberative and forward-looking perspective. As has been argued in Chapter 1, this conception of responsibility, like others, conflates the first-person perspective and forward-looking view with the third-person and backward-looking perspectives.

Because of this emphasis on attribution, the criticism advanced by Wolf[56] in terms of 'shallow' and 'deep' responsibility against aretaic attributive responsibility takes hold. According to Wolf, the 'real self view', or aretaic attributive

[56] Susan Wolf, *Freedom Within Reason* (OUP 1990).

responsibility, cannot distinguish between shallow and deep responsibility. Aretaic responsibility is causal. Let us think about an example to illustrate responsibility as causality. If you are a guest in my house and you break a precious glass due to your lack of care or attention, Watson would say that you are manifesting your valuational system with this action. By your actions, you are not valuing other people's property; rather, you are manifesting your indifference to it. According to Watson, you are *expressing or disclosing* your values and their connection to your practical identity.[57] The agent is willing to stand up for what she values, and this gives ethical depth to aretaic attributionism.[58] However, Wolf asserts that when we attribute responsibility to someone for an action, we do not say that she is a 'good-act' or 'bad-act' maker. In our example, Wolf would say that, according to Watson, you are responsible because you are a 'bad-act' maker, namely, you have broken a precious glass. In contrast, Wolf argues that the causalist conception of the aretaic model fails to grasp the deeper nature of attributions of responsibility. Thus, we say that the clock is a good clock as it operates well; similarly, we could say that people are good if they manifest their values. This kind of responsibility, Wolf tells us, is shallow.[59] However, responsibility extends beyond this superficial attribution. When we are attributing responsibility, we are saying something deeper, namely that you are indifferent or your actions are unconsidered.

However, Wolf is too quick to interpret aretaic responsibility in terms of a causal model of a 'good-act' or 'bad-act' maker. Her interpretation overlooks Watson's insight on the importance of the valuational system and focuses too quickly on the attributionist aspect of Watson's conception of aretaic responsibility. True, if the matter is only about attribution, then responsibility might look like a causal matter, with 'good-act' and 'bad-act' makers. However, if we look closely at the first-person perspective and forward-looking aspect of the agent, her struggles with her desires and valuational system, her thinking, descriptions, and re-descriptions of what she is doing, how she is doing it, and why she is doing what she is doing, then the picture becomes more complex. The causal and attributive conception of responsibility starts to look far too simplistic. Similarly, once we understand that Watson's view aims to bring our attention to the complexities of the valuational system and the way we manifest our values in our performance, then the criticism of 'deep' as opposed to 'shallow' also collapses. The issue lies in Watson's emphasis on the backward-looking perspective and attributionism, which tends to mask the complexities of the agent's struggle and her 'becoming' to conform to her valuational system. In my judgement, my proposal of focusing on the first-person or deliberative standpoint better grasps the depth and richness of the practical identity of the agent.

[57] Watson, 'Two Faces of Responsibility' (n 53) 267–71.
[58] ibid.
[59] Wolf (n 56) 35–45.

If we follow the thoughts advanced by aretaic attributionism, what can be said about negligence? Watson hints that there is an analogy between negligence and weakness of the will, and he argues that the latter is a matter of self-control.[60] However, this analogy is underdeveloped. Aretaic attributionism, arguably, can explain negligent actions as manifestations of our valuational system. We show a lack of concern for, or attention to, certain values as our evaluative judgements are disclosed in or expressed by our actions. For example, if a parent forgets that their child is in the bathtub, we would say that the parent shows a lack of concern for the value of their child's life. But this cannot be right, and Watson himself recognizes it.[61] Therefore, it appears that the conception of aretaic responsibility cannot illuminate cases of pure negligence. Parents care for their children, and they value their lives. In later sections, we will see how Smith, Scanlon, and Talbert's attributionist conceptions of responsibility can be used to explain responsibility for negligence. We will analyse this example to show the flaws and weaknesses of these theories of responsibility for negligence.

In his recent work, Watson has advanced his view on responsibility for inadvertent actions. He asserts that agential control is not necessarily voluntary control, but rather reason-responsive competence. Therefore, we are responsible for our negligent acts because our inadvertence is '*related in a special way to our reason-responsive competences*'.[62] However, this statement is too general to be explanatory, and we will discuss some challenges that the reason-responsive account faces because it relies on our competences and capacities in §8.3.4. More interestingly, in his recent work, Watson traces a negative path in our thinking about inadvertence. He delineates the way *we should not* think about inadvertence and pure negligence. He asserts that inadvertent action should not be equated to a glitch, something that 'just happens' to the agent, or a 'breakdown' of agency, which is the tendency of sceptical positions in responsibility for negligence. They tend to establish a stark binary option between voluntary action, ie deeds, and the corresponding retributive attitudes, and, on the other hand, non-voluntary actions, which are *mere glitches* or the agency's happenings. I agree with Watson on the way this negative path is delineated, and in this book I attempt to show a possible positive path for thinking about responsibility for negligence, ie *akrasia* as the underlying structure of practical reasoning in negligent acting.

My argument in this section can be summarized as follows: if we preserve Watson's insight on responsibility by focusing on the importance of the valuational system and enriching and expanding it, but ignore the 'attributive' part, then we

[60] Gary Watson, 'Scepticism About Weakness of the Will' in *Agency and Answerability: Selected Essays* (OUP 2004) 33, 52–53.

[61] Gary Watson, 'The Possibility of Pure Negligence' in Verónica Rodríguez-Blanco and George Pavlakos (eds), *Agency, Negligence and Responsibility* (CUP 2021) 99, 104–05.

[62] ibid 101.

might have the roots of an interesting and more psychologically realistic conception of responsibility.

§8.3.2 Attributionism as Answerability

Smith has defended a view of responsibility that downplays the role of choice and control. She instead focuses on attributions of responsibility that arise from the third-person or observer perspective, as well as the second-person perspective, when it aims at grasping the agent's *underlying* unreflective patterns of awareness of the evaluative judgements, and demands justificatory responses for the agent's actions or attitudes.

Smith's criticism of the control condition centres on the fact that we cannot control the agent's states that are sensitive to our judgements, ie the presence or absence of reasons in the circumstances, emotions such as fear, and other relevant states. Since attitudes depend on judgements about reasons, the former cannot change until our judgements change. We are not free to choose our attitudes. In other words, Smith tells us, '*we are not free to adopt, control or modify our attitudes in any way we choose*'.[63] Her positive position relies on the Scanlonian conception[64] that establishes that there is a class of judgement-sensitive attitudes that an ideally rational agent will come to have or reject, depending on their judgement of sufficient or insufficient reasons.[65] As a result, judgement-sensitive attitudes are a set of dispositions that make the agent react or act in certain ways. Furthermore, the agent is disposed to patterns of unreflective thoughts due to these judgement-sensitive attitudes. According to Smith, these attitudes underlie our evaluative judgements. Smith concentrates less on the Scanlonian ideally rational agent, placing more emphasis on the dispositional aspect together with the resulting patterns of underlying unreflective patterns of awareness.[66]

Smith's name for her own account varies; in some texts, she calls it the 'rational relation view'[67] because it focuses on the rational connection between the agent's actions, her attitudes, and evaluative judgements. For example, if Mr Potter II (see §8.2.2) acts in a way that overlooks truth and transparency in his relations with his clients, then this is an indication that Mr Potter II does not accept the evaluative judgement 'truth and transparency are important values when dealing with clients'. According to Smith, arguably, Mr Potter II does not 'choose' to act in a rude and

[63] A Smith, 'Attitudes, Tracing and Control' (n 47) 123.

[64] In her earlier work she relied on Watson's aretaic responsibility but in later work, she has come closer to Scanlon's conception of judgement-sensitive. In her earlier work she says that her account is self-expressive, which is the expression used by Watson.

[65] Scanlon, *What We Owe* (n 49) 20.

[66] Angela Smith, 'Responsibility for Attitudes' (2005) 115 Ethics 236, 241.

[67] Angela Smith, 'Control, Responsibility and Moral Assessment' (2008) 138 Philosophical Studies 367, 369; Angela Smith, 'Responsibility for Attitudes' (n 66) 240, 244–45.

inconsiderate manner. Rather, it is the case that his rude actions show, manifest, or express an unreflective pattern of awareness that underlies his evaluative judgements, ie indifference to truth and transparency. Smith oscillates between (i) an *expressivist* interpretation of this rational connection, ie the unreflective pattern of awareness expresses underlying evaluative judgements; (ii) a *constitutive* interpretation[68] of this rational connection, ie the unreflective pattern is constitutive of an evaluative judgement; and (iii) an *inferential* interpretation, ie an evaluative judgement reflects a particular mental state, and in light of the agent's spontaneous attitude and other explicit beliefs and judgements, an observer can infer that she has a particular evaluative judgement.[69]

In some of her work, Smith calls her position the 'answerability' view, as it focuses on the potential answers or responses that an agent could give if she were to ask why she is doing what she is doing.[70] More precisely, these are a set of answers that would emerge from moral criticism.[71] Furthermore, Smith believes that the answerability view of responsibility is basic,[72] and that reflections on adequate accountability towards, or sanctions, or punishments directed to the agent's actions depend on attributions of underlying evaluative judgements, ie attributivism as answerability.

The gist of responsibility, according to Smith, is that when we act, we need to confront others and answer *for* our actions in a justifying manner. This is possible because we are the kind of beings that have dispositions to act according to evaluative judgements. However, our actions do not depend on beliefs or other control mechanisms that we exercise over our bodily actions. On the contrary, our actions depend on our evaluative judgements, and on emerging and underlying unreflective patterns of awareness. Not surprisingly, the temporality of the agent is irrelevant. For Smith, it does not matter how our prior choices, valuing, and experiences determine our reasons for actions and beliefs, and how the latter shape our desires, values, and choices.[73] Judgements are presented as a matter of self-discovery. We find ourselves surprised by our reactions, emotions, and attitudes.[74] Consequently, one might infer that there are two steps in grasping the relevant

68 A Smith, 'Responsibility for Attitudes' (n 66) 244, fn 14.

69 ibid 255.

70 Angela Smith, 'Responsibility as Answerability' (2015) 58 Inquiry 99.

71 A Smith, Control, Responsibility and Moral Assessment' (n 67) 374.

72 A Smith, 'Responsibility as Answerability' (n 70) 102, fn 11. See also Gardner, who defends responsibility as answerability as primary or basic. John Gardner, 'The Mark of Responsibility' (2003) 23 Oxford Journal of Legal Studies 157. Smith rejects the distinction defended by Watson between accountability responsibility and aretaic responsibility. For Smith, any punishment, moral criticism, or sanction can be assessed once we have attributed basic responsibility in the sense defended by her, responsibility as answerability. A Smith, Control, Responsibility and Moral Assessment' (n 67) 379.

73 A Smith, 'Responsibility for Attitudes' (n 66) 239, 251. A Smith, Control, Responsibility and Moral Assessment' (n 67) 389.

74 A Smith, 'Responsibility for Attitudes' (n 66) 249. Smith asserts: 'Judgments are often things we discover about ourselves through our responses to questions or to situations.' ibid 252.

action and the idea of responsibility for the particular in Smith's account. First, the observer[75] or the second person, ie the person who has a claim on the actions and responses of the agent,[76] grasps the unreflective patterns of awareness that underlie the agent's evaluative judgements. Secondly, the observer or second person could potentially ask, or at least the agent is capable of being asked, for a justificatory response or answer for her action or pattern of awareness.

In early work, Smith does not appear to endorse the view that attributivism as answerability can be extended to non-intentional actions. Even cases of inattention are not interpreted as non-intentional, but rather, they are considered cases in which the agent intends '*to treat something with a particular form of (in)attention or (dis)respect*'.[77] According to Smith, what a person notices and neglects has an expressive significance. My interpretation is that intention for Smith is a dispositional mental state directed to an object. This line of thought is similar to Scanlon's view, as for him, '*actions are the kind of things for which normative reasons can be given only insofar as they are intentional, that is, are the expression of judgement-sensitive attitudes*'.[78]

Contrary to her early position, Smith in recent work[79] has attempted to show that attributivism can be applied to non-intentional omissions[80] or, as she calls them, 'unconscious' omissions. Her point of departure is Patricia Smith's view[81] which aims to establish that we are responsible for our non-intentional omissions because they involve a violation of or deviation from reasonable expectations according to a contextual standard. For Patricia Smith, it is a standard based on the community standard, ie the pattern of conduct of the community. Patricia Smith understands reasonable expectations in terms of what is probable or likely, but she recognizes the distinction between the probabilistic sense and the normative sense. However, she tends to dilute both senses and argues that these grounds are difficult to keep separated. Smith is concerned that Patricia Smith's account does not explain the rational connection between the agent and the omission. We do not know which omissions are truly attributable to the agent as failures of her acting and seeing as an active agent. For example, when I am nervous, I can bite

[75] I use the terms 'observer perspective' and the 'third-person perspective' as interchangeable.

[76] For further examination of the second-person perspective, see Stephen Darwall, *The Second-Person Standpoint* (Harvard UP 2009). The second-person view is the perspective of the individual who has a claim on the agent's actions. For example, if you step on my foot, I have a claim on you and can demand that you provide reasons for your actions.

[77] A Smith, 'Responsibility for Attitudes' (n 66) 242.

[78] Scanlon, *What We Owe* (n 49) 21.

[79] Angela Smith, 'Unconscious Omissions, Reasonable Expectations, and Responsibility' in Dana Kay Nelkin and Samuel C Rickless, *The Ethics and Law of Omissions* (OUP 2017) 36.

[80] To keep the discussion simple, I will use inadvertent actions, non-intentional omissions, and non-intentional actions as interchangeable. For a view that it does not make much sense to distinguish between actions and omissions, see Constantine Sandis, 'What Is It To Do Nothing?' in Verónica Rodríguez-Blanco and George Pavlakos, *Agency, Negligence and Responsibility* (CUP 2022) 187.

[81] Patricia Smith, 'Contemplating Failure: The Importance of Unconscious Omissions' (1990) 59 Philosophical Studies 159.

my nails, and my friends can reasonably expect me to bite my nails. However, one day, when I am nervous, against all reasonable expectations of my friends, I do not bite my nails. Have I committed an omission? According to Angela Smith, this and many similar cases show '*that people can fail to act in ways that it was reasonable (in an epistemic sense) to expect them to act without thereby committing omissions*'.[82] According to Angela Smith, what is really doing the work is not a norm in terms of reasonable expectation, but rather the idea that omissions depart from practical norms that give agents reasons for actions.

Angela Smith's view on responsibility, which emphasizes attributionism as answerability, suggests that the initial step is to ascertain whether non-intentional omissions can be attributed to agents. This type of responsibility is basic. After assessing basic responsibility, we can then engage in the question of whether the omission warrants a negative or critical response, ie sanction, punishment, or moral criticism. We must demonstrate (a) that the non-intentional omission can be rationally attributed to the agent, specifically by establishing a link between the omission, as the agent's failure to adhere to the practical norms, and the agent's underlying evaluative judgments; and (b) that the omission can be morally criticized because of the agent's ability to offer justifications for her omissions.[83] Furthermore, according to Angela Smith, the practical norm provides the agent with reasons that either require or favour doing a specific action, and the agent knows or should know this.[84] In this way, Smith expands her model of attributivism as answerability to inadvertent actions or non-intentional omissions.

Smith wants to emphasize that we are not passive victims of our characters,[85] and therefore the fact that attributionism cannot distinguish the bad agent from the blameworthy agent is an advantage.[86]

However, the attributionist theorist finds it difficult to comprehend why the agent is not passive regarding her character. It only assumes it because it perceives her action, performance, attitudes, feelings, and character as having a rational underpinning, and as a result, they belong to her. However, this is only an inference or conjecture. Therefore, character development and the way we are active concerning our characters remain a mystery within Smith's model of attributionism. Smith's proposal only views *reason in its effect, not its operation.* There is no genuine explanation for the existence of reason. It is mysterious whether it establishes boundaries or rather connects contingently to emotions and desires. Smith argues that there is a correlation between the mental state, emotion, attitude, intention, and the evaluative judgement or reasons. But this correlation is imposed by the observer or from the third-person perspective. Within this view, *reason cannot*

[82] A Smith, 'Unconscious Omissions' (n 79) 50.
[83] ibid 52–53.
[84] ibid 52.
[85] A Smith, Control, Responsibility and Moral Assessment' (n 67) 369.
[86] ibid 390.

shape emotions, desires, or intentions. They only *correlate*. When the state of mind is present, then the evaluative judgement *must* be present. It is unclear why this is so. Maybe it is because we are rational creatures that explains why there are 'patterns', but the nature of these patterns remains unexplained.

The bifurcation model of practical reason is present throughout the work of Smith. Scanlon's and Smith's position distinguishes reasons for belief or action from desires, which include attitudes, emotions, and passions. However, since the concept of reasons for actions requires spontaneity to show that reasons are involved with something we do, for Smith, spontaneity is assumed and explained as *unconscious or unreflective* patterns of awareness that underlie evaluative judgements or reasons. Smith asserts: '*We remember some things and forget others, particular considerations strike us as being relevant to the issue at hand, and we are moved spontaneously by various desires and inclinations*.'[87] Desires and emotions are created spontaneously, but they are judgement-dependent and Smith presents them as if they are *reducible* to reasons and evaluative judgements.[88] They manifest in tandem with our evaluative judgements, forming dispositions within our actions. However, Smith does not consider how we shape and transform these desires and emotions through our judgements. According to Smith, desires and emotions do not have independence or a partial independence from evaluative judgements. There is no explanation for how this reduction of desires to reasons operates or what the interaction between beliefs and desires *prior* to this reduction is, let alone the complex interaction between values, reasons, and desires.[89]

Smith presents us with a picture that is akin to a 'black box', where the input consists of the agent's evaluative judgements, along with the emotions and desires that are part of the evaluative judgements. On the other hand, we have the respective output, the expressions or manifestations of these evaluative judgements via unreflective patterns of awareness and the potential demands from either the

[87] A Smith, 'Responsibility for Attitudes' (n 66) 246.

[88] Smith points out: 'Attitudes such as contempt, jealousy, and regret seem to be partially constituted by certain kinds of evaluative judgements or appraisals. To feel contempt toward some person, for example, involves the judgement that she has some feature or has behaved in some way which makes her unworthy of one's respect, and to feel regret involves the judgment that something of value has been lost.' ibid 250.

[89] This bifurcation between desires and reasons and the ultimate reduction of desires to reason is also present in Scanlon. Furthermore, he believes that desires play no role in practical reasoning or thinking. Scanlon asserts: 'I will argue that desires, insofar as they are distinguished from the recognition of reasons, have a much less fundamental role in practical thinking than is commonly supposed. Indeed, I have become convinced that insofar as 'having a desire' is understood as a state that is distinct from 'seeing something as a reason', it plays almost no role in the justification and explanation of action.' Scanlon, *What We Owe* (n 49) 18. He has also defended the view that there is no distinction between practical and theoretical reasoning. ibid 23. Thus, desires motivate action because action has a belief-like component, and he regards cases of *akrasia* as the failure to give weight to specific reasons. Negligence is considered to be what happens when the agent ignores normative reasons and fails to make connections. ibid 30–51. He acknowledges that his position is similar to Davidson's view of weakness of the will. ibid 377, fn 18. Scanlon fails to explain the puzzling phenomenology of *akrasia*. For a discussion on Davidson's view on *akrasia*, see Chapter 6.

third-person or second-person perspective. Smith's account misses something important, which is our becoming. Responsibility plays a crucial role in our *becoming*, being possible by inhabiting aspirational perspectives. When we demand responses from others and when we express moral criticism, we express our reactive attitude *but also intend that the agent is able to inhabit a different perspective* concerning her actions, judgements, emotions, and desires, and take this new perspective into account in her future actions. We also desire that the agent reassess her entire self and explore new ways of looking at her actions and conduct. I have defended the view that changes and becoming are possible through our judgements and the transformation of our desires. We will expand on this in Chapter 9.

However, let us go back to and reflect on Wolf's criticism (see §8.3.1) that Smith's attributivism seems to be too close to a shallow conception of responsibility. Smith does not explain the agent's structure of thinking and valuing; this aspect remains obscure. We can attribute unreflective patterns of awareness to children, but they are not responsible in a deep or robust sense. Let us think about the following example. A young child named Pedro acts in an indifferent manner towards other children, being rude, cruel, and inconsiderate. He has behaved like this for a number of years, and, at the age of eight, Pedro stabs a friend at school. According to attributivism, Pedro is responsible because he has shown a pattern of unreflective awareness, which underlies his evaluative judgements. However, somehow, we do not make him responsible in the same way that we think Mr Potter II (see §8.2.2) is responsible for his rude and inconsiderate conduct. Pedro is responsible, arguably only for his unconscious awareness pattern, not for his actions. Mr Potter II is responsible for both his underlying pattern of unreflective awareness and his actions. The expression or manifestation of an underlying pattern of unreflective awareness cannot be the feature that guides us as to what responsibility is. Smith could argue that Pedro lacks evaluative judgements in the proper sense, and that his pattern of unreflective awareness does not reflect evaluative judgements in the proper sense. But this is difficult to defend. Pedro considers that he has reasons to be rude; he knows that in this way he can be feared and become powerful among his friends. Smith could also argue that it is not reasonable to demand justificatory responses from Pedro as to why he has done what he has done. True, but this means that it is only the answerability feature that enables us to distinguish between Pedro's case and Mr Potter II's case. Therefore, the first step of Smith's account, namely attribution in terms of underlying unreflective patterns of evaluative judgements, plays no role in demarcating the cases of Pedro and Mr Potter II. It is only the second step of Smith's account—being responsible if it is reasonable to ask justificatory responses for our actions and conduct—that plays the crucial role in distinguishing between Pedro's case and Mr Potter II's case.

Smith's account of basic responsibility for non-intentional omissions is also unsatisfactory and reflects the difficulties of her view of responsibility as attributionism for actions in general. Thus, the idea that the agent ought to have known the practical norm-generating reasons for action that apply to her does not illuminate the case of responsibility for inadvertent actions. Because Smith assumes a bifurcation between beliefs as reasons for actions and desires, her view is that the agent simply needs to engage with the respective beliefs as evaluative judgements to understand how the practical norm generates the respective reason for action. The position of the first-person perspective, the agent's temporality, her struggles between reason and desire, and her development and learning are ignored. Furthermore, ignoring the complexity of the interaction between desires and beliefs and focusing on a backward-looking perspective, namely the attribution of underlying unreflective patterns of awareness, has further consequences for the understanding of inadvertent action. A mismatch arises between (a) the underlying pattern of awareness of evaluative judgements, (b) the violation of the practical norm, and (c) potential answers to the question of why the agent did what she did or omitted to do what she ought to have done. Thus, we can correctly interpret that the agent has violated a practical norm that gives reasons for actions and say that she can be asked to answer for her omissions. Despite this, however, there could be a mismatch between *her* evaluative judgements and *our* attribution of the underlying pattern of awareness of evaluative judgements. Consequently, there would be no rational connection between *her* evaluative judgement and the violated practical norm, which grounds reasons for actions applicable to her. For example, in the case discussed in §8.2.1, *State v Williams*, the parents violated the practical norm of 'caring for their child' and therefore failed to follow the respective normative reason for actions that apply to them. We can grasp the fact that when Mrs Williams' child initially got ill, she did not seek medical advice. Days passed and the child's fever continued to increase to the point that it was dangerously high, but Mrs Williams still did not look for medical advice. From these facts, we can *attribute* to Mrs Williams an unreflective pattern of awareness that reflects or underlies the evaluative judgement 'I do not care about the health of my child'. Mrs Williams should have understood, based on Smith's account, that a combination of high temperature with other symptoms could signal a gangrenous infection. However, Mrs William's evaluative judgement was, 'I profoundly care for and love my child. I care for his health.' Thus, in this example, it is false that an unreflective pattern of awareness underlies Mrs Williams' evaluative judgement. It is unclear how Smith would defend the idea that Mrs Williams' agency is rationally connected to the violation of the practical norm and its corresponding normative reasons for actions.

The problem lies in the fact that Smith is not interested in the deliberative process, or the agent's choices and engagement in its temporality. Smith's focus is on attribution and the backward-looking perspective. Due to this limited focus, the complexity of both the agency and the first-person deliberative stance is lost. The only perspective that we can appreciate is the observer or second-person perspective, to the detriment of the first-person perspective and the forward-looking view.

Smith emphasizes the importance of our interactions and relations with other persons, and the importance of recognizing normative reasons in our interactions with other human beings. She asserts that failing to see the value of jazz or philosophy is different from failing to recognize or care about reasons that flow from other people's value.[90] People may criticize me for performing a piece of jazz music poorly, but this criticism differs from the criticism that stems from treating others rudely, inconsiderately, unkindly, and so on. When I attribute cruel conduct to others, I am not only implying that the person is bad, as a jazz performer is bad because she is performing poorly. Not only am I attributing a trait to her, but I am also demanding a justificatory response for her attitudes and conduct. Smith asserts: '*This demand by its very nature implies responsibility, for it is directed at his judgmental activity, activity for which we must regard him as responsible if we are to regard him as a moral agent in any case*.'[91] However, this assertion appears to draw a stark separation between activities and relationships or interactions with others. It overlooks the fact that the way we treat others, assess their values, develop, and learn valuing *is through our activities*.

In Chapter 4, I presented the analogy between craft and practical reason, demonstrating that, according to Aristotle, this analogy breaks down when we look at ethical or moral actions. In the case of craft, the standard of excellence is external to the crafter. For instance, for every carpenter there is a standard of excellence in working with wood, and for a jazz performer there is a standard of excellence in performing a specific piece of music. In ethics, however, the end is indeterminate, and Aristotle only tells us that in ethics, the right end is determined by the person who exercises practical reason. I have argued that when the agent deliberates in a narrow way, she is engaging with understanding and grasping the particular value in the circumstances, but there are also medium- and large-scale indeterminate ends and values that we are required to integrate. Therefore, we are asked to occupy a deliberative-aspirational perspective to shape the knowledge we gain from our substandard or narrow deliberation. This picture is dynamic and complex, emphasizing that through our activities, we also learn about the values that flow from other people. There is no stark separation between our activities and our relationships with others. If I am performing a jazz piece with a friend, I am learning to play the piece according to the standard of excellence, but I am also grasping the values of friendship, respect, consideration, and kindness. As a deliberator, the standard of my ethical actions is internal, and I give content and shape to my life according to the indeterminate conception of 'living well'. The standard of my performance of jazz is external, namely that there is a clear and external way of performing this piece in an excellent way. It is important to recognize that both activities and relationships are intricately linked. I may request that we set aside

[90] A Smith, Control, Responsibility and Moral Assessment' (n 67) 387.
[91] ibid 388.

the demand of achieving the external standard of excellence when performing this piece of jazz, as the values of friendship and kindness demand it *in this* particular situation. Through my activities, I gain a deeper understanding of valuing other people. The stark contrast between relationships and activities appears unjustified.

In his reply to Talbert's attributionism, Fitzpatrick makes a distinction between fittingness and deservingness. In the former case, we evaluate someone's moral views, and in virtue of this evaluation, we criticize, react, and respond to them; in the latter case, we say that the agent deserves a sanction, for example a reprimand, because of the way she has behaved.[92] According to Fitzpatrick, attributionists cannot capture the second sense of responsibility when we not only respond to or react to moral flaws and errors but also think that the actor deserves a punishment or sanction. Fitzpatrick rightly points out that Scanlon denies this and argues that his attributionism is about deservingness.[93] Fitzpatrick doubts that this position is coherent, and pressing further on this point, asks, '*how can we say that he deserves blame if he couldn't have helped being as he is*?'[94] Fitzpatrick tells us that the attributionist account gets wrong results in two key cases: (a) cases of indoctrination when there were no opportunities to learn and improve one's values and evaluations; and (b) cases of 'pure' negligence when the agent cares about and values the activity she is engaged with and/or takes care to avoid harm, but simply forgets to take the necessary precautions to avoid the harm. For example, consider a scenario where a mother neglects to change the smoke alarm's battery, resulting in a house fire that kills her family. She cares deeply about her family and their safety, but attributionists will say that her judgement shows the contrary, which is counterintuitive.

Daniel, who undergoes indoctrination by a sect and adopts strong homophobic views, exemplifies the first set of cases. But we can also use the previous cases of the women indoctrinated by the Taliban or the young men indoctrinated by the *Hitler-Jugend* programme (see §8.2.2). Fitzpatrick argues that in all these cases, attributionist accounts of deservingness and fittingness collapse together. Fitzpatrick argues that indoctrinated individuals are not deserving of punishment or sanction because they did not have the opportunity to develop and improve their moral judgements. For a correct judgement of deservingness, we need to show that at some point there was an opportunity for moral improvement that was not taken. By contrast, attributionists will say that these people deserve punishment, and it is fitting to reprimand them or react against them because they acted on *the basis of their values and wrong evaluations.* Fitzpatrick's core argument is that an explanation and understanding of the agency's temporal history are fundamental if we want to take responsibility for negligence or moral ignorance

92 Fitzpatrick, 'Unwitting Wrongdoing' (n 32) 33.
93 Tim Scanlon, *Moral Dimensions: Permissibility, Meaning, Blame* (Harvard UP 2008) 188.
94 Fitzpatrick, 'Unwitting Wrongdoing' (n 32) 34.

seriously, while offering a sound account of it. However, Fitzpatrick's idea that there is a *locus* at which the agent could reasonably expect to choose and improve his conceptions of values and moral beliefs relies on a simplistic model of deliberation, failing to capture the process of development and learning to become good.

Let us examine more closely the cases of indoctrination; there is no sufficient complexity in these cases offered by either attributionists or 'reasonable expectations' theorists. According to our proposal, the agent engages in narrow or sub-standard deliberation, the determination of *what* through determining the *how*, and it is through this engagement that she grasps *what* the end-value or end-desire looks like. This realization illuminates further deliberations, but also through criticism, friendship, engagement with others, and her own thinking, namely her description and re-description of her actions and valuing, she has the opportunity to avoid or recognize an aspirational perspective.

In the case of the indoctrinated individual, for example, a woman indoctrinated by the Taliban, the woman would have to decide, 'What shall I do?' regarding the education of her teenage daughter. She herself can write and read at a basic level, and she enjoyed learning when she was in primary school. She has grasped the value of reading and learning at a basic level, and now needs to decide whether or not to accept the Taliban's policy of not educating girls. In my proposal, the agent needs to inhabit the deliberative-aspirational perspective and either avoid or recognize the value of being educated. Like Murdoch's mother-in-law[95] she needs to engage in thinking, and describe and re-describe the situation and the positioning of her values, including other connected values within her indeterminate vision of 'living well'. She can avoid the aspirational perspective and say to herself that patriotism and loyalty to the religious convictions of her country are more important than her daughter's education. She can also adopt the deliberative-aspirational perspective, asserting that an authoritarian state, reflecting distorted religious beliefs and faith, cannot deny her daughter's education. She can take the view that faith cannot demand this from us and consider different interpretations of God and his benevolence. She can perhaps decide to escape. My point is that, *contra* Fitzpatrick, my proposal shows the complexity of deliberation; it shows how our desires and thinking are transformed while deciding what we should do and while succeeding or failing to inhabit a deliberative-aspirational perspective. This account of how practical reason operates is richer, presenting the different layers of our immersion in values and the exercise of our reasoning and thinking.

Our model in Chapter 6 also explains the case of pure negligence, demonstrating that the underlying structure of practical reasoning in cases of negligence is *akrasia*, which we explain in terms of an uneven development between character and our practical thinking. My proposal also demonstrates how our intelligent

[95] See §5.4.

thinking transforms desires and vice versa. In this way, we create a new conceptual space between attributionism and voluntarist accounts of responsibility for negligence and moral ignorance.

My proposal acknowledges the key insight of the 'reasonable expectations' view that we should not collapse deservingness and fittingness and that we need to explain the process of becoming good. However, I also argue that we need to take into account a more psychologically realistic view of our practical reason and deliberation. I acknowledge the role that values play in our lives, recognizing attributionists' emphasis on the significance of valuing while rejecting the view that we can grasp the richness of the interaction between reasons, values, and desires through mere attribution from the observer's or second-person point of view. I have rejected the reduction of the first-person perspective to the observer's or third-person perspective and the focus on the backward-looking perspective to the detriment of the forward-looking perspective.[96] Our emphasis is on the first-person perspective, arguing that mere attribution misses the agent's process of reasoning. Therefore, as we will see in Chapter 9, attribution misses how the law can help us grasp the good and the values of our lives and communities. In other words, it misses our aspirational citizenship.

§8.3.3 Sher and the Causality of Character: Physiological and Psychological Enabling Conditions

Scepticism about character concentrates on the problematic question of the source and possibility of controlling one's character. For example, Alexander and Ferzan emphasize that knowledge is key to control.[97] '*The law does not reach the negligent actor at the time he undertakes the negligent act... He cannot be guided at that moment*.'[98] Critics of character theory argue that the development of character is variable and contingent upon the psychological constitution of the agent and her situation; therefore, we cannot be responsible for our character, even if it plays a role in the causal history of our inadvertent actions. The key point is nicely summarized by Husak: '*The negligent actor need not have a defective character; only one act of carelessness will suffice for liability*.'[99]

In previous discussions, we learned that this way of putting the matter perpetuates the *myth of a* locus *of responsibility* and a bifurcation thesis. It emphasizes the assumption that we need to identify the control mechanism of action, and consequently, only the notions of choice, intention, belief, or consciousness can perform

[96] See Chapter 1 of this book for a detailed discussion of the first-person and third-person perspectives, as well as the backward-looking and forward-looking views.
[97] Alexander, Ferzan, and Morse (n 19) 78–79.
[98] ibid 80.
[99] Husak (n 10) 203.

such a task. If there is anything that belongs to the self outside this realm of conscious choice and intention, then it is purely contingent. Either we can control our actions through choice and intention, or our actions and patterns of conduct are contingent, making us immune to judgements of responsibility. Sher aims to resist this view and advances an account where character is central, though his position conceives character as a set of constitutive physiological and psychological features that play a causal role in our actions and patterns of conduct. Sher rejects this minimalist conception of the self based on control or knowledge because it is unable to explain responsibility for inadvertent actions. According to Sher, this contradicts our practice of responsibility. Therefore, it appears that if we want to avoid scepticism or a revisionary view of responsibility for inadvertence, we need to advance an explanation of responsibility for inadvertent action that is not minimalist. Sher provides several examples, such as the one from Chapter 1, to show that (a) agents acting inadvertently cannot fall under the minimalist conception, and (b) we tend to assign responsibility for inadvertent actions in our daily practices. Sher's example is as follows:

> *Hot Dog.* Alessandra, a soccer mom, has gone to pick-up her children at their elementary school. As usual, Alessandra is accompanied by the family's border collie, Bathsheba, who rides in the back of the van. Although it is very hot, the pick-up has never taken long, so Alessandra leaves Bathsheba in the van while she goes to gather the children. This time, however, Alessandra is greeted by a tangled tale of misbehavior, ill-considered punishment, and administrative bungling which requires several hours of indignant sorting out. During that time, Sheba languishes, forgotten in the locked car. When Alessandra and her children finally make it to the parking lot, they find Sheba unconscious from heat prostration.[100]

Sher argues that the minimalist self cannot explain our intuitions that attribute responsibility to Alessandra for leaving her dog in the vehicle and subsequently, almost dying of heatstroke. In fact, Alessandra's case demonstrates that Smith's and Scanlon's account, which focuses only on evaluative judgements, is not the correct account of responsibility for negligence, as Alessandra cares about her dog's well-being, and her evaluative judgements reflect this caring. According to Sher, there is a psychophysical structure that underpins her evaluative judgements; he argues that physiological and psychological features are constitutive of the self and have a causal role in what we do.

In opposition to the idea of the minimalist self, the 'maximalist conception' of the self incorporates all empirical features, including genetic composition. However, the grounding of responsibility in a maximalist conception of the self

[100] Sher (n 3) 24.

leads us to an over-inclusive account of responsibility, including responsibility for psychopathologies. However, this does not seem correct. Sher aims to look for a conception that occupies the logical space between the minimalist and the maximalist conceptions of the self, establishing that physiological and psychological features provide the enabling conditions for our reason-responsive capacities.

According to Sher, there are key reasons to believe that these features play a causal role. Hence, constitutive physiological and psychological features have a causal role in what we do because reason-responsiveness needs to respond to how the world is. Smith's and Scanlon's accounts of attributivism focus only on evaluative judgements, ignoring the causality of our psychological make-up, namely emotions, desires, and passions. According to Sher, the self is an enduring causal structure whose elements interact, and it is at the core of our explanation of responsibility for inadvertent action.[101] The interaction of physiological and psychological features '*determines the content of our conscious thoughts and deliberative activities*'.[102]

However, at other points, Sher asserts that physiological and psychological features *sustain* patterns of intellectual functioning.[103] Sher advances the view that these features, conceived as both causal and enabling of intellectual activity, define our practical identity and character. Moreover, any account of responsibility needs to make sense of both the judgements of the first-person perspective and the third-person or second-person perspective that focus on interpersonal relations. We need, consequently, as Sher tells us,[104] the premise of mental causation in order to understand others' mental states and to grasp an agent's actions and patterns. He argues that we cannot occupy other people's mental space because no one has access to their subjectivity. Attempting to understand others from our own subjectivity and mental space will not result in an interpersonal account. According to Sher, the only solution to this conundrum is to say that responsible selves *are the causes* of their subjectivity. Remember, this self is neither the maximal nor the minimal self, but a self constituted by physiological and psychological enabling conditions.

As a result, we can easily access these causes as they form an integral part of our empirical reality. The agent's actions stem from her beliefs, and her physiological and psychological constituencies causally explain her patterns of behaviour. From the observer's or second-person point of view, we can attribute reasonable beliefs and determine the content of such beliefs because there is an interaction between these beliefs and the world. The problem is, according to Sher, that the first-person

[101] ibid 121.
[102] ibid.
[103] ibid 123.
[104] ibid 125.

perspective is subjective and does not locate the self in the world; it is a non-empirical self.

The bifurcation thesis inevitably appears in Sher's account in a different manner. He distinguishes between emotions and desires *as enablers* of our intellectual activities. We have our intelligent thinking and beliefs, whose content is determined from the observer's point of view as causing the action and patterns of conduct resulting from interactions with the world; however, at no point do emotions and desires interact with intelligent thinking. One potential interpretation of this 'enabling' condition is to think in terms of the following analogy. As our tongue is an enabling condition of talking, our emotions and desires are enabling conditions of our intelligent thinking. However, our tongue does not shape our intelligent thinking. Similarly, neither does intelligent thinking shape our emotions and desires, nor vice versa. The vocabulary of enabling conditions remains obscure without a more detailed analysis of its implications.

Moreover, it is mysterious why physiological features play a crucial role in understanding how an agent's beliefs cause their actions. Finally, we have rejected the idea of subjectivity as a unique realm of the self, which only the agent can access. In Chapter 1, we demonstrated that the first-person perspective of the agent's own action entails 'seeing' the defective engagement of her practical reasoning when she sees the consequences or results of her actions. She does not look at her subjectivity or mental states *to infer or interpret her own actions.* The outcome of *her* action dawns on her because she recognizes the flawed engagement of her practical reasoning in her past action. Furthermore, our analysis of practical reason aims to demonstrate that the interaction of desires and emotions with our intelligent thinking is not causal but transformational. We have resisted the idea of viewing other minds as privileged subjectivities, while defending the view that we develop different perspectives through our thinking, and that through our thinking we transform our emotions, desires, and what we value. Contrary to Sher's account, my proposal advances the view that emotions and desires are not static; they are dynamic and can account for our changes, transformations, development, or becoming better people.

Sher's account is both incomplete and implausible. It is incomplete because we have no explanation of how and which physiological features are enabling and interacting to determine our intellectual activity. Is my propensity to sweat equally as important as my propensity to be lazy? What physiological features enable our intellectual activities? What criteria should we use to select these physiological features so that they can play an enabling role for our intelligent thinking? The account is implausible as it implies that our intelligent thinking *regarding normative and valuing issues* will differ based on our physiological characteristics. This would entail absurd views, such as the notion that my intelligent thinking about values and normative issues is influenced by factors like diabetes or obesity. Of course, this is not what Sher aims to convey. He wants to emphasize the importance of a broader conception of the self, in which physiological characteristics play a role in our agency's causal role. According to Sher, this conception of the self, which occupies a middle position between minimalist and maximalist views, would have implications for our theory of responsibility for inadvertent action. However, given the lack of a clear demarcation and criteria on which physiological features will be crucial for the causal and enabling role, we are left with the freedom to speculate and reach absurd conclusions. Sher leaves us without a clear understanding of this issue.

We will now turn to an analysis of the theories that aim to ground responsibility for negligence in the exercise of our rational capacities.

§8.3.4 Rational Capacity-Focused Theories

Capacity-focused theories rely on our general capacity for rational agency to ground responsibility for negligence. They advance the view that we have the capacity to be reason-responsive to information, evidence, norms, principles, and values. This is an important focus, and I have defended and emphasized the importance of our intelligent thinking and reason-responsiveness. However, this conception ignores the way in which our entire self, including emotions and desires, interacts with our reasons and transforms us. Consequently, it falls short in elucidating the actualization of our capacity and the intricate interplay between emotions, desires, intelligent thinking, and reason-responsiveness. In other words, it is an incomplete explanation of our rational agency.

Hart was one of the first authors in contemporary philosophy to argue that we are responsible for negligence due to the exercise of our rational capacities and their relevant relationship to our conduct. Thus, the negligent driver who drinks too much 'could have thought' before having too many drinks and getting into her vehicle. We say that the driver has acted below the standard expected of a reasonable person in the same situation[105] and she is responsible because she has the rational capacity to think about what she should do and could have acted differently. In other words, responsibility for negligence is about the functioning of her rational capacities in relation to her conduct. Raz continues with this line of thought on responsibility for negligence grounded in our rational capacities. Raz would say that we are responsible for our negligent actions because there is an appropriate connection between our actions and our rational agency 's capacity, and this capacity is a precondition for deserving praise or blame.[106]

[105] HLA Hart, *Punishment and Responsibility* (originally published in 1968, OUP 2008). Other authors have followed Hart's view in focusing on capacities to explain responsibility for negligence. See Anthony Duff, *Answering for Crime: Responsibility and Liability in the Criminal Law* (Hart 2007).

[106] Joseph Raz, 'Responsibility and the Negligence Standard' (2010) 30 Oxford Journal of Legal Studies 1.

The argument that the exercise of our capacities falls within the competence domain enriches Raz's rational capacity view. We cannot overlook the importance of the notion of competence. According to Raz, we cannot disavow the outcomes of our actions that fall within our competence domain. We are beings in the world who engage with actions and trust ourselves and others in performing such actions because we have certain competences. We hold ourselves responsible.[107] It is argued that we owe others the competent exercise of our competences, while also avowing the outcomes of our actions within our competence. This conception is part of our own self-understanding and the way we see ourselves in the world.[108] Raz gestures towards the idea that we are embodied and embedded agents, and the notion of competence plays a key role in explaining this embodiment. However, he does not engage with further explanations regarding what this competence domain entails[109] and how we might fail to exercise our rational capacities within our domain of competence.[110] The counterfactual test is used to reformulate Raz's capacity view, and this formulation might be as follows: if the agent had exercised her capacities that are within her domain of competence, then she would have thought and acted differently. The idea of failing to exercise a capacity does not explain *why she did not exercise*[111] her capacity, it only establishes *what would have happened* if she had exercised her capacity within her domain of competence.[112] Instead

107 Joseph Raz, *From Normativity to Responsibility* (OUP 2011) 245.

108 Joseph Raz, 'Being in the World' (2010) 23 Ratio 422.

109 Watson expresses a similar worry, as he thinks that we need an explanation concerning the defeating conditions of competence. Gary Watson, 'Raz on Responsibility' (2016) 10 Criminal Law and Philosophy 395.

110 Herstein advances an explanation of the concept of competence, as it relates to responsibility for negligence. He argues that negligence is the agent's failure to meet its own competence as required by some standard. As a result, the conduct expresses or manifests our failure. He refers to the idea of 'quality of agency'. This means that the agent is able to close the gap between her competency and success in her action. It is unclear, however, how this is *an explanation* of agency in terms of managing to reach successful performance on the basis of her competence. The account is susceptible to similar criticism in terms of lacking an explanation of how our capacities within competences truly operate. Ori Herstein, 'Nobody's Perfect: Moral Responsibility in Negligence' (2019) 32 Canadian Journal of Law and Jurisprudence 109.

111 Hurd and Moore criticize the capacity view and argue that capacity judgements are conditional, and it is usually very difficult to specify the respective conditionals as they are context-sensitive. My argument is along similar lines; I am asking why the agent did not exercise her capacities. Moore and Hurd pose the theoretical challenge in the following way: 'What the defense and the objection both depend on are capacity judgments that themselves depend on morally relevant factors that explain why an actor did not advert to the risk on the occasion in question. Was it because he was selfish, stupid, weak, or clumsy, either in general or at least on this occasion? If he can be blamed for these general defects or momentary lapses, then the relevant counterfactuals can be framed in which he lacks those defects, and in those possible worlds he would have adverted. And thus, one could infer, he could have adverted, in the relevant sense(s). But all the work here will be done by *the blameworthiness of these traits and lapses*, not by some general capacity or incapacity to advert to risks.' The emphasis is mine. Heidi Hurd and Michael Moore, 'Punishing the Awkward, the Stupid, the Weak and the Selfish: The Culpability of Negligence' (2011) 5 Criminal Law and Philosophy 147, 165.

112 ibid 161–65. Hurd and Moore ask: 'The question yet to be examined is whether the capacities involving changes in motivation, cognition, cognitive or motor skills are indeed desert bases for assessing moral culpability. That is the topic we examine in the next section. But before we turn to it, let us remind ourselves again of the implications of this section for the debate about negligence: contrary to HLA Hart's supposition, there is simply no defense to make of the blameworthiness of negligence in

of focusing on our general capacities for rational agency, we should consider the blameworthiness of specific traits. The rational capacity view must elucidate *what* and how changes and transformations operate, specifically the transition from a belief or desire to an action, *and distinguish it from* the capacity for its exercise.

It is true that our general capacities, and specifically and predominantly our rational capacity, determine *what* and *how* beliefs and desires transform or change. However, explaining the transformation or change of beliefs and desires does not equate to explaining the exercise of one's own capacity. Let us assume that the wind possesses the capacity to bend the tree, but neither its capacity nor its use of that ability can explain why and how this occurs. For example, it would be *no explanation* if, as a physics teacher, I said that the tree's bending is due to the capacity that the wind has. A further explanation is required, for example, of what this capacity *entails* when it is exercised. In the case of the wind, we would say that the trees convert the kinetic energy of the moving wind into the elastic potential energy of the wood fibres. We therefore need an explanation of *why* and *how* our rational capacity is exercised.

The agent's rational capacity reveals itself as she comprehends herself. This is the key difference between the example of the wind bending the tree and rational agency. This may sound cryptic, so allow me to clarify. When the agent acts, she establishes that certain reasons for her actions ground her acting. Explaining rational capacity involves elucidating how the agent reaches a grasp and understanding of her reasons for action, and why she fails to perform according to the exercise of her practical reasoning. The allure of the rational capacity view lies in its understanding that the agent settles the reasons for her actions from the deliberative, or self-understanding, point of view. Therefore, her practical reasoning starts with what she has learned or not learned. This means that judgements and attributions of responsibility begin with competences. However, this proposal does not explain how we might fail in our exercise as well as the complexity of the process of learning competences. For instance, there is a difference between being a good baseball player and having the competence of a good baseball player, and developing the competences of ethical conduct or virtue and becoming good. The former involves acquiring expertise that adheres to an external standard. Outside of the agent, the end is clear and determined. The latter is determined internally and involves, as we have shown in Chapters 4, 5, and 6, the transformation and change of the entire self.

terms of there being a culpability of unexercised capacity. But equally there is no objection to raise to the blameworthiness of negligence in terms of a lack of capacity to advert to risks in fact not adverted to.' Hurd and Moore (this note) 165. According to Hurd and Moore, capacity judgements depend on morally relevant factors that explain why the agent did not avert to the risk. It should be noted that all their examples, ie the agent cannot advert to the risk because he was selfish, stupid, weak, or clumsy, can be explained under my proposal, ie there is an uneven development between their emotions and desires and intelligent thinking about what they should do, which involves defective practical reasoning.

Furthermore, I have defended the view that practical wisdom and our capacity to become good and be reason-responsive regarding what is worthwhile and of value differ from our capacity to develop skills and crafts. Raz's concept of responsibility for negligence, rooted in our rational capacity within our domain of competences, fails to differentiate between craft and ethical action, particularly our capacity to develop and achieve excellence. In craft, the capacity is identified by the external standard, namely the end, determined externally. We have argued that external determination cannot determine the capacity to become good. The implication is that the standard is internal and therefore connected to our reason-responsiveness and thinking. However, this particular enabling condition necessitates a precise explanation. It is crucial to recognize and comprehend the distinction between competence in the skills of crafts and the ethical domain. It is true that both efforts require engagement with understanding and unfolding the end. They fall under the category of acquired capacities. However, skills and ethical conduct require a different kind of engagement, as demonstrated in Chapters 5 and 6. In the latter case, we must grasp values through both narrow and aspirational deliberation, and we must transform and shape our emotions and desires to align them with our intelligent thinking, or rational functioning.

Levy presents a criticism of the capacity view.[113] He asserts that it is not reasonable to expect to exercise our capacities when the conditions for their exercise are not present.[114] We cannot control what we are ignorant of. Levy then raises the question of whether capacity-view theorists would need a tracing account to identify the point at which the agent controlled the exercise of his capacity.[115] The explanation in terms of capacities does not move us forward, and the key issue or question reappears at a later stage of the explanation.

If temporality appears within capacity-focused theories, it is in order to distinguish between exercised or unexercised rational capacities within the diachronicity of our actions. However, this view does not explain how the transition from exercised to unexercised, or vice versa, truly happens. Within this account, the true dynamic, or diachronicity, of the nature of agency remains a mystery.

[113] He presents his argument as a criticism of Clarke's capacity view. See Randolph Clarke, *Omissions: Agency, Metaphysics and Responsibility* (OUP 2014). Levy, 'Culpable Ignorance and Moral Responsibility' (n 12); Matthew King, 'The Problem of Negligence' (2009) 35 Social Theory and Practice 577.

[114] Neil Levy, 'Methodological Conservatism and the Epistemic Condition' in Phillip Robichaud and Jan Willem Wieland (eds), *Responsibility: The Epistemic Condition* (OUP 2017) 252, 255.

[115] Sher also raises a similar criticism against Hart's capacity view and states that the capacity view as construed by Hart implies that 'what renders the negligent agent responsible is simply his act's failure to come up to some appropriate standard'. Sher (n 3) 83. For Sher, Hart's answer of responsibility for negligence as the failure to act according to the appropriate standard raises a further question, such as why the agent failed to exercise her capacity to advert or to investigate.

§8.4 Final Reflections on the Results of the Inquiry into Alternative Theories of Responsibility for Negligence

Ignoring the temporality of agency poses a problem as it fails to explain how the agent reaches maturity, resulting in the loss of the agent's own struggles, learning, and achievements. Any assessment of responsibility that overlooks the agent's temporality presents an artificially static picture of agency. On the other hand, if we accept the tracing strategy or the 'reasonable expectations' view where temporality is emphasized, then the picture of the operations and interactions of desire and beliefs is incomplete, as the becoming and transformations are either beliefs' changes or the will's execution. We cannot alter our will and desires without appropriate thought, and vice versa. Additionally, we need a proposal that provides a realistic psychological portrait of our operations in becoming good and transforming ourselves.

The proposal presented here aims to provide a comprehensive account of agency in negligence, as well as a psychologically realistic one. If we do not carefully examine the temporality of agency, blame, praise, punishment, and sanction for negligence seem unjustified or senseless. Our understanding of praise and blame as capable of guiding the agent into becoming better also becomes elusive. Not only does responsibility serve as a protest or a complaint, but it also serves as *a call for improvement* from the one imposing the blame to the one receiving it in the future. Our practices of responsibility are not only about a claim for the affected victim but also an invitation to carefully consider potential future victims and those whose actions can eventually harm others.

The bifurcation thesis and its corollary, the balancing view on deliberation, obscure our understanding of how we develop to become good or better or avoid being good or better, and how we can be responsible for the recognition or avoidance of an aspirational perspective. The bifurcation thesis also generates the *myth of the locus of responsibility*. This means that if agency's temporality is taken seriously, then we need to locate the *locus* of responsibility, ie the point at which we could choose and therefore at which our beliefs were present, resulting in being in control of our actions. In other words, the bifurcation paradigm identifies a specific time when we can locate our beliefs or form them. Conversely, disregarding temporality renders us oblivious to the interplay between reasons and desires. As a result, there is no directionality, and scepticism about the power of reasons to provide an account of agency arises.

Finally, we have shown that all accounts of responsibility for negligence, both those that focus on the temporality of agency and those that ignore it, come from backward-looking perspectives. They concentrate on the responses, yet they are unable to elucidate the interplay of thoughts and desires, and the intricate framework of agency during action. Therefore, they miss not only the forward-looking perspective but also the developmental and transformational role played by the interaction between beliefs and desires. They focus on *what* the responses are, not on *how* they are produced. The emphasis is on the response at a particular time, not the process of development or rational structure that generated the responses. We are presented as a cloven self; we witness the agent's responses, but her development, transformations, and becoming are veiled to us.

9

Revising the Puzzle of Negligence

Transforming the Citizen Towards Civic Maturity

§9.1 In Search of a Common Ground: Corrective Justice, Deliberation, and Practical Reason

At times, the outcomes of our actions might appear to be 'out of our control'. Appearance tells us that we can control our movements, but that beyond our bodily movements, things are beyond our control. There is no other domain of action in which this first impression is more palpable than in negligent action. Playing golf and other similar instantaneous voluntary movements with uncertain outcomes are the perfect example of an action that embodies the problem of indeterminacy of outcome. Thus, the golfer grasps her golf club, moves her arm, and hits the ball, but how things will turn out is beyond her control. If she hits another person, she is unlucky; if she gets close to the hole, she is lucky. In Chapter 7, we discussed the example of the two drivers, Fortunate and Fate, whose conduct is negligent, but only the action of one of them results in bad outcomes. The problem of control and luck spills over into our hopes for happiness or 'living well'. The idea that good, virtuous, or right action will lead to happiness is, as the sceptic tells us, illusory. 'Living well' depends on how things turn out and how the 'hap' in happiness and the 'daimon' in *eudaimonia* play their part.

Happiness, or *eudaimonia*, cannot be the ground for doing what is right or good. Kant rejected the idea that happiness and virtue guide our actions. He identified the control problem in the shaping of our will. How we shape our will defines how good or right our actions are. Kant located the will within a system of constraints and principles, which is a matter of internal freedom.[1] Kant contrasts the latter with so-called external freedom.[2] Kant's external freedom asks us to pay attention not to minimizing the 'hap' or 'daimon' via virtuous action but to look closely at the exercise of our external freedom, our movements and actions, in relation to others. Corrective justice theorists focus not on the shape of our will but on external freedom, where the exercise of an attribution by the judge is paramount,

[1] Immanuel Kant, *Metaphysics of Morals* (originally published in 1797, tr Mary Gregor, CUP 2017) 6:216–17 and 6:221.
[2] ibid 6:219–20.

Responsibility for Negligence in Ethics and Law. Verónica Rodríguez-Blanco, Oxford University Press.
 DOI: 10.1093/9780198948193.003.0009

and, in this way, they suppress the problem of moral luck rather than solving it in a satisfactory manner.

As discussed in Chapter 7, for corrective justice theorists, Kant's idea of external freedom provides the normative foundation for the losses and gains that are the outcome of human interaction and normatively grounds the restoration of these losses and gains. Your movements and actions have undermined my choices, and by exercising your external freedom, you have undermined mine, thus justifying judges' use of the law to restore inequality and exercise coercion. In other words, your illegitimate use of force on me justifies the law's force on you. The doctrinal content of tort law, including negligence law, is an evolving thought regarding this external freedom. The entire juridical doctrinal thought of the law of negligence, which includes concepts such as duty of care, standard of care, breach, causation, and injury, mirrors the structure of corrective justice. As a result, this model does not directly address the issue of moral luck and control; instead, it suppresses or obliterates it by focusing solely on the external exercise of our freedoms, replacing 'hap' and 'daimon' *with so-called external freedom as the only and legitimate concern of the jurist.* The shape of our will and what happens next as 'hap' or 'daimon' do not sit well within the domain of the law, or so we are told. According to the corrective justice theorist, the jurist only looks at what has already happened. The corrective justice theorist posits that the jurist retrospectively examines instances where my actions inflicted harm on you, impacted your property, or resulted in your suffering. They then interpret these actions and suffering through the prism of equality and autonomy.

Arguably, however, the question of justice is one for the citizen and her deep moral psychology, which includes her deliberation and engagement with values within the political community. She wishes her life to go well and seeks to avoid her own and others' suffering. She aims to act well and eschew acts of injustice that necessitate correction or reparation. She strives to prevent both her own suffering and mine. This represents the profound moral psychology of the citizen within the political community. She wishes her life to go well, deliberate, and choose well, but she also needs a political community whose members enjoy having their lives that 'go well'. However, since the citizen is compelled to participate in the world[3] and engage in action, it seems that she can only accomplish this through deliberation, or so we have attempted to demonstrate in Chapters 3 to 6. If we accept the premise that we must engage in deliberation, then deliberation is at the heart of doing. Previous chapters demonstrated the distinction between substandard or narrow deliberation and aspirational deliberation. If we define deliberation as '*the determination of the what through the determination of the how*' and the '*upward journey through the specification of the what*',[4] then it is difficult to imagine abstract

[3] I take this premise as commonplace in our experience.
[4] See Chapters 4 and 5.

concepts such as 'right and 'duty' playing any role in the citizen's deliberation, their deep moral psychology, and their political community.

Corrective justice theorists resist this way of thinking and focus on the subject matter of relational interaction. Two underlying presuppositions are fundamental to establishing the idea that only the normative framework of corrective justice in terms of relational interactions can provide the normative grounding of the tort of negligence law. First, the internal aspect, or 'internal logic' of corrective justice theory, establishes that we cannot resort to practical reason as deliberation in a narrow or aspirational manner. The citizen's search for an answer to the question, 'What shall I do?' is not relevant to the juridical mind because it lacks a relational component. When the citizen is facing the question 'What shall I do?', she is not confronted with another individual. She is not occupying the space of another's rational will. It may appear that juridical thinking does not need to engage with the citizen's 'living well', or narrow or aspirational deliberations. It appears that if tort law engages with the citizen's 'living well' or her deliberation, then tort law would need to resort to external ends, ie external ends manifested in values, being alien to corrective justice itself. Thus, the agent, in attempting to answer the question, 'What shall I do?' is not reasoning in juridical terms, such as the defendant's duties and plaintiff's rights, but rather in terms of values. As a result, this is essentially ethical reasoning, not 'corrective justice' reasoning. Additionally, according to corrective justice theorists, resorting to features or characteristics alien to the internal structure of corrective justice and negligence law undermines the intelligibility of the phenomena, namely the interaction between the plaintiff and the defendant. The doctrinal aspects of negligence law, akin to friendship or love, can only gain correct understanding and intelligibility through normativity, internal logic, and reasons for corrective justice, such as equality between persons and autonomy. Secondly, law and juridical thinking are matters of rights and duties. By contrast, ethical deliberation and practical reason are a matter of virtuous action, values, and what is good. We will refer to the first underlying presupposition as the 'internal logic' thesis. We will call the latter 'the separation of rights and values' thesis.

I aim to debunk both of these views and advance two key arguments. First, we must grasp the values embedded in the law through our 'doing' and in our engagement with the law.[5] This does not mean that these values are external and, therefore, that we make the internal logic of the negligence law unintelligible. Secondly, I will show that, from the forward-looking perspective of the citizen, there is no stark separation of rights and values. Judges take a backward-looking standpoint when engaging in decisions. They attribute liability grounded on the plaintiff's rights and the defendant's duties. However, in negligence law, judges

[5] See Verónica Rodríguez-Blanco and Pilar Zambrano, 'The Myth of the Classical Natural Law Theory: Reflecting on the 'Thin' View of Legal Positivism' (2018) 31 Ratio Juris 9 for further discussion on what engagement with the law means, and criticism of alternative possibilities.

advance values that play the role of *proleptic* thoughts, namely descriptions and re-descriptions of values that are part of the citizen's practical reasoning. We can understand both functions and roles because we understand that there is no stark separation of rights, duties, and values.

§9.1.1 The 'Internal Logic' Thesis

My arguments start with the thought that the internal logic of negligence law is not reducible to narrow juridical relational thinking but rather is a continuum with ethical and moral thinking and experience, where values play a key role. As the Aristotelian-inspired model has demonstrated, the values of tort law, like love or friendship, have an internal logic, but this internal logic is inescapably expansive and includes underlying moral and ethical values as learned and grasped through experience.

I will use the 'love' and 'friendship' analogies to undermine the narrow notion of an 'internal' logic of negligence law and corrective justice, as advocated by corrective justice theorists. For instance, if someone asks me why I love my friend, I would respond that it's because she is 'kind', 'gracious', and 'intelligent'. Because of all the experiences that we have shared, I have learned to describe and re-describe these features, which I then attribute to my friend. More precisely and following the Aristotelian-inspired model advanced in Chapters 3 to 6, my friend possesses these three features for me as a result of a development of my thinking together with what I have learned from our shared experiences, ie as a result of my own struggles in determining the correct descriptions and re-descriptions of our shared experiences, my actions, and her actions. My response is, so to speak, in accordance with the internal logic of the value of friendship. This means that I do not resort to scientific or empirical descriptions; I refer to the experience of love and friendship itself, as well as concepts related to or close to friendship, such as love and kindness.

However, my appreciation for my friend's love has a temporal dimension. I learned to grasp this set of values through both narrow and aspirational deliberation. Of course, if someone asks me to summarize my experience, I could say in a simple and abstract manner, 'I love my friend because she is kind, gracious, and intelligent.' My description fails to capture the intricacy of my deliberation, which is both narrow and aspirational, as well as the transformations and changes that have occurred in relation to my friendship. For instance, there have been moments when I have lost patience with my friend and needed to reflect on her best qualities, as well as moments when her gracious attitude and intelligence have manifested in unique ways. When I use the words 'kind', 'gracious', and 'intelligent', I use the internal logic of love and friendship, but this does not mean that other elements, including other values and the changes in my emotions, are not key in my grasping and correctly describing the phenomena. From the backward-looking perspective, I attribute the simple words 'kind', 'gracious', and 'intelligent' to describe my friend and the reasons behind my love for her. From the forward-looking perspective, however, when faced with decisions like being honest with my friend, telling her the truth, or telling her a noble lie about a situation, I must engage with her kindness and intelligence, which in turn shapes my love for her. My love for my friend stems from her kindness, graciousness, and intelligence, but it also requires me to consider other values like truth and honesty in our friendship.

Analogically, I argue that in law, the internal logic of the law of negligence has the appearance of doctrinal concepts and underlying abstract moral concepts such as rights and duties. Rights and duties operate as grounding reasons for my relationships and interactions with others.

From the backward-looking perspective, my attribution of the doing and the suffering that resulted from the negligent action, and the attribution of the judge of the negligent events, is in terms of the plaintiff's rights and the defendant's duties. The judge, in her attribution, resorts to the entire plethora of doctrinal concepts to attribute liability in negligence. However, from the forward-looking perspective, the citizen as agent, who has not yet caused the injury or damage, faces the question, 'What shall I do?' She needs to settle the question in order to act. As a result, she engages not only in substandard or narrow deliberation, but also aspirational deliberation. If our Aristotelian-inspired model of deliberation is sound, then from the forward-looking standpoint, the citizen cannot grasp the values of her actions, being unable to determine the *what* in terms of the *how*, being unable to avoid or recognize an aspirational point *unless* she determines the basic components of her action (ie features 'a_1' and 'a_2' as components of 'a', 'b_1', and 'b_2' as components of 'b', 'a', and 'b' to achieve 'x', and finally 'x' in order to achieve the end 'Y').[6] She also needs to transform her emotions and desires in light of her descriptions and thoughts about the indeterminate aim or end of 'living well'. Moreover, she must either recognize or avoid an aspirational point that confronts her. I argue that the forward-looking standpoint of her action and potential avoidance of harm or injury is not presented as an abstract right, duty, principle, or rule. However, this does not preclude formulating it as such, but rather necessitates settling the question, 'What shall I do?' This means that there is an internal logic in negligence law, but it is not reductive. From the backward-looking perspective, the judge will consider values that can only be learned and grasped through the forward-looking perspective. This new understanding of values will enrich the doctrinal concepts and be applied from the backward-looking perspective. To illustrate this, let us analyse a landmark case of negligence law.

[6] See §4.2 for a full analysis of this point.

In the case of *Donoghue v Stevenson*[7] Mrs May Donoghue went to a café where her friend ordered an ice cream and a bottle of ginger beer. They were supplied by the shopkeeper, who poured the ginger beer over the ice cream. Mrs Donoghue ate part of the ice cream and as she finished pouring the rest of the ginger beer, a decomposed snail floated out. As a result of consuming part of the liquid, Mrs Donoghue contracted a serious illness. The bottle was made of dark glass, so its contents could not have been determined by inspection. Mrs Donoghue initiated an action for negligence against the manufacturer, David Stevenson, who had produced a drink for general consumption by the public. The snail's presence rendered the product dangerous and harmful, and the plaintiff alleged that it was the duty of the manufacturer to avoid producing harmful and dangerous products.

The facts and circumstances of the case provide a concrete particularity to the value of physical integrity. The aim of the judge's reasoning is to determine the specific content of the plaintiff's rights, but she also has a forward-looking perspective. If her decision is intended to guide citizens, it must advance values that are manifested in particularities and provide appealing descriptions of values to guide citizens' actions.

Lord Atkin in *Donoghue v Stevenson* stated:

> But acts or omissions which any moral code would censure cannot in a practical world be treated so as to give a right to every person injured by them to demand relief. In this way rules of law arise which limit the range of complainants and the extent of their remedy. The rule that you are to love your neighbour becomes in law, you must not injure your neighbour; and the lawyer's question, Who is my neighbour? receives a restricted reply. You must take reasonable care to avoid acts or omissions which you can reasonably foresee would be likely to injure your neighbour. Who, then, in law is my neighbour? The answer seems to be—persons who are so closely and directly affected by my act that I ought reasonably to have them in contemplation as being so affected when I am directing my mind to the acts or omissions which are called in question.

In these passages, Lord Atkin states that there is a duty to avoid acts or omissions that would likely harm others, to the extent that 'I ought reasonably to have them in contemplation'. Lord Atkin establishes the general principle that 'you must not injure your neighbour'. This doctrinal duty is empty and abstract. However, it acquires special content in the particular circumstances and facts of the case, and due to the descriptions and re-descriptions of the judge. The judge applies his knowledge and grasp of values *as if he* were an agent. This means he is engaged in the question 'What shall I do?' in order to provide guidance to the citizen. However, simultaneously, the judge needs to look at the relational dimension of the case in

[7] [1932] UKHL 100.

order to determine whether the plaintiff's right has been violated and whether the defendant had a duty that has been breached. These attributions are sound and possible only if the judge understands the values that are at stake and can grasp the complexity of such values *as if he acted* from the forward-looking perspective.

Lord Atkin re-describes the facts of the case and the values at stake. This example demonstrates how judges present the realizability of specific values by describing them from a forward-looking perspective, similar to that of a citizen. We ask the citizen manufacturing a drink to consider the value of being attentive and *careful when producing an article of food*. This is put as follows:

> A manufacturer puts up an article of food in a container which he knows will be opened by the actual consumer. There can be no inspection by any purchaser and no reasonable preliminary inspection by the consumer. Negligently, in the course of preparation, he allows the contents to be mixed with poison. It is said that the law of England and Scotland is that the poisoned consumer has no remedy against the negligent manufacturer. If this were the result of the authorities, I should consider the result a grave defect in the law, and so contrary to principle that I should hesitate long before following any decision to that effect which had not the authority of this House.

The issue is now not only between Mr Stevenson, the manufacturer, and Mrs Donoghue, but between *any* manufacturer and any consumer. We ask the manufacturer to take into account the consumer's inability to inspect the bottle before purchasing it. The attribution is based on the consumer's rights and the manufacturer's duty. But the engagement, realizability, and determination of these abstract rights and duties are based on values, necessitating the sound deliberation and exercise of judges' and citizens' practical reasoning.[8]

We now turn to the 'separation of rights and values' thesis.

§9.1.2 The 'Separation of Values and Rights' Thesis

One could argue that the notion of 'right' is powerful and appealing. For example, Keating's forward-looking view attempts to show that negligence law is a matter of a violation of a primary norm, while only in a secondary sense is it a matter of reparation. Therefore, Keating argues that tort law theorists should prioritize respecting the rights of physical integrity and security of all individuals, rather than

[8] Some authors have explored the connection between the judges' perception and the development of her practical wisdom/practical reason to explain the complex and 'internal' task of the judge's adjudication. See Iris Van Dormeselaar, 'The Perceptive Judge' (2018) 9 Jurisprudence 71.

focusing on the remedy or reparation after the wrong has occurred. According to this viewpoint, the law is not about personal wrongs and our personal relationships with others, but rather about our rights. The law imposes rights on us, whether we like it or not, whether this is our choice of life, or whether we are able to deliberate correctly or defectively.

The concepts of rights and duties are also powerful and appealing within the theoretical framework of corrective justice. Kant's external freedom establishes the constraints and normative force of our deliberations and conduct. The focus is not on our *wrongful conduct*, but rather on the *wrongs* committed to others, thereby undermining their equality and autonomy. Keating's focus is on the forward-looking perspective of the citizen and *her right* to claim respect for *her security* and *physical* integrity. Weinrib and Ripstein concentrate on the backward-looking perspective of juridical thinking, which attributes liability for the wrong that has been committed. The normative justification is the defendant's autonomy, and we do not need to establish the content of the autonomous choice that deprived the victim. Similar to right and duty, we abstract the notion of autonomy from the citizen's values, her deliberations, and her response to the question, 'What shall I do?' Corrective justice theorists give prevalence to juridical thinking and adhere to the separation of values and rights.

However, let us consider how the citizen engages with rights, duties, and the exercise of her autonomy in her actions, all while exercising her practical reasoning. As an agent, the citizen participates in various activities, and her actions are characterized by her ability to deliberate from narrow or substandard perspectives to aspirational ones. At first glance, it might seem that activities require only technical or craft skills where the standard of excellence is external to them. For example, a doctor cures the patient's cancer according to the external standard of a healthy body. The doctor's goal is to remove cancer cells from the patient's body. The external standard determines the success of her enterprise. By contrast, as discussed in Chapter 4, ethical deliberation requires an internal standard. The aims of 'living well' are indeterminate for the agent, and the engagement with different values involves grasping the different aspects of specific values in the particular circumstances. For example, in Chapter 4, Beatrice gains a deeper understanding of her daughter's physical health in relation to her spiritual well-being after deliberating and reflecting on whether gymnastic or ballet classes would be better for her daughter. Values underpin both Beatrice's and the doctor's activities. The latter activity is a craft, with an external standard of excellence. Beatrice actively engages in living well and being a good mother, while the standard remains indeterminate and internal to her actions and deliberations. But this contrast might seem artificial. The doctor also aspires to lead a fulfilling life, and becoming a good doctor is closely linked to becoming a good man. To be a good doctor, he must also cultivate ethical virtues and values such as patience, compassion for his patients, and humility.

Example: The conductor of an orchestra

Let us imagine that you are the conductor of an orchestra and engage in settling the question, 'What shall I do?' in the context of preparing the orchestra for the next concert. While there is an external standard of excellence in musical performance, cultivating ethical values is also necessary to achieve the desired end of a good performance. For instance, the conductor must adapt daily practices to the musicians' needs and personalities, occasionally relaxing rigour to foster an imaginative understanding of the piece, and so on. Similarly, the conductor sees each musician as a person and aims to respect their individuality and capacity. Arguably, the performers' rights are not in the contemplation of the conductor. However, the conductor engages and deliberates with ethical and aesthetic values, ensuring that each action embodies the relationship's fundamental rights and duties. This implies that the performer's experiences and the temporality of their deliberation, both individually and collectively, shape the *content* of the rights and duties. The conductor does not respect the rights of the musicians in the abstract. The conductor's conduct, showing respect for these rights and adequate performance of his duties, is due to his grasping of the values, including the value of personhood, when he aims to answer the question 'What shall I do?' and engages in substandard, narrow, and aspirational deliberations.[9]

When we engage in ethical deliberation, we are attempting to determine the character and the right description of the respective value, as well as its role in shaping the indeterminate aim of 'living well'. At first glance, rights and duties operate differently. Their character is adversarial. When I assert my right to security and physical integrity, I am positioning myself against you. Within a political community, citizens position themselves against other citizens. Citizens demand respect for their rights, and the role of negligence law is to uphold these fundamental rights, specifically security and personal integrity. Similarly, if, due to your doings, you cause an injury, then you have breached the duty of care that you have towards me, and I have the right to claim a correction or reparation for the wrong. However, this description of the events, ie the doing, the injury, and the suffering, are abstracted from the agent's deliberative and forward-looking perspective.

[9] For a similar approach that aims to show how we combine the Kantian requirement of the categorical imperative with our intentional actions, see Verónica Rodríguez-Blanco, 'Dworkin's Dignity Under the Lens of the Magician of Königsberg' in Salman Khurshid, Lokendra Malik, and Verónica Rodríguez-Blanco (eds), *Dignity in Dworkin's Legal and Moral Philosophy* (OUP 2018).

Let us now return to the forward-looking perspective of the agent who engages in values-based activities. Upon first examination, this engagement differs from the judge's backward-looking perspective, which attributes legal liability based on rights and duties. To illustrate this point, let us look at one key example.

The example illustrates my key point. The backward-looking perspective is in continuity with the forward-looking perspective. As a result, the forward-looking perspective regarding the deliberation of values takes precedence over the grounding and abstract notions of rights and duties.

Thus far, I have defended the idea of grounding rights and duties whose content is determined by the values in the agent's deliberation. In other words, my proposal suggests that while rights and duties are empty and formal, the agent's deliberation process determines their realizability and manifestation. At the abstract level, rights and duties function as grounding. This explains why, at the moment of adjudication, they play a key role for judges, lawyers, and legal practitioners. However, this does not mean that values and deliberation play no role in delineating the shape of our responsibilities and legal liabilities. Attributions of responsibility aim not only to correct the wrong, but also to engage the citizen to recognize potential wrongful conduct and avoid it. Blameworthy judgements in ethics and liability judgments in law are not only a reaction to and protest against the injurer's actions or the plaintiff's actions, but a warning for future agents and citizens on how to engage with activities that inevitably, and due to the kind of creatures we are, involve values. These values are also acquired content through the agent's experiences and deliberation.

But now the question arises: how can the law be part of the agents' practical reasoning, while playing a role in the forward-looking perspective? I argue that the courts' decisions in negligence law mirror these complex, evolving values. They mirror the attributive juridical thinking exercised by judges, lawyers, and legal practitioners; but also court decisions play the role of advancing *proleptic* thoughts as forms of value descriptions and value re-descriptions in order to engage the citizen's practical reasoning so that she can recognize an aspirational-deliberative perspective. I now turn to the argument's analysis.

§9.2 Negligence Law as *Proleptic* Thoughts in Terms of Descriptions of Values that Engage the Citizen's Practical Reasoning

Both laypeople and legal practitioners have a common understanding of what court decisions are. People conceptualize court decisions as vessels that encompass all the necessary rules and principles. According to this image, the citizen only needs to discover the vessel's contents, and her action will follow. If her action fails, it is because she is not a law-abiding citizen and, consequently, has decided to disobey the law. This viewpoint threatens our understanding of negligence law because it reifies the law's content as something 'given'. Unsurprisingly, we struggle with understanding how negligence law can guide citizens.

In Chapter 7, we discussed the abstract, particularity, deterrence, and guidance challenges that any theory of negligence faces. These challenges stem from the impossibility of guidance in an abstract and non-specific law of negligence. This occurs when the law prioritizes principles or rules as guiding citizens' conduct, overlooks the essential elements of our agency and the exercise of practical reasoning, and views agency as empirical and influenced by incentives. The gist is to explain how practical reasoning, which is essentially engagement with values in their particular circumstances, can guide our actions and enable us to change and transform towards an aspirational-deliberative perspective. If the law serves as a vessel containing specific facts and values, and practical reasoning merely functions as a 'detecting' mechanism, it becomes challenging to assign responsibility for negligence. It seems natural to argue that the citizen, when acting negligently, had false or implicit beliefs, or that, at a certain time, the citizen failed to form the correct beliefs about the law's values.

In opposition to this view of law as a vessel, I will defend a very different picture of the role of court decisions in citizens' practical reasoning. I contend that the law of negligence presents citizens with *proleptic* thoughts on values *qua* descriptions and re-descriptions to be engaged with, namely unique ways of realizing the values of security and physical integrity in the particular circumstances of specific actions.[10] In doctrinal terms, we assert that negligence law invites the citizen to consider her duty in the context of the specific reasonable person in the respective situation, role, and activity. According to our theoretical account, negligence law requires citizens to engage in specific ways with values while exercising their practical reasoning. For instance, a doctor operating on a patient to cure her of cancer needs to look at ways of realizing diligence and care, carefully consider her peers' practice on treatments,[11] and critically evaluate the logic of her deliberations and decisions.[12] *Proleptic* thoughts, embodying specific values like the patient's health, present themselves to the citizen, while rights and duties used by judges in their attributive function ground the *proleptic* thoughts. However, the abstract grounding in terms of rights and duties plays no role in the citizen's practical reasoning unless she is able to engage with the specific realization of these values through her activities and actions, which mirrors the specific content of the *proleptic* thought. In the

[10] Finnis calls this the 'salient role' that the law plays. John Finnis, *Natural Law and Natural Rights* (Clarendon Press 1980).

[11] In English law, the so-called *Bolam* test establishes that in the exercise of their professional skills, like doctors, the person has not acted negligently if she has acted in accordance with a practice accepted at the time as proper by a responsible body of medical opinion. *Bolam v Friern Hospital Management Committee* [1957] 1 WLR 582 and *Montgomery v Lanarkshire Health Board* [2015] UKSC 11.

[12] The *Bolitho* case establishes that, when applying the *Bolam* test, the practice must demonstrate that it is based on logic and is defensible. *Bolitho v City & Hackney Health Authority* [1997] 3 WLR 1151.

case of *Donoghue v Stevenson*, the manufacturers recognize the value of consumers' physical integrity by meticulously handling the bottles and ensuring the utmost quality of inspection. Practices would need to be changed. For instance, the manufacturer and retailer introduce clear bottles for inspection, and package warnings on packages should be tailored to the specific product and its intended use.

§9.3 Back to Moral Luck: Law and Learning Towards Aspirational Deliberation

At the outset of this final chapter, I provided a summary of how corrective justice theorists dissolve the problem of moral luck. They focus on our bodily movements and the wrongs that we commit when we injure or harm others. These bodily movements are the outcome of our rational will. Thus, Kant's external freedom provides the theoretical foundation for the necessary repair or correction that arises from the inequality of losses and gains resulting from human interaction, ie the clash of rational wills and the materialization of bodily movements. When you act in a way that harms me, we should not view it solely as an empirical fact, but rather as a collision of two rational wills. Prior to the injury or harm occurring, one person had a duty to act in a certain way, such as being careful and thoughtful, in order to avoid harm, but has breached that duty, and the other party had a right to be protected in her security and physical integrity, as these are constitutive of her autonomy. When our rational wills are confronted, the wrong becomes apparent. When you, as a person, demand from me a remedy to repair the loss that I have imposed on you, then juridical thinking emerges. Prior to that, we might assume that there was no juridical thinking involved in this particular performance of the action.

In his book *From Personal Lives to Private Law*[13] Gardner complains that the idea of right is too adversarial to reflect the complex guidance and role that the law of negligence (and tort law) play in our personal lives. Gardner's goal is to demonstrate that our personal lives are also public, and focusing solely on the corrective and adversarial dimensions of tort law will not allow us to understand and make intelligible our 'living well' and plurality of choices. My interpretation is that he is attempting to show that, even before any harm or injury occurred, the law was already in place, showing values, shaping the content of our responsibilities, and providing corrective measures for our wrongful conduct.

Honoré and Gardner, like other corrective justice theorists, also suppress the moral luck problem. They argue that the outcomes are inherent in our actions. Goldberg and Zipursky also suppress the problem as they rely on a characterization

[13] John Gardner, *From Personal Life to Private Law* (OUP 2018).

of action that already implies embracing the outcomes of our actions. However, sceptics are unsatisfied with these answers, and rightly so. The problem of moral luck does not disappear if we simply reformulate or re-describe action to incorporate outcomes when the phenomenology of action tells us otherwise.

In Chapter 7, we discussed the example of the two drivers presented at the abstract level. Both Fortunate and Fate acted wrongly, but only Fate is legally liable because she has harmed another person. According to the sceptical views discussed in Chapter 2, the problem appears to stem from 'glitches' or something that is beyond our control. We have no control over our character, attentiveness, or carefulness. Worse, the question of transformation or becoming is already posed in a sceptical manner. Even if we could, as Rosen attempts to demonstrate, control of character lies in the obscure account of *akrasia*. In contrast to Rosen, I have attempted to demonstrate in this book that there exists a precise and correct account of *akrasia*, which serves as the underlying structure of a negligent action.

To suppress the problem of moral luck, however, is to give further strength to sceptical positions. Corrective justice theorists, along with Gardner, Honoré, Goldberg, and Zipursky, commonly employ an argumentative strategy that divides the temporality of the negligent act into two distinct parts. First, we have the *ex-ante* part, which refers to anything that occurs before the clashing of two rational wills or before the occurrence of the outcome or injury. Secondly, we have the *ex-post* element, where responsibility emerges following the occurrence of injury, suffering, or harm. These theorists focus on the latter, although Gardner and Honoré suggest that outcomes form part of our identity.[14] However, they fail to establish a connection between this identity and our ability to shape it—that is, to become and transform ourselves. Zipursky and Goldberg introduce the key idea of practice as constitutive of the directive, but this appears too thin to be able to guide the citizen's conduct.[15] This approach artificially suppresses the problem of moral luck. In other words, Honoré, Gardner, Goldberg, and Zipursky do not recognize the problem of moral luck and its challenges in all their robustness and complexity. According to corrective justice theorists, the focus should be on the normative foundation of the unequal relation, which results in the loss of one part and the normative gain on the other. According to Honoré and Gardner, it is a matter of

[14] John Gardner, 'What is Tort Law For?' (2011) 30 Law and Philosophy 1; Tony Honoré, *Responsibility and Fault* (Hart 1999).

[15] John Goldberg and Benjamin Zipursky, *Recognizing Wrongs* (Harvard UP 2020). To be fair, in recent work, Zipursky defends resultant moral luck in terms of 'response norm concepts', establishing a parallel between morality and law. This is an intriguing position that differs from the 'practice-based' view. According to Zipursky, there is a parallel between the domains of legal liability and moral blameworthiness. They involve 'response norm concepts', which acknowledge that individuals respond differently to the nature and character of others. As a result, response norm concepts play a role in distinguishing justifiable from unjustifiable occasions for such responses. Benjamin Zipursky, 'Response Norm Concepts in Law and Morality: A Qualified Defense of Moral Luck' in Daniel Peixoto-Murata, Verónica Rodríguez-Blanco, and Julieta Rábanos (eds), *Bernard Williams on Law and Responsibility: From Agency and Responsibility to Methodology* (Hart/Bloomsbury 2025).

correctly understanding and describing the negligent action, which should be in terms of an injury-inclusive description. According to Goldberg and Zipursky, it is a matter of providing a description of the action that mirrors the legal directive.

However, if we closely examine the phenomenology of the example presented in Chapter 7 regarding the discussion of moral luck, it becomes clear that both Fortunate and Fate acted wrongly, specifically driving at a high speed and acting negligently, but only one of them bears liability. Corrective justice theorists will deny that the negligence law is about wrongful conduct. Therefore, according to corrective justice theorists, the issue is not whether Fortunate and Fate drove at high speed and acted wrongly; rather, the wrong *is in the interaction*. It is a relational wrong related to another rational will. Goldberg and Zipursky demonstrate that the legal directive, as a practice, shapes the relation between persons and the content of the wrong, while Honoré and Gardner focus on the outcomes of our actions as the correct descriptions of our negligent actions. When we act, we make wagers; like a golf player, we are lucky if the ball does not hit another person and gets close to the hole, unlucky otherwise. Our agency and identity require us to embrace outcomes. However, these accounts do not offer solutions to the issue of moral luck; rather, they serve as escapes or unsatisfactory suppressions of a genuine problem in practical reason and theory of action.

From Chapters 3 to 6, I demonstrated that we need to deliberate in order to act, and that deliberation comprises narrow and aspirational deliberation. The latter is characterized by descriptions and re-descriptions of what we do, and it entails recognizing or avoiding taking an aspirational-deliberative point of view. As we have said in the context of negligence law, courts' decisions invite us to consider an aspirational-deliberative point of view via a *proleptic* mechanism. We can either recognize or avoid this aspirational perspective.

Furthermore, the recognition or avoidance does not happen as a glitch or at a particular *locus*, but rather as a result of a *diachronic* engagement with values, descriptions, and re-descriptions of values within both the substandard and aspirational perspectives. This engagement, I have also argued, is on the part of both the citizen and the judge. As a result, values emerge from our engagement with them. I have also argued that corrective justice theorists are correct in emphasizing the harm or injury caused, ensuring that the relational aspect is central to any theory of negligence law. However, the notions of right and duty are too abstract to play any role in the citizens' practical reasoning when they act.

It might appear, however, that my account cannot illuminate the problem of moral luck. Upon examining Fate and Fortunate, my account fails to address the phenomenological issue, which is the sense of unfairness or injustice we experience when we solely make Fate responsible and force her to compensate for the wrong she has committed.

In other words, if we say that both Fate and Fortunate committed a wrongful action because they both acted *akratically* and did not sufficiently engage with an aspirational-deliberative perspective, then why is it the case that only in the case of Fate do we impose liability? The reasoning seems flawed. Criminal law states that attempts to commit a crime are punishable. If the civil law equivalent of a sanction is the duty to compensate the defendant, ie 'to put the defendant in the same position as if the wrong has not been committed', then, by analogy to this reasoning and guided by the logic of wrongful conduct, we should surely assert that an award of nominal damages should be made. Let's say Fortunate was on the verge of running someone over. However, in the context of negligence law, the law does not award nominal damages for mere wrongful conduct and does not give the victim empowerment to a civil recourse in negligence unless there is actionable damage. Therefore, negligence and breach of duty are not actionable per se. To be actionable, the damage needs to be more than negligible.

The 'suppressed' argumentative strategy regarding the moral luck problem by theorists in the context of negligence law seems then to be sound. We need to explain and focus on an answer to the question of why the law regards harm as fundamental. My position, by contrast, focuses on the citizen's forward-looking perspective, her engagement with values, the *proleptic* role of negligence law, and the *akratic* underlying structure of the negligent or inadvertent act. My position, as an objector might advance, neither offers a satisfactory answer to the problem of moral luck, nor presents a suppressive strategy that is theoretically intelligible or appealing. Furthermore, an objector might argue that the suppressive strategy is the only sound response to this pugnacious puzzle. It also provides a strong normative foundation, namely Kant's concept of external freedom.

However, I argue that it is true that the law does impose liability only when there is injury or harm and only when the respective negligent or inadvertent action results in harm or suffering to other people or property. Conversely, the *proleptic* role of the law of negligence necessitates the provision of opportunities for learning from the law of negligence and its inherent logic. This allows us to interact with precise descriptions and re-descriptions of values.

Consequently, we can confront and reflect on our failure to transform ourselves because we have avoided inhabiting the deliberative-aspirational perspective. The process of learning, becoming, and making mistakes is possible, and even permissible, in light of the law of negligence, as long as we do not harm or injure others by performing the particular action. If we do so, then we are responsible for our inadvertent or negligent action because we acted *akratically*; specifically, we avoided inhabiting the deliberative-aspirational perspective. Moreover, courts' decisions are grounded on the plaintiff's duty of care and the defendant's right to personal security and safety. As previously explained, the abstraction of the duty-right enters the judges' practical reasoning at this stage. Hence, the *proleptic* function of the law serves as both an invitation to contemplate the description and re-description of values that will be part of the citizen's practical reasoning, as well as the learning process that the citizen must engage in to achieve the deliberative-aspirational perspective.

Some commentators on Aristotle's *Nichomachean Ethics* assert that Aristotle '*sees the law not, primarily, as the set of prescriptions which the state has the right or duty to enforce through sanctions threatened and executed, but rather as providing a positive guidance for moral development in accordance with values of which law is the institutional expression (Cf. NE X9)*'.[16] The law of negligence considers the misdemeanours of citizens as learners, and sees the process of becoming, and gives opportunities for the citizen to engage with '*the upward journey through the specification of the what*'. This engagement offers the opportunity to consider our wrongful actions within a spectrum that goes from immature to mature civic citizenship. The law conveys to both immature and mature agents the same message: 'this is worth', 'this is the way of thinking about it'.

§9.4 The Law and Civic Maturity

One could argue that my account overstates our deliberative and transformational capacities, particularly the potential to inhabit an aspirational-deliberative perspective. This can be expressed in the following manner: my account suggests that taking responsibility for one's actions is a sign of maturity, which includes civic maturity. Civic maturity is the maturity of citizens who live in a specific community or state and robustly and fully engage with their laws as they shape their citizenship and exercise their practical reasoning. According to some authors, my position might be problematic. For example, Williams rejects the view that when we are responsible for our actions, which entails deliberation and sustained control, we are also concerned with the full development of the requirements of deliberation, including self-knowledge and, in my own terminology, inhabiting the deliberative-aspirational perspective. He states: '*if we are addressing the ideas of being held responsible or regarded as a responsible agent, it is not clear why such an ideal should be relevant*'.[17] He continues by asserting that when we are dealing with responsibility for our actions that involve self-control, we are dealing with questions of justice. Thus, questions of justice arise among people living under a '*common system of justice*',[18] when we deal with strangers. Williams tells us: '*these people do not, just from this perspective, have any interest in one another's power of self-understanding, that is, in the ideal of maturity*'.[19]

However, Williams precisely assumes the position that I have attempted to refute, namely, that on one side we have self-control, which necessitates minimum

[16] Sarah Broadie, *Ethics with Aristotle* (OUP 1991) 127.
[17] Bernard Williams, 'Voluntary Acts and Responsible Agents' in *Making Sense of Humanity* (CUP 1995) 22, 29.
[18] ibid 29.
[19] ibid.

agency, and, on the other side, we are able to experience the full development and realization of the mature agent. Williams argues that there is no connection between these two different aspects of our agency. Against this view, I have tried to demonstrate that there is continuity; that when we deliberate at the substandard or immersive level, we are also forced to bring this substandard way of deliberating into other aspects of our actions, in our relations to others, and inevitably are forced to either recognize or avoid inhabiting a deliberative-aspirational perspective.

In the legal context, when we engage with the court decisions and the courts ask us to be responsible, the courts require us to engage with specific values safeguarded by negligence law. The judges' task involves settling the question, 'What shall I do?' in specific circumstances. The citizen is able to grasp and incorporate the judges' response into her own response to the same question and in similar circumstances. By reasoning and engaging with values in the particularities of the legal case, the judge upholds the institution of the law and what they deem right, good, and dutiful. At the same time, they address the condition of their own agency as if they were to act in a forward-thinking manner.

When the judge engages with and thinks about values, they themselves undergo a transformation, and they invite the citizen to change through *proleptic* thinking. To put it another way, judges are both the subject and the object when they make decisions. To reach an answer to the question, 'What is the correct way of approaching this particular case?' and therefore 'What should the citizen have done?', she needs to answer a prior question, 'What should I have done in this particular case?' and she needs self-understanding in terms of values and her own engagement. In this manner, she provides the citizen with an answer that stems from her own engagement with values and experience. If the judge is to impose self-control and answer the question, 'What should the citizen have done in this particular case?', the judge and the citizen need to become mature agents or learners of the good and rightful. In other words, in the context of law, we cannot ignore the question of mature agency and citizenship.

My position assumes that the citizen's action occurs within the paradigm of civic maturity and that the power of self-understanding and 'making sense' of our institutions and actions is fundamental and somehow inescapable. If Williams is correct in suggesting that we should separate self-control from the ideal of civic maturity in the public sphere, limiting the question of justice and responsibility to the politics of self-control, then my perspective on the continuity between self-control and self-understanding (and maturity) is flawed.

What are Williams' arguments to sustain this separation? He rejects Irwin's Aristotelian interpretation of responsibility[20] which argues that reason can reshape our characters, and defends his position in his essay 'Voluntary Acts and

[20] ibid 27.

Responsible Agents'.[21] He argues that Irwin's intellectualist interpretation of Aristotle discards the most important insight of Aristotle, namely, the psychological realism of Aristotle's view on practical reason, focusing on desires and character.[22] Irwin's proposal, according to Williams, clings to the hopeless fantasy of total deliberative control over our dispositions. However, Williams acknowledges the plausibility of a moderate version of this position, where the agent possesses evaluative attitudes that align with his desires and results in effective control.[23] According to Williams, this ideal is the *mature* agent and is an 'aspiration for human growth'.[24] However, Williams questions how *this* ideal can underlie everyday actions, such as taking the bus. How can this 'aspiration for human growth' relate to the assertion 'You are responsible for this action'?[25]

Williams argues that the confusion stems from the belief that freedom, which involves control over our actions and therefore being responsible for them in everyday life, equates to 'responsibility for self', where the agent is responsible for herself and has a specific understanding of herself. The ideal can be defined as 'certain way or condition of life'.[26] According to Williams, the agent having self-control and being responsible for their actions on the one hand and the mature agent on the other *do not coincide*. The former is capable of deliberation and has self-control with minimal agency. However, at no point does Williams explain what he understands by 'deliberation'. He also introduces another idea, namely that when we deal with strangers and live under a common system of justice, responsibility as self-control is what matters. In the sphere of justice, we only care that other people have the power of self-control, not that they have self-understanding and are becoming mature. Of course, Williams tells us, this power of self-control would include people deliberating together on what the law should be.[27] However, there is a tension between Williams' idea of self-control and minimum agency and his view that we deliberate together on what the law should be. One way to reconcile both positions is to say that this deliberation of 'what the law should be' is within the confines of minimal agency, namely, a non-defective person. However, it is unclear

[21] ibid.

[22] ibid.

[23] He attributes this moderate version to Charles Taylor, 'Self-Interptreting Animals' in *Human Agency and Language* (CUP 1985) 45; Charles Taylor, 'What is Human Agency?' in *Human Agency and Language* (CUP 1985)15; and Harry Frankfurt, 'Freedom of the Will and Concept of a Person' (1971) 68 Journal of Philosophy 5. However, it leaves the matter there. It is unclear what he means here, but we can assume that my proposal is a moderate version of Irwin's more ambitious deliberative control. In any case, Williams aims to reject both moderate and ambitious deliberative control.

[24] Williams, 'Voluntary Acts' (n 17) 28.

[25] My interpretation is that Williams returns to a common theme in his view on ethics and responsibility. Aspirations and ideals are abstract and entail a deep engagement with reflection. However, if we engage deeply in reflection, we might lose the character of the ethical action. See Bernard Williams, *Ethics and the Limits of Philosophy* (Fontana Press 1993).

[26] Williams, 'Voluntary Acts' (n 17) 29.

[27] ibid 30.

how we should understand the notion of a non-defective person. According to Williams, even when we engage in communal deliberation, we do not require the engagement of the mature citizen. He states this point as follows:

> Already at this level, the level of persons subject to the law, there is a model of people understanding the requirements of society, and an interest in whether their general set is to conform or not, and this brings into play a certain notion of a responsible agent, one that does *not go far beyond the minimum requirement of an adult, non-defective person.* [my emphasis][28]

Williams strips away any hopes for a 'reconciliation' strategy, where society could reasonably hope that what its citizens '*will be like*' will align with what they ideally '*want to be*'. In this manner, according to Williams, scepticism, freedom, rationality, virtue, citizenship, and individuality will not coincide.[29] Williams argues that we cannot force the aspirations of the ideal into the notion of responsibility.

The problem lies, however, in Williams' association between the mature agent, even in its weakest version, and the idea that we can control our desires and character from top to bottom, from our aspirations to our lower desires. According to Williams, since we cannot control our desires and character, we must live with the truth that *we are not our deliberations.* Unintentional actions, such as desires and character, exist, and the agent must recognize that her responsibility extends beyond voluntary actions. However, this perspective prematurely disregards the relationship between our values-infused thinking, the world we experience, and our shift towards a deliberative-aspirational viewpoint.

My proposal aims to establish a bridge between self-control, minimal agency, and mature agency precisely by providing a more complex picture of how this minimal agency functions, ultimately leading to a more aspirational stance. My proposal also upholds Aristotle's psychological realism by encouraging us to consider the intricate nature of our active mind and our value-based thinking.

A key underlying premise of my position requires explanation and justification. *Contra* Williams, I have attempted to demonstrate that responsibility for oneself is not a choice or 'certain way or condition of life'.[30] My central premise is that citizens and judges must adopt a deliberative perspective and values. This entails the perspective that, as agents, we must 'make sense' of our actions, a process that inevitably involves engaging with values within the particularity of those actions. The process of 'making sense' occurs at both the immersive or substandard level and the aspirational-deliberative level. This premise is grounded in our agency's phenomenology, emphasizing that we lack complete clarity about our ends and what

[28] ibid 31.
[29] ibid 31.
[30] ibid 29.

'living well' means until we actively integrate values in our deliberations and experiences. We understand values in their particulars, and we apply what we know about them to medium- and larger-scale goals, all while keeping an aspirational perspective. Deliberation seems inescapable because we are in the world and need to act, and acting means answering the question, 'What shall I do?'

If Williams is correct, we could determine the rightness or wrongness of actions solely as a matter of self-control, without engaging in immersive and aspirational deliberations, and, thus, without settling on an answer to the question, 'What shall I do?' This picture may closely resemble Kant's concept of external freedom, which urges individuals to exercise their freedom within the boundaries of other's freedom and use their means in a way that is compatible with other individuals' use of their means. However, we are unable to know, *ex ante*, the performance of the action, how this should be done, or what it entails. We cannot 'make sense' of this in particular or concrete terms, from the point of view of our experience and being in the world.

If Williams is right and self-control is what matters (and let us assume this should be cashed out in terms of the idea of Kantian external freedom), then we also need to discard the idea that the law of negligence has any relevance in our forward-looking perspective and that it can guide our conduct. However, of course, Williams would reject any Kantian path to understanding responsibility in terms of minimal agency.[31] We must find an alternative interpretation.

I propose the following interpretative reading of Williams' text. Williams is trying to propose a mature agent who is *personally responsible* for character and desires. This means that the mature agent needs to 'take responsibility' for character and desires, including those beyond deliberative action—the result of deliberative failure, construed in a narrow manner. We have the lives we live, Williams would say, not just because of what we do intentionally or through deliberation. William offers his final move in this argumentative dialectic by denying that this ideal of maturity as *personal responsibility* can ever coincide with the ideal of maturity in the *public sphere*. The institutions of control or coercion, such as law and community, will hold the mature agent responsible for her flawed deliberation and minimal agency. The former kind of responsibility, namely, personal responsibility, will only be present when she is in her private domain and within the confines of her personal life. She can then own all of her deeds, including those that are voluntary and those that result from actions outside of her control.

In this book, however, I attempt to demonstrate that the opposite of this view is a sound way of thinking about responsibility. I have argued that there is no such thing as private deliberation. What is this 'personal' space where I can be responsible for

[31] Williams' criticisms of Kantian practical philosophy are threaded throughout his work, and, in interpretative holistic terms, it would be uncharitable to read him in these passages as defending a version of Kantian external freedom.

my deeds? This is more likely to occur in the realm of friends and family. However, this is precisely the question that the public sphere of private law aims to scrutinize and answer. If our engagement with values, our immersed deliberation, begins at the personal level and, subsequently, we can transition to inhabit an aspirational perspective, it appears that we must rely on our understanding of values at the personal level and how they extend from the personal to the public sphere. There is, in other words, a continuity between immersed and aspirational deliberation, self-control, and mature deliberation, a deep and constant interaction between judges valuing and 'making sense' and citizens 'valuing' and 'making sense', and finally a continuity between the personal and public spheres. Let me explain this point further.

Bernard Williams presents a pugnacious puzzle about civic maturity. If we ask the citizen to 'take responsibility' then this demonstrates precisely that the citizen either has not shown maturity or is not mature. A sign of maturity means taking responsibility based on our own realizations and reflections, not because *someone else has told us to do so*.

If the law advances *proleptic* thoughts and ways of engaging with values so that the citizen is able to inhabit a deliberative-aspirational perspective that reflects civic maturity, then there is a tension between the idea of civic maturity itself and ethical and legal responsibility for negligence or inadvertent actions, as we have delineated. Let us recall that we have argued that legal and ethical responsibility are a matter of engaging with deliberative-aspirational perspectives and that the transformation of oneself is possible due to ways of engaging with the law as courts describe and re-describe values in particular circumstances. This may imply that the necessity of the law stems from the *citizens' lack of maturity*. The coercive nature of the law is different from the advice of a friend. The law *forces* us to engage with particular values.

This presents a challenge to my own account. If my account of narrow and aspirational deliberation is sound, then the *proleptic* aspect of the law is an important way through which the citizen becomes a mature agent. Williams concludes that the outcomes of our actions determine our responsibility, and we cannot reconcile this with the ideal of civic maturity. The latter is a matter of self-knowledge or self-awareness. Psychologically realistic politics is the politics of justice and not the politics of civic maturity since we cannot reconcile our agency as being responsible with the ideal of civic maturity. Williams thinks it is psychologically unrealistic to imagine that we can deliberate, be in control of our actions, and at the same time achieve self-knowledge and become mature citizens. We must settle for a modest understanding of responsibility, requiring citizens to be responsible for the outcomes of their actions, even if they are not intended, because *this responsibility encompasses the harm we inflict upon others.*

The aspirational point of the law, which holds us responsible due to our possession or potential for civic maturity, is an illusion. Arguably, in a possible interpretation, we could say that the coercive nature of the law only forces us to 'try' to exercise self-control so that we do not harm others. According to Williams, to assume the possibility of mature agency within the sphere of justice is to hold on to the psychologically unrealistic presupposition that we can control most of our actions, our characters, and our desires through our deliberations.

By contrast, we *can* reconcile, I argue, the politics of civic maturity and the politics of justice. The engagement of the citizen with the values of the law, presented in negligence law through *proleptic* thoughts, such as value descriptions and re-descriptions, and value-based reasoning by courts, achieves the former. Descriptions and re-descriptions of values based on the judges' reasoning are in the background of the attributions. Nevertheless, I accept Williams' point that we need a psychologically realistic account of ethical and legal responsibility. I have demonstrated how the conception of deliberation can be psychologically realistic. We begin with a basic engagement with values in concrete and particular circumstances. We develop our knowledge of these values through experience. We describe and re-describe our values using practical reasoning's 'internal logic'. However, the phenomenology of our temporal actions and thoughts teaches us that we do not stop here. It is not psychologically realistic to assume that we do not undergo change and become. We transform ourselves and produce more precise and accurate—or perhaps, at times, less precise and accurate—re-descriptions of our values, projects, ends, and commitments. We become and transform ourselves, taking on either an aspirational or a less-than-aspirational perspective on our values. The law belongs to the 'internal logic' of values, which form an integral part of citizens' practical reasoning via our *proleptic* thoughts.

An objector may assert that my view is problematic. Following the steps of Williams' reasoning, my view assumes that we can all become mature citizens, and the position necessitates a transformation of our desires. It disregards the contingencies and intricacies of our social and educational environment. In Chapter 8, I attempted to demonstrate precisely the paradoxical nature of this line of thinking. For instance, in the case of *State v Williams*, the argument posited that the native American parents could not have known that high fever was a sign of a more severe illness and should have sought medical advice. Contrary to this position, I demonstrate that the agent can engage in narrow deliberation, specially focusing on the value of a child's health in particular circumstances; valuing knowledge; learning basic first aid skills; and reflecting from other parents, friends, or educational programmes. Additionally, the agent can take up invitations to inhabit the deliberative-aspirational perspective to avoid inadvertence or negligent action. The law plays a similar role to friends, other parents, and educational programmes in the example. It forces us to contemplate the importance of engaging with values and seek a specific way of thinking about an answer to the question, 'What shall I do?' The position that we aim to defend is not too demanding; the law of negligence does not ask citizens to take sudden and implausible steps beyond what any reasonable layperson can feasibly think and do. It builds upon our daily deliberations and experiences, which are narrow or substandard, and considers how we describe and re-describe the embedded values in our own situation in relation to our own actions. It asserts that this is what we do; we take a stance on matters of value, whether we like it or not.

We either avoid or recognize better, more proximate descriptions and re-descriptions of the values at stake and their role in our actions. Like the example of Murdoch's mother-in-law discussed in Chapter 6, our shared experiences with family and friends invite us to re-describe our evaluations, and this also inevitably forces us to re-describe certain values that will be present in future deliberations, both narrow or substandard and aspirational.

The law of negligence puts forward a *proleptic* thought in the form of descriptions of values. For instance, in the case of *State v Williams*, Mr Williams should engage with specific values in his deliberations. These values include caring for his children when they are ill, as well as being vigilant about fevers.

§9.5 The Challenges of Abstraction, Particularity, Deterrence, and Guidance and the New Way of Thinking about Responsibility in the Law of Negligence

§9.5.1 The Abstract Challenge

In Chapter 7, I argue that Weinrib's and Ripstein's corrective theories face the abstract challenge, which advances the view that the abstract pair right and duty cannot be part of the citizen's practical reasoning because abstract concepts do not enter our practical reasoning when we are engaging in the forward-looking perspective. A similar criticism applies to Keating's formulation of an omnilateral right *ex ante* the wrongful act. Thus, the abstract right of 'not to be harmed' appears as empty and plays no role in the citizen's forward-looking practical reasoning.

The criticism doesn't mean abstraction can't become particularity. The criticism does not aim to show that when the citizen engages in forward-looking thinking, she cannot think in terms of abstract rights and duties and subsequently provide more concrete manifestations of these abstract rights and duties in the context of the particular case. Rather, the proposal is sceptical of the role of abstract concepts in practical reasoning. It establishes that we engage with deliberation in an immersive or substandard manner, attempting to assess the values at stake and the particular content of these values in relation to the circumstances and particularities. However, when the judge or citizen poses the question, 'What shall I do?', she also engages with an aspirational perspective, considering the knowledge and insights she has gained from the immersive deliberation. This necessitates engagement with a description and re-description of the values at stake in a more aspirational manner. The key argument is that only particulars, ie the description and re-description of values, enter into the citizen's practical reasoning from the forward-looking perspective. This view implies that when the agent adopts the forward-looking perspective, abstract rights and duties do not factor as part of the citizen's practical reasoning at all. Of course, this does not deny the importance and role of abstract formulations of rights, duties, principles, and rules. However, the abstract formulation of rights and duties, principles, and rules is possible *after* the respective particulars have been grasped, ie via description and re-description of values. Furthermore, if judges undertake the task of attributing and determining whether a violation of duties has caused suffering and harm, they must engage with the particularity of the victim's suffering and losses to assess the remedy.

I have also attempted to advance a sound conception of practical reasoning in the context of negligence law. It aims to consider the complexities of judges' and citizens' forward-looking and backward-looking perspectives, demonstrating that there is space for thinking about the role of right and duty. However, the abstract pair of right and duty plays a crucial role when judges attribute liability for negligence, reflecting on the plethora of doctrinal categories and concepts to shed light on the facts of the specific case. Nevertheless, the abstract pair of right and duty cannot play any role in the forward-looking perspective, as learning and becoming towards an aspirational perspective can only occur through the engagement with descriptions and re-descriptions of values within the specific particularity. The underlying premise of this view is that values are present in our daily lives in a concrete manner, manifesting in our ordinary way of thinking about matters, and in the phenomenology of our experiences. Values are lived out and experienced. It also follows from this that the task of ethics and normative philosophy in general is to excavate and articulate the relationships and the internal connections of these values and their concepts. Displaying imagination and resources to re-imagine, describe, and re-describe these values is key to achieving accuracy and avoiding idiosyncratic descriptions. Accuracy in descriptions of values aims to minimize or even, at times, dissolve the illusion of private values and private goods, avoiding the temptation of fantasizing about values. Accurate descriptions seem key to articulating our objective values and creating appropriate moral visions or outlooks. Furthermore, judges engage with this task of re-imagining, describing, and re-describing values as experienced and lived by the citizens and by themselves.

The courts' task in negligence law is to invite citizens to consider specific values from an aspirational perspective. It is a *proleptic* role that anticipates thoughts, namely, descriptions and re-descriptions of values, to inform the citizen's practical reasoning. However, the grounding of the courts' decisions relies on rights and duties. Rights and duties also play a role in the backward-looking perspective of judges' decisions. Rights and duties establish the contours and shapes regarding the content of the specific values at stake in legal decisions. If abstraction plays a role in judges' juridical thinking, it is because the judge has already grasped the sound—and perhaps, on occasion, less sound—description and re-description of the values at stake in the particular decision.

My proposal overcomes the abstract challenge and shows how particularity plays a fundamental role in practical reasoning. However, the proposal does not completely eliminate the role of abstract rights and duties. On the contrary, it locates it within the correct perspective, where it plays a pivotal role, namely, the backward-looking perspective.

My proposal also demonstrates that there is a natural development from our daily experiences with values and modern legal liability rules. Negligence law, it has been argued, plays a *proleptic* role in citizens' practical reasoning and the way that aspirational descriptions, re-imagining, and re-descriptions operate. However, at the same time, description and re-description of the values by judges bring to our awareness the *salience* of the victim's injury. The abstract concepts of right and duty, along with the courts' backward-looking reasoning, reveal another aspect regarding the suffering and the injury, which is its grounding in more abstract terms.

It is now clear that the expansive 'internal logic' of negligence law is doing most of the work in terms of citizens' and judges' practical reasoning from both forward-looking and backward-looking perspectives. The courts expand the 'internal logic' of negligence law by advancing new ways of describing and re-describing the values in particular circumstances, as well as by describing the abstract violated duties and rights. Furthermore, to be more precise, the expansion of 'the internal logic' occurs as a result of practical reasoning. Thus, we must exercise practical reasoning from both forward-looking and backward-looking perspectives[32] to grasp the content of the negligence law and its underlying values.

It is now clear why trying to ground the relationality element of the right and duty pair or the engagement with practical reasoning and values of the 'internal logic' of negligence law as something external, namely, Kant's external freedom, a contractualist arrangement, or economic rationality, reflects a misunderstanding of the nature of the 'internal logic' of the law of negligence. From the forward-looking

[32] Stone aims to show as against Posner (Richard Posner, 'The Concept of Corrective Justice in Recent Theories of Tort Law' (1981) 10 Journal of Legal Studies 187) and Weinrib (Ernest Weinrib, *The Idea of Private Law* (OUP 2012)) that there is no gap in the Aristotelian conception of corrective justice and therefore no need to look for an external 'foundation' or normative ground for corrective justice. As stated differently, we cannot fill any gap without considering our particular reasons. The confusion lies, Stone argues, in thinking that corrective justice and its normative foundations are a *test or aim* that the law of negligence or tort law 'gets right'. In other words, there is no need for a procedure external to the dialectic and 'internal logic' of corrective justice itself that normatively grounds corrective justice and its determination. See Martin Stone, 'The Significance of Doing and Suffering' in Gerald Postema (ed), *Philosophy and the Law of Torts* (CUP 2001) 131, 167, 260. Like Stone, some authors argue in favour of the internal structure of the deployment of practical reason in law. See eg Nigel Simmonds, *The Decline of Juridical Reason: Doctrine and Theory in the Legal Order* (Manchester UP 1984); Lon L Fuller, *The Law in Quest of Itself* (originally published in 1940, Beacon Press 2012); Joseph Raz, 'The Inner Logic of the Law' in *Ethics in the Public Domain* (OUP 1995) and Verónica Rodríguez-Blanco, 'Tracing Finnis's Criticism of Hart's Internal Point of View' in Torben Spaak and Patricia Mindus (eds), *Cambridge Companion to Legal Positivism* (CUP 2020) 695.

perspective, we have re-imaginings, descriptions, and re-descriptions of values advanced by the courts. From the backward-looking perspective, judges resort to rights and duties. There is no 'foundational' aspect but a continuity of thinking in terms of our values in daily experiences and the abstract grounding of rights and duties as they are manifested in the specific particulars and circumstances of the legal case and as seen, described, and grasped by the judges.

Judges' descriptions and re-descriptions of values, as well as their descriptions and re-descriptions of the content of rights and duties, do not require any further completion or groundwork. We only need to settle through immersed and aspirational deliberation the sound or approximately correct description and re-description of the values and content of rights and duties at stake in the specific particulars and circumstances. Of course, we can formulate general principles, norms, rules, and directives, but their origin lies in the way judges and citizens engage in their immersed and aspirational deliberations.

The emphasis is on our values as experienced. For instance, when a doctor violates a duty and causes harm and suffering to a patient, we can clearly 'see' that the key values that manifest in these particular circumstances also apply to all future doctors facing similar situations. The idea of more or less suffering has no meaning in abstraction; the person abstracted from her particular roles, jobs, relationships, moral vision, aspirations, projects, and goals cannot suffer. How can we grasp all the aspects of loss through abstract thinking?

Thus, judges intertwine the abstract pair of right and duty with specific descriptions of values, generating a decision and advancing *proleptic* thoughts that can permeate citizens' practical reasoning. Once descriptions and re-descriptions are formulated, values and the content of rights and duties become visible, intelligible, and part of our reasoning. However, the temptation is to think that there is something else grounding the law of negligence.

§9.5.2 The Particularity Challenge

In Chapter 7, we scrutinized a corollary of the abstract challenge, the particularity challenge. It establishes that rules, principles, and norms cannot be part of the citizen's practical reasoning when the citizen adopts the forward-looking perspective. This means that if the model of immersive and aspirational deliberation is sound, then rules, principles, and norms cannot play the prescribed role in deliberation, and *ex ante*, the action is performed.

Justice as formulated by norms, principles, and rules cannot be specified independently of the exercise of practical reasoning in its immersive and aspirational perspective and its forward-looking and backward-looking stances. The internal point of view is not only a 'mirror' of our social practice, but it also reflects an 'internal logic', evolving and displaying itself. It forces itself into expansion because practical reasoning is quintessentially deliberation. Practical reasoning necessitates settling an answer to the question, '*What*?' in terms of '*How*?', and it also involves recognizing or avoiding a deliberative-aspirational perspective. Consequently, the possibility of settling an answer cannot be achieved from an outside or external point of view. Furthermore, the possibility of settling an answer to the question 'What shall I do?' for the judge and the citizen cannot be achieved through abstract general principles, norms, rules, and/or determinate grand ends. If we understand practical reason and its internal logic in terms of rules, norms, principles, and determinate 'grand ends',[33] then we overlook the crucial way in which immersed and aspirational deliberation function. We ignore this at the peril of simplifying practical reasoning and deliberation. We also do violence to, and misunderstand, the way we engage with values in our daily lives and how this influences courts' decisions. Naturally, once we grasp the values in particulars, we can formulate general rules and principles, the content of abstract rights and duties, and determinate ends. However, they will only play a role in the practical reasoning from the backward-looking perspective, when the courts *attribute* responsibility for negligent acts or wrongs. Nevertheless, I contend that the judge had already engaged with and grasped the values prior to this backward-looking reasoning and attribution. Thus, from the forward-looking perspective, the judge has formulated descriptions and re-descriptions of the values in the particular circumstance and, more importantly, the description and re-description of the specific values in their aspirational form. The judge can now resort to principles or rules and abstract rights and duties to ground her backward-looking deliberation.

According to Goldberg and Zipursky,[34] practices ground legal directives and establish the content of the wrongful act, which should not be severed from the injury. Legal practice provides a description of the legal directive's content. However, legal practice is not understood in robust normative terms. If immerse and aspirational deliberation serve as a means of engaging with values in particularities and specific circumstances, it can be challenging to comprehend the role of practices and, moreover, legal directives within this model. Perhaps our practices and the resulting directives exist at different levels. The way we describe and re-describe values reflects our legal practices. However, the judges have the ability to modify this description and re-describe values. Thus, legal practices have a diachronic and dynamic dimension that is under-described and over-simplified by Goldberg's and Zipursky's theory of civil recourse. Furthermore, the problem of principles and rules playing no role in our deliberation from the forward-looking perspective is a challenge to Goldberg's and Zipursky's view, which aims to ground negligence law on legal directives that emanate from practices. Their theory overlooks the complexity of practical reasoning's function.

[33] See §4.3.
[34] Goldberg and Zipursky (n 15).

The character of the wrongness of negligence law is illuminated by the description and re-description of values advanced by courts in their proleptic function, as well as the role of abstract rights and duties in their backward-looking perspective.

We can now confidently state that the failure of the citizen to engage with the legal directive does not accurately characterize negligence. Instead, the problem lies in the citizen's failure to recognize the aspirational perspective that the courts present through *proleptic* thoughts. Consequently, there exists both a legal and an ethical wrong. Both are in continuity because judges describe and re-describe ethical values in a *juridical form.* We present law as advancing our own ends and values, describing and re-describing it in ways that rational beings can comprehend. Of course, there ought to be a struggle on the part of the judge to define the direction of the particular values at stake and to capture them correctly and according to a sound description and re-description.

From the citizen's point of view, the process is *similar* to the phenomenon of counterprivacy. This implies that when we are confronted with a fresh outlook, perspective, or new 'making sense' of a normative reality, this new vision is inescapably 'seen', or even imposed on us. In the domain of virtues, the phenomenon of counterprivacy is particularly evident. Feeling envy or gratitude is only possible after a confrontation with another person. Similarly, the courts' decisions present *proleptic* thoughts, and description of values are presented to the citizen.

From the perspective of the citizen, grasping values is, of course, incomplete and anticipates potential wrongs and suffering. The citizen uses *this valuational presentation to move* herself forward. There is the possibility of either recognizing or avoiding this aspirational stance. If the citizen maintains her existing outlook and avoids a new 'making sense' or re-describing the values in their particularity, she is potentially avoiding an aspirational perspective. In other words, the citizen avoids the new rational thought advanced by the judge.

Let us recall the example of Murdoch's mother-in-law in Chapter 5. The mother-in-law perceives her daughter-in-law as beneath his son's social class; however, she encounters friends from a different social class who challenge her snobbish attitudes. Similarly, judges put forward to the manufacturer, to the employer, to the doctor, to the lawyer, to the teacher, or to the parent ways of looking and 'making sense' of their activities and the values that are involved in the particularities of their activities. These descriptions and re-descriptions become an integral part of the citizen's immersed and aspirational deliberations.

The citizen is required to transform herself through her thinking and 'seeing' through 'grasping' the respective value in the particularity through the judge's description or re-description. We have argued that desiring and thinking go together, and an alignment of both will enable the citizen to inhabit an aspirational perspective and avoid *akrasia*, which is the phenomenon that underlies a negligent act. Our attitudes—desires and emotions—reorient themselves towards the description and re-description of the respective values in their particularities.

Given that humans are inherently dependent on others for self-direction, one could argue that the citizens need the law. The citizen is in the position of the learner, either through avoidance or recognition of the aspirational perspective. For example, the doctor engages with how other doctors perform a medical procedure,[35] as well as scrutinizing the logical foundation of this medical procedure.[36] She comprehends that this is the way to proceed, and through thinking, she refines her desires of adjusting to sound procedures guided by both common practices and logic.

Goldberg and Zipursky also endeavour to establish the view that a description of the wrong action in negligence cannot be severed from the injury. Therefore, the legal directive mirrors this non-severance between doing and suffering. However, we cannot explain and justify the non-severance between the wrong action and the injury solely in terms of legal practices and legal directives that reflect these practices.

We have argued that the *proleptic* function of the law of negligence can explain the distinction between an agent who acts wrongly without injuring anyone and an agent who acts equally wrongly and whose actions result in injuring another person. Only in the latter case is the performer of the negligent act legally liable, and this can be explained because the law of negligence plays a role in our becoming and learning to be good. It directs us towards an aspirational perspective that we need to engage with, as well as giving us opportunities to learn. If no injury or harm results from our learning, when we are trying to be careful, thoughtful, and engage with values in particularities, yet the outcomes are awkward, clumsy, and inexact, then the law does not impose on us any sanction. The law enables us to learn and engage with an aspirational perspective. As a result, my proposal is more consistent with both a sound understanding of philosophy of action and practical reason, and it takes the moral luck problem seriously.

Furthermore, it would be strange to say that our normal way of speaking in respect of our negligent actions is in error or is different from legal or juridical thinking. Thus, our ordinary way to think about the two drivers, Fate and Fortune, is that *both* have committed wrongful actions, but only one was lucky. Arguably, we can say that our ordinary language reflects an error; the truth is that only one driver, the one who caused an injury, acted wrongly, and that our ordinary language is mistaken or in error in not reflecting this. We would say that only Fate has done a wrong.

But this idea is counter-intuitive; we think that it is not only a matter of our moral or ethical language but also a matter of conduct, justice, and responsibility. Both acts can be described in exactly the same manner; both Fate and Fortunate

[35] *Bolam v Friern Hospital Management Committee* [1957] 1 WLR 582; *Montgomery v Lanarkshire Health Board* [2015] UKSC 11.

[36] *Bolito v City & Hackney Health Authority* [1997] 3 WLR 1151.

acted carelessly, but different results ensued. Therefore, the law of negligence will sanction only one of them.

Goldberg and Zipursky could counter-argue that the legal meaning, whose content is determined by legal practice and the legal directive, is different from our ordinary ethical or moral meaning. The directive establishes that only when there is injury or harm must the defendant compensate the plaintiff. But the question that arises is why the legal meaning diverges from the ordinary ethical and moral meaning. Goldberg and Zipursky may answer that it is because this meaning and understanding of action is the result of legal practices. But if practices include the way we deliberate and engage with values, they are under-describing both legal and ethical practice.

§9.5.3 The Deterrence Challenge

Chapter 7 presents the aims-centred theories of negligence that concentrate on the aims and goals of our institutions, and therefore, the authors of these theories see their task as identifying the most efficient way to achieve these aims or goals. The advantage of this position is that these theories effectively explain the deterrence element of the law of negligence. Specifically, they argue that the laws of negligence provide incentives for citizens to comply with the law. However, these theories are only attractive if it is true that the model of practical deliberation and practical reasoning can be reduced to purely theoretical reasoning construed as a calculation of the costs and benefits of certain actions from the point of view of the deliberator. However, this approach lacks moral and psychological realism. The aims-centred theories[37] assume that the agent and her process of rational decision-making involve the bifurcation of beliefs and desires and assume that these are 'given' and clear to the agent. There is no process of 'making sense' of or understanding value-ends or desire-ends. However, when we engage in activities, we do not calculate benefits and costs because this would assume that we have clarity on the content of our beliefs and desires.

This view assumes the truth of the balancing view, which is a corollary of the bifurcation thesis as demonstrated in Chapter 3. It assumes that reasons and desires are clear to us, and that, therefore, our sole task is to balance them and think about the benefits versus the costs. However, when a citizen engages in a specific activity, the judge mandates that she carefully consider the description of the respective value(s) and the other-regarding values that are at stake when she performs her actions. The judge makes salient a normative reality and invites the citizen to inhabit

[37] eg Mitchell Polinsky and Steven Shavell, 'The Theory of Public Enforcement' in Mitchell Polinsky and Steven Shavell (eds), *Handbook of Law and Economics* (Elsevier 2007) 403; Steven Shavell, 'Liability for Accidents' in *Handbook of Law and Economics* 139.

this normative reality. The costs and benefits of the activities are only derivatively grasped as the result of our engagement with the particularities of the values in the respective activities. We cannot present costs and benefits to the citizen *ex ante* before they engage in both immersive and aspirational deliberations.

§9.5.4 The Guidance Challenge

The underlying ideas of the wrongful act in negligence either as a 'glitch' or as entailing implicit false beliefs, unconscious desires, inattention, lack of memory, distractions, or similar mechanisms that would explain the agency of inadvertence are the premise of the bifurcation thesis discussed in Chapter 3. This premise, I argue, mistakenly establishes a stark opposition between our beliefs and desires. Consequently, we portray beliefs and desires as 'given' mental states without elucidating their possible interplay or how our desires and values, both immersive and aspirational, shape and transform us.

If the bifurcation thesis holds true, and the correct explanation for inadvertence in negligent action is in terms of 'glitches' or mechanisms such as unconscious beliefs, implicit false beliefs, unconscious desires, distractions, and inattention, then it becomes obscure and mysterious why the agent should be responsible for her negligent actions. As the sceptical views of negligence discussed in Chapter 2 clearly demonstrate, these mechanisms simply occur to the agent.[38] The sceptic tells us that she is not in control of her actions. All these mechanisms, or 'glitches', can appear at any point of her engagement with deliberation, while exercising her practical reasoning. If this is the correct view, negligence law has no role in guiding our conduct. The sceptical views will have an upper hand, and alternative solutions to the law of negligence to avoid 'accidents', such as a comprehensive system of non-fault legal liability,[39] will acquire a natural and logical appeal.

In contrast to the sceptical position, I have argued that this is not how our agency functions. There is no 'glitch' or mechanism that just happens to us. The inadvertence arises from the lack of recognition of descriptions and re-descriptions of our values from an aspirational perspective. Furthermore, our agency is characterized by a diachronic dimension, a process of transformation, and a becoming that is immersed in values and experiences. However, we have the ability to move towards an aspirational perspective, using the valuational resources we have

[38] eg Alexander, Ferzan, and Morse assert that the agent cannot be culpable for not adverting to dangerous aspects because they have failed to form a belief, lack the intention or motivation, etc. Larry Alexander, Kim Ferzan, and Stephen Morse, *Crime and Culpability* (CUP 2009). This view presupposes the bifurcation model, see discussion in Chapter 3.

[39] See the Report of the New Zealand Royal Commission of Inquiry, *Compensation for Personal Injury in New Zealand* (New Zealand, 1967) (Chair: Mr Justice Owen Woodhouse). See also *The Royal Commission on Civil Liability and Compensation for Personal Injury* (England, 1978) (Pearson Report).

gained by grasping values at the immersive level. Our proposal emphasizes the becoming and transformation of agency, the changes of perspectives, the 'making sense' of things from different stances, and the *proleptic* role of the law in this process of becoming and transformation. The wrongness of negligent agency is due to the citizen avoiding inhabiting an aspirational perspective that is presented by the courts' decisions. I have also argued that underlying negligence is the phenomenon of *akrasia*, in which there is an uneven development of character and thinking about values.

Furthermore, the guidance provided by the law is realistic, feasible, and in accordance with our nature as agents and learners. The judges' decisions present us with particular descriptions of values, but they also base their decisions on descriptions of the specific content of rights and duties. It is the judges' descriptions of values that play the anticipatory—*proleptic*—and aspirational perspective which the citizen is requested to inhabit. The citizens can avoid the descriptions of these values or recognize them. These are invitations for thinking about and 'making sense' of the values in the particular circumstances and in the legal context. The citizen is invited to grasp these descriptions, and failure to do so entails acting inadvertently. But the law provides opportunities for transformation and learning, as previously explained. This way, we undermine the sceptical view.

Contrary to the sceptic, we have demonstrated that there is no 'glitch' or mechanism that simply happens to the citizen, and, as a result, the nature of our agency and rationality can secure negligence law.

Thus, it is a sound explanation of our agency's complexity that enables us to ground negligence law. Judges' law-making means that there is an adjustment to the way we exercise our practical reasoning and deliberate. There is a plight of inescapability in our agency in engaging with values at both immersive and aspirational levels, and our institutions reflect this condition. Practical reason forms an extended temporal dialogue with others. Law is, arguably, an 'institutional other' that shapes practical reason and deliberation. By discarding negligence law, we eliminate one form of dialogue. Of course, there is room for bad or inaccurate descriptions of values or for judges to propose disvalues. My proposal explains the entire spectrum, from paradigmatic to a defective law of negligence.[40]

One additional advantage of the proposal is that there is no distance between the deliberator, the object, and the action. This is a key aspect of immersive deliberation. On the other hand, the deliberative perspective enables us to liberate ourselves from fantasies, wrong descriptions, and illusions of a unique and private sense of the good. A good law invites us to liberate ourselves from this through *proleptic* reasoning. Negligence law as *proleptic* prompts us to consider others, taking

[40] For further reflections on this, see Finnis (n 10) ch 1.

into account how their activities and values are intertwined with our activities and values in particularity.

This invitation as a description of values might be formulated in the abstract as 'reasonable risk' or 'unreasonable risk', or assert that 'foreseeability' is a function of 'risk'. However, this terminology does not imply that the issue is a risk calculation or merely an epistemic problem. On the contrary, if our model of agency and exercise of deliberation is correct, there is no epistemic position that enables us to 'calculate risk' and therefore act correctly.

The term 'reasonable person' seems to better capture the complexity of judges' and citizens' forward-looking and backward-looking deliberations. Not surprisingly, there is an attempt to establish that risk is really a normative and moral concept.[41] The imposition of a risk is a threat to our autonomy, as we do not need to show that there has been a completed wrong, namely, an injury. However, if the proposed model of deliberation as immersed and aspirational is correct, the abstract concept of autonomy cannot guide us.

The agent must inescapably discern her choices based on values, as well as grasp these values through descriptions and re-descriptions of particularities. There could be explanations *post*-performance of the action in terms of risk and violation of autonomy, but they do not do any work at the *ex-ante* stage, or from the forward-looking perspective, when the agent is engaged in both immersive and aspirational deliberations.[42]

§9.6 A Potential Objection: The Deliberative-Aspirational Model and Scepticism About Practical Reason

In this section, I address a potential objection to the Aristotelian-inspired model of the deliberative-aspirational stance, which is a pillar of the book's argumentative structure. An objector may assert that practical reason is portrayed as a 'flow of our practical reasoning', leading to ambiguity and a lack of clarity regarding how we grasp objective goods and become *phronimos*. Furthermore, the objector may

[41] Oberdiek asserts that 'risk' is not an epistemic problem but rather a moral issue. Impervious risk imposition is a breach of the person's autonomy. He distinguishes between the wrong and the negligent act. The wrong is in the risk. Oberdiek denies that the duty is to avoid carelessly causing material harm. See John Oberdiek, *Imposing Risk: A Normative Framework* (OUP 2017) and John Oberdiek, 'The Wrong in Negligence' (2021) 41 Oxford Journal of Legal Studies 1174. However, exposure to risk is not how a citizen sees the matter and engages with the world, as I have attempted to demonstrate in this book.

[42] Some authors, eg Perry, talk about pure and impure risk. Impure risk leads to physical harm. Stephen Perry, 'The Moral Foundations of Tort Law' (1992) 77 Iowa Law Review 449. However, we need to explain both how the agent engages with this kind of risk and how the law of negligence guides the citizen. The concept of risk is too abstract and detached from deliberation to effectively contribute to the agent's deliberation exercise. Arguably, this way of thinking perpetuates the bifurcation model, as beliefs will be sufficient to explain a negligent act.

argue that the book fails to address certain meta-ethical assumptions, resulting in a gap regarding the relationship between practical knowledge and objective moral goods. We can formulate three different versions of this objection, which are the following.

§9.6.1 Mackie-Style Scepticism About Practical Reason

First, we can adopt a sceptical viewpoint, inspired by Mackie's philosophy,[43] which argues that it is absurd to believe in the existence of objective values or moral facts. According to this perspective, there are no moral facts in the universe that can *cause* our actions *qua* normative. To put it simply, according to the deliberative-aspirational model, when I engage in thoughts about whether an end 'Y' is good, and after deliberating, I also engage in acting to pursue 'Y'. However, a Mackie-style objection may state that this is simply the mere 'flowing of my reasoning'. There is no objective or factual existence of anything as 'moral' or 'ethical', as part of the 'furniture of the universe'. To assert that objective moral facts, which dictate both the what and the how of my actions, and an objective aspirational perspective, *cause* the correctness of my thoughts and actions would be 'queer'. Therefore, there is no such thing as an 'aspirational' perspective *qua* objective good. The deliberative-aspirational approach merely represents the 'flowing of my thoughts'. Naturally, the critic may argue that we might acknowledge the notion that we speak as if we are acting in accordance with the good and inhabiting an 'objective' aspirational stance. However, this would only demonstrate that our ethical language is neither true nor false. Our ethical concepts and terms do not refer to anything. The ethical language is in error. Alternatively, the deliberative-aspirational model collapses into a wholly subjective perspective. This latter view is also examined in §9.6.3.

However, this kind of scepticism muddles the fundamental inquiry of practical reason, as if it were a matter of theoretical reason. The objection is fallacious, as it assumes that the sole kind of objectivity is limited to objectivity in theoretical reasoning. Allow me to elucidate.

We can depict this image, which emphasizes the 'naturalness' of our thoughts and the pursuit of the good, as follows: you immediately contemplate an end 'Y'. Therefore, you are ready to recommend it or desire it, leading to making 'Y' occur through your bodily movements and your grasp of the means. This 'ethical' quality resides within you, requiring no transformation of your desires, emotions, and passions. Moreover, every individual has this inherent quality of immediately apprehending the good, the rightful, and the dutiful inside themselves. If this were a genuine possibility at all, the sole requirement for action would be the grasping of

[43] John Mackie, *Ethics: Inventing Right and Wrong* (Penguin 1977).

objective goods, followed by the physical motion of our body. However, this would be *the opposite of practical reason*. Based on this image, there is no need for practical reason's mediation. Unlike theoretical reasoning and any possible reduction of practical reason to theoretical reason, as recently discussed, practical reason's inquiry seeks to establish the character and substance of the standard of the particular action. Only by settling the series of actions connecting the indeterminate end and the means to it, as outlined in the aspirational-deliberative model, can one determine the objective good, which serves as the standard of practical reason in ethical action. The indeterminate end is comprised of components, whose basic elements determine the initiation of the action. Once we start acting, the indeterminate end illuminates the *how* of the action, and vice versa (see Chapter 5). It is a constant 'flowing' of our reasoning that includes *the transformation of our character*. As a result, any objection to robust practical reason must consider the suggested argument's structure while refraining from imposing the structure and methods of theoretical reasoning.

A Mackie-style objection prevents any interpretation of reasoning as involving the interaction of desires, including emotions and passions, and reason, which is precisely what has been proposed. According to the proposed model, practical reasoning is 'seeking' and settling what the good is in relation to the *how* of the action. A Mackie-style argument asserts that it would be 'queer' to postulate an entity in the world that would *cause* the pursuit of our actions to be a practical necessity. However, Mackie's argument assumes that the mind, beliefs, or thoughts can immediately grasp the objective good, thereby leading to action as a practical necessity or imperative requirement, specifically 'what I ought to do' or 'what I ought to pursue'. In contrast to this position, my core argument is that our inherent animal nature compels us to engage with the particularity and contingency of our actions. However, we can also elevate ourselves to an aspirational perspective, transforming our desires, passions, and emotions through their alignment with our thoughts about what is good, dutiful, and rightful. The journey towards a more aspirational perspective is neither a *sudden leap nor an immediate apprehension of an ethical reality*, but rather a constant and diachronic shift of stance or perspective through interactions with others and engagement with evaluative concepts and ethical language.

Our ethical and legal language, along with its respective practices, constitutes a thick web that does not have an external reference beyond its form, logical connections, or internal structure. As a result, the theoretical distinction between subjective and objective viewpoints is equally artificial. This distinction is predominantly intelligible when we are engaging with theoretical reasoning. Let us suppose that we investigate a virus's cellular structure. If our theoretical framework or the scientist's beliefs are the sole factor determining the character of the virus's cellular structure, the statements are subjective. Arguably, the cell's structure is merely a construction of our theoretical framework and, hence, subjective, as we have no empirical evidence supporting the reality of the virus's cellular structure. In contrast, if we assert that the cell's structure genuinely exists in the universe, then the virus's DNA sequence is not only a mere construct but rather a fact, as evidenced by our experiments. Hence, this statement is an objective statement. Practical reason, in contrast to theoretical reason, *does not depict anything in this way*. It aims to establish the series of reasonable actions that would lead us to what is good, dutiful, and rightful.

According to robust practical reason and the deliberative-aspirational model, the objectivity or standard of excellence is ascertained by the abilities of human beings that have learnt to 'see' the good. This model assumes that we possess the *ability to transform ourselves* and act accordingly. However, a critic could contest this view, arguing that evolutionary biology demonstrates that we are merely physical-biological entities, our physical form and cognitive functions subject to scientific laws and principles. Within a scientific paradigm, how we learn to transform ourselves to become good remains mysterious. I will approach this challenge as a second version of scepticism about practical reason.

§9.6.2 Incompatibility Between Science and Practical Reason

A critic may argue that the deliberative-aspirational model that I have defended in this book is incompatible with scientific laws and principles, including recent theoretical discoveries. The objector may contend that we are primarily beings that are governed by scientific laws and principles. Therefore, the concept of 'human being' construed as having the capacity to transform herself through thoughts about what is valuable or good is a helpless fantasy or illusion. Furthermore, evolutionary theory has taught us that our species is in constant adaptation to environmental changes. The cognitive functions and emotional attitudes that we possess are the result of this evolutionary adaptation. Reason, not least 'practical' reason, appears to play no role in mediating between our apprehension of the good and the right, and our continuous transformation. Rather, our adaptative capacities play the key role in our transformation.[44] While ethical language and conduct might be necessary to develop and foster cooperative and more effective actions, they do not inherently imply or allude to anything that is objectively good. Practical reason serves as an explanation of how we tend to cooperate, engaging with ends as believed 'good', to obtain advantages and benefits.

The core of this challenge lies in our conceptions of human nature. Serious engagement with this view would entail a thorough examination of the way our biological mechanisms interact with other aspects of our nature and constitution.

[44] See eg Richard Joyce, *The Evolution of Morality* (MIT Press 2007).

However, I can identify some shortcomings in this type of scepticism, while also acknowledging the need for a more thorough examination of this challenge. This view cannot provide an intelligible explanation of the high forms of meaning in our lives, as well as the high forms of human expression such as the arts, love, friendship, political community, and so on. It is unable to explain the diverse and intricate ways in which human society expresses itself and develops. Indeed, while it may highlight some important truths about our nature as living beings, it lacks the resources to explain all the different levels of our acting, encompassing the physical-biological, psychological, ethical, and spiritual aspects, as well as their intricate interplay. It is unclear why we need to postulate the dominance of the physical-biological. The relationship between the physical-biological and other aspects of our constitution, such as the ethical, intellectual, psychological, and spiritual, is also unclear. We need to be able to recognize ourselves in these explanations if they are considered successful. However, a scientific explanation of phenomena such as the beauty of a piece of artwork or the overwhelming experience of parental love will be deficient and limited in scope. It is not properly 'human'. It diminishes the depth and intricacy of our ethical, intellectual, psychological, and spiritual experiences.

The objector may argue that any advances regarding the interaction of the different aspects of our constitution would be due to our scientific progress. Hence, a more sophisticated account of who we are awaits us as we make progress in scientific discoveries, exploration, and innovation. However, I have endeavoured to argue in favour of the existence of an irreducible level of our constitution, encompassing ethical, intellectual, and psychological aspects, which manifest our ability to learn and undergo personal transformations through our thoughts about what is valuable or good. The ethical, intellectual, and psychological dimensions of our actions and constitution cannot be learnt or explained by scientific discoveries. This is because we are creatures who reason and think about what is valuable. We create states of affairs in the world by settling our own thoughts about what is good, rightful, beautiful, and duty-bound. As a result, to explain this fundamental nature of our existence and be acknowledged as pertaining to what is 'human', theorists must engage with a method that departs from a scientific approach or methodology.

§9.6.3 Moral Knowledge, Meta-Ethical Debates, and Practical Reason

Another version of the potential objection regarding scepticism about robust practical reason stems from the idea that moral facts do not exist. In the absence of moral facts, acquiring moral knowledge becomes impossible. As a result, practical reasoning does not yield practical knowledge. The position holds that practical reasoning does not lead to moral truths, just as grasping moral facts does not.

Practical reasoning is not knowledge at all. As a corollary, the sole form of knowledge is theoretical knowledge, which allows us to grasp facts about our world and the universe.

Over the last four decades, there has been an extensive literature on moral realism, including a rich and sophisticated debate on meta-ethics involving proponents of moral realism and moral anti-realism. Moral realism asserts that there are moral facts that can be either natural or non-natural. Moral anti-realists deny that there are moral facts.

However, it is a mistake to think that practical reason aims to grasp moral facts as part of the natural world or as non-natural facts. In a similar vein, it is not accurate to claim that practical reason is solely the result of our intentions, will, or creation of reasons, leading to the satisfaction of desires or ends.

Meta-ethical debates, as formulated in the literature, distort what the practical reason is. The dialectic of these debates aims to give credibility to practical knowledge and hence to advance an emaciated version of practical reason that focuses on the formation of intentions as mental states, reasons for actions, or will that 'grasp' normative reasons or moral facts. Conversely, anti-realists, specifically Humean or neo-Humean anti-realists, maintain that reason serves to establish logical connections—theoretical reasoning—to the satisfaction of desires. Both are simplified and weak versions of practical reasoning. According to the Humean perspective, desires are neutral; they are devoid of rationality or irrationality. They are unresponsive to reasons. Desires and passions are neither true nor false. They do not represent anything. Consequently, moral anti-realists assert that there is no knowledge of 'moral facts'. Therefore, our ethical language is an expression of our desires, emotions, and passions—attitudes—or a shadow of our internal attitudes and emotions, and might involve the formation of our mental states, such as intention, that have no reference to any reality.

However, the dialectic between moral realists and moral anti-realists is an obstacle to the full understanding of robust practical reason. In Chapter 4, I have attempted to argue that the Humean view has dominated our conceptions of beliefs and desires within action theory, providing the core premise in our philosophizing about practical reason. The bifurcation thesis is the underlying premise. The thesis asserts the separation and non-interaction of desires and reasons. Consequently, this view holds that beliefs and our thinking about values do not shape our character, including our desires and passions. The debate between moral realists and moral anti-realists shifts this discussion to a more abstract level, while continuing to ignore the question pertaining to the interaction between desires and beliefs. The meta-ethical debate replicates the bifurcation between desires and beliefs at a more abstract level. At the meta-ethical level, the bifurcation is between, on the one hand, the idea that we can 'grasp' moral facts as either part of the natural universe or as non-natural facts, and, on the other hand, the idea that our ethical language refers to a mere subjective expression or representation with no reference to what is good, dutiful, or rightful.

My defence of robust practical knowledge has focused on the idea that practical knowledge involves the development and maturation of certain capacities and virtues in human beings. Simply put, the agent's changes enable her to understand the object in the *right light*. There is a grasp of objective goods, but this objectivity is only appreciated as the result of a specific effort in deliberation, involving comprehension by exercising excellence in practical reason. Excellence in practical reason involves a complete shift of the self. It includes our animality, namely our passions and emotions, as well as our reasoning. All human beings have the genuine possibility to embody excellence and mature. The deliberative-aspirational model demonstrates how we engage our animality with values through piecemeal reasoning, focusing on the particular character of the action, but we are also able to progress towards a broader and aspirational perspective.

However, a critic may state that this is circular. Arguably, we now have a 'test' to recognize or identify excellence in practical reason. The agent, through appropriate development and maturation, is able to determine the objective good of particular actions. Simultaneously, the objective good is defined as something that is grasped by the mature agent, who has undergone personal transformation. However, I argue that this is an innocuous circularity. The idea that we need a foundation outside the agent's development of capacities towards maturity and transformation presupposes that there is a 'test' or a 'process' that provides the ultimate justification for our actions. I will now turn to analysing this different version of scepticism about practical reason.

§9.6.4 The Need of a Process to Justify the End as Objective Good and Scepticism About Practical Reason

In science, we have methods or procedures that ensure the objectivity of the results of the scientific inquiry. In parallel fashion, an objector may demand a similar procedure to determine and justify whether an action is good, right, or dutiful. It is the idea that there ought to be 'an authoritative argument' that compels all of us to act and deliberate in a certain manner. The authoritative argument would deliver the required justification. It might be that deliberation is presented as a procedure—by analogy to a scientific method—that guarantees justified decisions and actions. This conception assumes that *we are able* to formulate a procedure to construct justified and right actions and decisions. I am thinking about some interpretations of Kant's categorical imperative and utilitarianism.

However, this view assumes that we need 'a procedure' to recognize what is good, dutiful, or right. I have tried to demonstrate precisely the opposite. Transforming ourselves by engaging with what is good, rightful, and dutiful entails the learning of new capacities and ways of 'seeing' values through our interactions with others, including the involvement of practical deliberation. Excellence in practical reason is precisely achieved because we possess the capacity to shift perspectives and acquire new ways of appreciating and learning what is good, right, and dutiful. It is erroneous to believe that there is a specific time, while we are learning and maturing, at which we grasp what is objectively good in a particular end or action. It is inaccurate to believe that there exists a 'procedure' or 'method' that guarantees the goodness, righteousness, or dutifulness of the action and its outcome. Learning, maturing, and transforming our entire selves happen in a diachronic manner through our lives, experiences, and interactions. The incessant movement of reason reveals a substantive aspect of reality—values embodied in the particular—through its descriptions and re-descriptions.

I conclude this book with a brief note regarding the importance of reassessing and reconsidering the comparison between scientific methodologies, theoretical and philosophical reasoning. My responses to the significant challenges of scepticism about practical reason aim to address the issue of method in philosophizing. I urge caution over the widespread extrapolation of scientific methods and theoretical reasoning in all spheres of our human experience and existence. Engaging with philosophy and humanistic ways of thinking is essential for the betterment of humanity. The underlying view that I advocate is that philosophical inquiry, including developing and refining the descriptions and re-descriptions of what is good, rightful, and dutiful, leads to a shift in our ethical and legal outlook, as well as being crucial for developing institutions and practices, including law and legal practice, that are just, right, and good.

Bibliography

Alexander L, Ferzan KK, and Morse S, *Crime and Culpability* (CUP 2009)
Allan D, *The Philosophy of Aristotle* (OUP 1952)
Allan DJ, 'The Practical Syllogism', in Auguste Mansion (ed), *Autour d'Aristote* (Publications Universitaires de Louvain 1955) 325
Altham J, 'The Legacy of Emotivism' in *Fact, Science and Morality: Essays on A.J. Ayer's Language, Truth and Logic* (Blackwell 1986) 275
Annas J, *Intelligent Virtue* (OUP 2011)
Anscombe E, *Intention* (Basil Blackwell 1957, reprinted by Harvard UP 2000)
——'Modern Moral Philosophy' (1958) 33 Philosophy 1
——'On Brute Facts' (1958) 18 Analysis 69
Aquinas T, *Summa Theologica* (tr Thomas Gilby, CUP 2006)
Aristotle, *Eudemian Ethics* (tr H Rackham, Harvard UP, Loeb Classical Library 1989)
——*Nichomachean Ethics* (trs Sarah Broadie and Christopher Rowe, OUP 2002)
Armstrong D, *A Materialist Theory of Mind* (Routledge 1968)
Arpaly N, *Unprincipled Virtue* (OUP 2003)
Austin J, 'A Plea for Excuses' in John L Austin, Geoffrey J Warnock, and James O Urmson (eds), *Philosophical Papers* (OUP 1979) 175
Bagnoli C, 'Respect and Loving Attention' (2003) 33 Canadian Journal of Philosophy 483
Betzler M, 'Personal Projects and Reasons for Partiality' (2014) 40 Social Theory and Practice 683
Blackburn S, *Essays in Quasi-Realism* (OUP 1993)
Bobonich C, 'Plato and Akrasia and Knowing Our Own Mind' in Christopher Bobonich and Pierre Destrée (eds), *Akrasia in Greek Philosophy: From Socrates to Plotinus* (Brill 2007) 41
Bradley D, 'Thomas Aquinas on Weakness of the Will' in Tobias Hoffman (ed), *Weakness of Will from Plato to Present* (The Catholic University of America Press 2008) 82
Bratman M, *Intention, Plans and Practical Reason* (CUP 1987)
——*Faces of Intention* (CUP 1999)
Brickhouse T, 'Aristotle on Corrective Justice' (2014) 18 Journal of Ethics 187
—— and Smith N, 'Socrates on Akrasia' in Christopher Bobonich and Pierre Destrée (eds), *Akrasia in Greek Philosophy: From Socrates to Plotinus* (Brill 2007) 1
Broadie S, *Ethics with Aristotle* (OUP 1991)
Burnyeat M, 'Aristotle on Learning to be Good' in Amélie Rorty (ed), *Essays on Aristotle's Ethics* (University of California Press 1980) 69
Calabresi G, *The Cost of Accidents* (Yale UP 1970)
Callard A, 'Ignorance and Akrasia-Denial in the Protagoras' in Brad Inwood (ed), *Oxford Studies in Ancient Philosophy* (OUP 2014) 31
——'The Enkrates Phronimos' (2017) 99 Archiv für Geschichte der Philosophie 31
——'Aristotle on Deliberation' in Ruth Chang and Kurt Sullivan (eds), *Routledge Handbook of Practical Reason* (Routledge 2021) 126
Cavell S, *The Claim of Reason: Wittgenstein, Scepticism, Morality and Tragedy* (OUP 1979)
Chang R, 'Grounding Practical Normativity: Going Hybrid' (2013) 164 Philosophical Studies 163
Charles D, *Aristotle's Philosophy of Action* (Cornell UP 1984)
Clarke R, *Omissions: Agency, Metaphysics and Responsibility* (OUP 2014)
Coleman JL, 'Property, Wrongfulness and the Duty to Compensate' (1987) 63 Chicago-Kent LR 451
——*Risks and Wrongs* (CUP 1993)
——'The Practice of Corrective Justice' in David Owen (ed), *Philosophical Foundations of Tort Law* (OUP 1995)

——*The Practice of Principle* (OUP 2003)
Cooper J, *Reason and the Human Good in Aristotle* (Hackett 1975)
Curzer HJ, 'Aristotle's Practical Syllogisms' (2015) 46 The Philosophical Forum 129
Dahl N, *Practical Reason, Aristotle, and Weakness of the Will* (University of Minnesota Press 1984)
Dancy J, *Practical Reality* (OUP 2000)
——*Practical Shape: A Theory of Practical Reasoning* (OUP 2018)
Darwall S, *The Second-Person Standpoint* (Harvard UP 2009)
Davidson D, 'Actions, Reasons and Causes' (1963) 60 The Journal of Philosophy 685
——'How is Weakness of the Will Possible?' in *Essays on Actions and Events* (Clarendon Press 2001, first published in 1969) 21
Donnelly-Lazarov B, *A Philosophy of Criminal Attempts* (CUP 2015)
Dorion L-A, 'Plato and Enkrateia' in Christopher Bobonich and Pierre Destrée (eds), *Akrasia in Greek Philosophy: From Socrates to Plotinus* (Brill 2007) 119
Dorsey D, 'Hume's Internalism Reconsidered' (2007) 2 Journal of Ethics and Social Philosophy 1
Duff A, *Intention, Agency and Criminal Liability* (Blackwell 1990)
——'Choice, Character and Criminal Liability' (1993) 12 Law and Philosophy 345
——*Answering for Crime: Responsibility and Liability in the Criminal Law* (Hart 2007)
Enç B, 'Hume's Unreasonable Desires' (1996) 13 History and Philosophical Quarterly 239
Engberg-Pedersen T, *Aristotle's Theory of Moral Insight* (Clarendon Press 1983)
Enoch D and Marmor A, 'The Case Against Moral Luck' (2007) 26 Law and Philosophy 405
Ferzan K, 'Opaque Recklessness' (2001) 91 The Journal of Criminal Law and Criminology 597
Finnis J, *Natural Law and Natural Rights* (Clarendon Press 1980)
——'"The Thing I Am": Personal Identity in Aquinas and Shakespeare' (2005) 22 Social Philosophy and Policy 250
——'Practical Reasons's Foundations' in *Reason in Action. Collected Essays:* vol I (OUP 2011) 19
Fisher JM and Tognazzini N, 'The Truth About Tracing' (2009) 43 Nous 531
Fitzpatrick W, 'Moral Responsibility and Normative Ignorance: Answering a New Skeptical Challenge' (2008) 118 Ethics 589
——'Unwitting Wrongdoing, Reasonable Expectations, and Blameworthiness' in Phillip Robichaud and Jan Willem Wieland (eds), *Responsibility: The Epistemic Condition* (OUP 2017) 29
——'Varieties of Negligence and Complications for Moral Blameworthiness' in Verónica Rodríguez-Blanco and George Pavlakos (eds), *Agency, Negligence and Responsibility* (CUP 2021) 75
Flannery K, *Action and Character According to Aristotle* (The Catholic University of America 2013)
Fletcher GP, 'Fairness and Utility in Tort Law' (1972) 85 Harvard Law Review 537
Flikschuh K, 'The Morality of External Freedom' in *Kant and Modern Political Philosophy* (CUP 2000) 80
Frankfurt H, 'Freedom of the Will and Concept of a Person' (1971) 68 Journal of Philosophy 5
Fried C, *An Anatomy of Values: Problems of Personal and Social Choice* (Harvard UP 1970)
Fuller LL, *The Law in Quest of Itself* (Beacon Press 2012, originally published in 1940)
Gadamer H, *The Idea of the Good in Platonic-Aristotelian Philosophy* (Yale UP 1986)
Gardner J, 'Obligations and Outcomes in the Law of Torts' in Peter Cane and John Gardner (eds), *Relating to Responsibility: Essays in Honour of Tony Honoré on his 80th Birthday* (Hart/Bloomsbury 2001)
——'The Mark of Responsibility' (2003) 23 Oxford Journal of Legal Studies 157
——'What is Tort Law For?' (2011) 30 Law and Philosophy 1
——*From Personal Life to Private Law* (OUP 2018)
Goldberg J and Zipursky B, 'Replies to Commentators' (2021) 41 Law and Philosophy 127
——'Seeing Tort Law From the Internal Point of View: Holmes and Hart on Legal Duties' (2006) 75 Fordham Law Review 1563
——*Recognizing Wrongs* (Harvard UP 2020)
Gould C, 'A Puzzle About the Possibility of Aristotelian Enkrateia' (1994) 39 Phronesis 174

Guyer P, 'Kant's Deductions of the Principles of Right' in *Kant's Metaphysics of Morals: Interpretative Essays* (Clarendon Press 2022) 23
Hampshire S, *Freedom of the Individual* (Princeton UP 1975)
Hampton J, 'Does Hume Have an Instrumental Conception of Practical Reason' (1995) 21 Hume Studies 57
Hardie WFR, 'Aristotle on Moral Weakness' in Mortimore, G (ed), *Weakness of Will* (MacMillan 1971) 69
——*Aristotle's Ethical Theory* (Clarendon Press 2004, originally printed in 1968)
Hare R, *The Language of Morals* (Clarendon Press 1952)
—— 'Weakness of Will' in Lawrence Becker and Charlotte Becker (eds), *The Encyclopedia of Ethics* (Routledge 2001) 1789
Harman E, 'Does Moral Ignorance Exculpate?' (2011) 24 Ratio 443
Hart HLA, *Punishment and Responsibility* (OUP 2008, originally published in 1968)
Herschovitz S, 'Harry Potter and the Trouble with Tort Theory' (2010) 63 Stanford Law Review 67
—— 'Tort as a Substitute for Revenge' in John Oberdiek (ed), *Philosophical Foundations of the Law of Torts* (OUP 2014) 86
Herstein O, 'Responsibility in Negligence: Why the Duty of Care is Not a Duty To Try' (2010) 23 Canadian Journal of Law and Jurisprudence 403
—— 'Responsibility in Negligence: Discussion of From Normativity to Responsibility' (2013) 8 Jerusalem Review of Legal Studies 167
—— 'Nobody's Perfect: Moral Responsibility in Negligence' (2019) 32 Canadian Journal of Law and Jurisprudence 109
—— 'Reasons to Try' in Haris Psarras and Sandy Steel (eds), *Private Law and Practical Reason: Essays on John Gardner's Private Law Theory* (OUP 2023)
Heuer U, 'Luck and Responsibility according to Bernard Williams' in András Szigeti and Matthew Talbert (eds), *Morality and Agency: Themes from Bernard Williams* (OUP 2022)
Hill T, 'Weakness of Will and Character' (1986) 14 Philosophical Topics 93
Hills A, 'The Principle of Right: Practical Reason and Justification in Kant's Ethical and Political Philosophy' (2007) 3 Politics and Ethics Review 24
Holton R, *Willing, Wanting and Waiting* (OUP 2009)
Honoré T, *Responsibility and Fault* (Hart 1999)
Hooker B and Little MO, *Moral Particularism* (OUP 2000)
Hume D, *Treatise of Human Nature* (Penguin Classics 1985, first published in 1739)
Hurd, H and Moore M, 'Punishing the Awkward, the Stupid, the Weak and the Selfish: The Culpability of Negligence' (2011) 5 Criminal Law and Philosophy 147
Husak D, 'Negligence, Belief, Blame and Criminal Liability: The Special Case of Forgetting' (2011) 5 Criminal Law and Philosophy 199
——*Ignorance of Law* (OUP 2016)
Hyman J, *Action, Knowledge and Will* (OUP 2015)
Irwin T, 'Reason and Responsibility in Aristotle' in Amélie Rorty (ed), *Essays in Aristotle's Ethics* (University of California Press 1980) 117
——'Some Rational Aspects of Incontinence' (1988) 27 The Southern Journal of Philosophy 49
——'Ethics with Aristotle by Sarah Broadie' (1993) 90 The Journal of Philosophy 329
——'Aristotle Reads the Protagoras' in Tobias Hoffman (ed), *Weakness of Will from Plato to the Present* (The Catholic University of America Press 2008) 22
Jeffrey R, *The Logic of Decision* (Chicago UP 1965)
Jimenez M, *Aristotle on Shame and Learning to be Good* (OUP 2020)
Joachim H, *Aristotle, The Nichomachean Ethics. A Commentary* (Clarendon Press 1951)
Joyce R, *The Evolution of Morality* (MIT Press 2007)
Kant I, *Metaphysics of Morals* (tr Mary Gregor, CUP 2017, originally published in 1797)
Keating G, 'Reasonableness and Rationality in Negligence Tort Theory' (1996) 48 Stanford Law Review 311
——'The Priority of Respect Over Repair' (2012) 18 Legal Theory 293

——and Esper D, 'Putting Duty in Its Place: A Reply to Professor Goldberg and Zipursky' (2008) 41 Loyola-Los Angeles Review 1225
Kenny A, 'The Practical Syllogism and Incontinence' (1966) 11 Phronesis 163
——'The Ends of Life' in *Aristotle on the Perfect Life* (OUP 1992) 199
Kent B, 'Transitory Vice: Thomas Aquinas on Incontinence' (1989) 27 Journal of the History of Philosophy 199
King M, 'The Problem of Negligence' (2009) 35 Social Theory and Practice 577
Korsgaard C, 'Scepticism about Practical Reason' (1986) 83 The Journal of Philosophy 5
Kosman A, *Virtues of Thought* (Harvard UP 2014)
Kraut R, 'In Defense of the Grand End View' (1993) 103 Ethics 361
Lawrence G, 'Acquiring Character: Becoming Grown Up' in *Moral Psychology and Human Action in Aristotle* (OUP 2011) 233
Levy N, 'Culpable Ignorance and Moral Responsibility: A Reply to Fitzpatrick' (2009) 119 Ethics 729
——'Methodological Conservatism and the Epistemic Condition' in Phillip Robichaud and Jan Willem Wieland (eds), *Responsibility: The Epistemic Condition* (OUP 2017) 252
Lewis D, 'Desire as Belief' (1988) 97 Mind 323
Lillehammer H, 'The Doctrine of Internal Reason' (2000) 34 The Journal of Value Inquiry 507
Lord E, *The Importance of Being Rational* (OUP 2018)
MacIntyre A, 'Rival Aristotles: Aristotle against Some Modern Aristotelians' in *Ethics and Politics: Selected Essays* (CUP 2006) 22
——'Conflicts of Desire' in Tobias Hoffman (ed), *Weakness of Will From Plato to the Present* (The Catholic University of America Press 2008) 276
Mackie J, *Ethics: Inventing Right and Wrong* (Penguin 1977)
McDowell J, 'Are Moral Requirements Hypothetical Imperatives?' (1978) 52 Proceedings of the Aristotelian Society, Supplementary Volume 13
——'Virtue and Reason' (1979) 62 The Monist 331
——'Comments on Irwin's "Some Rational Aspects of Incontinence"' (1989) 27 The Southern Journal of Philosophy 49
——'Deliberation and Moral Development in Aristotle's Ethics' in Stephen Engstrom and Jennifer Whiting (eds), *Aristotle, Kant and the Stoics: Rethinking Happiness and Duty* (CUP 1996)
——'Some Issues in Aristotle's Moral Psychology' in *Mind, Value and Reality* (Harvard UP 1998) 23
Milgram E, 'Practical Reasoning: the Current State of Play' in Elijah Milgram (ed), *Varieties of Practical Reasoning* (MIT Press 2001) 1
Miller P and Pojanowski J, 'The Internal Point of View in Private Law' (2022) 67 American Journal of Jurisprudence 247
Moore C, *Socrates and Self-Knowledge* (OUP 2015)
Moore G, 'Moore's Paradox' in Tom Baldwin (ed), *G.E. Moore: Selected Writings* (Routledge 1993) 207
——*Principia Ethica* (CUP 1993)
Moran R, *Authority and Estrangement: An Essay on Self-Knowledge* (Princeton UP 2001)
——'Iris Murdoch and Existentialism' in *The Philosophical Imagination: Selected Essays* (OUP 2017) 169
Moss J, *Aristotle on the Apparent Good* (OUP 2012)
Mulhall S, *Inheritance and Originality* (OUP 2001)
Murdoch I, 'The Darkness of Practical Reason' in *Existentialists and Mystics* (Penguin 1950) 193
——'Nostalgia for the Particular' in *Existentialists and Mystics* (Penguin 1950) 43
——'Metaphysics and Ethics' in *Existentialists and Mystics* (Penguin 1950) 59
——'The Sublime and the Good' in *Existentialists and Mystics* (Penguin 1950) 205
——'The Idea of Perfection' in *Existentialists and Mystics* (Penguin 1950) 299
——'Thinking and Language' in *Existentialists and Mystics* (Penguin 1950) 33
——'Vision and Choice in Morality' in Existentialists and Mystics (Penguin 1950) 76.

Metaphysics as a Guide to Morals (Penguin 1993)
Nagel T, *The Possibility of Altruism* (Princeton UP 1970)
——'Moral Luck' 50 Proceedings of the Aristotelian Society (1976) 137
——*The View From Nowhere* (OUP 1986)
Newhouse M, 'The Legislative Authority' (2019) 24 Kantian Review 531
Nielsen K, 'Deliberation as Inquiry: Aristotle's Alternative to the Presumption of Open Alternatives' (2011) 120 The Philosophical Review 383
Nussbaum M, 'Virtue Ethics: A Misleading Category?' (1999) 3 The Journal of Ethics 163
——'The Protagoras: A Science of Practical Reasoning' in Elijah Milgram (ed), *The Varieties of Practical Reasoning* (MIT Press 2001) 153
Oberdiek J, 'Structure and Justification in Contractualist Tort Theory' in John Oberdiek (ed), *Philosophical Foundations of the Law of Torts* (OUP 2014) 103
——*Imposing Risk: A Normative Framework* (OUP 2017)
——'The Wrong in Negligence' (2021) 41 Oxford Journal of Legal Studies 1174
Olfert C, *Aristotle on Practical Truth* (OUP 2017)
Parfit D, 'Reasons and Motivations' (1997) 71 Proceedings of the Aristotelian Society 94
Patterson D, 'The Metaphysics of Formalism' (1992) 77 Iowa Law Review 741
Pauer-Studer H, '"A Community of Rational Beings". Kant's Realm of Ends and the Distinction Between Internal and External Freedom' (2016) 107 Kant Studien 125
Pavlakos G, 'Agent-Relativity without Control: Grounding Negligence on Normative Relations' in Verónica Rodríguez-Blanco and George Pavlakos (eds), *Agency, Negligence and Responsibility* (CUP 2021) 118
Peels R and Blaauw M, *The Epistemic Dimensions of Ignorance* (CUP 2017)
Perry S, 'The Moral Foundations of Tort Law' (1992) 77 Iowa Law Review 449
Pickavé M and Whiting J, 'Nichomachean Ethics 7.3 on Akratic Ignorance' in David Sedley (ed), *Oxford Studies in Ancient Philosophy* (OUP 2008) 323
Plato, *Charmides* (Harvard UP 1927, Loeb Classical Library)
——*Protagoras* (tr Christopher C Taylor, Clarendon Press 1976)
Polinsky AM and Shavell S, 'The Theory of Public Enforcement' in *Handbook of Law and Economics* (Elsevier 2007) 403
Posner R, 'A Theory of Negligence' (1972) 1 The Journal of Legal Studies 29
——'The Concept of Corrective Justice in Recent Theories of Tort Law' (1981) 10 Journal of Legal Studies 187
——'The Path Away from the Law' (1997) 110 Harvard Law Review 1039
Price A, 'The Practical Syllogism: A New Interpretation' (2008) 11 History of Philosophy and Logical Analysis 151
Psarras H, 'Corrective Justice, the Continuity Thesis, and the Duty of Care in Negligence: Lessons from John Gardner's From Personal Life to Private Law' (2019) 19 Jerusalem Review of Legal Studies 34
Rabinowicz W and Ronnow-Rasmussen T, 'The Strike of the Demon: On Fitting Pro-Attitudes and Values' (2004) 114 Ethics 391
Rawls J, *A Theory of Justice* (Harvard UP 1999, originally published in 1971)
Raz J, 'The Inner Logic of the Law' in *Ethics in the Public Domain* (OUP 1995)
——'Being in the World' (2010) 23 Ratio 422
——'Responsibility and the Negligence Standard' (2010) 30 Oxford Journal of Legal Studies 1
——*From Normativity to Responsibility* (OUP 2011)
Reeve C, *Action, Contemplation and Happiness* (Harvard UP 2012)
Ripstein A, *Equality, Responsibility and the Law* (CUP 2012)
——*Private Wrongs* (Harvard UP 2016)
Robichaud P and Wieland JW, *Responsibility: The Epistemic Condition* (OUP 2017)
Robinson R, 'L'Acrasie, selon Aristote' (1955) 145 Revue Philosophique de la France et de l'Etranger 261
Rodríguez-Blanco V, *Law and Authority Under the Guise of the Good* (Hart/Bloomsbury 2014)

—— 'Dworkin's Dignity Under the Lens of the Magician of Königsberg' in Salman Khurshid, Lokendra Malik, and Verónica Rodríguez-Blanco (eds), *Dignity in Dworkin's Legal and Moral Philosophy* (OUP 2018)
—— 'Tracing Finnis's Criticism of Hart's Internal Point of View' in Torben Spaak and Patricia Mindus (eds), *Cambridge Companion to Legal Positivism* (CUP 2020) 695
—— 'The Law of Negligence, Blameworthy Action and the Relationality Thesis: A Dilemma for Goldberg and Zipursky's Civil Recourse of Tort Law' (2021) 41 Law and Philosophy 63
—— and Zambrano P, 'The Myth of the Classical Natural Law Theory: Reflecting on the "Thin" View of Legal Positivism' (2018) 31 Ratio Juris 9
Rorty A, 'Akrasia and Pleasure: Nichomachean Ethics Book 7' in Amélie Rorty (ed), *Essays on Aristotle's Ethics* (University of California Press 1980) 267
Rosen G, 'Scepticism About Moral Responsibility' (2004) 18 Philosophical Perspectives 295
—— 'The Problem of Pure Negligence' in Verónica Rodríguez-Blanco and George Pavlakos (eds), *Agency, Negligence and Responsibility* (CUP 2022) 15
Ross W, *Aristotle* (Routledge 1949)
Saarinen R, 'Walter Burley on Akrasia: Second Thoughts' (1999) 37 Vivarium 60
Sandis C, 'What Is It To Do Nothing?' in Verónica Rodríguez-Blanco and George Pavlakos (eds), *Agency, Negligence and Responsibility* (CUP 2022) 187
Sarch A, *Criminally Ignorant* (OUP 2019)
Sauvé Meyer S, 'Living for the Sake of an Ultimate End' in Jon Miller (ed), *Aristotle's Nichomachean Ethics: A Critical Guide* (CUP 2011) 47
Scanlon T, *What We Owe to Each Other* (Harvard UP 1998)
—— *Moral Dimensions: Permissibility, Meaning, Blame* (Harvard UP 2008)
Schroeder M, 'The Importance of Being in a Position to Know' (2020) 100 Philosophy and Phenomenological Research 457
Scott D, *Levels of Argument* (OUP 2015)
Segvic H, *From Protagoras to Aristotle* (Princeton UP 2008)
Setiya K, 'Hume on Practical Reason' (2004) 18 Philosophical Perspectives 365
Shavell S, 'Liability for Accidents' in *Handbook of Law and Economics* (Elsevier 2007) 139
Sher G, 'Out of Control' (2006) 116 Ethics 285
—— *Who Knew* (OUP 2009)
Sherman N, *The Fabric of Character* (Clarendon Press 1989)
Shield C, 'Unified Agency and Akrasia in Plato's Republic' in Christopher Bobonich and Pierre Destrée (eds), *Akrasia in Greek Philosophy: From Socrates to Plotinus* (Brill 2007) 61
Shoemaker D, *Responsibility from the Margins* (OUP 2015)
Shoemaker S, 'Self-Knowledge and the Inner Sense' (1994) 54 Philosophy and Phenomenological Research 249
Simester A, 'Responsibility for Inadvertent Acts' (2005) 2 Ohio State Journal of Criminal Law 601
Simmonds N, *The Decline of Juridical Reason: Doctrine and Theory in the Legal Order* (Manchester UP 1984)
Smith A, 'Responsibility for Attitudes' (2005) 115 Ethics 236
—— 'Control, Responsibility and Moral Assessment' (2008) 138 Philosophical Studies 367
—— 'Attitudes, Tracing and Control' (2015) 32 Journal of Applied Philosophy 115
—— 'Responsibility as Answerability' (2015) 58 Inquiry 99
—— 'Unconscious Omissions, Reasonable Expectations, and Responsibility' in Dana Kay Nelkin and Samuel C Rickless (eds), *The Ethics and Law of Omissions* (OUP 2017) 36
Smith H, 'Culpable Ignorance' (2003) 92 Philosophical Review 61
Smith M, 'The Humean Theory of Motivation' (1987) 96 Mind 33
—— *The Moral Problem* (Blackwell 1994)
Smith P, 'Contemplating Failure: The Importance of Unconscious Omissions' (1990) 59 Philosophical Studies 159
Stark F, *Culpable Carelessness: Recklessness and Negligence in the Criminal Law* (CUP 2016)
Stevenson C, *Ethics and Language* (Yale UP 1994)

Stone M, 'The Significance of Doing and Suffering' in Gerald Postema (ed), *Philosophy and the Law of Torts* (CUP 2001) 131
Sultana M, *Self-Deception and Akrasia* (Editrice Pontificia Universitá Gregoriana 2006)
Talbert M, 'Akrasia, Awareness and Blameworthiness' in Phillip Robichaud and Jan Willem Wieland (eds), *Responsibility: The Epistemic Condition* (OUP 2017) 47
Taylor C, 'Self-Interpreting Animals' in *Human Agency and Language* (CUP 1985) 45
——'What is Human Agency?' in *Human Agency and Language* (CUP 1985) 15
Teichman R, 'How Should One Live: Williams on Practical Deliberation and Reasons for Acting' in Sophie Grace Chappell and Marcel Van Ackeren (eds), *Ethics Beyond the Limits: New Essays on Bernard Williams' Ethics and the Limits of Philosophy* (Routledge 2018)
Van Dormeselaar I, 'The Perceptive Judge' (2018) 9 Jurisprudence 71
Vargas M, 'The Trouble with Tracing' (2005) 29 Midwest Studies in Philosophy 269
——'On the Importance of History for Responsible Agency' (2006) 127 Philosophical Studies 351
Velleman D, 'The Guise of the Good' (1992) 26 Nous 3
Vigo A, 'Deliberación y Decisión Segun Aristóteles' (2012) 43 Tópicos: Revista de Filosofía 51
Vogt K, *Desiring the Good* (OUP 2017)
Von Wright G, *Norm and Action* (Routledge and Kegan 1963)
Waldron J, 'Moments of Careless and Massive Loss' in David Owen (ed), *Philosophical Foundations of Tort Law* (OUP 1995) 387
Walker M, 'Moral Luck and the Virtues of Impure Agency' (1991) 22 Metaphilosophy 14
Wallace J, 'Virtue, Reason and Principle' (1991) 21 Canadian Journal of Philosophy 469
Walsh J, Aristotle's Conception of Moral Weakness (Columbia UP 1963)
Watson G, 'Free Agency' in *Agency and Answerability: Selected Essays* (Clarendon Press 2004) 13
——'Scepticism About Weakness of the Will' in *Agency and Answerability: Selected Essays* (OUP 2004) 33
——'Two Faces of Responsibility' in *Agency and Answerability: Selected Essays* (Clarendon Press, 2004) 260
——'Raz on Responsibility' (2016) 10 Criminal Law and Philosophy 395
—— 'The Possibility of Pure Negligence' in Verónica Rodríguez-Blanco and George Pavlakos (eds), *Agency, Negligence and Responsibility* (CUP 2021) 99
Weinman M, *Pleasure in Aristotle's Ethics* (Continuum 2007)
Weinrib E, *The Idea of Private Law* (OUP 2012)
Whitting J, 'Human Nature and Intellectualism in Aristotle' (1986) 68 Archiv für Geschichte der Philosophie 70
Wiggins D, 'Deliberation and Practical Reason' in Amélie Rorty (ed), *Essays on Aristotle's Ethics* (University of California Press 1980) 221
Williams B, 'Internal and External Reasons for Actions' in *Moral Luck* (CUP 1981) 101
——'Moral Luck' in *Moral Luck* (CUP 1981) 20
——*Ethics and the Limits of Philosophy* (Fontana Press 1993)
——'Voluntary Acts and Responsible Agents' in *Making Sense of Humanity* (CUP 1995) 22
Wittgenstein L, *Philosophical Investigations* (Blackwell 2009, originally published in 1953)
Wolf S, *Freedom Within Reason* (OUP 1990)
Wood A, 'The Final Form of Kant's Practical Philosophy' in Mark Timmons (ed), *Kant's Metaphysics of Morals: Interpretative Essays* (Clarendon Press 2002) 1
Yaffe G, 'How Could You? The Moral Import of Obliviousness' in Verónica Rodríguez-Blanco and George Pavlakos (eds), *Agency, Negligence and Responsibility* (CUP 2021) 57
Young C, 'Aristotle on Temperance' (1988) 97 Philosophical Review 521
Zimmerman M, 'Moral Responsibility and Ignorance' (1997) 107 Ethics 410
Zipursky B, 'Sleight of Hand' (2007) 48 William and Mary Law Review 2033
—— 'Response Norm Concepts in Law and Morality: A Qualified Defense of Moral Luck' in Daniel Peixoto-Murata, Verónica Rodríguez-Blanco, and Julieta Rábanos (eds), *Bernard Williams on Law and Responsibility: From Agency and Responsibility to Methodology* (Hart/ Bloomsbury 2025)

Commissioned Reports

New Zealand

New Zealand Royal Commission of Inquiry, The New Zealand Plan, Compensation for Personal Injury in New Zealand (New Zealand 1967) (Chair Mr Justice Owen Woodhouse)

United Kingdom

Pearson M, *Royal Commission on Civil Liability and Compensation for Personal Injury* (Her Majesty's Stationary Office 1978)

Index

For the benefit of digital users, indexed terms that span two pages (e.g., 52–53) may, on occasion, appear on only one of those pages.